ACCA

PRACTICE & REVISION KIT

PAPER F5

PERFORMANCE MANAGEMENT

BPP Learning Media is an **ACCA Approved Content Provider** for the ACCA qualification. This means we work closely with ACCA to ensure our products fully prepare you for your ACCA exams.

In this Practice & Revision Kit, which has been reviewed by the **ACCA examination team,** we:

- Discuss the **best strategies** for revising and taking your ACCA exams
- Ensure you are well **prepared** for your exam
- Provide you with **lots of great guidance** on tackling questions
- Provide you with **three** mock exams
- Provide **ACCA exam answers** as well as our own for selected questions

Our **Passcard** product also supports this paper.

FOR EXAMS FROM 1 SEPTEMBER 2015 TO 31 AUGUST 2016

BPP
LEARNING MEDIA

First edition 2008

Ninth edition April 2015

ISBN 9781 4727 3202 6
(previous ISBN 9781 4727 2688 9)

e-ISBN 9781 4727 3279 8

British Library Cataloguing-in-Publication Data
A catalogue record for this book
is available from the British Library

Published by

BPP Learning Media Ltd
BPP House, Aldine Place
London W12 8AA

www.bpp.com/learningmedia

Printed in the United Kingdom by

Ashford Colour Press Ltd
Gosport
Hants

We are grateful to the Association of Chartered Certified Accountants for permission to reproduce past examination questions. The suggested solutions in the practice answer bank have been prepared by BPP Learning Media Ltd, except where otherwise stated.

Your learning materials, published by BPP Learning Media Ltd, are printed on paper obtained from traceable sustainable sources.

Contents

A note about copyright

Dear Customer

What does the little © mean and why does it matter?

Your market-leading BPP books, course materials and e-learning materials do not write and update themselves. People write them: on their own behalf or as employees of an organisation that invests in this activity. Copyright law protects their livelihoods. It does so by creating rights over the use of the content.

Breach of copyright is a form of theft – as well as being a criminal offence in some jurisdictions, it is potentially a serious breach of professional ethics.

With current technology, things might seem a bit hazy but, basically, without the express permission of BPP Learning Media:

- Photocopying our materials is a breach of copyright
- Scanning, ripcasting or conversion of our digital materials into different file formats, uploading them to Facebook or emailing them to your friends is a breach of copyright

You can, of course, sell your books, in the form in which you have bought them – once you have finished with them. (Is this fair to your fellow students? We update for a reason.) Please note the e-products are sold on a single user licence basis: we do not supply 'unlock' codes to people who have bought them secondhand.

And what about outside the UK? BPP Learning Media strives to make our materials available at prices students can afford by local printing arrangements, pricing policies and partnerships which are clearly listed on our website. A tiny minority ignore this and indulge in criminal activity by illegally photocopying our material or supporting organisations that do. If they act illegally and unethically in one area, can you really trust them?

Question index

The headings in this checklist/index indicate the main topics of questions, but questions often cover several different topics.

Questions set under the old syllabus *Financial Management and Control* and *Performance Management* papers are included because their style and content are similar to those which appear in the F5 exam. The questions have been amended to reflect the current exam format.

BPP
LEARNING MEDIA

Part D: Performance measurement and control

Topic index

Listed below are the key Paper F5 syllabus topics and the numbers of the questions in this Kit covering those topics.

If you need to concentrate your practice and revision on certain topics or if you want to attempt all available questions that refer to a particular subject, you will find this index useful.

Helping you with your revision

BPP Learning Media – Approved Learning Partner – content

As an ACCA **Approved Content Provider**, BPP Learning Media gives you the **opportunity** to use **exam team reviewed** revision materials. By incorporating the examination team's comments and suggestions regarding syllabus coverage, the BPP Learning Media Practice & Revision Kit provides excellent, **ACCA-approved** support for your revision.

Tackling revision and the exam

Using feedback obtained from the ACCA exam team review:

- We look at the dos and don'ts of revising for, and taking, ACCA exams
- We focus on Paper F5; we discuss revising the syllabus, what to do (and what not to do) in the exam, how to approach different types of question and ways of obtaining easy marks

Selecting questions

We provide signposts to help you plan your revision.

- A full **question index**
- A **topic index** listing all the questions that cover key topics, so that you can locate the questions that provide practice on these topics, and see the different ways in which they might be examined

Making the most of question practice

At BPP Learning Media we realise that you need more than just questions and model answers to get the most from your question practice.

- Our **top tips** included for certain questions provide essential advice on tackling questions, presenting answers and the key points that answers need to include.
- We show you how you can pick up **easy marks** on some questions, as we know that picking up all readily available marks often can make the difference between passing and failing.
- We include **marking guides** to show you what the examiner rewards.
- We include **comments from the examiners** to show you where students struggled or performed well in the actual exam.
- We refer to the **BPP Study Text for exams between 1 September 2015 and 31 August 2016** for detailed coverage of the topics covered in questions.
- In a bank at the end of this Kit we include the **official ACCA answers** to the June and December 2014 exams. Used in conjunction with our answers they provide an indication of all possible points that could be made, issues that could be covered and approaches to adopt.

Attempting mock exams

There are three mock exams that provide practice at coping with the pressures of the exam day. We strongly recommend that you attempt them under exam conditions. **Mock exams 1 and 2** reflect the question styles and syllabus coverage of the exam; **Mock exam 3** is the December 2014 exam paper.

Revising F5

Topics to revise

All questions are compulsory so you must revise the **whole** syllabus. Since the exam includes 20 multiple choice questions, you should expect questions to cover a large part of the syllabus. Selective revision **will limit** the number of questions you can answer and hence reduce your chances of passing. It is better to go into the exam knowing a reasonable amount about most of the syllabus rather than concentrating on a few topics to the exclusion of the rest.

Question practice

Practising as many exam-style questions as possible will be the key to passing this exam. You must do questions under **timed conditions** and ensure you write full answers to the discussion parts as well as doing the calculations.

Avoid looking at the answer until you have finished a question. Your biggest problem with F5 questions may be knowing how to start, and this needs practice.

Also ensure that you attempt all three mock exams under exam conditions.

Passing the F5 exam

Displaying the right qualities

- You are expected to have a core of management accounting knowledge from your previous studies of F2.
- You will be required to identify the requirements of multiple choice questions quickly, so that you can make your answers confidently within the available time.
- You will be required to carry out calculations, with clear workings and a logical structure.
- You will be required to interpret data.
- You will be required to explain management accounting techniques and discuss whether they are appropriate for a particular organisation.
- You must be able to apply your skills in a practical context.
- You must understand what numbers tell you about the performance of a business.

Avoiding weaknesses

- There is no choice in this paper, all questions have to be answered. You must therefore study the entire syllabus, there are no short-cuts.
- Ability to answer multiple choice questions improves with practice. Try to get as much practice with these questions as you can.
- The longer questions will be based on simple scenarios and answers must be focused and specific to the organisation.
- Answer plans for the longer questions will help you to focus on the requirements of the question and enable you to manage your time effectively – but there will not be much time.
- Answer all parts of the longer questions. Even if you cannot do all the calculation elements, you will still be able to gain marks in the discussion parts.

Using the reading time

- Speed read through the question paper, jotting down any ideas that come to you about any of the questions.
- Decide the order in which you are likely to tackle questions (possibly the multiple choice questions first, but possibly last). Decide the order in which you will tackle the longer questions (probably easiest questions first, most difficult questions last).
- Spend the remainder of the reading time looking at the questions in detail analysing scenarios, jotting down answer plans to longer questions. (Any plans written on the question paper should be reproduced in the answer booklet.)
- When you can start writing get straight on with the questions you have planned to tackle first. One approach may be to answer first of all the multiple choice questions you think you can answer, and leave those you are less certain about until later. You can return to these after you have answered the longer questions in Section B of the paper.

Gaining the easy marks

Easy marks in this paper tend to fall into three categories.

Multiple choice questions

Some MCQs are easier than others. Answer those that you feel fairly confident about as quickly as you can. Come back later to those you find more difficult. This could be a way of making use of the time in the examination most efficiently and effectively.

Many MCQs will not involve calculations. Make sure that you understand the wording of 'written' MCQs before selecting your answer.

Calculations in Section B questions

There may be some relatively straightforward calculations at the start of the question and they will then probably get progressively more difficult. If you get stuck, make an assumption, state it and move on.

Discussions in Section B questions

A Section B question may separate discussion requirements from calculations, so that you do not need to do the calculations first in order to answer the discussion part. This means that you should be able to gain marks from making sensible, practical comments without having to complete the calculations.

Discussions that are focused on the specific organisation in the question will gain more marks than regurgitation of knowledge. Read the question carefully and more than once, to ensure you are actually answering the specific requirements.

Pick out key words such as 'describe', 'evaluate' and 'discuss'. These all mean something specific.

- 'Describe' means to communicate the key features of
- 'Evaluate' means to assess the value of
- 'Discuss' means to examine in detail by argument

Clearly label the points you make in discussions so that the marker can identify them all rather than getting lost in the detail.

Provide answers in the form requested. Use a report format if asked for and give recommendations if required.

Exam formulae

Set out below are the formulae **which you will be given in the exam** in a formulae sheet. You should learn to use them. If you are not sure what the symbols mean, or how the formulae are used, you should refer to the appropriate chapter in the Study Text.

Exam formulae	*Chapter in Study Text*
Demand curve	5

$P = a - bQ$

$b = \dfrac{\text{Change in price}}{\text{Change in quantity}}$

a = price when $Q = 0$

$MR = a - 2bQ$

Learning curve	10

$Y = ax^b$

Where Y = the cumulative average time per unit to produce X units

a = the time taken for the first unit of output

x = the cumulative number of units

b = the index of learning (log LR/log 2)

LR = the learning rate as a decimal

Exam information

Format of the exam

All questions are compulsory.

20 multiple choice questions in Section A, each worth 2 marks

Five compulsory questions in Section B. Three of these are 10-mark questions and two are 15-mark questions.

Time allowed: 3 hours plus 15 minutes reading time.

The two 15-mark questions will come from the decision-making techniques, budgeting and control, or performance measurement and control areas of the syllabus. The Section A questions and the 10-mark Section B questions can cover any areas of the syllabus.

Additional information

The Study Guide provides more detailed guidance on the syllabus.

Useful websites

The websites below provide additional sources of information of relevance to your studies for *Performance Management.*

- www.accaglobal.com

  ACCA's website. The students' section of the website is invaluable for detailed information about the qualification, past issues of Student Accountant (including technical articles) and a free downloadable Student Planner App.

- www.bpp.com

  Our website provides information about BPP products and services, with a link to the ACCA website.

Questions

SPECIALIST COST AND MANAGEMENT ACCOUNTING TECHNIQUES

Questions 1 to 17 cover Specialist cost and management accounting techniques, the subject of Part A of the BPP Study Text for Paper F5.

MCQ bank 1

36 mins

1.1 The following statements have been made about activity based costing.

(1) Unlike traditional absorption costing, ABC identifies variable overhead costs for allocation to product costs.

(2) ABC can be used as an information source for budget planning based on activity rather than incremental budgeting.

Which of the above statements is/are true?

A 1 only
B 2 only
C Neither 1 nor 2
D Both 1 and 2

(2 marks)

1.2 When machine time is a binding constraint on production output, which one of the following will have **no effect** on the throughput accounting ratio for a product that the machine is used to manufacture?

A Obtaining a lower purchase price for materials for the product
B Reducing factory costs
C Increasing the selling price of the product
D None of the above

(2 marks)

1.3 The following statements have been made about life cycle costing.

(1) Life cycle costing can be applied to products with a short life cycle.
(2) Product life cycle costing is not particularly well-suited for use as part of budgetary control systems.

Which of the above statements is/are true?

A 1 only
B 2 only
C Neither 1 nor 2
D Both 1 and 2

(2 marks)

1.4 Product X is made in a production process where machine time is a bottleneck resource. One unit of Product X requires 0.1 machine hours. The costs and selling price of Product X are as follows:

	$
Materials	6
Labour (0.25 hours)	3
Other factory costs	5
	14
Sales price	15
Profit	1

In a system of throughput accounting, what is the return per factory hour?

A $90
B $60
C $10
D $4

(2 marks)

1.5 The following statements have been made about target costing.

(1) Target costing makes the business look at what competitors are offering at an early stage in the new product development process.

(2) Cost control is emphasised at the new product design stage so any engineering changes must happen before production starts.

Which of the above statements is/are true?

A 1 only
B 2 only
C Neither 1 nor 2
D Both 1 and 2

(2 marks)

1.6 The following statements have been made about target costing.

(1) Target costing is inappropriate for a new product that has no existing market.

(2) It may be acceptable for a target cost for a new product to be exceeded during the growth stage of its life cycle.

Which of the above statements is/are true?

A 1 only
B 2 only
C Neither 1 nor 2
D Both 1 and 2

(2 marks)

1.7 Given the following information, what is the target cost gap for product X?

Product X target selling price per unit	$10
Target profit	25% on cost
Current cost	$8.40 per unit

A $0.40
B $0.60
C $0.90
D $1.60

(2 marks)

1.8 Which one of the following environmental management accounting techniques would include an assessment of clean-up costs and costs of decontamination when a project comes to an end?

A Environmental activity based costing
B Flow cost accounting
C Input-output analysis
D Life cycle costing

(2 marks)

1.9 MN manufactures automated industrial trolleys, known as TRLs. Each TRL sells for $2,000 and the material cost per unit is $800. There is no limit to sales demand. Costs next year will be $264,000 for factory labour, $834,000 for production overheads, and $265,000 for marketing and administrative costs.

The trolleys are made on two different machines. Machine X can produce the parts for 40 TRLs each week but it is old and unreliable and it breaks down from time to time. It is estimated that on average 15% of production time on this machine is lost. Machine Z, which is reasonably reliable, can process and assemble 30 TRLs per week.

The company has recently introduced a just-in-time (JIT) system and it is company policy to hold little work-in-progress and no finished goods inventory from week to week. The company operates a 40-hour week, 48 weeks a year.

Required

The throughput accounting ratio for the key resource for an average hour next year will be:

A 1.078
B 1.268
C 1.338
D 1.574

(2 marks)

1.10 The following statements have been made about throughput accounting.

(1) When throughput accounting (TA) is used, the aim should be to have sufficient inventories to overcome bottlenecks in production.

(2) Throughput accounting is based on the assumption that in the short run, most factory costs, other than materials, are fixed.

Which of the above statements is/are true?

A 1 only
B 2 only
C Neither 1 nor 2
D Both 1 and 2

(2 marks)
(Total = 20 marks)

MCQ bank 2 — 36 mins

2.1 The following statements have been made about activity based costing.

(1) Implementation of ABC is unlikely to be cost effective when variable production costs are a low proportion of total production costs.

(2) In a system of ABC, for costs that vary with production levels, the most suitable cost driver is likely to be direct labour hours or machine hours.

Which of the above statements is/are true?

A 1 only
B 2 only
C Neither 1 nor 2
D Both 1 and 2

(2 marks)

2.2 Product X is made in a production process where machine time is a bottleneck resource. One unit of Product X requires 0.3 machine hours. The costs and selling price of Product X are as follows:

	$
Materials	8
Labour (0.4 hours)	4
Other factory costs	2
	14
Sales price	18
Profit	4

In a system of throughput accounting, what is the throughput accounting ratio for Product X?

A 1.29
B 1.67
C 3.00
D 4.00

(2 marks)

2.3 In the theory of constraints and throughput accounting, which of the following methods may be used to elevate the performance of a binding constraint?

(1) Acquire more of the resource that is the binding constraint
(2) Improve the efficiency of usage of the resource that is the binding constraint

A 1 only
B 2 only
C 1 and 2
D Neither 1 nor 2

(2 marks)

2.4 Which one of the following environmental costs should **not** be included in an environmental cost budget?

A Cost of cleaning up contaminated sites
B Costs of using pollution-prevention methods and technology
C Cost of fines for environmental contamination
D Cost of recycling waste

(2 marks)

2.5 The following statements have been made about life cycle costing.

(1) Life cycle costing is more useful for planning than for control purposes.

(2) Most of the life cycle costs for a product are determined by decisions taken in the early stage of a product's life cycle.

Which of the above statements is/are true?

A 1 only
B 2 only
C Neither 1 nor 2
D Both 1 and 2

(2 marks)

2.6 The following statements have been made about activity based costing.

(1) Activity based costs are not the same as relevant costs for the purpose of short-run decision making.
(2) Activity based costing is a form of absorption costing.

Which of the above statements is/are true?

A 1 only
B 2 only
C Neither 1 nor 2
D Both 1 and 2

(2 marks)

2.7 According to the United Nations Division for Sustainable Development (UNDSD), environmental costs may be described as comprising costs incurred to protect the environment (such as pollution reduction measures), and also:

A Costs of wasted materials, capital and labour
B Energy costs
C Costs of detecting damage to the environment
D Costs to the general public of environmental damage

(2 marks)

2.8 The following statements have been made about throughput accounting and the theory of constraints.

(1) When an existing bottleneck is overcome ('elevated'), a new bottleneck will appear.

(2) In any commercial organisation, it should be expected that the throughput accounting ratio for any product will exceed 1.

Which of the above statements is/are true?

A 1 only
B 2 only
C Neither 1 nor 2
D Both 1 and 2

(2 marks)

2.9 In material flow cost accounting (MFCA), manufacturing costs are categorised into material costs, waste treatment costs and:

A System costs and energy costs
B Positive product costs
C Negative product costs
D Positive products costs and negative product costs

(2 marks)

2.10 A manufacturing company uses throughput accounting. It has identified Labour Grade A as its bottleneck resource. Which one of the following measures might enable the company to improve its total throughput?

(1) Reduce the selling prices of some products in order to increase sales demand.
(2) Improve the efficiency of machine usage by cutting down wastage.
(3) Pay Grade A labour overtime at a premium of $4 per hour in order to work additional hours.

A Measure 1
B Measure 2
C Measure 3
D None of the measures will increase throughput

(2 marks)
(Total = 20 marks)

MCQ bank 3 — 36 mins

3.1 The following statements have been made about activity based costing.

(1) In a system of ABC, apportionment of some overhead costs may need to be done on an arbitrary basis.

(2) The costs of introducing and maintaining an activity based costing system may exceed the benefits of such a costing system.

Which of the above statements is/are true?

A 1 only
B 2 only
C Neither 1 nor 2
D Both 1 and 2

(2 marks)

3.2 The following statements have been made about target costing.

(1) Target costing ensures that new product development costs are recovered in the target price for the product.

(2) A cost gap is the difference between the target price and the target cost.

Which of the above statements is/are true?

A 1 only
B 2 only
C Neither 1 nor 2
D Both 1 and 2

(2 marks)

3.3 In which of the following ways might financial returns be improved over the life cycle of a product?

(1) Maximising the breakeven time
(2) Minimising the time to market
(3) Minimising the length of the life cycle

A 1 and 2 only
B 1 and 3 only
C 2 only
D 2 and 3 only

(2 marks)

3.4 According to one definition of environmental management accounting (EMA), EMA involves identifying, collecting, analysing and using monetary information about environment-related costs and savings, and also:

A Investment returns on environmentally friendly investment

B Physical information about the use and flows of energy, water and materials, including waste and emissions

C Impacts on the environment for which the organisation does not incur any direct cost

D The profitability of products, allowing for environmental costs

(2 marks)

3.5 The following statements have been made about environmental management accounting.

(1) A system of environmental management accounting provides environmental information for internal use by management, but not for external reporting.

(2) Environmental management accounting systems typically make use of life cycle costing.

Which of the above statements is/are true?

A 1 only
B 2 only
C Neither 1 nor 2
D Both 1 and 2

(2 marks)

3.6 The following statements have been made about throughput accounting and the theory of constraints.

(1) A principle of throughput accounting is that a buffer inventory should be built up for output from the bottleneck resource.

(2) Unless output capacity is greater than sales demand, there will always be a binding constraint.

Which of the above statements is/are true?

A 1 only
B 2 only
C Neither 1 nor 2
D Both 1 and 2

(2 marks)

3.7 One of the products manufactured by a company is Product X, which sells for $40 per unit and has a material cost of $10 per unit and a direct labour cost of $7 per unit. The total direct labour budget for the year is 50,000 hours of labour time at a cost of $12 per hour. Factory overheads are $2,920,000 per year.

The company is considering the introduction of a system of throughput accounting. It has identified that machine time as the bottleneck in production. Product X needs 0.01 hours of machine time per unit produced. The maximum capacity for machine time is 4,000 hours per year.

What is the throughput accounting ratio for Product X?

A $3.41
B $2.80
C $2.10
D $1.90

(2 marks)

3.8 The following statements have been made about material flow cost accounting.

(1) In material flow cost accounting, waste is treated as a negative product and given a cost.

(2) Material flow cost accounting should encourage management to focus on ways of achieving the same amount of finished output with less material input.

Which of the above statements is/are true?

A 1 only
B 2 only
C Neither 1 nor 2
D Both 1 and 2

(2 marks)

3.9 The following statements have been made about target costing.

(1) Target costing is better suited to assembly orientated industries than service industries that have a large fixed cost base.

(2) Costs may be reduced in target costing by removing product features that do not add value.

Which of the above statements is/are true?

A 1 only
B 2 only
C Neither 1 nor 2
D Both 1 and 2

(2 marks)

3.10 Budget information relating to a company that manufactures four products is as follows.

Product	*Maximum sales demand*	*Machine hours per unit*	*Maximum machine hours required*	*Sales price per unit*	*Material cost per unit*
	Units			$	$
A	1,000	0.1	100	15	6
B	500	0.2	100	21	10
C	2,000	0.3	600	18	9
D	1,000	0.2	200	25	16
			1,000		

Only 750 machine hours are available during the period. Applying the principles of throughput accounting, how many units of Product B should be made if the company produces output to maximise throughput and profit?

A 0 units
B 250 units
C 375 units
D 500 units

(2 marks)
(Total = 20 marks)

MCQ bank 4 **36 mins**

4.1 The following statements have been made about activity based costing.

(1) Implementation of ABC is unlikely to be cost effective when variable production costs are a low proportion of total production costs.

(2) In a system of ABC, for costs that vary with production levels, the most suitable cost driver is likely to be direct labour hours or machine hours.

Which of the above statements is/are true?

A 1 only
B 2 only
C Neither 1 nor 2
D Both 1 and 2

(2 marks)

4.2 The following statements have been made about activity based costing.

(1) Activity based costs are not the same as relevant costs for the purpose of short-run decision making.
(2) Activity based costing is a form of absorption costing.

Which of the above statements is/are true?

A 1 only
B 2 only
C Neither 1 nor 2
D Both 1 and 2

(2 marks)

4.3 The following statements have been made about target costing.

(1) A target cost gap is the difference between the target cost for a product and its projected cost.
(2) Products should not be manufactured if there is a target cost gap.

Which of the above statements is/are true?

A 1 only
B 2 only
C Neither 1 nor 2
D Both 1 and 2

(2 marks)

4.4 The costs for design and development of a new product are expected to be $800,000. The time from original product concept to market launch will be 8 months. The expected selling price for the product is $8 per unit and the unit cost of sale will be $5. Expected sales per month in the period after product launch are:

Month	*Sales units*
1	40,000
2	60,000
3	80,000
4	100,000

What is the breakeven time for this product?

A 4 months
B 8 months
C 10 months
D 12 months

(2 marks)

4.5 The following statements have been made about throughput accounting and the theory of constraints.

(1) The production capacity of a bottleneck resource should determine the production schedule for the organisation as a whole.

(2) Idle time should be avoided in areas of production that are not a bottleneck resource.

Which of the above statements is/are true?

A 1 only
B 2 only
C Neither 1 nor 2
D Both 1 and 2

(2 marks)

4.6 The following statements have been made about activity based costing.

(1) The cost driver for quality inspection is likely to be batch size.

(2) The cost driver for materials handling and despatch costs is likely to be the number of orders handled.

Which of the above statements is/are true?

A 1 only
B 2 only
C Neither 1 nor 2
D Both 1 and 2

(2 marks)

4.7 The following statements have been made about target costing.

(1) A risk with target costing is that cost reductions may affect the perceived value of the product.
(2) An effective way of reducing the projected cost of a new product is to simplify the design.

Which of the above statements is/are true?

A 1 only
B 2 only
C Neither 1 nor 2
D Both 1 and 2

(2 marks)

4.8 The following statements have been made about life cycle costing.

(1) A product is usually most profitable during the growth phase of its life cycle.
(2) Life cycle costing is useful for deciding the selling price for a product.

Which of the above statements is/are true?

A 1 only
B 2 only
C Neither 1 nor 2
D Both 1 and 2

(2 marks)

4.9 The following statements have been made about throughput accounting.

(1) Inventory has no value and should be valued at $0.
(2) Efficiency is maximised by utilising direct labour time and machine time to full capacity.

Which of the above statements is/are true?

A 1 only
B 2 only
C Neither 1 nor 2
D Both 1 and 2

(2 marks)

4.10 The following information relates to the expected cost of a new product over its expected three-year life.

	Year 0	*Year 1*	*Year 2*	*Year 3*
Units made and sold		25,000	100,000	75,000
R&D costs	$850,000	$90,000		
Production costs				
Variable per unit		$30	$25	$20
Fixed costs		$500,000	$500,000	$500,000
Selling and distribution costs				
Variable per unit		$6	$5	$4
Fixed costs		$700,000	$500,000	$300,000
Customer service costs				
Variable per unit		$4	$3	$2

What is the expected average life cycle cost per unit?

A $35.95
B $46.25
C $48.00
D $50.95

(2 marks)
(Total = 20 marks)

MCQ bank 5 — 36 mins

5.1 The following statements have been made about activity based costing.

(1) In the short run, all the overhead costs for an activity vary with the amount of the cost driver for the activity.

(2) A cost driver is an activity based cost.

Which of the above statements is/are true?

A 1 only
B 2 only
C Neither 1 nor 2
D Both 1 and 2

(2 marks)

5.2 The following statements have been made about target costing.

(1) The value of target costing depends on having reliable estimates of sales demand.

(2) Target costing may be applied to services that are provided free of charge to customers, such as costs of call centre handling.

Which of the above statements is/are true?

A 1 only
B 2 only
C Neither 1 nor 2
D Both 1 and 2

(2 marks)

5.3 The following statements have been made about life cycle costing.

(1) An important use of life cycle costing is to decide whether to go ahead with the development of a new product.

(2) Life cycle costing encourages management to find a suitable balance between investment costs and operating expenses.

Which of the above statements is/are true?

A 1 only
B 2 only
C Neither 1 nor 2
D Both 1 and 2

(2 marks)

5.4 The following statements have been made about life cycle costing.

(1) Project management is often an important aspect of life cycle costing.
(2) Customer life cycles are similar to product life cycles.

Which of the above statements is/are true?

A 1 only
B 2 only
C Neither 1 nor 2
D Both 1 and 2

(2 marks)

5.5 The following estimates have been produced for a new product with an expected life of four years.

	Year 1	*Year 2*	*Year 3*	*Year 4*
Units made and sold	5,000	10,000	25,000	10,000
	$	$	$	$
R&D costs	0.9 million	0.3 million		
Marketing costs	0.3 million	0.3 million	0.1 million	0.1 million
Production cost per unit	80	40	30	30
Customer service cost per unit	20	15	10	5
Disposal costs				0.2 million

What is the expected life cycle cost per unit?

A $48.00
B $57.50
C $88.00
D $92.00

(2 marks)

5.6 The following statements have been made about throughput accounting.

(1) Direct labour should always be treated as a factory cost when measuring throughput.

(2) If machine time is the bottleneck resource, there is no value in taking measures to improve direct labour efficiency.

Which of the above statements is/are true?

A 1 only
B 2 only
C Neither 1 nor 2
D Both 1 and 2

(2 marks)

5.7 The following statements have been made about throughput accounting.

(1) A factor other than a production resource may be a binding constraint in throughput accounting.

(2) Production must be limited to the capacity of the bottleneck resource, but this resource should be utilised fully.

Which of the above statements is/are true?

A 1 only
B 2 only
C Neither 1 nor 2
D Both 1 and 2

(2 marks)

5.8 In environmental costing, the future cost of cleaning up operations for a product or activity may be classified as a:

A Carbon footprint
B Contingent cost
C Hidden cost
D Relationship cost

(2 marks)

5.9 Value engineering is applied in target costing to identify those aspects of a product that do not add value. 'Value' is said to consist of both the use value of a product (its function) and its:

A Complexity value
B Cost value
C Esteem value
D Quality value

(2 marks)

5.10 The following statements have been made about traditional absorption costing and activity based costing.

(1) Traditional absorption costing may be used to set prices for products, but activity based costing may not.

(2) Traditional absorption costing tends to allocate too many overhead costs to low-volume products and not enough overheads to high-volume products.

Which of the above statements is/are true?

A 1 only
B 2 only
C Neither 1 nor 2
D Both 1 and 2

(2 marks)
(Total = 20 marks)

6 Linacre Co (12/05 amended) 18 mins

Linacre Co operates an activity based costing system and has forecast the following information for next year.

Cost pool	*Cost*	*Cost driver*	*Number of drivers*
Production set-ups	$105,000	Set-ups	300
Product testing	$300,000	Tests	1,500
Component supply and storage	$25,000	Component orders	500
Customer orders and delivery	$112,500	Customer orders	1,000

General fixed overheads such as lighting and heating, which cannot be linked to any specific activity, are expected to be $900,000 and these overheads are absorbed on a direct labour hour basis. Total direct labour hours for next year are expected to be 300,000 hours.

Linacre Co expects orders for Product ZT3 next year to be 100 orders of 60 units per order and 60 orders of 50 units per order. The company holds no inventories of Product ZT3 and will need to produce the order requirement in production runs of 900 units. One order for components is placed prior to each production run. Four tests are made during each production run to ensure that quality standards are maintained. The following additional cost and profit information relates to product ZT3:

Component cost:	$1.00 per unit
Direct labour:	10 minutes per unit at $7.80 per hour
Profit mark up:	40% of total unit cost

Required

(a) Calculate the activity based recovery rates for each cost pool. **(2 marks)**

(b) Calculate the total unit cost and selling price of Product ZT3. **(8 marks)**

(Total = 10 marks)

7 Jola Publishing Co (6/08 amended) 18 mins

Jola Publishing Co publishes two forms of book.

The company publishes a children's book (CB), which is sold in large quantities to government controlled schools. The book is produced in only four large production runs but goes through frequent government inspections and quality assurance checks.

The paper used is strong, designed to resist the damage that can be caused by the young children it is produced for. The book has only a few words and relies on pictures to convey meaning.

The second book is a comprehensive technical journal (TJ). It is produced in monthly production runs, 12 times a year. The paper used is of relatively poor quality and is not subject to any governmental controls and consequently only a small number of inspections are carried out. The TJ uses far more machine hours than the CB in its production.

The directors are concerned about the performance of the two books and are wondering what the impact would be of a switch to an activity based costing (ABC) approach to accounting for overheads. They currently use absorption costing, based on machine hours for all overhead calculations. They have produced an analysis for the coming year as follows:

	CB		*TJ*
	$ per unit		$ per unit
Paper (400g @ $2 per kg)	0.80	(100g @ $1 per kg)	0.10
Printing ink (50 ml @ $30 per litre)	1.50	(150 ml @ $30 per litre)	4.50
Machine costs (6 mins @ $12 per hour)	1.20	(10 mins @ $12 per hour)	2.00
Overheads (6 mins @ $24 per hour)	2.40	(10 mins @ $24 per hour)	4.00
Total cost	5.90		10.60
Selling price	9.30		14.00
Margin	3.40		3.40

The main overheads involved are:

Overhead	*% of total overhead*	*Activity driver*
Property costs	75.0%	Machine hours
Quality control	23.0%	Number of inspections
Production set up costs	2.0%	Number of set ups

If the overheads for the previous accounting year were reallocated under ABC principles then the results would be that the overhead allocation to CB would be $0.05 higher at $2.45 per unit, and the overhead allocated to TJ would be $0.30 lower at $3.70 per unit.

Required

(a) Explain why the overhead allocations have changed in the way indicated above. **(7 marks)**

(b) Briefly explain the implementation problems often experienced when ABC is first introduced. **(3 marks)**

(Total = 10 marks)

8 The Gadget Co (12/10 amended) 18 mins

The Gadget Co produces three products, A, B and C, all made from the same material. Until now, it has used traditional absorption costing to allocate overheads to its products. The company is now considering an activity based costing system in the hope that it will improve profitability. Information for the three products for the last year is as follows:

	A	*B*	*C*
Production and sales volumes (units)	15,000	12,000	18,000
Selling price per unit	$7.50	$12	$13
Raw material cost per unit	$2.40	$3.60	$4.80
Direct labour cost per unit	$1.48	$2.22	$2.96
Machine hours per unit	0.5	0.7	0.9
Number of production runs per annum	16	12	8
Number of purchase orders per annum	24	28	42
Number of deliveries to retailers per annum	48	30	62

Using an overhead absorption rate of $28.30 per direct labour hour, the unit costs of each product using traditional absorption costing were $6.71 for Product A, $10.07 for Product B and $13.42 for Product C.

The company is considering an activity based costing system in the hope that it will improve profitability. The annual overhead costs for the last year were as follows:

	$
Machine set up costs	26,550
Machine running costs	66,400
Procurement costs	48,000
Delivery costs	54,320

Required

(a) Calculate the full cost per unit of each product in the last year using activity based costing. Do your calculations to two decimal places. **(6 marks)**

(b) Explain briefly how activity based costing may help The Gadget Co improve the profitability of each product. **(4 marks)**

(Total = 10 marks)

9 Duff Co (6/14 amended) 18 mins

Duff Co manufactures three products, X, Y and Z. Demand for products X and Y is relatively elastic whilst demand for product Z is relatively inelastic. Each product uses the same materials and the same type of direct labour but in different quantities. For many years, the company has been using full absorption costing and absorbing overheads on the basis of direct labour hours. Selling prices are then determined using cost plus pricing. This is common within this industry, with most competitors applying a standard mark-up.

Budgeted production and sales volumes for X, Y and Z for the next year are 20,000 units, 16,000 units and 22,000 units respectively.

The budgeted direct costs of the three products are shown below:

Product	*X*	*Y*	*Z*
	$ per unit	$ per unit	$ per unit
Direct materials	25	28	22
Direct labour ($12 per hour)	30	36	24

In the next year, Duff Co also expects to incur indirect production costs of $1,377,400, which are analysed as follows:

Cost pools	$	*Cost drivers*
Machine set up costs	280,000	Number of batches
Material ordering costs	316,000	Number of purchase orders
Machine running costs	420,000	Number of machine hours
General facility costs	361,400	Number of machine hours
	1,377,400	

The following additional data relate to each product:

Product	*X*	*Y*	*Z*
Batch size (units)	500	800	400
No of purchase orders per batch	4	5	4
Machine hours per unit	1.5	1.25	1.4

Duff Co wants to boost sales revenue in order to increase profits but its capacity to do this is limited because of its use of cost plus pricing and the application of the standard mark-up. The finance director has suggested using activity based costing (ABC) instead of full absorption costing, since this will alter the cost of the products and may therefore enable a different price to be charged.

Required

Calculate the budgeted full production cost per unit of each product using activity based costing. All workings should be to two decimal places. **(10 marks)**

10 Target costing (6/12 amended) 18 mins

The newly appointed financial controller of a company that operates a number of private schools comes from a manufacturing background and has extensive experience with target costing and target pricing. She believes that introducing a target costing system into the company will help with the control of costs and ensure that the schools operate at a surplus of revenue over expenditure. Her chief executive officer is not convinced, believing target costing to be only really suitable in manufacturing companies.

Required

(a) Explain the main steps involved in developing a target price and target cost for a product in a typical manufacturing company. **(6 marks)**

(b) Explain four key characteristics that distinguish services from manufacturing. **(4 marks)**

(Total = 10 marks)

11 UHS (6/12 amended) 18 mins

The Universal Health System (UHS) provides the entire healthcare service to residents in Illopia. The UHS is funded centrally through revenues from taxpayers. The UHS is largely managed regionally by a number of self-governing trusts, such as the Sickham UHS Trust.

The Sickham UHS Trust runs one hospital in Sickham and, like other trusts in Illopia, receives 70% of its income largely from the UHS's 'payments by results' scheme, which was established two years ago. Under this scheme, the trust receives a pre-set tariff (fee income) for each service it provides. If the Trust manages to provide any of its services at a lower cost than the pre-set tariff, it is allowed to use the surplus as it wishes. Similarly, it has to bear the cost of any deficits itself.

Currently, the Trust knows that a number of its services simply cannot be provided at the tariff it receives and accepts that these always lead to a deficit. Similarly, other services always seem to create a surplus. This is partly because different trusts define their services and account for overheads differently. Also, it is partly due to regional differences in costs, which are not taken into account by the scheme, which operates on the basis that 'one tariff fits all'.

The remaining 30% of the Trust's income comes from transplant and heart operations. Since these are not covered by the scheme, the payment the Trust receives is based on the actual costs it incurs in providing the operations. However, the Trust is not allowed to exceed the total budget provided for these operations in any one year.

Over recent years, the Trust's board of directors has become increasingly dissatisfied with the financial performance of the Trust and has blamed it on poor costing systems, leading to an inability to control costs. The newly appointed financial controller believes that the introduction of a target costing system at the Sickham UHS Trust is an answer to the problem.

Required

(a) Describe how the Sickham UHS Trust is likely, in current circumstances, to try to derive:

(i) A target cost for the services that it provides under the 'payment by results' scheme; and **(2 marks)**

(ii) A target cost for transplants and heart operations. **(2 marks)**

(b) Discuss **three** of the particular difficulties that the Sickham UHS Trust may find in using target costing in its service provision. **(6 marks)**

(Total = 10 marks)

12 Edward Limited — 18 mins

Edward Limited assembles and sells many types of radio. It is considering extending its product range to include digital radios. These radios produce a better sound quality than traditional radios and have a large number of potential additional features not possible with the previous technologies (station scanning, more choice, one touch tuning, station identification text and song identification text etc).

A radio is produced by assembly workers assembling a variety of components. Production overheads are currently absorbed into product costs on an assembly labour hour basis.

Edward Limited is considering a target costing approach for its new digital radio product.

A selling price of $44 has been set in order to compete with a similar radio on the market that has comparable features to Edward Limited's intended product. The board have agreed that the acceptable margin (after allowing for all production costs) should be 20%.

Cost information for the new radio is as follows:

Component 1 (Circuit board) – these are bought in and cost $4.10 each. They are bought in batches of 4,000 and additional delivery costs are $2,400 per batch.

Component 2 (Wiring) – in an ideal situation 25 cm of wiring is needed for each completed radio. However, there is some waste involved in the process as wire is occasionally cut to the wrong length or is damaged in the assembly process. Edward Limited estimates that 2% of the purchased wire is lost in the assembly process. Wire costs $0.50 per metre to buy.

Other material – other materials cost $8.10 per radio.

Assembly labour – these are skilled people who are difficult to recruit and retain. Edward Limited has more staff of this type than needed but is prepared to carry this extra cost in return for the security it gives the business. It takes 30 minutes to assemble a radio and the assembly workers are paid $12.60 per hour. It is estimated that 10% of hours paid to the assembly workers is for idle time.

Production overheads – recent historical cost analysis has revealed the following production overhead data:

	Total production overhead	*Total assembly labour hours*
	$	
Month 1	620,000	19,000
Month 2	700,000	23,000

Fixed production overheads are absorbed on an assembly hour basis based on normal annual activity levels. In a typical year 240,000 assembly hours will be worked by Edward Limited.

Required

Calculate the expected cost per unit for the radio and identify any cost gap that might exist. **(10 marks)**

13 Fit Co (12/11 amended) — 18 mins

Fit Co specialises in the manufacture of a small range of hi-tech products for the fitness market. They are currently considering the development of a new type of fitness monitor, which would be the first of its kind in the market. It would take one year to develop, with sales then commencing at the beginning of the second year. The product is expected to have a life cycle of two years, before it is replaced with a technologically superior product. The following cost estimates have been made.

	Year 1	*Year 2*	*Year 3*
Units manufactured and sold		100,000	200,000
Research and development costs	$160,000		
Product design costs	$800,000		
Marketing costs	$1,200,000	$1,000,000	$1,750,000
Manufacturing costs:			
Variable cost per unit		$40	$42
Fixed production costs		$650,000	$1,290,000
Distribution costs:			
Variable cost per unit		$4	$4.50
Fixed distribution costs		$120,000	$120,000
Selling costs:			
Variable cost per unit		$3	$3.20
Fixed selling costs		$180,000	$180,000
Administration costs	$200,000	$900,000	$1,500,000

Note. You should ignore the time value of money.

Required

(a) Calculate the life cycle cost per unit. **(6 marks)**

(b) Briefly discuss the benefits of life cycle costing for pricing, performance management and decision making. **(4 marks)**

(Total = 10 marks)

14 Cam Co (6/13 amended) — 18 mins

Cam Co manufactures webcams, devices which can provide live video and audio streams via personal computers. It has recently been suffering from liquidity problems and hopes that these will be eased by the launch of its new webcam, which has revolutionary audio sound and visual quality.

The webcam is expected to have a product life cycle of two years. Market research has already been carried out to establish a target selling price and projected lifetime sales volumes for the product. Cost estimates have also been prepared, based on the current proposed product specification. Cam Co uses life cycle costing to work out the target costs for its products. You are provided with the following relevant information for the webcam:

Projected lifetime sales volume	50,000 units
Target selling price per unit	$200
Target profit margin (35% selling price)	$70
Target cost per unit	$130
Estimated lifetime cost per unit (see note below for detailed breakdown)	$160

Note. Estimated lifetime cost per unit:

	$	$
Manufacturing costs		
Direct material (bought in parts)	40	
Direct labour	26	
Machine costs	24	
Quality control costs	10	
		100
Non-manufacturing costs		60
Estimated lifetime cost per unit		160

The company needs to close the cost gap of $30 between the target cost and the estimated lifetime cost. The following information has been identified as relevant:

(1) Direct material cost: all of the parts currently proposed for the webcam are bespoke parts. However, most of these can actually be replaced with standard parts costing 55% less. However, three of the bespoke parts, which currently account for 20% of the estimated direct material cost, cannot be replaced, although an alternative supplier charging 10% less has been sourced for these parts.

(2) Direct labour cost: the webcam uses 45 minutes of direct labour, which costs $34.67 per hour. The use of more standard parts, however, will mean that whilst the first unit would still be expected to take 45 minutes, there will now be an expected rate of learning of 90% (where 'b' = – 0.152). This will end after the first 100 units have been completed.

Required

Recalculate the estimated lifetime cost per unit for the webcam after taking into account points 1 and 2 above.

(10 marks)

15 Sapu — 18 mins

Sapu makes and sells a number of products. Products A and B are products for which market prices are available at which Sapu can obtain a share of the market as detailed below. Estimated data for the forthcoming period is as follows.

Product data

	Product A	*Product B*	*Other products*
Production/sales (units)	5,000	10,000	40,000
	$'000	$'000	$'000
Total direct material cost	80	300	2,020
Total direct labour cost	40	100	660

Variable overhead cost is $1,500,000 of which 40% is related to the acquisition, storage and use of direct materials and 60% is related to the control and use of direct labour.

It is current practice in Sapu to absorb variable overhead cost into product units using overall company wide percentages on direct material cost and direct labour cost as the absorption bases.

Market prices for Products A and B are $75 and $95 per unit respectively.

Required

(a) Prepare estimated unit product costs for Product A and Product B where variable overhead is charged to product units, using an activity based costing approach where cost drivers have been estimated for material and labour related overhead costs as follows.

	Product A	*Product B*	*Other products*
Direct material related overheads – cost driver is material bulk. The bulk proportions per unit are:	4	1	1.5
Direct labour related overheads – cost driver is number of labour operations (not directly time related). Labour operations per product unit are:	6	1	2

(6 marks)

(b) Explain how Sapu could make use of target costing in conjunction with activity based costing with respect to Products A and B. **(4 marks)**

(Total = 10 marks)

16 Environmental — 18 mins

A company is currently developing a system of environmental costing.

Required

(a) Describe the key features of an environmental management system. **(5 marks)**

(b) Explain the difference between internalised environmental costs and externalised environmental impacts and state **two** examples of each. **(5 marks)**

(Total = 10 marks)

17 Yam Co (6/09 amended) — 18 mins

Yam Co is involved in the processing of sheet metal into products A, B and C using three processes, pressing, stretching and rolling. Like many businesses Yam faces tough price competition in what is a mature world market.

The factory has 50 production lines each of which contain the three processes: Raw material for the sheet metal is first pressed then stretched and finally rolled. The processing capacity varies for each process and the factory manager has provided the following data:

	Processing time per metre in hours		
	Product A	*Product B*	*Product C*
Pressing	0.50	0.50	0.40
Stretching	0.25	0.40	0.25
Rolling	0.40	0.25	0.25

The factory operates for 18 hours each day for five days per week. It is closed for only two weeks of the year for holidays when maintenance is carried out. On average one hour of labour is needed for each of the 225,000 hours of factory time. Labour is paid $10 per hour.

The raw materials cost per metre is $3.00 for product A, $2.50 for product B and $1.80 for product C. Other factory costs (excluding labour and raw materials) are $18,000,000 per year. Selling prices per metre are $70 for product A, $60 for product B and $27 for product C.

Yam carries very little inventory.

Required

(a) Calculate the throughput accounting ratio (TPAR) for each product assuming that the bottleneck process is fully utilised. **(7 marks)**

(b) Assuming that the TPAR of product C is less than 1, suggest how Yam could improve the TPAR of product C. **(3 marks)**

(Total = 10 marks)

18 Thin Co (6/11 amended) **18 mins**

Thin Co is a private hospital offering three types of surgical procedures known as A, B and C. Each of them uses a pre-operative injection given by a nurse before the surgery. Thin Co currently rent an operating theatre from a neighbouring government hospital. The Managing Director of Thin Co is keen to maximise profits and has heard of something called 'throughput accounting', which may help him to do this. The following information is available:

(1) All patients go through a five step process, irrespective of which procedure they are having. This process involves an adviser, nurse, anaesthetist, surgeon and recovery specialist.

(2) The price of each of procedures A, B and C is $2,700, $3,500 and $4,250 respectively.

(3) The only materials' costs relating to the procedures are for the pre-operative injections given by the nurse, the anaesthetic and the dressings. These are as follows:

	Procedure A	*Procedure B*	*Procedure C*
	$ per procedure	*$ per procedure*	*$ per procedure*
Pre-operative nurse's injections	700	800	1,000
Anaesthetic	35	40	45
Dressings	5.60	5.60	5.60

(4) There are five members of staff employed by Thin Co. Each works a standard 40-hour week for 47 weeks of the year, a total of 1,880 hours each per annum. Their salaries are as follows:

-- Adviser: $45,000 per annum;
-- Nurse: $38,000 per annum;
-- Anaesthetist: $75,000 per annum;
-- Surgeon: $90,000 per annum;
-- Recovery specialist: $50,000 per annum.

The only other hospital costs (comparable to 'factory costs' in a traditional manufacturing environment) are general overheads, which include the theatre rental costs, and amount to $250,000 per annum.

(5) Maximum annual demand for A, B and C is 600, 800 and 1,200 procedures respectively. Surgeon's hours have been correctly identified as the bottleneck resource.

Time spent by the surgeon on each procedure is as follows:

Procedure A	*Procedure B*	*Procedure C*
Hours	*Hours*	*Hours*
per procedure	*per procedure*	*per procedure*
0.75	1.00	1.25

Part hours are shown as decimals eg 0.24 hours = 14.4 minutes (0.24 × 60).

Required

(a) Calculate the throughput accounting ratio for procedure C.

Note. It is recommended that you work in hours rather than minutes. **(5 marks)**

(b) The return per factory hour for products A and B has been calculated and is $2,612.53 and $2,654.40 respectively. The throughput accounting ratio for A and B has also been calculated and is 8.96 and 9.11 respectively.

Calculate the optimum product (procedure) mix and the maximum profit per annum. **(5 marks)**

(Total = 10 marks)

19 Solar Systems (12/13 amended) **18 mins**

Solar Systems Co (S Co) makes two types of solar panels at its manufacturing plant: large panels for commercial customers and small panels for domestic customers. All panels are produced using the same materials, machinery and a skilled labour force. Production takes place for five days per week, from 7am until 8pm (13 hours), 50 weeks of the year. Each panel has to be cut, moulded and then assembled using a cutting machine (Machine C), a moulding machine (Machine M) and an assembly machine (Machine A).

Due to poor productivity levels, late orders and declining profits over recent years, the finance director has suggested the introduction of throughput accounting within the organisation, together with a 'Just in Time' system of production.

Material costs and selling prices for each type of panel are shown below.

	Large panels	*Small panels*
	$	$
Selling price per unit	12,600	3,800
Material costs per unit	4,300	1,160

The company has committed itself to a government contract for the production of 1,000 small panels per year for the next two years, with no increase in panel prices.

Total factory costs, which include the cost of labour and all factory overheads, are $12 million each year at the plant.

Out of the 13 hours available for production each day, workers take a one hour lunch break. For the remaining 12 hours, Machines M is utilised 90% of the time. The unproductive time arises either as a result of routine maintenance or because of staff absenteeism, as each machine needs to be manned by skilled workers in order for the machine to run.

The following information is available for Machine M, which has been identified as the bottleneck resource:

	Large panels	*Small panels*
	Hours per unit	Hours per unit
Machine M	1.4	0.6

There is currently plenty of spare capacity on Machines C and A. Maximum annual demand for large panels and small panels is 1,800 units and 1,700 units respectively.

Required

(a) Calculate the throughput accounting ratio for large panels and for small panels and explain what they indicate to S Co about production of large and small panels. **(6 marks)**

(b) Suggest **two** ways in which S Co could try to increase its production capacity and hence increase throughput in the next year without making any additional investment in machinery. **(4 marks)**

(Total = 10 marks)

20 Corrie **18 mins**

Corrie produces three products, X, Y and Z. The capacity of Corrie's plant is restricted by process alpha. Process alpha is expected to be operational for eight hours per day and can produce 1,200 units of X per hour, 1,500 units of Y per hour, and 600 units of Z per hour.

Selling prices and material costs for each product are as follows.

Product	*Selling price*	*Material cost*	*Throughput*
	$ per unit	$ per unit	$ per unit
X	150	70	80
Y	120	40	80
Z	300	100	200

Conversion costs are $720,000 per day.

Required

(a) Calculate the throughput accounting ratio for each product. **(4 marks)**

(b) In the absence of demand restrictions for the three products, advise Corrie's management on the optimal production plan. **(2 marks)**

(c) State **four** actions that management could consider to improve the throughput accounting ratio of a particular product. **(4 marks)**

(Total = 10 marks)

DECISION-MAKING TECHNIQUES

Questions 18 to 38 cover Decision-making techniques, the subject of Part B of the BPP Study Text for Paper F5.

MCQ bank 1

36 mins

21.1 For which one of the following reasons would the choice of penetration pricing be **unsuitable** for a product during the initial stage of its life cycle?

A To discourage new entrants to the market
B To increase the length of the initial stage of the life cycle
C To achieve economies of scale
D To set a price for a product that has a high price elasticity of demand

(2 marks)

21.2 The following statements have been made about the use of expected values for decision making under conditions of uncertainty.

(1) Expected values are used to support a risk-averse attitude to decision making.

(2) Expected values are more valuable as a guide to decision making where they refer to outcomes which will occur many times over.

Which of the above statements is/are true?

A 1 only
B 2 only
C Neither 1 nor 2
D Both 1 and 2

(2 marks)

21.3 Which of the following statements about relevant costing is/are correct?

(1) An opportunity cost is defined as the relevant cost of taking a business opportunity.
(2) Business decisions should be taken on the basis of whether they improve profit or reduce costs.

A 1 only is correct
B 2 only is correct
C Neither 1 nor 2 is correct
D Both 1 and 2 are correct

(2 marks)

21.4 Which of the following statements about market research is/are correct?

(1) Market research is a source of primary data.
(2) Market research provides information about risk and uncertainty.

A 1 only is correct
B 2 only is correct
C Neither 1 nor 2 is correct
D Both 1 and 2 are correct

(2 marks)

21.5 A company is budgeting to sell 200,000 units of its product next year at a price of $15 per unit. Fixed costs will be $1,232,000 and the variable cost/sales ratio is 44%.

What is the breakeven sales revenue figure and what is the margin of safety in the budget?

A Breakeven $2,200,000, margin of safety 26.7%
B Breakeven $2,200,000, margin of safety 36.4%
C Breakeven $2,800,000, margin of safety 6.7%
D Breakeven $2,800,000, margin of safety 7.1%

(2 marks)

21.6 A manufacturing company has the following monthly budget.

	$	$
Sales		480,000
Direct materials	140,000	
Direct labour	110,000	
Variable overheads	50,000	
Fixed overheads	130,000	
Total costs		430,000
Profit		50,000

Sales can be increased by 15% per month if an extra work shift is added, but the sales price would have to be reduced by 3% on all units sold in order to sell the extra volume. Direct labour is a variable cost, but work in the extra shift would have to be paid an extra 50% per hour on top of the normal hourly rate. Increased purchases of materials means that a bulk purchase discount of 2% will be available on all materials purchased. Additional fixed overheads would be $2,000 per month.

If the additional work shift is added, what will be the monthly profit?

A $51,400
B $52,150
C $53,410
D $60,060

(2 marks)

21.7 The following statements have been made about linear programming analysis.

(1) The sales price of units produced and sold may be a constraint in a linear programming problem.

(2) If a constraint is $0.04x + 0.03y \leq 2{,}400$, the boundary line for the constraint can be drawn on a graph by joining up the points y = 0, x = 80,000 and x = 0, y = 60,000 with a straight line.

Which of the above statements is/are true?

A 1 only
B 2 only
C Neither 1 nor 2
D Both 1 and 2

(2 marks)

21.8 The following statements have been made about the demand for products.

(1) Demand for a product will increase when the price of a substitute product falls.
(2) Demand for a product will fall when the price of a complementary product falls.

Which of the above statements is/are true?

A 1 only
B 2 only
C Neither 1 nor 2
D Both 1 and 2

(2 marks)

21.9 In a manufacturing plant, the work force is operating at full capacity. The work force is paid a fixed rate of $12 per hour for a 35-hour week. This is a fixed weekly wage, although for the purpose of management accounting, direct labour costs are treated as a variable cost. A customer has asked for a special job to be done that would involve taking employees off regular work that earns a contribution of $15 per hour, after allowing for direct labour cost and variable overheads at $2 per hour. The special job would take 10 hours of labour time.

The company must decide whether to agree to the customer's request for the work, and to set a price. What would be the relevant cost of labour for this job?

A $150
B $170
C $270
D $290

(2 marks)

21.10 A company produces three components on the same machine. The components are used in the manufacture of a finished product. The budget for next year indicates a requirement for 3,000 units of each component, but only 60,000 of machine time will be available. Additional components and be purchased from an external supplier to meet any production shortfall.

Component	*Machine hours per unit*	*Variable production cost per unit*	*Purchase price from external supplier*
		$ per unit	$ per unit
A	9	45	65
B	5	70	78
C	12	56	80

What is the minimum total variable cost at which the 3,000 units of all three components can be obtained?

A $537,000
B $543,000
C $549,000
D $553,000

(2 marks)

(Total = 20 marks)

MCQ bank 2 **36 mins**

22.1 The demand curve for a product is expressed by the formula P = 24 – 0.004Q, where P is the selling price and Q is the quantity demanded per week at that price. At the current sales price of $10 per unit, demand per week is 3,500 units.

By how much could the company raise the selling price per unit in order to increase total sales revenue per week, before total sales revenue per week from the product begins to go into decline?

A By $2 per unit
B By $4 per unit
C By $10 per unit
D By $12 per unit

(2 marks)

22.2 In which one of the following circumstances would the choice of a market skimming pricing policy be **unsuitable** for a product during the initial stage of its life cycle?

A The product is protected by a patent
B Expected demand and the price sensitivity of customers for the new product are unknown
C When the product is expected to have a long life cycle
D To maximise short-term profitability

(2 marks)

22.3 The following statements have been made about relevant costing.

(1) Sunk costs can never be a relevant cost for the purpose of decision making.

(2) If a company charges the minimum price for a product or service, based on relevant costs, it will not improve its overall profitability.

Which of the above statements is/are true?

A 1 only
B 2 only
C Neither 1 nor 2
D Both 1 and 2

(2 marks)

22.4 A company has a sales budget of $1.6 million and budgeted fixed costs of $840,000. Its contribution/sales ratio is 60%. It is considering a change in the production method, requiring no investment outlay, that would reduce variable costs by 10% but increase fixed costs by 20%.

What would be the effect of introducing the change in production method?

A The breakeven point would be higher and the margin of safety would be higher
B The breakeven point would be higher and the margin of safety would be lower
C The breakeven point would be lower and the margin of safety would be higher
D The breakeven point would be lower and the margin of safety would be lower

(2 marks)

22.5 Production output by a manufacturing company is restricted by a shortage of supplies of Material X and skilled labour Y. Material X costs $10 per kilogram.

It has been determined using linear programming that at the profit-maximising level of output, all available quantities of Material X would be fully utilised and the shadow price (dual price) of Material X would be $6 per kilogram. Skilled labour Y has a shadow price of $0, but existing staff would be willing to work overtime for an additional $2 per hour.

Another supplier has now offered to supply additional quantities of Material X, but at a price of $14 per kilogram.

Would the company increase profits by (1) purchasing Material X at the higher price or (2) employing skilled labour Y to work overtime?

	Buy extra Material X	*Pay labour Y to work overtime*
A	No	Yes
B	No	No
C	Yes	Yes
D	Yes	No

(2 marks)

22.6 The following statements have been made about multi-product profit-volume charts.

(1) A multi-product profit-volume chart can be drawn, and breakeven revenue calculated, only if a constant sales mix is assumed.

(2) A multi-product profit-volume chart can be drawn that shows the contribution of each product to the breakeven sales volume.

Which of the above statements is/are true?

A 1 only
B 2 only
C Neither 1 nor 2
D Both 1 and 2

(2 marks)

22.7 The following statements have been made about full cost plus pricing.

(1) Charging prices at full cost plus a fixed margin for profit will ensure that the business will make a profit in each period.

(2) Full cost plus pricing can lead to under- and overpricing of products.

Which of the above statements is/are true?

A 1 only
B 2 only
C Neither 1 nor 2
D Both 1 and 2

(2 marks)

22.8 Skilled labour at a manufacturing plant is in short supply, and all available skilled labour time is fully utilised. A customer has asked for a special job that will cost $400 in direct materials and will require 15 hours of skilled labour time. Skilled labour costs $8 per hour and variable production overhead is $2 per hour. Fixed production overheads are absorbed at a rate of $20 per skilled labour hour. If the job is undertaken the skilled labour will be withdrawn from work on making items that earn a contribution of $25 per skilled labour hour.

What is the minimum price that should be charged if this special job is undertaken?

A $775
B $895
C $925
D $1,225

(2 marks)

22.9 A company wishes to decide on a selling price for a new product, and wants to choose the price that will provide the most satisfactory weekly total contribution. Weekly sales of each product will depend on the price charge and also on customers' response to the new product. The following pay-off table has been prepared.

	Probability	*Price P1*	*Price P2*	*Price P3*	*Price P4*
		$	$	$	$
Price		5.00	5.50	6.00	6.50
Unit contribution		3.00	3.50	4.00	4.50
Weekly demand		Units	Units	Units	Units
Best possible	0.3	10,000	9,000	8,000	7,000
Most likely	0.5	8,000	7,500	7,000	6,000
Worst possible	0.2	6,000	5,000	4,000	3,000

If the choice of selling price is based on a maximax decision rule, which price would be selected?

A P1
B P2
C P3
D P4

(2 marks)

22.10 The constraints in a linear programming problem are as follows:

3x + 4.8y	≤	120,000	(Grade A labour hours)
5x + 4y	≤	160,000	(Grade B labour hours)
x	≤	30,000	(Sales demand product X)
y	≤	20,000	(Sales demand Product Y)
x, y	≥	0	

The objective function is to maximise total contribution: 20x + 30y. A graph of the constraints is as follows.

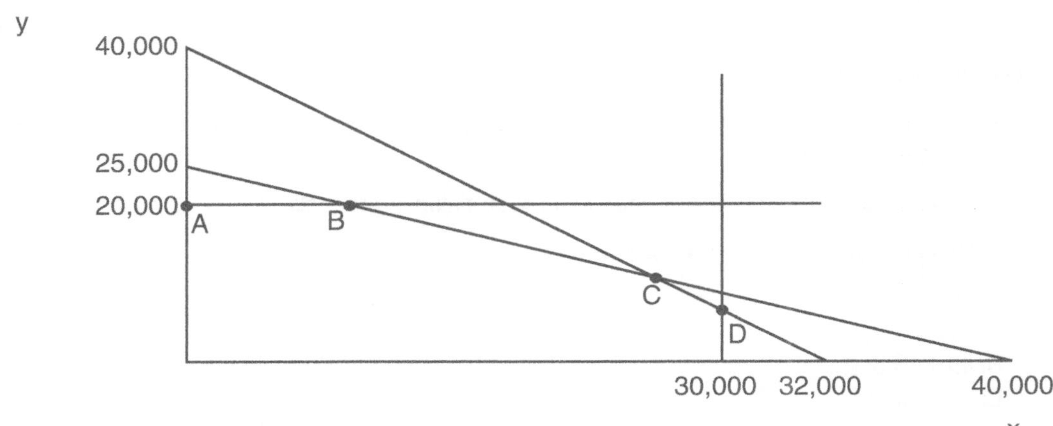

Where is the optimal solution to the linear programming problem?

A Point A
B Point B
C Point C
D Point D

(2 marks)

(Total = 20 marks)

MCQ bank 3 — 36 mins

23.1 A decision tree is a way of representing decision choices in the form of a diagram. It is usual for decision trees to include probabilities of different outcomes.

The following statements have been made about decision trees.

(1) Each possible outcome from a decision is given an expected value.
(2) Each possible outcome is shown as a branch on a decision tree.

Which of the above statements is/are true?

A 1 only
B 2 only
C Neither 1 nor 2
D Both 1 and 2

(2 marks)

23.2 The following statements have been made about price elasticity of demand.

(1) When sales demand is inelastic, a company can increase profits by raising the selling price of its product.

(2) Price elasticity of demand is measured as the amount of change in sales price (measured as a percentage of the current sales price) divided by the amount of change in quantity demanded (measured as a percentage of the current sales volume)

Which of the above statements is/are true?

A 1 only
B 2 only
C Neither 1 nor 2
D Both 1 and 2

(2 marks)

23.3 The following statements have been made about cost plus pricing.

(1) A price in excess of full cost per unit will ensure that a company will cover all its costs and make a profit.

(2) Cost plus pricing is an appropriate pricing strategy when jobs are carried out to customer specifications.

Which of the above statements is/are true?

A 1 only
B 2 only
C Neither 1 nor 2
D Both 1 and 2

(2 marks)

23.4 A company has fixed costs of $1.3 million. Variable costs are 55% of sales up to a sales level of $1.5 million, but at higher volumes of production and sales, the variable cost for incremental production units falls to 52% of sales.

What is the breakeven point in sales revenue, to the nearest $1,000?

A $1,977,000
B $2,027,000
C $2,708,000
D $2,802,000

(2 marks)

23.5 The following statements have been made about solving linear programming problems for budgeting purposes.

(1) Slack occurs when less than the maximum available of a limited resource is required.

(2) When the linear programming problem includes a constraint for minimum sales demand for a product, there may be a surplus for sales demand in the optimal solution.

Which of the above statements is/are true?

A 1 only
B 2 only
C Neither 1 nor 2
D Both 1 and 2

(2 marks)

23.6 The following budgeted data has been prepared for a company that manufactures four products.

Product	*W*	*X*	*Y*	*Z*
	$ per unit	$ per unit	$ per unit	$ per unit
Sales price	9.0	6.0	4.0	8.0
Variable cost	5.5	4.0	2.2	4.0
Budgeted sales units	20,000	25,000	50,000	12,500
Direct labour hours per unit	0.5	0.25	0.3	0.8

If the total available direct labour hours in the period is 24,000 hours and the company plans to maximise profit, which products should it make and sell in the period?

A W, X and Y
B W, X and Z
C W, Y and Z
D Y and Z only

(2 marks)

23.7 The main purpose of sensitivity analysis is to:

A Predict the future outcome from an uncertain situation
B Determine the outcome from a situation in the event of the worst possible outcome
C Determine the expected value of an outcome that is uncertain
D Gain insight into which assumptions or variables in a situation are critical

(2 marks)

23.8 A company is selling a product for $180. At this price it sells 50,000 units per month. The variable cost of sale per unit is $125 and monthly fixed costs are $2 million. It has been estimated that for every $10 increase or reduction in price, sales demand will fall or increase by 4,000 units.

At what selling price per unit will the monthly profit be maximised?

A $135
B $180
C $215
D $248.75

(2 marks)

23.9 The following information is available for identifying the relevant cost of materials for a job for a customer. The company's management wants to establish a minimum price at which it is prepared to take on the job.

Material	*Total quantity required*	*Currently in inventory*	*Carrying value per kg*	*Realisable value per kg*	*Replacement cost per kg*
	kg	kg	$	$	$
W	500	0	–	–	8
X	500	300	5	3	7
Y	500	400	8	9	11
Z	100	100	10	12	15

Material Y is in regular use by the company. Materials X and Z are no longer in regular use. There is no alternative use for Material X but the 100 kg of Material Z could be used instead of 150 kg of Material V on a different job. Material V costs $9 per kg and there is currently none of this material in inventory.

What is the relevant cost of these materials for the job under consideration?

A $10,850
B $11,350
C $12,200
D $13,150

(2 marks)

23.10 A company wishes to decide on a selling price for a new product. Weekly sales of each product will depend on the price charge and also on customers' response to the new product. The following pay-off table has been prepared.

	Probability	*Price P1*	*Price P2*	*Price P3*	*Price P4*
		$	$	$	$
Price		5.00	5.50	6.00	6.50
Unit contribution		3.00	3.50	4.00	4.50
Weekly demand		units	units	units	units
Best possible	0.2	10,000	9,000	8,000	7,000
Most likely	0.5	8,000	7,500	7,000	6,000
Worst possible	0.3	6,000	5,000	4,000	3,000

If the choice of selling price is based on the expected value decision rule, which price would be selected?

A P1
B P2
C P3
D P4

(2 marks)

(Total = 20 marks)

MCQ bank 4 — 36 mins

24.1 The following statements have been made about decision making under conditions of uncertainty.

(1) Expected value is a more reliable basis for decision making where the situation and outcome will occur many times than for a one-off decision.

(2) A risk-averse decision maker avoids all risks in decision making.

Which of the above statements is/are true?

A 1 only
B 2 only
C Neither 1 nor 2
D Both 1 and 2

(2 marks)

24.2 Which method of pricing is most easily applied when two or more markets for the product or service can be kept entirely separate from each other?

A Price discrimination
B Product line pricing
C Skimming
D Volume discounting

(2 marks)

24.3 A company wishes to go ahead with one of three mutually exclusive projects, but the profit outcome from each project will depend on the strength of sales demand, as follows.

	Strong demand Profit/(Loss)	*Moderate demand Profit*	*Weak demand Profit/(Loss)*
	$	$	$
Project 1	70,000	10,000	(7,000)
Project 2	25,000	12,000	5,000
Project 3	50,000	20,000	(6,000)
Probability of demand	0.1	0.4	0.5

What is the value to the company of obtaining this perfect market research information, ignoring the cost of obtaining the information?

A $3,000
B $5,500
C $6,000
D $7,500

(2 marks)

24.4 A manufacturing company makes two joint products, CP1 and CP2, in a common process. These products can be sold at the split-off point in an external market, or processed further in separate processes to produce products FP1 and FP2. Details of these processes are shown in the diagram.

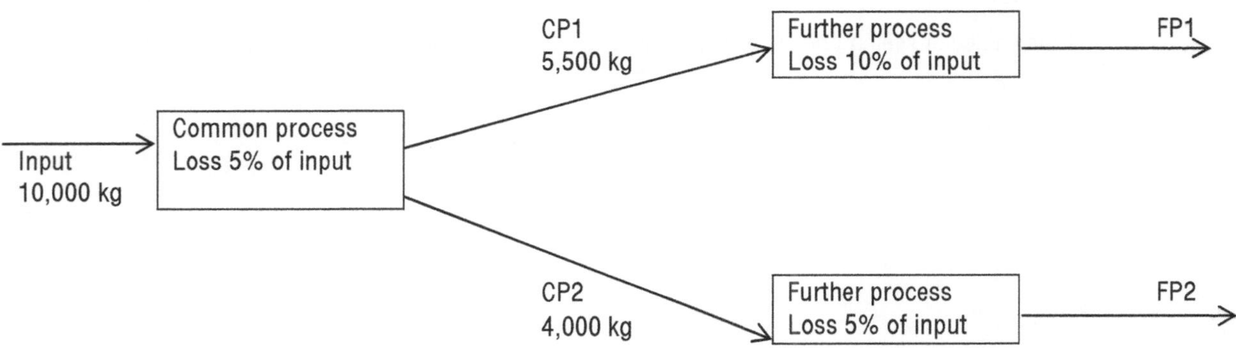

CP1 has a market price of $6 per kg and CP2 has a market price of $5 per kg. Relevant further processing costs are $2 per input kg in the process to make FP1 and $3 per input kg in the process to make FP2. Both FP1 and FP2 sell for $9 per kg.

For each 10,000 kg input to the common process, how much additional profit is obtained by further processing each of the joint products instead of selling them at the split-off point?

A $2,750
B $4,450
C $8,750
D $9,500

(2 marks)

24.5 A company is selling a product at a price of $120 per unit. At this price it is selling 200,000 units per period. It has been estimated that for every $5 increase or reduction in price, sales demand will fall or increase by 10,000 units.

At what selling price will total sales revenue per period be maximised?

A $80
B $90
C $100
D $110

(2 marks)

24.6 A company produces and sells a single product. Budgeted sales are $2.4 million, budgeted fixed costs are $360,000 and the margin of safety is $400,000. What are budgeted variable costs?

A $1.640 million
B $1.728 million
C $1.968 million
D $2.040 million

(2 marks)

24.7 The following statements have been made about cost plus pricing.

(1) A weakness of cost plus pricing is that it fails to recognise the effect of sales price on sales demand. A price in excess of full cost per unit will ensure that a company will cover all its costs and make a profit.

(2) A weakness of full cost plus pricing is that the bases used for apportionment of overhead costs between products or jobs may be arbitrary or inappropriate.

Which of the above statements is/are true?

A 1 only
B 2 only
C Neither 1 nor 2
D Both 1 and 2

(2 marks)

24.8 Which of the following statements about decision trees is/are correct?

(1) A decision tree can be used to identify the preferred decision choice using the minimax regret decision rule.

(2) A decision tree is likely to present a simplified representation of reality.

A 1 only is correct
B 2 only is correct
C Neither 1 nor 2 is correct
D Both 1 and 2 are correct

(2 marks)

24.9 The price elasticity of demand for a product at its current price level is inelastic. What will happen if the price of the product is reduced?

A Total revenue will fall and profit will fall
B Total revenue will fall and profit may either increase or fall
C Total revenue will increase and profit will increase
D Total revenue will increase and profit may either increase or fall

(2 marks)

24.10 A company makes two products, X and Y, on the same type of direct labour and production capacity per period is restricted to 60,000 direct labour hours. The contribution per unit is $8 for Product X and $6 for Product Y. The following constraints apply to production and sales:

x	≤ 10,000	(Sales demand for Product X)
y	≤ 12,000	(Sales demand for Product Y)
5x + 4y	≤ 60,000	(Direct labour hours)

The contribution-maximising output is to produce and sell 10,000 units of Product X and 2,500 units of Product Y.

What is the shadow price per direct labour hour and for how many additional hours of labour does this shadow price per hour apply?

A $1.50 per hour for the next 38,000 direct labour hours
B $1.50 per hour for the next 47,500 direct labour hours
C $1.60 per hour for the next 38,000 direct labour hours
D $1.60 per hour for the next 47,500 direct labour hours

(2 marks)

(Total = 20 marks)

MCQ bank 5 — 36 mins

25.1 The following statements have been made about marginal cost plus pricing.

(1) Marginal cost plus pricing is used extensively in retailing.

(2) Marginal cost plus pricing, with prices determined by a fixed mark-up on marginal cost, allows for market conditions more than full cost plus pricing.

Which of the above statements is/are true?

A 1 only
B 2 only
C Neither 1 nor 2
D Both 1 and 2

(2 marks)

25.2 A company makes and sells four products. Direct labour hours are a scarce resource, but the company is able to sub-contract production of any products to external suppliers. The following information is relevant.

Product	*W*	*X*	*Y*	*Z*
	$ per unit	$ per unit	$ per unit	$ per unit
Sales price	10	8	12	14
Variable cost	8	5	8	12
Cost of external purchase	9	7.1	10	13
Direct labour hours per unit	0.1	0.3	0.25	0.2

In what order of priority should the company make these products in-house, rather than purchase them externally?

A W, Y, X then Z
B W, Z, X then Y
C X, Z, W then Y
D Z, X, Y then W

(2 marks)

25.3 The following statements have been made about solving linear programming problems for budgeting purposes using the graphical method.

(1) When the objective function is to minimise total variable costs, the optimal solution is at the point where an iso-cost line touches the feasible region at a point nearest to the origin of the graph.

(2) A constraint that may have an effect on the optimal solution is show by a line on the graph that helps to determine the shape of the feasible region.

Which of the above statements is/are true?

A 1 only
B 2 only
C Neither 1 nor 2
D Both 1 and 2

(2 marks)

25.4 In a linear programming problem to determine the contribution-maximising production and sales volumes for two products, X and Y, the following information is available.

	Product X per unit	*Product Y per unit*	*Total available per period*
Direct labour hours	2 hours	4 hours	10,000 hours
Material X	4 kg	2 kg	14,000 kg
Contribution per unit	$12	$18	

The profit-maximising level of output and sales is 3,000 units of Product X and 1,000 units of Product Y.

What is the shadow price of a direct labour hour?

A $1.00
B $2.40
C $4.00
D $4.50

(2 marks)

25.5 A company makes and sells a single product. When sales per month are $6.8 million, total costs are $6.56 million. When sales per month are $5.2 million, total costs are $5.44 million. There is a step cost increase of $400,000 in fixed costs when sales are $6.0 million, but variable unit costs are constant at all levels of output and sales.

What is the breakeven point for sales revenue per month?

A $6.0 million
B There are two breakeven points: $5.64 million and $6.36 million
C $5.64 million only
D $6.36 million only

(2 marks)

25.6 A benefit sacrificed by taking one course of action instead of the most profitable alternative course of action is known as:

A An incremental cost
B An opportunity cost
C A relevant cost
D A sunk cost

(2 marks)

25.7 A special job for a customer will required 8 tonnes of a Material M. The company no longer uses this material regularly although it holds 3 tonnes in inventory. These originally cost $44 per tonne, and could be resold to a supplier for $35 per tonne. Alternatively these materials could be used to complete another job instead of using other materials that would cost $126 to purchase. The current market price of Material M is $50 per tonne.

The company must decide whether to agree to the customer's request for the work, and to set a price. What would be the relevant cost of Material M for this job?

A $250
B $355
C $376
D $382

(2 marks)

25.8 A company wishes to decide on a selling price for a new product. Weekly sales of each product will depend on the price charge and also on customers' response to the new product. The following pay-off table has been prepared.

	Probability	*Price P1*	*Price P2*	*Price P3*	*Price P4*
		$	$	$	$
Price		5.00	5.50	6.00	6.50
Unit contribution		3.00	3.50	4.00	4.50
Weekly demand		units	units	units	units
Best possible	0.3	10,000	9,000	8,000	7,000
Most likely	0.5	8,000	7,500	7,000	6,000
Worst possible	0.2	6,000	5,000	4,000	3,000

If the choice of selling price is based on a maximin decision rule, which price would be selected?

A P1
B P2
C P3
D P4

(2 marks)

25.9 Analysing the range of different possible outcomes from a particular situation, with a computer model that uses random numbers is known as:

A Probability analysis
B Sensitivity analysis
C Simulation modelling
D Stress testing

(2 marks)

25.10 The following decision tree shows four decision options: 1, 2, 3 and 4

Option	*Probability*	*Benefit* $
1	1.0	9,500
2	0.3	14,000
	0.3	10,000
	0.4	5,000
3	0.4	10,000
	0.6	9,000
4	0.7	8,000
	0.3	14,000

Using the expected value rule, which choice should be made so as to optimise the expected benefit?

A Choice 1
B Choice 2
C Choice 3
D Choice 4

(2 marks)

(Total = 20 marks)

MCQ bank 6

36 mins

26.1 What method of uncertainty or risk analysis is also called 'What if?' analysis?

A Decision tree analysis
B Sensitivity analysis
C Simulation modelling
D Stress testing

(2 marks)

26.2 The following statements have been made about the price elasticity of demand for a product.

(1) Price elasticity of demand may be reduced by means of advertising and sales promotion activities.

(2) When elasticity of demand is very inelastic customers are not sensitive to either price or advertising and sales promotion activities.

Which of the above statements is/are true?

A 1 only
B 2 only
C Neither 1 nor 2
D Both 1 and 2

(2 marks)

26.3 A company wants to decide whether to make its materials in-house or whether to sub-contract production to an external supplier. In the past it has made four materials in-house, but demand in the next year will exceed in-house production capacity of 8,000 units. All four materials are made on the same machines and require the same machine time per unit: machine time is the limiting production factor.
The following information is available.

Material	*W*	*X*	*Y*	*Z*
Units required	4,000	2,000	3,000	4,000
Variable cost of in-house manufacture	$8 per unit	$12 per unit	$9 per unit	$10 per unit
Directly attributable fixed cost expenditure	$5,000	$8,000	$6,000	$7,000
Cost of external purchase	$9 per unit	$18 per unit	$12 per unit	$12 per unit

Directly attributable fixed costs are fixed cash expenditures that would be saved if production of the material in-house is stopped entirely.

If a decision is made solely on the basis of short-term cost considerations, what materials should the company purchase externally?

A 4,000 units of W and 1,000 units of Z
B 4,000 units of W and 4,000 units of Z
C 3,000 units of Y and 2,000 units of Z
D 1,000 units of Y and 4,000 units of Z

(2 marks)

26.4 A company wishes to decide on a selling price for a new product. Weekly sales of each product will depend on the price charge and also on customers' response to the new product. The following pay-off table has been prepared.

	Probability	*Price P1*	*Price P2*	*Price P3*	*Price P4*
		$	$	$	$
Price		5.00	5.50	6.00	6.50
Unit contribution		3.00	3.50	4.00	4.50
Weekly demand		Units	Units	Units	Units
Best possible	0.3	10,000	9,000	8,000	7,000
Most likely	0.5	8,000	7,500	7,000	6,000
Worst possible	0.2	6,000	5,000	4,000	3,000

If the choice of selling price is based on a minimax regret decision rule, which price would be selected?

A P1
B P2
C P3
D P4

(2 marks)

26.5 A company wishes to go ahead with one of two mutually exclusive projects, but the profit outcome from each project will depend on the strength of sales demand, as follows.

	Strong demand	*Moderate demand*	*Weak demand*
	Profit	*Profit*	*Profit/(Loss)*
	$	$	$
Project 1	80,000	50,000	(5,000)
Project 2	60,000	25,000	10,000
Probability of demand	0.2	0.4	0.4

The company could purchase market research information, at a cost of $4,500. This would predict demand conditions with perfect accuracy.

What is the value to the company of obtaining this perfect market research information?

A $1,500
B $3,500
C $4,500
D $6,000

(2 marks)

26.6 A company uses linear programming to decide on the production and sales budget that will maximise total contribution and profit for a financial period. The optimal solution involves using all available direct labour hours, for which the shadow price is $4.50 per hour, and machine hours, for which the shadow price is $3 per machine hour. Direct labour is paid $8 per hour.

If the objective of the company is to maximise total contribution and profit in each period, how much should the company be willing to pay per hour to obtain additional direct labour hours of production capacity?

A Up to but not including $4.50
B Up to but not including $9.50
C Up to but not including $12.50
D Up to but not including $15.50

(2 marks)

26.7 A company budgets to sells its three products A, B and C in the ratio 2:3:5 respectively, measured in units of sales. Unit sales prices and variable costs are as follows.

Product	*A*	*B*	*C*
	$ per unit	$ per unit	$ per unit
Sales price	20	18	24
Variable cost	11	12	18

Budgeted fixed costs are $1.2 million. What sales will be needed to achieve a target profit of $400,000 for the period, to the nearest $1,000?

A $5.188 million
B $5.101 million
C $4.939 million
D $4.724 million

(2 marks)

26.8 Market research into demand for a product indicates that when the selling price per unit is $145, demand in each period will be 5,000 units and if the price is $120, demand will be 11,250 units. It is assumed that the demand function for this product is linear. The variable cost per unit is $27.

What selling price should be charged in order to maximise the monthly profit?

A $83
B $84
C $95
D $96

(2 marks)

26.9 The demand for a product at its current price has a price elasticity greater than 1.0 (ignoring the minus sign). Which of the following statements must be correct?

(1) A reduction in the sales price will increase total revenue.

(2) A reduction in the sales price by x% will result in a percentage increase in sales demand which is greater than x%.

(3) An increase in the selling price will increase total profit.

A Statements 1 and 2 only must be correct
B Statements 1 and 3 only must be correct
C Statements 2 and 3 only must be correct
D All three statements must be correct

(2 marks)

26.10 A company makes and sells three products. The budget for the next period is as follows:

Product	*A*	*B*	*C*
	$ per unit	$ per unit	$ per unit
Sales price	12	18	20
Variable cost	3	6	11
	9	12	9
Fixed cost	6	9	6
Profit	3	3	3
Number of units	30,000	40,000	10,000

What is the breakeven point in sales, to the nearest $1,000?

A $640,000
B $739,000
C $914,000
D $1,500,000

(2 marks)

(Total = 20 marks)

27 Devine Desserts — 18 mins

You are the Assistant Accountant of Devine Desserts plc, a newly formed food manufacturer. The Board of Directors is concerned that its operational managers may not be fully aware of the importance of understanding the costs incurred by the business and the effect that this has on their operational decision making.

In addition, the operational managers need to be aware of the implications of their pricing policy when trying to increase the volume of sales.

You are scheduled to make a presentation to the operational managers to explain to them the different costs that are incurred by the business, the results of some research that has been conducted into the implications for pricing and the importance of understanding these issues for their decision making. **The diagram has already been prepared for the presentation.**

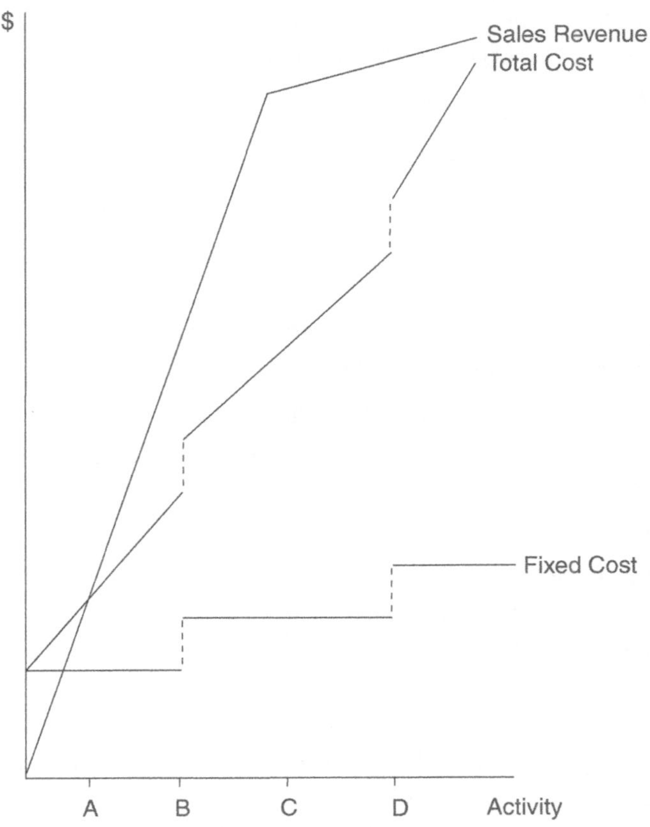

Required

Interpret the diagram and explain how it illustrates issues that the operational managers should consider when making decisions. (**Note.** Your answer must include explanations of the Sales Revenue, Total Cost and Fixed Cost lines, and the significance of each of the activity levels labelled A, B, C, D.) **(10 marks)**

28 Cut and Stitch (6/10 amended) 18 mins

Cut and Stitch (CS) make two types of suits using skilled tailors (labour) and a delicate and unique fabric (material). Both the tailors and the fabric are in short supply and so the accountant at CS has correctly produced a linear programming model to help decide the optimal production mix.

The model is as follows:

Variables:

Let W = the number of work suits produced
Let L = the number of lounge suits produced

Constraints

Tailors' time: $7W + 5L \leq 3,500$ (hours) – this is line T on the diagram
Fabric: $2W + 2L \leq 1,200$ (metres) – this is line F on the diagram
Production of work suits: $W \leq 400$ – this is line P on the diagram

Objective is to maximise contribution subject to:

$C = 48W + 40L$

On the diagram provided the accountant has correctly identified OABCD as the feasible region and point B as the optimal point.

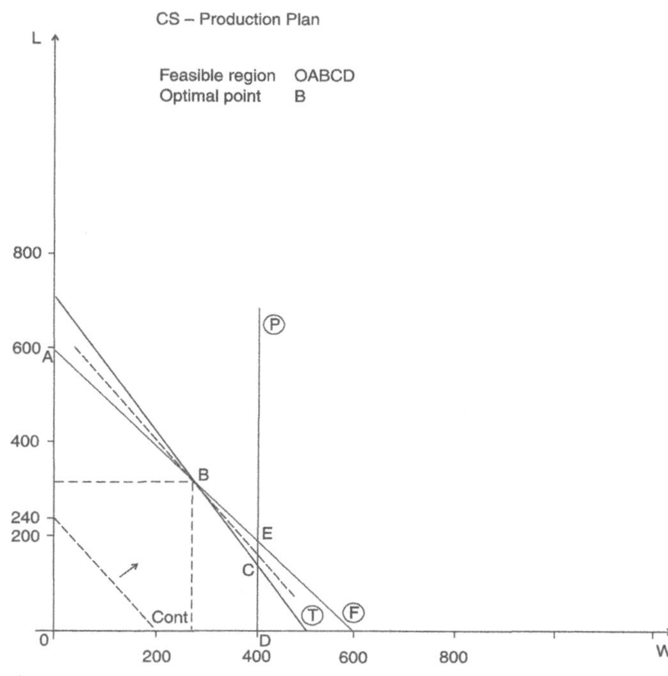

Required

(a) Find by appropriate calculation the optimal production mix and related maximum contribution that could be earned by CS. **(4 marks)**

(b) Calculate the shadow prices of the fabric per metre and the tailor time per hour. **(6 marks)**

(Total = 10 marks)

29 RB Co — 18 mins

Just over two years ago, RB Co was the first company to produce a specific 'off-the-shelf' accounting software package. The pricing strategy, decided on by the managing director, for the packages was to add a 50% mark-up to the budgeted full cost of the packages. The company achieved and maintained a significant market share and high profits for the first two years.

Budgeted information for the current year (Year 3) was as follows.

Production and sales	15,000 packages
Full cost	$400 per package

At a recent board meeting, the finance director reported that although costs were in line with the budget for the current year, profits were declining. He explained that the full cost included $80 for fixed overheads. This figure had been calculated by using an overhead absorption rate based on labour hours and the budgeted level of production of 15,000 packages. He pointed out that this was much lower than the current capacity of 25,000 packages.

The marketing director stated that competitors were beginning to increase their market share. He also reported the results of a recent competitor analysis which showed that when RB Co announced its prices for the current year, the competitors responded by undercutting them by 15%. Consequently, he commissioned an investigation of the market. He informed the board that the market research showed that at a price of $750 there would be no demand for the packages but for every $10 reduction in price the demand would increase by 1,000 packages.

The managing director appeared to be unconcerned about the loss of market share and argued that profits could be restored to their former level by increasing the mark-up.

Required

(a) Discuss the managing director's pricing strategy in the circumstances described above. **(4 marks)**

(b) Suggest and explain two alternative strategies that could have been implemented at the launch of the packages. **(4 marks)**

(c) Based on the data supplied by the market research, derive a straight line demand equation for the packages. **(2 marks)**

(Total = 10 marks)

30 Heat Co (6/11 amended) — 18 mins

Heat Co specialises in the production of a range of air conditioning appliances for industrial premises. It is about to launch a new product, the 'Energy Buster', a unique air conditioning unit which is capable of providing unprecedented levels of air conditioning using a minimal amount of electricity. The technology used in the Energy Buster is unique so Heat Co has patented it so that no competitors can enter the market for two years. The company's development costs have been high and it is expected that the product will only have a five-year life cycle.

Heat Co is now trying to ascertain the best pricing policy that they should adopt for the Energy Buster's launch onto the market. Demand is very responsive to price changes and research has established that, for every $15 increase in price, demand would be expected to fall by 1,000 units. If the company set the price at $735, only 1,000 units would be demanded.

The costs of producing each air conditioning unit are as follows:

	$	
Direct materials	42	
Labour	12	(1.5 hours at $8 per hour. See note below)
Fixed overheads	6	(based on producing 50,000 units per annum)
Total cost	60	

Note.

The first air conditioning unit took 1.5 hours to make and labour cost $8 per hour. A 95% learning curve exists, in relation to production of the unit, although the learning curve is expected to finish after making 100 units. Heat Co's management have said that any pricing decisions about the Energy Buster should be based on the time it takes to make the 100th unit of the product. You have been told that the learning co-efficient, b = –0.0740005.

All other costs are expected to remain the same up to the maximum demand levels.

Required

(a) Establish the demand function (equation) for air conditioning units. **(2 marks)**

(b) Calculate the marginal cost for each air conditioning unit after adjusting the labour cost as required by the note above. **(6 marks)**

(c) Equate marginal cost and marginal revenue in order to calculate the optimum price and quantity. **(2 marks)**

(Total = 10 marks)

31 Metallica Ltd **18 mins**

Metallica Ltd, an engineering company manufactures a range of products and components. One of the company's suppliers has announced that the amount of M1, one of the materials it currently supplies, will be limited to 1,000 square metres in total for the next three-month period because there will be insufficient M1 to satisfy demand.

The only items manufactured using M1 and their production costs and selling prices (where applicable) are shown below.

	Product P4	*Product P6*	*Component C3*	*Component C5*
	$/unit	$/unit	$/unit	$/unit
Selling price	125	175	n/a	n/a
Direct materials:				
M1*	15	10	5	10
M2	10	20	15	20
Direct labour	20	30	16	10
Variable overhead	10	15	8	5
Fixed overhead**	20	30	16	10
Total cost	75	105	60	55

* Material M1 is expected to be limited in supply during the next three months. These costs are based on M1 continuing to be available at a price of $20 per square metre.

** Fixed overhead is absorbed as a percentage of direct labour cost.

Products P4 and P6 are sold externally. Components C3 and C5 are used in other products made by the company. These other products do not require any further amounts of material M1.

The estimated total demand for these products and components during the next three months is as follows.

P4 2,000 units
P6 1,500 units
C3 500 units
C5 1,000 units

Components C3 and C5 are essential components. They would have to be bought in if they could not be made internally. They can be purchased from external suppliers for $75 and $95 per unit respectively. The bought in components are of the same quality as those manufactured by the company. The product they are used in have sufficient margins to remain financially worthwhile if C3 and C5 are bought in at these prices.

Required

(a) Prepare calculations to show the most profitable course of action for the company for the next three months, assuming that there are no other suppliers of material M1. **(7 marks)**

(b) Outline **three** other factors that Metallica should consider before making its decision. **(3 marks)**

(Total = 10 marks)

32 Ennerdale **18 mins**

Ennerdale has been asked to quote a price for a one-off contract. The company's management accountant has asked for your advice on the relevant costs for the contract. The following information is available:

Materials

The contract requires 3,000 kg of material K, which is a material used regularly by the company in other production. The company has 2,000 kg of material K currently in inventory which had been purchased last month for a total cost of $19,600. Since then the price per kilogram for material K has increased by 5%.

The contract also requires 200 kg of material L. There are 250 kg of material L in inventory which are not required for normal production. This material originally cost a total of $3,125. If not used on this contract, the inventory of material L would be sold for $11 per kg.

Labour

The contract requires 800 hours of skilled labour. Skilled labour is paid $9.50 per hour. There is a shortage of skilled labour and all the available skilled labour is fully employed in the company in the manufacture of product P. The following information relates to product P:

	$ per unit	*$ per unit*
Selling price		100
Less:		
Skilled labour	38	
Other variable costs	22	
		(60)
		40

Required

(a) Prepare calculations showing the total relevant costs for making a decision about the contract in respect of the following cost elements:

(i) Materials K and L

(ii) Skilled labour **(5 marks)**

The company also manufactures three joint products (M, N and P) from the same common process. In a typical month, output from the common process consists of 25,000 litres of M, 15,000 litres of N and 45,000 litres of P, in fixed proportions. The monthly costs of the common process are $480,000.

Each one of the products can be sold immediately after the common process, but each one of them can be further processed individually before being sold. The following further processing costs and selling prices per litre are expected:

Product	*Selling price after common process* $/litre	*Selling price after further processing* $/litre	*Further variable processing cost* $/litre
M	6.25	8.40	1.75
N	5.20	6.45	0.95
P	6.80	7.45	0.85

(b) Evaluate the viability of the common process, and determine the optimal processing plan for each of the three products, showing appropriate calculations. **(5 marks)**

(Total = 10 marks)

33 Hair (12/12 amended) 27 mins

Hair Co manufactures three types of electrical goods for hair: curlers (C), straightening irons (S) and dryers (D). The budgeted sales prices and volumes for the next year are as follows:

	C	*S*	*D*
Selling price	$110	$160	$120
Units	20,000	22,000	26,000

Each product is made using a different mix of the same materials and labour. The budgeted sales volumes for all the products have been calculated by adding 10% to last year's sales.

The standard cost card for each product is shown below.

	C	*S*	*D*
	$	$	$
Materials	20	50	42
Labour	30	54	50

Labour costs are variable. The general fixed overheads are expected to be $640,000 for the next year.

Required

(a) Calculate the weighted average contribution to sales ratio for Hair Co.

Note. Round all workings to two decimal places. **(4 marks)**

(b) Calculate the total break-even sales revenue for the next year for Hair Co.

Note. Round all workings to two decimal places. **(2 marks)**

(c) Using the graph paper provided, draw a multi-product profit-volume (PV) chart showing clearly the profit/loss lines assuming:

(i) You are able to sell the products in order of the ones with the highest ranking contribution to sales ratios first; and

(ii) You sell the products in a constant mix.

Note. Only one graph is required. **(9 marks)**

(Total = 15 marks)

34 Higgins Co (6/08 amended) 27 mins

Higgins Co (HC) manufactures and sells pool cues and snooker cues. The cues both use the same type of good quality wood (ash) which can be difficult to source in sufficient quantity. The supply of ash is restricted to 5,400 kg per period. Ash costs $40 per kg.

The cues are made by skilled craftsmen (highly skilled labour) who are well known for their workmanship. The skilled craftsmen take years to train and are difficult to recruit. HC's craftsmen are generally only able to work for 12,000 hours in a period. The craftsmen are paid $18 per hour.

HC sells the cues to a large market. Demand for the cues is strong, and in any period, up to 15,000 pool cues and 12,000 snooker cues could be sold. The selling price for pool cues is $41 and the selling price for snooker cues is $69.

Manufacturing details for the two products are as follows:

	Pool cues	*Snooker cues*
Craftsmen time per cue	0.5 hours	0.75 hours
Ash per cue	270 g	270 g
Other variable costs per cue	$1.20	$4.70

The contribution per unit is $20 for pool cues and $40 per unit for snooker cues.

HC does not keep inventory.

Required

(a) Determine the optimal production plan for a typical period assuming that HC is seeking to maximise the contribution earned. You should use a linear programming graph, identify the feasible region and the optimal point and accurately calculate the maximum contribution that could be earned using whichever equations you need. **(10 marks)**

(b) Explain the meaning of a shadow price (dual price) and calculate the shadow price of both the labour (craftsmen) and the materials (ash). **(5 marks)**

(Total = 15 marks)

35 The Cosmetic Co (12/10 amended) — 27 mins

The Cosmetic Co is a company producing a variety of cosmetic creams and lotions. The creams and lotions are sold to a variety of retailers at a price of $23.20 for each jar of face cream and $16.80 for each bottle of body lotion. Each of the products has a variety of ingredients, with the key ones being silk powder, silk amino acids and aloe vera. Six months ago, silk worms were attacked by disease causing a huge reduction in the availability of silk powder and silk amino acids. The Cosmetic Co had to dramatically reduce production and make part of its workforce, which it had trained over a number of years, redundant.

The company now wants to increase production again by ensuring that it uses the limited ingredients available to maximise profits by selling the optimum mix of creams and lotions. Due to the redundancies made earlier in the year, supply of skilled labour is now limited in the short term to 160 hours (9,600 minutes) per week, although unskilled labour is unlimited. The purchasing manager is confident that they can obtain 5,000 grams of silk powder and 1,600 grams of silk amino acids per week. All other ingredients are unlimited. The following information is available for the two products:

	Cream	*Lotion*
Materials required: silk powder (at $2.20 per gram)	3 grams	2 grams
– Silk amino acids (at $0.80 per gram)	1 gram	0.5 grams
– Aloe vera (at $1.40 per gram)	4 grams	2 grams
Labour required: skilled ($12 per hour)	4 minutes	5 minutes
– Unskilled (at $8 per hour)	3 minutes	1.5 minutes

Each jar of cream sold generates a contribution of $9 per unit, whilst each bottle of lotion generates a contribution of $8 per unit. The maximum demand for lotions is 2,000 bottles per week, although demand for creams is unlimited. Fixed costs total $1,800 per week. The company does not keep inventory although if a product is partially complete at the end of one week, its production will be completed in the following week.

Required

(a) On the graph paper provided, use linear programming to calculate the optimum number of each product that the Cosmetic Co should make per week, assuming that it wishes to maximise contribution. Calculate the total contribution per week for the new production plan. All workings **must** be rounded to two decimal places. **(10 marks)**

(b) Calculate the shadow price for silk powder and the slack for silk amino acids. All workings **must** be rounded to two decimal places. **(5 marks)**

(Total = 15 marks)

36 LD Co — 27 mins

LD Co provides two cleaning services for staff uniforms to hotels and similar businesses. One of the services is a laundry service and the other is a dry cleaning service. Both of the services use the same resources, but in different quantities. Details of the expected resource requirements, revenues and costs of each service are shown below.

		Laundry	*Dry cleaning*
		$ per service	$ per service
Selling price		5.60	13.20
Cleaning materials	($10.00 per litre)	2.00	3.00
Direct labour	($6.00 per hour)	1.20	2.00
Variable machine cost	($3.00 per hour)	0.50	1.50
Fixed costs *		1.15	2.25
Profit		0.75	4.45

* Total annual fixed costs are $32,825.

The maximum resources expected to be available in December 20X3 are

Cleaning materials	5,000 litres
Direct labour hours	6,000 hours
Machine hours	5,000 hours

LD Co has one particular contract which it entered into six months ago with a local hotel to guarantee 1,200 laundry services and 2,000 dry cleaning services every month. If LD Co does not honour this contract it has to pay substantial financial penalties to the local hotel.

The maximum demand for laundry is expected to be 14,000 services and for dry cleaning 9,975 services.

Required

(a) Assuming that a graphical linear programming solution is to be used to maximise profit:

(i) State the constraints and objective function. **(4 marks)**

(ii) Determine the maximum profit that can be made. **(7 marks)**

(b) Calculate the shadow price of a machine hour and explain what this means for LD Co. **(4 marks)**

(Total = 15 marks)

37 Tablet Co (6/14 amended) 27 mins

Tablet Co makes two types of tablet computer, the Xeno (X) and the Yong (Y). X currently generates a contribution of $30 per unit and Y generates a contribution of $40 per unit. There are three main stages of production: the build stage, the program stage and the test stage. Each of these stages requires the use of skilled labour which, due to a huge increase in demand for tablet computers over recent months, is now in short supply. The following information is available for the two products:

Stage	*Xeno (X)* Minutes per unit	*Yong (Y)* Minutes per unit
Build ($10 per hour)	24	20
Program ($16 per hour)	16	14
Test ($12 per hour)	10	4

Tablet Co is now preparing its detailed production plans for the next quarter. During this period it expects that the skilled labour available will be 30,000 hours (1,800,000 minutes) for the build stage, 28,000 hours (1,680,000 minutes) for the program stage and 12,000 hours (720,000 minutes) for the test stage. The maximum demand for X and Y over the three-month period is expected to be 85,000 units and 66,000 units respectively. Fixed costs are $650,000 per month.

Due to rapid technological change, the company holds no inventory of finished goods.

Required

On the graph paper provided, use linear programming to calculate the optimum number of each product which Tablet Co should make in the next quarter assuming it wishes to maximise contribution. Calculate the total profit for the quarter. **(15 marks)**

38 T Co (12/11 amended) 27 mins

The Telephone Co (T Co) is a company specialising in the provision of telephone systems for commercial clients. There are two parts to the business:

- Installing telephone systems in businesses, either first time installations or replacement installations;
- Supporting the telephone systems with annually renewable maintenance contracts.

T Co has been approached by a potential customer, Push Co, who wants to install a telephone system in new offices it is opening. Whilst the job is not a particularly large one, T Co is hopeful of future business in the form of replacement systems and support contracts for Push Co. T Co is therefore keen to quote a competitive price for the job. The following information should be considered:

(1) One of the company's salesmen has already been to visit Push Co, to give them a demonstration of the new system, together with a complimentary lunch, the costs of which totalled $400.

(2) The installation is expected to take one week to complete and would require three engineers, each of whom is paid a monthly salary of $4,000. The engineers have just had their annually renewable contract renewed with T Co. One of the three engineers has spare capacity to complete the work, but the other two would have to be moved from contract X in order to complete this one. Contract X generates a contribution of $5 per engineer hour. There are no other engineers available to continue with Contract X if these two engineers are taken off the job. It would mean that T Co would miss its contractual completion deadline on Contract X by one week. As a result, T Co would have to pay a one-off penalty of $500. Since there is no other work scheduled for their engineers in one week's time, it will not be a problem for them to complete Contract X at this point.

(3) T Co's technical adviser would also need to dedicate eight hours of his time to the job. He is working at full capacity, so he would have to work overtime in order to do this. He is paid an hourly rate of $40 and is paid for all overtime at a premium of 50% above his usual hourly rate.

(4) Two visits would need to be made by the site inspector to approve the completed work. He is an independent contractor who is not employed by T Co, and charges Push Co directly for the work. His cost is $200 for each visit made.

(5) T Co's system trainer would need to spend one day at Push Co delivering training. He is paid a monthly salary of $1,500 but also receives commission of $125 for each day spent delivering training at a client's site.

(6) 120 telephone handsets would need to be supplied to Push Co. The current cost of these is $18.20 each, although T Co already has 80 handsets in inventory. These were bought at a price of $16.80 each. The handsets are the most popular model on the market and frequently requested by T Co's customers.

(7) Push Co would also need a computerised control system called 'Swipe 2'. The current market price of Swipe 2 is $10,800, although T Co has an older version of the system, 'Swipe 1', in inventory, which could be modified at a cost of $4,600. T Co paid $5,400 for Swipe 1 when it ordered it in error two months ago and has no other use for it. The current market price of Swipe 1 is $5,450, although if Push Co tried to sell the one they have, it would be deemed to be 'used' and therefore only worth $3,000.

(8) 1,000 metres of cable would be required to wire up the system. The cable is used frequently by T Co and it has 200 metres in inventory, which cost $1.20 per metre. The current market price for the cable is $1.30 per metre.

(9) You should assume that there are four weeks in each month and that the standard working week is 40 hours long.

Required

Prepare a cost statement, using relevant costing principles, showing the minimum cost that T Co should charge for the contract. Make **detailed** notes showing how each cost has been arrived at and **explain** why each of the costs above has been included or excluded from your cost statement. **(15 marks)**

39 Robber Co (6/12 amended) 27 mins

Robber Co manufactures control panels for burglar alarms, a very profitable product. Every product comes with a one year warranty offering free repairs if any faults arise in this period.

It currently produces and sells 80,000 units per annum, with production of them being restricted by the short supply of labour. Each control panel includes two main components – one key pad and one display screen. At present, Robber Co manufactures both of these components in-house. However, the company is currently considering outsourcing the production of keypads and/or display screens. A newly established company based in Burgistan is keen to secure a place in the market, and has offered to supply the keypads for the equivalent of $4.10 per unit and the display screens for the equivalent of $4.30 per unit. This price has been guaranteed for two years.

The current total annual costs of producing the keypads and the display screens are:

	Keypads	*Display screens*
Production	80,000 units	80,000 units
	$'000	$'000
Direct materials	160	116
Direct labour	40	60
Heat and power costs	64	88
Machine costs	26	30
Depreciation and insurance costs	84	96
Total annual production costs	374	390

Notes

1 Materials costs for keypads are expected to increase by 5% in six months' time; materials costs for display screens are only expected to increase by 2%, but with immediate effect.

2 Direct labour costs are purely variable and not expected to change over the next year.

3 Heat and power costs include an apportionment of the general factory overhead for heat and power as well as the costs of heat and power directly used for the production of keypads and display screens. The general apportionment included is calculated using 50% of the direct labour cost for each component and would be incurred irrespective of whether the components are manufactured in-house or not.

4 Machine costs are semi-variable; the variable element relates to set up costs, which are based upon the number of batches made. The keypads' machine has fixed costs of $4,000 per annum and the display screens' machine has fixed costs of $6,000 per annum. Whilst both components are currently made in batches of 500, this would need to change, with immediate effect, to batches of 400.

5 60% of depreciation and insurance costs relate to an apportionment of the general factory depreciation and insurance costs; the remaining 40% is specific to the manufacture of keypads and display screens.

Required

(a) Advise Robber Co whether it should continue to manufacture the keypads and display screens in-house or whether it should outsource their manufacture to the supplier in Burgistan, assuming it continues to adopt a policy to limit manufacture and sales to 80,000 control panels in the coming year. **(8 marks)**

(b) Robber Co takes 0.5 labour hours to produce a keypad and 0.75 labour hours to produce a display screen. Labour hours are restricted to 100,000 hours and labour is paid at $1 per hour. Robber Co wishes to increase its supply to 100,000 control panels (ie 100,000 each of keypads and display screens).

Advise Robber Co as to how many units of keypads and display panels they should either manufacture and/or outsource in order to minimise their costs. **(7 marks)**

(Total = 15 marks)

40 Stay Clean (12/09 amended) 27 mins

Stay Clean manufactures and sells a small range of kitchen equipment. Specifically the product range contains a dishwasher (DW), a washing machine (WM) and a tumble dryer (TD). The TD is of a rather old design and has for some time generated negative contribution. It is widely expected that in one year's time the market for this design of TD will cease, as people switch to a washing machine that can also dry clothes after the washing cycle has Completed.

Stay Clean is trying to decide whether or not to cease the production of TD now **or** in 12 months' time when the new combined washing machine/drier will be ready. To help with this decision the following information has been provided:

(1) The normal selling prices, annual sales volumes and total variable costs for the three products are as follows:

	DW	*WM*	*TD*
	$	$	$
Selling price per unit	200	350	80
Material cost per unit	70	100	50
Labour cost per unit	50	80	40
Contribution per unit	80	170	-10
Annual sales	5,000 units	6,000 units	1,200 units

(2) It is thought that some of the customers that buy a TD also buy a DW and a WM. It is estimated that 5% of the sales of WM and DW will be lost if the TD ceases to be produced.

(3) All the direct labour force currently working on the TD will be made redundant immediately if TD is ceased now. This would cost $6,000 in redundancy payments. If Stay Clean waited for 12 months the existing labour force would be retained and retrained at a cost of $3,500 to enable them to produce the new washing/drying product. Recruitment and training costs of labour in 12 months' time would be $1,200 in the event that redundancy takes place now.

(4) Stay Clean operates a just in time (JIT) policy and so all material cost would be saved on the TD for 12 months if TD production ceased now. Equally, the material costs relating to the lost sales on the WM and the DW would also be saved. However, the material supplier has a volume based discount scheme in place as follows:

Total annual expenditure	*Discount*
$	%
0 – 600,000	0
600,001 – 800,000	1
800,001 – 900,000	2
900,001 – 960,000	3
960,001 and above	5

Stay Clean uses this supplier for all its materials for all the products it manufactures. The figures given above in the cost per unit table for material cost per unit are net of any discount Stay Clean already qualifies for.

(5) The space in the factory currently used for the TD will be sublet for 12 months on a short-term lease contract if production of TD stops now. The income from that contract will be $12,000.

(6) The supervisor (currently classed as an overhead) supervises the production of all three products spending approximately 20% of his time on the TD production. He would continue to be fully employed if the TD ceases to be produced now.

Required

(a) Calculate whether or not it is worthwhile ceasing to produce the TD now rather than waiting 12 months (ignore any adjustment to allow for the time value of money). **(11 marks)**

(b) Explain two pricing strategies that could be used to improve the financial position of the business in the next 12 months assuming that the TD continues to be made in that period. **(4 marks)**

(Total = 15 marks)

41 Bits and Pieces (6/09 amended) 27 mins

Bits and Pieces (B&P) operates a retail store selling spares and accessories for the car market. The store has previously only opened for six days per week for the 50 working weeks in the year, but B&P is now considering also opening on Sundays.

The sales of the business on Monday through to Saturday averages at $10,000 per day with average gross profit of 70% earned.

B&P expects that the gross profit % earned on a Sunday will be 20 percentage points lower than the average earned on the other days in the week. This is because they plan to offer substantial discounts and promotions on a Sunday to attract customers. Given the price reduction, Sunday sales revenues are expected to be 60% **more than** the average daily sales revenues for the other days. These Sunday sales estimates are for new customers only, with no allowance being made for those customers that may transfer from other days.

B&P buys all its goods from one supplier. This supplier gives a 5% discount on **all** purchases if annual spend exceeds $1,000,000.

It has been agreed to pay time and a half to sales assistants that work on Sundays. The normal hourly rate is $20 per hour. In total five sales assistants will be needed for the six hours that the store will be open on a Sunday. They will also be able to take a half-day off (four hours) during the week. Staffing levels will be allowed to reduce slightly during the week to avoid extra costs being incurred.

The staff will have to be supervised by a manager, currently employed by the company and paid an annual salary of $80,000. If he works on a Sunday he will take the equivalent time off during the week when the assistant manager is available to cover for him at no extra cost to B&P. He will also be paid a bonus of 1% of the extra sales generated on the Sunday project.

The store will have to be lit at a cost of $30 per hour and heated at a cost of $45 per hour. The heating will come on two hours before the store opens in the 25 'winter' weeks to make sure it is warm enough for customers to come in at opening time. The store is not heated in the other weeks.

The rent of the store amounts to $420,000 per annum.

Required

(a) Calculate whether the Sunday opening incremental revenue exceeds the incremental costs over a year (ignore inventory movements) and on this basis reach a conclusion as to whether Sunday opening is financially justifiable. **(11 marks)**

(b) Briefly discuss whether offering substantial price discounts and promotions on Sunday is a good suggestion. **(4 marks)**

(Total = 15 marks)

42 BDU Co 27 mins

BDU Co is a manufacturer of baby equipment and is planning to launch a revolutionary new style of sporty pushchair. The company has commissioned market research to establish possible demand for the pushchair and the following information has been obtained.

If the price is set at $425, demand is expected to be 1,000 pushchairs, at $500 it will be 730 pushchairs and at $600 it will be 420 pushchairs. Variable costs are estimated at either $170, $210 or $260.

A decision needs to be made on what price to charge.

A table showing the expected contribution for each of the nine possible outcomes has been prepared, as follows.

		Price		
		$425	$500	$600
	$170	255,000 (W1)	240,900 (W3)	180,600
Variable cost	$210	215,000 (W2)	211,700	163,800
	$260	165,000	175,200	142,800

Workings

(1) $(425 - 170) \times 1{,}000 = \$255{,}000$
(2) $(425 - 210) \times 1{,}000 = \$215{,}000$
(3) $(500 - 170) \times 730 = \$240{,}900$

Required

(a) Explain what is meant by maximax, maximin and minimax regret decision rules, using the information in the scenario to illustrate your explanations. **(10 marks)**

(b) Explain the use of expected values and sensitivity analysis and suggest how BDU could make use of such techniques. **(5 marks)**

(Total = 15 marks)

43 Gym Bunnies (6/13 amended) 27 mins

Gym Bunnies (GB) is a health club. It currently has 6,000 members, with each member paying a subscription fee of $720 per annum. The club is comprised of a gym, a swimming pool and a small exercise studio.

A competitor company is opening a new gym in GB's local area, and this is expected to cause a fall in GB's membership numbers, unless GB can improve its own facilities. Consequently, GB is considering whether or not to expand its exercise studio in a hope to improve its membership numbers. Any improvements are expected to last for three years.

Option 1

No expansion. In this case, membership numbers would be expected to fall to 5,250 per annum for the next three years. Operational costs would stay at their current level of $80 per member per annum.

Option 2

Expand the exercise studio. The capital cost of this would be $360,000.The expected effect on membership numbers for the next three years is as follows:

Probability	*Effect on membership numbers*
0.4	Remain at their current level of 6,000 members per annum
0.6	Increase to 6,500 members per annum

The effect on operational costs for the next three years is expected to be:

Probability	*Effect on operational costs*
0.5	Increase to $120 per member per annum
0.5	Increase to $180 per member per annum

Required

(a) Using the criterion of expected value, prepare and fully label a decision tree that shows the two options available to GB. Recommend the decision that GB should make.

Note. Ignore time value of money. **(11 marks)**

(b) Calculate the maximum price that GB should pay for perfect information about the expansion's exact effect on **membership numbers**. **(4 marks)**

(Total = 15 marks)

44 SH (12/08 amended) 27 mins

Shifters Haulage (SH) is considering changing some of the vans it uses to transport crates for customers. The new vans come in three sizes; small, medium and large. SH is unsure about which type to buy. The capacity is 100 crates for the small van, 150 for the medium van and 200 for the large van.

Demand for crates varies and can be either 120 or 190 crates per period, with the probability of the higher demand figure being 0.6.

The sale price per crate is $10 and the variable cost $4 per crate for all van sizes subject to the fact that if the capacity of the van is greater than the demand for crates in a period then the variable cost will be lower by 10% to allow for the fact that the vans will be partly empty when transporting crates.

SH is concerned that if the demand for crates exceeds the capacity of the vans then customers will have to be turned away. SH estimates that in this case goodwill of $100 would be charged against profits per period to allow for lost future sales regardless of the number of customers that are turned away.

Depreciation charged would be $200 per period for the small, $300 for the medium and $400 for the large van.

SH has in the past been very aggressive in its decision making, pressing ahead with rapid growth strategies. However, its managers have recently grown more cautious as the business has become more competitive.

Required

(a) Prepare a profits table showing the **six** possible profit figures per period. **(9 marks)**

(b) Using your profit table from (b) above discuss which type of van SH should buy taking into consideration the possible risk attitudes of the managers. **(6 marks)**

(Total = 15 marks)

45 Gam Co (6/14, amended) 27 mins

Gam Co sells electronic equipment and is about to launch a new product onto the market. It needs to prepare its budget for the coming year and is trying to decide whether to launch the product at a price of $30 or $35 per unit. The following information has been obtained from market research:

Price per unit $30		*Price per unit $35*	
Probability	*Sales volume*	*Probability*	*Sales volume*
0.4	120,000	0.3	108,000
0.5	110,000	0.3	100,000
0.1	140,000	0.4	94,000

Notes

1 Variable production costs would be $12 per unit for production volumes up to and including 100,000 units each year. However, if production exceeds 100,000 units each year, the variable production cost per unit would fall to $11 for all units produced.

2 Advertising costs would be $900,000 per annum at a selling price of $30 and $970,000 per annum at a price of $35.

3 Fixed production costs would be $450,000 per annum.

Required

(a) Calculate each of the six possible profit outcomes which could arise for Gam Co in the coming year. **(8 marks)**

(b) Calculate the expected value of profit for each of the two price options and recommend, on this basis, which option Gam Co would choose. **(4 marks)**

(c) Briefly explain the maximin decision rule and identify which price should be chosen by management if they use this rule to decide which price should be charged. **(3 marks)**

(Total = 15 marks)

BUDGETING AND CONTROL

Questions 39 to 67 cover Budgeting and control, the subject of Part C of the BPP Study Text for Paper F5.

MCQ bank 1 — 36 mins

46.1 Which of the following statements about setting budget targets is/are correct?

(1) Setting 'ideal standards' as targets for achievement should motivate employees to perform to the best of their ability.

(2) Setting low standards as targets for achievement should motivate employees because they should usually achieve or exceed the target.

A 1 only is correct
B 2 only is correct
C Neither 1 nor 2 is correct
D Both 1 and 2 are correct

(2 marks)

46.2 A company produces a blended drink product from two ingredients, Ingredient A and Ingredient B. Ingredient A is more expensive per litre than Ingredient B. During the most recent period, the company produced fewer litres of finished drink product than budgeted, and it used a larger than expected proportion of Ingredient A in the materials mix than expected.

Which one of the following statements is correct about materials variances in the period?

A The materials mix variance is adverse and the materials yield variance is also adverse

B The materials mix variance is adverse but the materials yield variance cannot be measured with the available data

C The materials mix variance is favourable and the materials yield variance is also adverse

D The materials mix variance is favourable but the materials yield variance cannot be measured with the available data

(2 marks)

46.3 A company began producing a new product in batches four months ago. When production commenced the first batch took 45 hours. The actual learning rates observed were as follows.

Month	*Total batches produced to date*	*Actual learning rate*
1	1	
2	2	75%
3	4	75%
4	8	90%

What was the average production time per batch for the first eight batches?

A 18.98 hours
B 22.78 hours
C 39.06 hours
D 32.81 hours

(2 marks)

46.4 Extracts from the flexible budgets of a manufacturing company are as follows.

Production and sales quantity	5,000 units	7,000 units
Budget cost allowance	$'000	$'000
Materials costs	50	70
Labour costs	65	77
Production overheads	80	84
Administration costs	35	35
Selling and distribution costs	15	19
Total cost allowance	245	285

What would be the total expenditure incurred in a period when 6,000 units are produced and 5,500 units are sold?

A $234,000
B $250,500
C $263,500
D $264,000

(2 marks)

46.5 A control system that reacts to changes in the business environment, usually to maintain a desired state of operations, is known as:

A Feedback control
B Feedforward control
C A rolling budget
D Top-down control

(2 marks)

46.6 The following statements have been made about zero base budgeting.

(1) The zero base budgeting process seeks to identify long-term benefits and improvements, even if they are sometimes made at the expense of short-term profitability.

(2) A restriction on the use of zero base budgeting is that management do not have the skills to apply it.

Which of the above statements is/are true?

A 1 only
B 2 only
C Neither 1 nor 2
D Both 1 and 2

(2 marks)

46.7 The following statements have been made about the use of spreadsheets for budgeting.

(1) A problem with spreadsheets for budgeting is that managers are tempted to accept figures produced from the model without questioning them.

(2) Spreadsheets have greater practical application to budgeting for complex organisations than for smaller business operations.

Which of the above statements is/are true?

A 1 only
B 2 only
C Neither 1 nor 2
D Both 1 and 2

(2 marks)

46.8 A mix of three materials into a process produces 0.9 litres of a finished product, with 10% loss of input in the process. Standard material costs are as follows per 0.9 litres of output.

Material		$
X	0.5 litres at $2 per litre	1.00
Y	0.4 litres at $1.50 per litre	0.60
Z	0.1 litres at $4 per litre	0.40
		2.00

During a control period, 4,000 litres of output were produced. These used 2,810 litres of Material X; 1,910 litres of Material Y; and 380 litres of Material Z.

What is the materials yield variance?

A $195 (F)
B $1,116 (A)
C $1,311 (A)
D $2,200 (A)

(2 marks)

46.9 The following statements have been made about planning and operational variances.

(1) No one may accept responsibility for planning variances.

(2) It is usually easy to identify in retrospect what prices and quantities were, but not nearly so easy to identify what they should have been.

Which of the above statements is/are true?

A 1 only
B 2 only
C Neither 1 nor 2
D Both 1 and 2

(2 marks)

46.10 A standard product takes 0.4 hours of direct labour time for which the original standard wage rate is $14 per hour. During the most recent month, 8,000 units of the product were manufactured and these took 3,500 hours to make. It is recognised that the work force had been given a large pay rise to $16.50 per hour, which applied throughput the recent month, but which had not been included in the standard hourly rate.

What is the labour rate planning variance, if it is chosen to use planning and operational variances for reporting performance?

A $4,200 (A)
B $8,000 (F)
C $8,750 (F)
D $8,750 (A)

(2 marks)

(Total = 20 marks)

MCQ bank 2 — 36 mins

47.1 The following statements have been made about activity based budgeting (ABB).

(1) The amount of an activity in the budget is decided according to how many resources the organisation has decided to allocate to it.

(2) ABB is based on the principle that activities drive costs and the aim is to control the causes (drivers) of costs rather than the costs themselves.

Which of the above statements is/are true?

A 1 only
B 2 only
C Neither 1 nor 2
D Both 1 and 2

(2 marks)

47.2 The following statements have been made about standard costing.

(1) Standard costing is well suited to organisations that produce items to customer specifications.

(2) Predetermined standards conflict with a philosophy of continual improvement and Total Quality Management.

Which of the above statements is/are true?

A 1 only
B 2 only
C Neither 1 nor 2
D Both 1 and 2

(2 marks)

47.3 The following budgeted and actual sales information relates to a budget period for a company that makes and sells three products.

Product	*Budgeted sales*	*Budgeted sales price per unit*	*Actual sales*
	Units	$	Units
X	5,000	20	5,800
Y	3,000	35	2,700
Z	2,000	40	1,800

The standard contribution per unit for each product is 40% of the standard sales price.

What was the sales quantity variance for the period?

A $1,000 (A)
B $3,420 (F)
C $3,800 (F)
D $8,550 (F)

(2 marks)

47.4 A standard batch of 10 litres of input materials to a process should produce 9 litres of finished output. There are three input materials into each batch, as follows.

Material		$
X	5 litres at $3 per litre	15
Y	2 litres at $6 per litre	12
Z	3 litres at $4 per litre	12
		39

In one month, 100 batches of finished output were produced. Input materials were 523 litres of Material X, 238 litres of Material Y and 239 litres of Material Z.

What is the materials mix variance?

A $53 (A)
B $53 (F)
C $433 (F)
D $433 (A)

(2 marks)

47.5 Which one of the following is **not** a common criticism of incremental budgeting?

A It assumes that all current activities and costs are still needed.
B There is no requirement for managers to justify existing costs.
C There is no incentive for managers to reduce costs.
D There are no performance targets for managers.

(2 marks)

47.6 For which of the following reasons is budgeting more difficult in public sector organisations (such as government and the police force) than in private sector companies?

Reason
1 Difficulty in quantifying objectives
2 Spending limits imposed by government
3 Difficulty in quantifying outputs

A Reasons 1 and 2 only
B Reasons 1 and 3 only
C Reasons 2 and 3 only
D Reasons 1, 2 and 3

(2 marks)

47.7 If workers are paid a bonus on the basis of labour efficiency in a period, which type of standard would be most appropriate as a basis for deciding the amount of bonuses payable?

A Attainable standard
B Basic standard
C Current standard
D Ideal standard

(2 marks)

47.8 A company has estimated that an 85% learning curve will apply to the production of a new item for which the time to produce the first unit was 800 hours.

What is the expected time to produce the ninth unit?

A 370.86 hours
B 417.61 hours
C 477.92 hours
D 491.30 hours

(2 marks)

47.9 Budgeting has been criticised extensively by the Beyond Budgeting Round Table (BBRT). Which one of the following is **not** a criticism of traditional budgeting by the BBRT?

A Budgets protect rather than reduce costs
B Budgets focus in sales targets rather than customer satisfaction
C Managers do not give budgeting enough of their time
D Budgets discourage innovation and initiative

(2 marks)

47.10 Apply the high-low method to the following data to establish a fixed cost per period and a variable cost per unit.

Period	*Activity level*	*Cost*
	Units	$
1	35,000	233,200
2	48,000	274,800
3	32,000	225,200
4	45,000	277,200
5	42,000	256,300

Estimated costs are:

A $97,200 fixed costs + $4.00 per unit variable cost
B $117,700 fixed costs + $3.30 per unit variable cost
C $121,200 fixed costs + $3.20 per unit variable cost
D $126,000 fixed costs + $3.10 per unit variable cost

(2 marks)

(Total = 20 marks)

MCQ bank 3 36 mins

48.1 In which one of the following ways might a budgetary control **not** act as a disincentive to management to achieve targeted performance?

A Targets are too strict
B Budgets are imposed by senior management
C Targets are not communicated
D Control reports are provided too late

(2 marks)

48.2 The following statements have been made about planning and operational variances

(1) Operational variances should be a realistic measure of what the causes of the variances have cost the organisation.

(2) The causes of planning variances need not be investigated.

Which of the above statements is/are true?

A 1 only
B 2 only
C Neither 1 nor 2
D Both 1 and 2

(2 marks)

48.3 A sales volume variance can sometimes be analysed into a market size variance and a market share variance. The following statements have been made about these variances.

(1) In a competitive market, a market share variance is controllable by sales management.
(2) In a competitive market, a market size variance is not controllable by sales management.

Which of the above statements is/are true?

A 1 only
B 2 only
C Neither 1 nor 2
D Both 1 and 2

(2 marks)

48.4 Apply the high-low method to the following data to establish a fixed cost per period and a variable cost per unit.

Period	*Activity level*	*Cost*
	Units	$
1	34,000	257,200
2	38,000	282,000
3	37,000	284,700
4	24,000	247,000
5	25,000	242,700

Estimated costs are:

A $187,000 fixed costs + $2.50 per unit variable cost
B $177,400 fixed costs + $2.90 per unit variable cost
C $167,700 fixed costs + $3.00 per unit variable cost
D $155,200 fixed costs + $3.50 per unit variable cost

(2 marks)

48.5 The first batch of a new product is expected to take 5 hours to manufacture (at a labour cost of $10 per hour) and the expected material cost is $10 per batch. An 80% learning curve is expected to apply, but it is planned to establish a standard cost at the time required to produce the 40th batch of the product. When the learning curve is expressed as a formula $Y = ax^b$, the value of b is –0.3219281.

What will be the standard variable cost per batch?

A $12.46
B $20.38
C $25.24
D $25.37

(2 marks)

48.6 The following statements have been made about rolling budgets.

(1) Rolling budgets may be used to alter plans instead of encouraging managers to focus on improving performance.

(2) Rolling budgets are not worth preparing unless there is a persistent and large amount of uncertainty about the future.

Which of the above statements is/are true?

A 1 only
B 2 only
C Neither 1 nor 2
D Both 1 and 2

(2 marks)

48.7 The following statements have been made about zero base budgeting.

(1) The ranking process for activities is a critically important part of the zero base budgeting process.

(2) Zero base budgeting is time consuming and can be costly; therefore it is inappropriate to use this budgeting method every financial year.

Which of the above statements is/are true?

A 1 only
B 2 only
C Neither 1 nor 2
D Both 1 and 2

(2 marks)

48.8 A mix of three materials into a process produces one litre of a finished product, with some loss of input in the process. Standard material costs are as follows per litre of output.

Material		$
X	0.3 litres at $2 per litre	0.60
Y	0.6 litres at $3 per litre	1.80
Z	0.3 litres at $1 per litre	0.30
		2.70

During a control period, 5,000 litres of output were produced. These used 1,400 litres of Material X; 3,100 litres of Material Y; and 1,250 litres of Material Z.

What is the materials yield variance?

A $412.50 (A)
B $150 (F)
C $469 (F)
D $562.50 (F)

(2 marks)

48.9 A manufacturer produces Product X from three input raw materials, P, Q and R. There is some loss in the process, usually about 5% of input. Results for the most recent month are as follows.

Which one of the following performance measurements is accurate?

A Rate of wastage = 6.7%
B Average cost of input = $3.88 per kg
C Output: input conversion ratio = 6.25%
D Materials yield variance = $1,938 (A)

(2 marks)

48.10 In which one of the following ways might an operational manager try to improve labour efficiency and achieve favourable labour efficiency variances?

A Increase output volumes
B Increase inspection and testing of products
C Provide workers with training
D Arrange for overtime working

(2 marks)

(Total = 20 marks)

MCQ bank 4 — 36 mins

49.1 A company operates in export and import markets, and its operational cash flows are affected by movements in exchange rates, which are highly volatile. As a result, the company has great difficulty in establishing a budgeting system that is reliable for more than three months ahead. Which one of the following approaches to budgeting would be most appropriate for this company's situation?

A Flexible budget
B Incremental budget
C Rolling budget
D Zero based budget

(2 marks)

49.2 What general term is used for information about output from an operation that is used to control the operation?

A Feedback
B Feedforward
C Key performance indicators
D Variances

(2 marks)

49.3 Which of the following weaknesses in a budgeting system is most likely to be found in a top-down system of budgeting?

A Management budgets may include excessive amounts of 'slack' (unnecessary budget spending allowances)

B Budgets may be inconsistent with the long-term strategy of the organisation

C Management budgets may not be realistic in practice

D All of the above

(2 marks)

49.4 The following statements have been made about learning curves.

(1) Standard costs are not applicable in industries where a learning curve applies.

(2) When a learning curve applies to production, a company may choose to sell early units of a new product at a loss in order to create sales demand.

Which of the above statements is/are true?

A 1 only
B 2 only
C Neither 1 nor 2
D Both 1 and 2

(2 marks)

49.5 The first item of a new product took 2,000 hours to manufacture (at a labour cost of $15 per hour). A 90% learning curve was expected to apply, and it was decided to establish a standard time as the time required to manufacture the 50th item of the product, rounded to the nearest hour. The 50th item actually took 980 hours.

What was the labour efficiency variance for the 50th unit produced?

A $645 (A)
B $43 (A)
C $1,860 (F)
D $1,905 (F)

(2 marks)

49.6 Which one of the following is the **least** likely reason why standard costs might not easily be applied to road haulage and distribution services.

A It is difficult to measure labour times reliably
B Variable costs are negligible
C It is difficult to identify a standard item for costing
D Standard costing applies to manufacturing industries only

(2 marks)

49.7 In which of the following circumstances should the operational manager of a budget centre, rather than the purchasing managers, be held accountable for material price variances?

Circumstance	
1	When the operational centre uses excessive quantities of materials
2	When the operational manager buys materials directly from suppliers
3	When materials are purchased at short notice, at the urgent request of the operational manager

A Circumstances 1 and 2 only
B Circumstances 1 and 3 only
C Circumstances 2 and 3 only
D Circumstances 1, 2 and 3

(2 marks)

49.8 The following information is given about standard and actual material costs during one month for a production process.

Material	*Standard cost* per kg	*Actual cost* per kg	*Standard mix*	*Actual mix* kg
P	3.00	3.50	10%	820
Q	2.50	2.75	20%	1,740
R	4.00	3.50	30%	2,300
S	5.25	5.00	40%	2,640
				7,500

What was the materials mix variance?

A $720 (A)
B $720 (F)
C $880 (A)
D $880 (F)

(2 marks)

49.9 For which one of the following variances should a production manager usually be held responsible?

A Material price planning variance
B Material price operational variance
C Material usage planning variance
D Material usage operational variance

(2 marks)

49.10 The following statements have been made about standard mix and yield variances.

(1) Mix variances should be calculated whenever a standard product contains two or more direct materials.
(2) When a favourable mix variance is achieved, there may be a counterbalancing adverse yield variance.

Which of the above statements is/are true?

A 1 only
B 2 only
C Neither 1 nor 2
D Both 1 and 2

(2 marks)

(Total = 20 marks)

MCQ bank 5 — 36 mins

50.1 The following statements have been made about flexible budgets.

(1) Flexible budgets enable proper comparisons to be made between actual and expected revenues and costs.

(2) In every variance reporting system with flexible budgets that compares budgeted and actual profit, there must be a sales volume variance.

Which of the above statements is/are true?

A 1 only
B 2 only
C Neither 1 nor 2
D Both 1 and 2

(2 marks)

50.2 A company sells two products X and Y. Product X sells for $30 per unit and achieves a standard contribution of $12 per unit, which is 40% of the selling price. Product Y, a new product, sells for $80 per unit and achieves a standard contribution of just $10 per unit, which is 12.5% of the selling price. Budgeted sales are 5,000 units of X and 3,000 units of Y.

However the sudden cancellation of an advertising campaign for Product Y has meant that sales for the product will be well below budget, and there has been some price discounting in an attempt to obtain sales for the product. Sales of X were in line with the budget.

Which one of the following sales variances, if calculated, would you expect to show a favourable variance for the period?

A Sales mix variance
B Sales price variance
C Sales quantity variance
D Sales volume variance

(2 marks)

50.3 Which one of the following provides the most suitable definition of the controllability principle in business?

A A fundamental principle of management is the responsibility to control the organisation

B Managers should be held accountable only for costs and revenues over which they have some influence or control

C Organisations should be divided into budget centres for the purpose of operational control

D Performance measures should be reported to managers to enable them to control operations

(2 marks)

50.4 The following statements have been made about standard mix and yield variances.

(1) Mix and yield variances enable management to resolve problems with the quality of production output.

(2) Persistent adverse mix variances may have an adverse effect on sales volume variances and direct labour efficiency variances.

Which of the above statements is/are true?

A 1 only
B 2 only
C Neither 1 nor 2
D Both 1 and 2

(2 marks)

50.5 The following statements have been made about the application of standard costing systems.

(1) Standard costing systems are compatible with a Total Quality Management approach to operations.

(2) Standard costing systems are less commonly used in an industry that operates in a rapidly changing environment.

Which of the above statements is/are true?

A 1 only
B 2 only
C Neither 1 nor 2
D Both 1 and 2

(2 marks)

50.6 The following statements have been made about learning curves.

(1) Learning curves are easier to apply in companies with a high labour turnover than those with a lower rate of staff turnover.

(2) Learning rates are not affected by time gaps between the production of additional units of a product.

Which of the above statements is/are true?

A 1 only
B 2 only
C Neither 1 nor 2
D Both 1 and 2

(2 marks)

50.7 The following statements have been made about the use of expected values in budgeting.

(1) Expected values may not be expected to occur, which means that probabilistic budgets are of limited value for budgetary control.

(2) The use of expected values and probabilities in budgeting is most useful when there is a high level of uncertainty about the future.

Which of the above statements is/are true?

A 1 only
B 2 only
C Neither 1 nor 2
D Both 1 and 2

(2 marks)

50.8 A company makes and sells three products. Budgeted and actual results for the period just ended were as follows.

Product	*Budgeted sales*	*Budgeted profit per unit*	*Actual sales*	*Actual profit per unit*
	Units	$	Units	$
X	800	10	700	8
Y	1,000	6	1,200	6
Z	600	12	350	16
	2,400		2,250	

What was the sales mix variance?

A $1,475 (A)
B $1,475 (F)
C $1,800 (A)
D $1,800 (F)

(2 marks)

50.9 Which one of the following statements about standard costing is **incorrect**?

A Standard costing is less applicable in a modern manufacturing environment where a large proportion of total costs are overhead costs that are fixed in the short term

B Managers expect to access up-to-date performance information online, and standard costing systems do not easily provide this

C Management may prefer alternative methods of performance reporting instead of standard costing

D Managers no longer rely on formal budgetary control reports to monitor performance

(2 marks)

50.10 For which one of the following reasons is zero based budgeting (ZBB) often considered more suitable for public sector service organisations than for private sector companies?

A ZBB is more suited to costs where there is little discretionary spending, as in the public sector services

B The public sector is better able to afford the high cost of ZBB

C ZBB is used in a top-down approach to budgeting, which is more common in the public sector than the private sector

D It is easier to put public sector activities into decision packages because they are more easily definable than in the private sector

(2 marks)

(Total = 20 marks)

MCQ bank 6 **36 mins**

51.1 The following statements have been made about the use of spreadsheets for budgeting.

(1) Spreadsheets greatly assist sensitivity analysis during the planning process.

(2) Spreadsheets greatly assist the budgeting process by facilitating the preparation of alternative draft budgets.

Which of the above statements is/are true?

A 1 only
B 2 only
C Neither 1 nor 2
D Both 1 and 2

(2 marks)

51.2 Which type of standard cost is most useful for monitoring trends in performance over time?

A Attainable standard
B Basic standard
C Current standard
D Ideal standard

(2 marks)

51.3 The following statements have been made about sales mix and quantity variances.

(1) Sales mix and quantity variances are inappropriate for control report purposes when different managers have responsibility for sales of different products.

(2) Sales mix variances can provide useful information for a company that wants to persuade customers to upgrade from a lower-cost and cheaper product to a higher quality and more expensive version.

Which of the above statements is/are true?

A 1 only
B 2 only
C Neither 1 nor 2
D Both 1 and 2

(2 marks)

51.4 A standard product uses 3 kilograms of direct material costing $4 per kg. During the most recent month, 120 units of the product were manufactured. These required 410 kilograms of material costing $4.50 per kg. It is decided in retrospect that the standard usage quantity of the material should have been 3.5 kg, not 3 kg.

What is the materials operational usage variance, if it is chosen to use planning and operational variances for reporting performance?

A $270 (A)
B $240 (A)
C $40 (F)
D $60 (A)

(2 marks)

51.5 For which of the following types of budget is a rolling budget most likely to be appropriate?

A Cash
B Direct labour
C Materials purchases
D Sales

(2 marks)

51.6 Managers may show a negative attitude to budgetary control reports they receive, and it should be the responsibility of senior management and management accountants to do what they can to reduce such negativity. Which one of the following measures is **least** likely to be within the ability of the management accountant to implement?

A Control reports should use less technical terminology and jargon
B Managers should not be held accountable for variances they cannot control
C Control reports should not be used as pressure devices to push managers into performing better
D The information in control reports should be timely, accurate and reliable

(2 marks)

51.7 The following statements have been made about budgets.

(1) Annual budgets provide a link between long-term business planning and short-term operational concerns.

(2) Budgets establish targets for achievement within a framework for monitoring achievement.

Which of the above statements is/are true?

A 1 only
B 2 only
C Neither 1 nor 2
D Both 1 and 2

(2 marks)

51.8 What name is given to a method of budgeting in which managers decide what is needed to achieve their planned objectives, and their budgets are combined to establish total operating budget?

A Bottom-up budgeting
B Feedforward control
C Incremental budgeting
D Zero based budgeting

(2 marks)

51.9 The following statements have been made about incremental budgeting.

(1) Incremental budgets encourage managers to review and question the continuing need for certain activities.

(2) Incremental budgeting is best suited to budgets for discretionary items of spending.

Which of the above statements is/are true?

A 1 only
B 2 only
C Neither 1 nor 2
D Both 1 and 2

(2 marks)

51.10 A company makes and sells three products. Budgeted and actual results for the period just ended were as follows.

Product	*Budgeted sales*	*Budgeted profit per unit*	*Actual sales*	*Actual profit per unit*
	Units	$	Units	$
X	800	10	700	8
Y	1,000	6	1,200	6
Z	600	12	350	16
	2,400		2,250	

What was the sales quantity variance?

A $1,227 (A)
B $1,325 (A)
C $2,800 (F)
D $3,600 (F)

(2 marks)

(Total = 20 marks)

52 GH Consultancy **18 mins**

G and H have recently formed a consultancy business, and have sought your advice concerning costs and fees. G and H each wish to receive a salary of $20,000 in the first year of trading.

G and H each expect to work for eight hours per day, five days per week for 45 weeks per year. They refer to this as **available time**. 25% of the available time is expected to be used dealing with administrative matters related to their own business, and in the first year it is expected that there will be idle time which will average 22.5% of the available time. The remainder of the available time is expected to be chargeable to clients.

In order that the consultancy business breaks even after paying the required salaries, classify the costs are classified between professional services and vehicle costs, and the available time is then analysed into travelling time and productive time.

G and H agreed that their fee structure should comprise the following.

(1) An hourly rate for productive client work
(2) An hourly rate for travelling to/from clients
(3) A rate per mile travelled to/from clients

They expect that the travelling time will equal 25% of their chargeable time, and will amount to a total of 18,000 miles. They have agreed that this time should be charged at one-third of their normal hourly rate.

G and H have estimated their other costs for the first 12 months as follows:

Professional services costs: $62,100
Vehicle costs: $10,080

Required

(a) Calculate the following.

(i) An hourly rate for productive client work
(ii) An hourly rate for travelling to/from clients
(iii) A rate per mile travelled to/from clients **(6 marks)**

(b) Explain how G and H may monitor their income and costs during the year to see if they are achieving their objectives. **(4 marks)**

(Total = 10 marks)

53 Sauce Co (6/12 amended) **18 mins**

Sauce Co manufactures and sells cartons of cooking sauces, which deteriorate over time and must be used within three months. Over the last two years, Sauce Co has experienced all kinds of problems. The financial and sales directors believe these to be a result of persistently unrealistic sales targets imposed by the managing director, who makes forecasts based on his own subjective and overly optimistic views about future sales. Production volumes are currently based on anticipated sales rather than actual orders.

Whilst an incentive scheme is in place for employees, the company has not hit its targets for the last three years, so no bonuses have been paid out.

Required

Discuss the likely impact that the budgeting style and inaccurate sales forecasts have had on the staff and business of Sauce Co. **(10 marks)**

54 Wargrin (12/08 amended) **18 mins**

Wargrin designs, develops and sells many digital games. Games have a short life cycle lasting around three years only. Performance of the games is measured by reference to the profits made in each of the expected three years of popularity. Wargrin accepts a net profit of 35% of turnover as reasonable. A rate of contribution (sales price less variable cost) of 75% is also considered acceptable.

Wargrin has a large centralised development department which carries out all the design work before it passes the completed game to the sales and distribution department to market and distribute the product.

Wargrin has developed a brand new game called Stealth and this has the following budgeted performance figures.

The selling price of Stealth will be a constant $30 per game. Analysis of the costs show that at a volume of 10,000 units a total cost of $130,000 is expected. However at a volume of 14,000 units a total cost of $150,000 is expected. If volumes exceed 15,000 units the fixed costs will increase by 50%.

Stealth's budgeted volumes are as follows:

	Year 1	*Year 2*	*Year 3*
Sales volume	8,000 units	16,000 units	4,000 units

In addition, marketing costs for Stealth will be $60,000 in year one and $40,000 in year two. Design and development costs are all incurred before the game is launched and has cost $300,000 for Stealth. These costs are written off to the income statement as incurred (ie before year 1 above).

Required

(a) Produce the budgeted results for the game 'Stealth' and briefly assess the game's expected performance, taking into account the whole lifecycle of the game. **(6 marks)**

(b) Explain why incremental budgeting is a common method of budgeting and outline the main problems with such an approach. **(4 marks)**

(Total = 10 marks)

55 Learning (12/11 amended) **18 mins**

A company has been estimating the cost of a new product over its expected two-year life cycle. Expected production and sales are 100,000 units in the first year and 200,000 units in the second year. The original estimate for the variable manufacturing cost per unit was $40 in the first year and $42 in the second year: this includes a cost for 0.5 hours of labour. The remainder of the variable manufacturing cost is not driven by labour hours. The first year cost per hour for labour is $24 and the second year cost is $26 per hour.

The original cost estimate has been reviewed and it is now estimated that, although the first unit is expected to take 0.5 hours, a learning curve of 95% is expected to occur until the 100th unit has been completed. The learning rate for a learning curve of 95% = –0.0740005

Required

Calculate the revised life cycle cost for labour in each of the first and second years, taking into account the effect of the learning curve. Calculate the average labour cost per unit over the two-year period. **(10 marks)**

56 HC (12/08 amended) **18 mins**

Henry Company (HC) provides skilled labour to the building trade. They have recently been asked by a builder to bid for a kitchen fitting contract for a new development of 600 identical apartments. HC has not worked for this builder before. Cost information for the new contract is as follows:

Labour for the contract is available. HC expects that the first kitchen will take 24 man-hours to fit but thereafter the time taken will be subject to a 95% learning rate. After 200 kitchens are fitted the learning rate will stop and the time taken for the 200th kitchen will be the time taken for all the remaining kitchens. Labour costs $15 per hour.

Overheads are absorbed on a labour hour basis. HC has collected overhead information for the last four months and this is shown below:

	Hours worked	*Overhead cost*
		$
Month 1	9,300	115,000
Month 2	9,200	113,600
Month 3	9,400	116,000
Month 4	9,600	116,800

HC normally works around 120,000 labour hours in a year.

HC uses the high low method to analyse overheads.

The learning curve equation is $y = ax^b$, where $b = \frac{\text{Log LR}}{\text{Log 2}} = -0.074$

Required

Calculate the total cost including all overheads for HC that it can use as a basis of the bid for the new apartment contract. **(10 marks)**

57 Mic Co (12/13 amended) — 18 mins

Mic Co produces microphones for mobile phones and operates a standard costing system. Before production commenced, the standard labour time per batch for its latest microphone was estimated to be 200 hours. The standard labour cost per hour is $12 and resource allocation and cost data were therefore initially prepared on this basis.

Production of the microphone started in July and the number of batches assembled and sold each month was as follows:

Month	*No of batches assembled and sold*	*Cumulative production quantity (batches)*
July	1	1
August	1	2
September	2	4
October	4	8
November	8	

The first batch took 200 hours to make, as anticipated, but, during the first four months of production, a learning effect of 88% was observed, although this finished at the end of October. The learning formula is shown on the formula sheet and at the 88% learning rate the value of b is –0.1844245.

Mic Co uses 'cost plus' pricing to establish selling prices for all its products. Sales of its new microphone in the first five months have been disappointing. The sales manager has blamed the production department for getting the labour cost so wrong, as this, in turn, caused the price to be too high.

Required:

(a) Calculate the actual total monthly labour costs for producing the microphones for each of the five months from July to November. **(8 marks)**

(b) Discuss briefly the implications of the learning effect coming to an end for Mic Co, with regard to costing and budgeting. **(2 marks)**

(Total = 10 marks)

58 Lock Co (6/12 amended) **18 mins**

Lock Co makes security locks and uses standard costing. Unit costs comprise of direct materials, direct labour, variable overheads and fixed production overheads.

The budgeted sales and profit for two of the company's latest products, the Devil Lock and the Power Lock are as follows:

	Sales	*Revenue*	*Costs*	*Profit*	*Profit per unit*
	Units	$	$	$	$
Power Lock	800	16,000	12,000	4,000	5
Devil Lock	600	24,000	22,200	1,800	3
	1,400			5,800	

Actual sales were 560 units of Power Lock and 1,260 units of Devil Lock. Company management are able to control the relative sales of each product through the allocation of sales effort, advertising and sales promotion expenses.

Required

(a) Calculate the sales volume variance, the sales mix variance and the sales quantity variance. **(6 marks)**

(b) Comment on the likely reasons for the variances in part (a). **(4 marks)**

(Total = 10 marks)

59 Standard costing and TQM (6/12 amended) **18 mins**

The production director at an engineering company believes that the way to persistently increase market share in the long term is to focus on quality, and is hoping to introduce a 'Total Quality Management' (TQM) approach. The finance director also shares this view and has said that 'standard costing will no longer have a place within the organisation if TQM is introduced.'

Required

Discuss the view that there is no longer a place for standard costing if TQM is introduced at Lock Co.

(10 marks)

60 Choc Co (12/11 amended) **18 mins**

Choc Co is a company which manufactures and sells three types of biscuits in packets. One of them is called 'Ooze' and contains three types of sweeteners: honey, sugar and syrup. The standard materials usage and cost for one unit of 'Ooze' (one packet) is as follows:

		$
Honey	20 grams at $0.02 per gram	0.40
Sugar	15 grams at $0.03 per gram	0.45
Syrup	10 grams at $0.025 per gram	0.25
		1.10

In the three months ended 30 November 20X1, Choc Co produced 101,000 units of 'Ooze' using 2,200 kg of honey, 1,400 kg of sugar and 1,050 kg of syrup. Note: there are 1,000 grams in a kilogram (kg).

Required

Calculate the following variances for materials in Ooze:

(a) Total materials usage variance; **(2 marks)**

(b) Total materials mix variance; **(4 marks)**

(c) Total materials quantity (yield) variance. **(4 marks)**

(Total = 10 marks)

61 DIY **18 mins**

HR is a paint manufacturer that produces a range of paints which it sells to trade and retail outlets.

The standard material cost for 100 litres of white paint is given below.

Raw material	*Volume (litres)*	*Standard cost per litre*	*Standard cost*
		$	$
A	28	1.40	39.20
B	27	1.20	32.40
C	8	3.65	29.20
D	42	2.60	109.20
	105		210.00

During February, HR produced 7,800 litres of white paint using the following raw materials.

Raw material	*Volume (litres)*	*Actual cost per litre*
		$
A	2,800	1.50
B	2,700	1.30
C	1,000	4.00
D	1,900	2.50
	8,400	

There was no opening or closing inventory of raw materials.

Required

Prepare a statement that reconciles the standard material cost to the actual material cost for February. Your statement should include the individual material price variances, the individual material mix variances and the total material yield variance. **(10 marks)**

62 Valet Co (6/14 amended) **18 mins**

Valet Co is a car valeting (cleaning) company. It operates in the country of Strappia, which has been badly affected by the global financial crisis. Petrol and food prices have increased substantially in the last year and the average disposable household income has decreased by 30%. Recent studies have shown that the average car owner keeps their car for five years before replacing it, rather than three years as was previously the case. Figures over recent years also show that car sales in Strappia are declining whilst business for car repairs is on the increase.

Valet Co offers two types of valet – a full valet and a mini valet. A full valet is an extensive clean of the vehicle, inside and out; a mini valet is a more basic clean of the vehicle. Until recently, four similar businesses operated in Valet Co's local area, but one of these closed down three months ago after a serious fire on its premises. Valet Co charges customers $50 for each full valet and $30 for each mini valet and this price never changes. Their budget and actual figures for the last year were as follows:

	Budget		*Actual*	
Number of valets:				
Full valets	3,600		4,000	
Mini valets	2,000		3,980	
	$	$	$	$
Revenue		240,000		319,400
Variable costs:				
Staff wages	(114,000)		(122,000)	
Cleaning materials	(6,200)		(12,400)	
Energy costs	(6,520)		(9,200)	
		(126,720)		(143,600)
Contribution		113,280		175,800

	Budget		Actual	
	$	$	$	$
Fixed costs:				
Rent, rates and depreciation		(36,800)		(36,800)
Operating profit		76,480		139,000

The budgeted contribution to sales ratios for the two types of valet are 44·6% for full valets and 55% for mini valets.

Required

(a) Using the data provided for full valets and mini valets, calculate:

(i) The total sales mix contribution variance **(4 marks)**

(ii) The total sales quantity contribution variance **(4 marks)**

(b) Briefly describe the sales mix contribution variance and the sales quantity contribution variance. **(2 marks)**

(Total = 10 marks)

63 PC Co (12/11 amended) 27 mins

You have recently been appointed as an assistant management accountant in a large company, PC Co. When you meet the production manager, you overhear him speaking to one of his staff, saying:

'Budgeting is a waste of time. I don't see the point of it. It tells us what we can't afford but it doesn't keep us from buying it. It simply makes us invent new ways of manipulating figures. If all levels of management aren't involved in the setting of the budget, they might as well not bother preparing one.'

Required

(a) Identify and explain briefly FIVE objectives of a budgetary control system. **(6 marks)**

(b) Discuss the concept of a participative style of budgeting in terms of the five objectives identified in part (a). **(9 marks)**

(Total = 15 marks)

64 ZBB (12/10 amended) 27 mins

Some commentators argue that: 'With continuing pressure to control costs and maintain efficiency, the time has come for all public sector organisations to embrace zero-based budgeting. There is no longer a place for incremental budgeting in any organisation, particularly public sector ones, where zero-based budgeting is far more suitable anyway.'

Required

(a) Discuss the particular difficulties encountered when budgeting in public sector organisations compared with budgeting in private sector organisations, drawing comparisons between the two types of organisations. **(4 marks)**

(b) Explain the terms 'incremental budgeting' and 'zero-based budgeting'. **(2 marks)**

(c) State the main stages involved in preparing zero-based budgets. **(3 marks)**

(d) Discuss the limitations and possible advantages of ZBB within a public sector organisation. **(6 marks)**

(Total = 15 marks)

65 Northland (6/09 amended) 27 mins

Northland's major towns and cities are maintained by local government organisations (LGO), which are funded by central government. The LGOs submit a budget each year which forms the basis of the funds received.

You are provided with the following information as part of the 20X2 budget preparation.

Overheads

Overhead costs are budgeted on an incremental basis, taking the previous year's actual expenditure and adding a set % to allow for inflation. Adjustments are also made for known changes. The details for these are:

Overhead cost category	*20X1 cost*	*Known changes*	*Inflation adjustment between 20X1 and 20X2*
	$		
Property cost	120,000	None	+5%
Central wages	150,000	Note 1 below	+3%
Stationery	25,000	Note 2 below	0%

Note 1. One new staff member will be added to the overhead team; this will cost $12,000 in 20X2.
Note 2. A move towards the paperless office is expected to reduce stationery costs by 40% on the 20X1 spend.

Road repairs

In 20X2 it is expected that 2,000 metres of road will need repairing but a contingency of an extra 10% has been agreed.

In 20X1 the average cost of a road repair was $15,000 per metre repaired, but this excluded any cost effects of extreme weather conditions. The following probability estimates have been made in respect of 20X2:

Weather type predicted	*Probability*	*Increase in repair cost*
Good	0.7	0
Poor	0.1	+10%
Bad	0.2	+25%

Inflation on road repairing costs is expected to be 5% between 20X1 and 20X2.

New roads

New roads are budgeted on a zero base basis and will have to compete for funds along with other capital projects such as hospitals and schools.

Required

(a) Calculate the overheads budget for 20X2. **(3 marks)**

(b) Calculate the budgets for road repairs for 20X2. **(6 marks)**

(c) Explain the problems associated with using expected values in budgeting by an LGO and explain why a contingency for road repairs might be needed. **(6 marks)**

(Total = 15 marks)

66 Big Cheese Chairs (12/09 amended) 27 mins

Big Cheese Chairs (BCC) manufactures and sells executive leather chairs. They are considering a new design of massaging chair to launch into the competitive market in which they operate.

They have carried out an investigation in the market and using a target costing system have targeted a competitive selling price of $120 for the chair. BCC wants a margin on selling price of 20% (ignoring any overheads).

The frame and massage mechanism will be bought in for $51 per chair and BCC will upholster it in leather and assemble it ready for despatch.

Leather costs $10 per metre and two metres are needed for a complete chair although 20% of all leather is wasted in the upholstery process.

The upholstery and assembly process will be subject to a learning effect as the workers get used to the new design. BCC estimates that the first chair will take two hours to prepare but this will be subject to a learning rate (LR) of 95%. The learning improvement will stop once 128 chairs have been made and the time for the 128th chair will be the time for all subsequent chairs. The cost of labour is $15 per hour.

The learning formula is shown on the formula sheet and at the 95% learning rate the value of b is –0.074000581.

Required

(a) Calculate the average cost for the first 128 chairs made and identify any cost gap that may be present at that stage. **(5 marks)**

(b) Assuming that a cost gap for the chair exists suggest four ways in which it could be closed. **(4 marks)**

The production manager denies any claims that a cost gap exists and has stated that the cost of the 128th chair will be low enough to yield the required margin.

(c) Calculate the cost of the 128th chair made and state whether the target cost is being achieved on the 128th chair. **(6 marks)**

(Total = 15 marks)

67 Designit (12/12 amended) 27 mins

Designit is a small company providing design consultancy to a limited number of large clients. The business is mature and fairly stable year on year. It has 30 employees and is privately owned by its founder. Designit prepares an annual fixed budget. The company's accounts department consists of one part-qualified accountant who has a heavy workload. He prepares the budget using spreadsheets. The company has a November year end.

Designit pays each of its three sales managers an annual salary of $150,000, plus an individual bonus based on sales targets set at the beginning of the year. There are always two levels of bonus that can be earned, based on a lower and an upper level of fee income. For the year ended 30 November 20X2, for example, each of the sales managers was given a lower target of securing $1.5m of fee income each, to be rewarded by an individual bonus equating to 20% of salary. If any of the managers secured a further $1.5m of fee income, their bonus would increase by 5% to the upper target of 25%. None of the managers achieved the upper target but all of them achieved the lower one.

This is the same every year and Designit finds that often the managers secure work from several major clients early in the year and reach the $1.5m target well before the year has ended. They then make little effort to secure extra fees for the company, knowing that it would be almost impossible to hit the second target. This, together with a few other problems that have arisen, has made the company consider whether its current budgeting process could be improved and whether the bonus scheme should also be changed.

Designit is now considering replacing the fixed budget with a monthly rolling budget, which Designit believes will make the budgeting process more relevant and timely and encourage managers to focus on the future rather than the past. It would also prevent the problem of targets being met too early on in the year by the sales managers because the targets would be set for monthly performance rather than annual performance. For example, a manager could be given a target of securing $200,000 fee income in the first month for a reward of 2% of salary. Then, depending on what is happening both within the business and in the economy as a whole, at the end of the first month, a different target fee income could be set for the second month.

Required

(a) Explain what a monthly rolling budget is and how it would operate at Designit. **(4 marks)**

(b) Discuss the problems that may be encountered if Designit decides to introduce monthly rolling budgets together with a new bonus scheme, such as the one outlined above. **(5 marks)**

(c) Discuss the problems with the current bonus scheme and, assuming that the company decides against introducing rolling budgets, describe and justify an alternative, more effective bonus scheme that could be introduced. **(6 marks)**

(Total = 15 marks)

68 Newtown School (6/13 amended) — 27 mins

Newtown School's head teacher has prepared the budget for the year ending 31 May Year 2. The government pays the school $1,050 for each child registered at the beginning of the school year, which is June 1, and $900 for any child joining the school part-way through the year. The school does not have to refund the money to the government if a child leaves the school part-way through the year. The number of pupils registered at the school on 1 June Year 1 is 690.

Based on past experience, the probabilities for the number of pupils starting the school part-way through the year are as follows:

Probability	*No. of pupils joining late*
0.2	50
0.3	20
0.5	26

The head teacher admits to being 'poor with numbers' and does not understand probabilities so, when calculating budgeted revenue, he just calculates a simple average for the number of pupils expected to join late. His budgeted revenue for the year ending 31 May Year 2 is therefore as follows:

	Pupils	*Rate per pupil*	*Total income*
Pupils registered at beginning of school year	690	$1,050	$724,500
Average expected number of new joiners	32	$900	$28,800
			$753,300

The head teacher uses incremental budgeting to budget for his expenditure, taking actual expenditure for the previous year as a starting point and simply adjusting it for inflation, as shown below.

	Note	*Actual cost for y/e 31 May Year 1*	*Inflationary adjustment*	*Budgeted cost for y/e 31 May Year 2*
		$		$
Repairs and maintenance	1	44,000	+ 3%	45,320
Salaries	2	590,000	+ 2%	601,800
Capital expenditure	3	65,000	+ 6%	68,900
Total budgeted expenditure				716,020
Budget surplus				37,280

Notes

1 $30,000 of the costs for the year ended 31 May Year 1 related to standard maintenance checks and repairs that have to be carried out by the school every year in order to comply with government health and safety standards.

These are expected to increase by 3% in the coming year. In the year ended 31 May Year 1, $14,000 was also spent on redecorating some of the classrooms. No redecorating is planned for the coming year.

2 There were no salary increases in the year to 31 May Year 1. A 2% pay rise will be given to all staff with effect from 1 December Year 1.

3 The full $65,000 actual costs for the year ended 31 May Year 1 related to improvements made to the school gym. This year, the canteen is going to be substantially improved, although the extent of the improvements and level of service to be offered to pupils is still under discussion. There is a 0.7 probability that the cost will be $145,000 and a 0.3 probability that it will be $80,000. These costs must be paid in full before the end of the year ending 31 May Year 2.

The school's board of governors, who review the budget, are concerned that the budget surplus has been calculated incorrectly. They believe that it should have been calculated using expected income, based on the probabilities provided, and using expected expenditure, based on the information provided in notes 1 to 3. They believe that incremental budgeting is not proving a reliable tool for budget setting in the school since, for the last three years, there have been shortfalls of cash despite a budget surplus being predicted.

Required

(a) Considering the views of the board of governors, recalculate the budget surplus/deficit for the year ending 31 May Year 2. **(5 marks)**

(b) Discuss the advantages and disadvantages of using incremental budgeting. **(4 marks)**

(c) Discuss the extent to which zero-based budgeting could be used by Newtown School to improve the budgeting process. **(6 marks)**

(Total = 15 marks)

69 Spike Limited (12/07 amended) 27 mins

Spike Limited manufactures and sells good quality leather bound diaries. Each year it budgets for its profits, including detailed budgets for sales, materials and labour. If appropriate, the departmental managers are allowed to revise their budgets for planning errors.

In recent months, the managing director has become concerned about the frequency of budget revisions. At a recent board meeting he said 'There seems little point budgeting any more. Every time we have a problem the budgets are revised to leave me looking at a favourable operational variance report and at the same time a lot less profit than promised.'

Two specific situations have recently arisen, for which budget revisions were sought:

Materials

A local material supplier was forced into liquidation. Spike Limited's buyer managed to find another supplier, 150 miles away at short notice. This second supplier charged more for the material and a supplementary delivery charge on top. The buyer agreed to both the price and the delivery charge without negotiation. 'I had no choice', the buyer said, 'the production manager was pushing me very hard to find any solution possible!' Two months later, another, more competitive, local supplier was found.

A budget revision is being sought for the two months where higher prices had to be paid.

Labour

During the early part of the year, problems had been experienced with the quality of work being produced by the support staff in the labour force. The departmental manager had complained in his board report that his team were 'unreliable, inflexible and just not up to the job'.

It was therefore decided, after discussion of the board report, that something had to be done. The company changed its policy so as to recruit only top graduates from good quality universities. This has had the effect of pushing up the costs involved but increasing productivity in relation to that element of the labour force.

The support staff departmental manager has requested a budget revision to cover the extra costs involved following the change of policy.

Required

(a) Discuss each request for a budget revision, putting what you see as both sides of the argument and reach a conclusion as to whether a budget revision should be allowed. **(7 marks)**

The market for leather bound diaries has been shrinking as the electronic versions become more widely available and easier to use. Spike Limited has produced the following data relating to leather bound diary sales for the year to date:

Budget

Sales volume	180,000 units
Sales price	$17.00 per unit
Standard contribution	$7.00 per unit

The total market for diaries in this period was estimated in the budget to be 1.8m units. In fact, the actual total market shrank to 1.6m units for the period under review.

Actual results for the same period

Sales volume	176,000 units
Sales price	$16.40 per unit

Required

(b) Calculate the total sales price and total sales volume variance. **(4 marks)**

(c) Analyse the total sales volume variance into components for market size and market share. **(4 marks)**

(Total = 15 marks)

70 Carat — 27 mins

Carat, a premium food manufacturer, is reviewing operations for the year of 20X3. The company operates a standard marginal costing system and manufactures one product, ZP, for which the following standard revenue and cost data per unit of product is available:

Selling price	$12.00
Direct material A	2.5 kg at $1.70 per kg
Direct material B	1.5 kg at $1.20 per kg
Direct labour	0.45 hrs at $6.00 per hour

Actual data for the 12-month period was as follows:

Sales and production	48,000 units of ZP were produced and sold for $580,800
Direct material A	121,951 kg were used at a cost of $200,000
Direct material B	67,200 kg were used at a cost of $84,000
Direct labour	Employees worked for 18,900 hours, but 19,200 hours were paid at a cost of $117,120

Budgeted sales for the three-month period were 50,000 units of Product ZP.

A recession in 20X3 meant that the market for the ZP declined by 5%.

Required

(a) Calculate the following variances.

  (i) Sales volume variance
  (ii) Planning and operational variances for sales volume
  (iii) Price, mix and yield variances **(9 marks)**

(b) Suggest possible explanations for the variances calculated in part (a). **(6 marks)**

(Total = 15 marks)

71 Crumbly Cakes (6/09 amended) — 27 mins

Crumbly Cakes make cakes, which are sold directly to the public. The new production manager (a celebrity chef) has argued that the business should use only organic ingredients in its cake production. Organic ingredients are more expensive but should produce a product with an improved flavour and give health benefits for the customers. It was hoped that this would stimulate demand and enable an immediate price increase for the cakes.

Crumbly Cakes operates a responsibility based standard costing system which allocates variances to specific individuals. The individual managers are paid a bonus only when net favourable variances are allocated to them.

The new organic cake production approach was adopted at the start of March 20X9, following a decision by the new production manager. No change was made at that time to the standard costs card. The variance reports for February and March are shown below (Fav = Favourable and Adv = Adverse).

Manager responsible	*Allocated variances*	*February variance*	*March variance*
		$	$
Production manager	Material price (total for all ingredients)	25 Fav	2,100 Adv
	Material mix	0	600 Adv
	Material yield	20 Fav	400 Fav
Sales manager	Sales price	40 Adv	7,000 Fav
	Sales contribution volume	35 Adv	3,000 Fav

The production manager is upset that he seems to have lost all hope of a bonus under the new system. The sales manager thinks the new organic cakes are excellent and is very pleased with the progress made.

Crumbly Cakes operate a JIT inventory system and holds virtually no inventory.

Required

(a) Assess the performance of the production manager and the sales manager and indicate whether the current bonus scheme is fair to those concerned. **(7 marks)**

In April 20X9 the following data applied:

Standard cost card for one cake (not adjusted for the organic ingredient change)

Ingredients	Kg	$
Flour	0.10	0.12 per kg
Eggs	0.10	0.70 per kg
Butter	0.10	1.70 per kg
Sugar	0.10	0.50 per kg
Total input	0.40	
Normal loss (10%)	(0.04)	
Standard weight of a cake	0.36	

The budget for production and sales in April was 50,000 cakes. Actual production and sales was 60,000 cakes in the month, during which the following occurred:

Ingredients used	Kg	$
Flour	5,700	$741
Eggs	6,600	$5,610
Butter	6,600	$11,880
Sugar	4,578	$2,747
Total input	23,478	$20,978
Actual loss	1,878	
Actual output of cake mixture	21,600	

All cakes produced must weigh 0.36 kg as this is what is advertised.

Required

(b) Calculate the material price, mix and yield variances for April. You are not required to make any comment on the performance of the managers. **(8 marks)**

(Total = 15 marks)

72 Secure Net (12/09 amended) — 27 mins

Secure Net (SN) manufacture security cards that restrict access to government owned buildings around the world.

The standard cost for the plastic that goes into making a card is $4 per kg and each card uses 40 g of plastic after an allowance for waste. In November 100,000 cards were produced and sold by SN and this was well above the budgeted sales of 60,000 cards.

The actual cost of the plastic was $5.25 per kg and the production manager (who is responsible for all buying and production issues) was asked to explain the increase. He said 'World oil price increases pushed up plastic prices by 20% compared to our budget and I also decided to use a different supplier who promised better quality and increased reliability for a slightly higher price. I know we have overspent but not all the increase in plastic prices is my fault. The actual usage of plastic per card was 35 g per card and again the production manager had an explanation. He said 'The world-wide standard size for security cards increased by 5% due to a change in the card reader technology, however, our new supplier provided much better quality of plastic and this helped to cut down on the waste.'

SN operates a just in time (JIT) system and hence carries very little inventory.

Required

(a) Analyse the variances into planning and operational variances. **(8 marks)**

(b) Assess the performance of the production manager. **(7 marks)**

(Total = 15 marks)

73 Carad Co (12/10 amended) — 27 mins

Carad Co is an electronics company which makes two types of televisions – plasma screen TVs and LCD TVs. It operates within a highly competitive market and is constantly under pressure to reduce prices and develop new products. Carad Co operates a standard costing system and performs a detailed variance analysis of both products on a monthly basis. Extracts from the management information for the month of November are shown below:

		Note
Total number of units made and sold	1,400	1
Material price variance	$28,000 A	2

Notes

1 The budgeted total sales volume for TVs was 1,180 units, consisting of an equal mix of plasma screen TVs and LCD screen TVs. Actual sales volume was 750 plasma TVs and 650 LCD TVs. Standard sales prices are $350 per unit for the plasma TVs and $300 per unit for the LCD TVs. The actual sales prices achieved during November were $330 per unit for plasma TVs and $290 per unit for LCD TVs. The standard contributions for plasma TVs and LCD TVs are $190 and $180 per unit respectively.

2 The sole reason for this variance was an increase in the purchase price of one of its key components, X. Each plasma TV made and each LCD TV made requires one unit of component X, for which Carad Co's standard cost is $60 per unit. Due to a shortage of components in the market place, the market price for November went up to $85 per unit for X. Carad Co actually paid $80 per unit for it.

Required

(a) Calculate the following for the month of November, showing all workings clearly:

(i) The sales volume contribution variance, the sales mix variance and the sales quantity variance. **(7 marks)**

(ii) The material price planning variance and material price operational variance. **(3 marks)**

(b) Explain the reasons why Carad Co would be interested in the material price planning variance and the material price operational variance. **(5 marks)**

(Total = 15 marks)

74 Noble (6/11 amended) — 27 mins

Noble is a restaurant that is only open in the evenings, on **six** days of the week. It has eight restaurant and kitchen staff, each paid a wage of $8 per hour on the basis of hours actually worked. It also has a restaurant manager and a head chef, each of whom is paid a monthly salary of $4,300. Noble's budget and actual figures for the month of May was as follows:

	Budget		*Actual*	
Number of meals	1,200		1,560	
	$	$	$	$
Revenue: Food	48,000s		60,840	
Drinks	12,000		11,700	
		60,000		72,540

	Budget		Actual	
	$	$	$	$
Variable costs:				
Staff wages	(9,216)		(13,248)	
Food costs	(6,000)		(7,180)	
Drink costs	(2,400)		(5,280)	
Energy costs	(3,387)		(3,500)	
		(21,003)		(29,208)
Contribution		38,997		43,332
Fixed costs:				
Manager's and chef's pay	(8,600)		(8,600)	
Rent, rates and depreciation	(4,500)	(13,100)	(4,500)	(13,100)
Operating profit		25,897		30,232

The budget above is based on the following assumptions:

(1) The restaurant is only open six days a week and there are four weeks in a month. The average number of orders each day is 50 and demand is evenly spread across all the days in the month.

(2) The restaurant offers two meals: Meal A, which costs $35 per meal and Meal B, which costs $45 per meal. In addition to this, irrespective of which meal the customer orders, the average customer consumes four drinks each at $2.50 per drink. Therefore, the average spend per customer is either $45 or $55 including drinks, depending on the type of meal selected. The May budget is based on 50% of customers ordering Meal A and 50% of customers ordering Meal B.

(3) Food costs represent 12.5% of revenue from food sales.

(4) Drink costs represent 20% of revenue from drinks sales.

(5) When the number of orders per day does not exceed 50, each member of hourly paid staff is required to work exactly six hours per day. For every incremental increase of five in the average number of orders per day, each member of staff has to work 0·5 hours of overtime for which they are paid at the increased rate of $12 per hour. You should assume that all costs for hourly paid staff are treated wholly as variable costs.

(6) Energy costs are deemed to be related to the total number of hours worked by each of the hourly paid staff, and are absorbed at the rate of $2.94 per hour worked by each of the eight staff.

Required

(a) Prepare a flexed budget for the month of May, assuming that the standard mix of customers remains the same as budgeted. **(11 marks)**

(b) After preparation of the flexed budget, you are informed that the following variances have arisen in relation to total food and drink sales:

Sales mix contribution variance	$1,014 Adverse
Sales quantity contribution variance	$11,700 Favourable

Briefly describe the sales mix contribution variance and the sales quantity contribution variance. Identify why each of them has arisen in Noble's case. **(4 marks)**

(Total = 15 marks)

75 Block Company (6/13 amended) 27 mins

Block Company (Block) operates an absorption costing system and sells two types of product – Commodity 1 and Commodity 2. Like other competitors operating in the same market, Block is struggling to maintain revenues and profits in face of the economic recession which has engulfed the country over the last two years. Sales prices fluctuate in the market in which Block operates.

Consequently, at the beginning of each quarter, a market specialist, who works on a consultancy basis for Block, sets a budgeted sales price for each product for the quarter, based on his expectations of the market. This then becomes the 'standard selling price' for the quarter. The sales department itself is run by the company's sales manager, who negotiates the actual sales prices with customers.

At the end of each quarter, a revised standard price is obtained from the average market price per unit for the quarter.

The following budgeted figures are available for the quarter ended 31 May Year 1.

Product	*Budgeted production and sales units*	*Standard selling price per unit*	*Standard variable production costs per unit*
Commodity 1	30,000	$30	$18
Commodity 2	26,000	$41.60	$26.40

Block uses absorption costing. Standard fixed production overhead costs are $2.80 per unit for Commodity 1 and $3.20 per unit for Commodity 2.
The following data shows the actual sales prices and volumes achieved for each product by Block for the quarter ended 31 May Year 1 and the average market prices per unit.

Product	*Actual production and sales units*	*Actual selling price per unit*	*Average market price per unit*
Commodity 1	29,840	$31	$32.20
Commodity 2	25,600	$40.40	$39.10

The following variances have already been correctly calculated for Commodity 1:

Sales price operational variance: $35,808 Adverse
Sales price planning variance: $65,648 Favourable

Required

(a) Calculate, for Commodity 2, the sales price operational variance and the sales price planning variance. **(4 marks)**

(b) Using the data provided for Commodities 1 and 2, calculate the total sales mix variance and the total sales quantity variance. **(7 marks)**

(c) Briefly discuss the performance of the sales manager for the quarter ended 31 May Year 1. **(4 marks)**

(Total = 15 marks)

76 Bedco (12/13 amended) — 27 mins

Bedco manufactures bed sheets and pillowcases which it supplies to a major hotel chain. It uses a just-in-time system and holds no inventories.

The standard cost for the cotton which is used to make the bed sheets and pillowcases is $5 per m2.

Each bed sheet uses 2 m2 of cotton and each pillowcase uses 0.5 m2. Production levels for bed sheets and pillowcases for November were as follows:

	Budgeted production levels	*Actual production levels*
	Units	Units
Bed sheets	120,000	120,000
Pillow cases	190,000	180,000

The actual cost of the cotton in November was $5.80 per m2. 248,000 m2 of cotton was used to make the bed sheets and 95,000 m2 was used to make the pillowcases.

The world commodity prices for cotton increased by 20% in the month of November. At the beginning of the month, the hotel chain made an unexpected request for an immediate design change to the pillowcases. The new design required 10% more cotton than previously. It also resulted in production delays and therefore a shortfall in production of 10,000 pillowcases in total that month.

The production manager at Bedco is responsible for all buying and any production issues which occur, although he is not responsible for the setting of standard costs.

Required

(a) Calculate the following variances for the month of November, for both bed sheets and pillow cases, and in total:

(i) Total material price planning variance; **(2 marks)**
(ii) Total material price operational variance; **(2 marks)**
(iii) Total material usage planning variance; **(2 marks)**
(iv) Total material usage operational variance. **(2 marks)**

(b) Assess the performance of the production manager for the month of November. **(7 marks)**

(Total = 15 marks)

> **PERFORMANCE MEASUREMENT AND CONTROL**
>
> Questions 68 to 96 cover Performance measurement and control, the subject of Part D of the BPP Study Text for Paper F5.

MCQ bank 1 — 36 mins

77.1 Product quality or service quality is generally associated with which perspective of performance in a balanced scorecard?

A Customer perspective
B Financial perspective
C Innovation and learning perspective
D Internal business perspective

(2 marks)

77.2 A company sells a subscription service to customers, and a key performance measure for the company is the churn rate, which is the rate at which customers cease their subscriptions. The following information is available for the year just ended.

Number of subscribers at the beginning of the year	5.6 million
New subscribers during the year	1.0 million
Customers ceasing their subscription	0.6 million
Number of subscribers at the end of the year	6.0 million

What was the churn rate for the year?

A 6.9%
B 7.1%
C 10.0%
D 10.3%

(2 marks)

77.3 In terms of performance measurement, 'divisionalisation' refers to:

A The delegation of profit-making responsibility
B Incentives for improving performance
C Return on investment
D Transfer pricing

(2 marks)

77.4 The planning and control system within an organisation for ensuring that resources are used efficiently and effectively for achieving the organisation's objectives is known as:

A Corporate planning
B Management control
C Operational planning
D Strategic planning

(2 marks)

77.5 Which one of the following terms best describes an information system that provides extensive information to management, of both a financial and non-financial nature, from sources both internal and external to the organisation?

A Enterprise resource management system
B Executive information system
C Strategic management accounting system
D Strategic planning system

(2 marks)

77.6 The following statements have been made about data and information.

(1) Information obtained from market research that has been commissioned by a company for use by its sales and marketing team is an example of primary internal data.

(2) Information obtained from external sources is generally more reliable than information produced internally.

Which of the above statements is/are true?

A 1 only
B 2 only
C Neither 1 nor 2
D Both 1 and 2

(2 marks)

77.7 Which one of the following is the most useful measure of performance for a bus company (transport company), for comparing performance between different parts of the business and over a period of time?

A Cost per bus route
B Cost per journey
C Cost per passenger
D Cost per passenger kilometre travelled

(2 marks)

77.8 Which one of the following is a dimension of performance in a service business, as identified by Fitzgerald and Moon?

A Controllability
B Innovation
C Rewards
D Standards

(2 marks)

77.9 The following statements have been made about divisionalisation and performance measurement.

(1) In a divisionalised performance system, it is not usually possible to make a fair comparison of the performance of different divisions when their non-current assets are valued at net book value.

(2) When performance is measured by ROI, the figure for profit is calculated after deducting interest on capital employed.

Which of the above statements is/are true?

A 1 only
B 2 only
C Neither 1 nor 2
D Both 1 and 2

(2 marks)

77.10 One of the divisions in a large industrial company reported the following results for the financial year.

	$'000
Revenue	920
Cost of sales	330
Gross profit	590
Other costs	
Attributable to divisional activities	(70)
Attributable to the division	(30)
Apportioned head office costs	(40)
Divisional profit	450

In a responsibility accounting system, for what amount of divisional profit should the divisional manager be held personally responsible?

A $590,000
B $520,000
C $490,000
D $450,000

(2 marks)

(Total = 20 marks)

MCQ bank 2 — 36 mins

78.1 The following statements have been made about a transfer pricing system where Division A transfers output to Division B.

(1) Internal transfers should be preferred when there is an external market for the transferred item, because there will be more control over quality and delivery.

(2) The transfer price will determine how profits will be shared between the two divisions.

Which of the above statements is/are true?

A 1 only
B 2 only
C Neither 1 nor 2
D Both 1 and 2

(2 marks)

78.2 The following statements have been made about performance measurements in not-for-profit organisations.

(1) Not-for-profit organisations do not have financial objectives.

(2) The outputs produced by not-for-profit organisations are easier to measure than output of commercial companies.

Which of the above statements is/are true?

A 1 only
B 2 only
C Neither 1 nor 2
D Both 1 and 2

(2 marks)

78.3 Which one of the following figures would be the most suitable for divisional profit for the purpose of performance measurement?

A Gross profit
B Profit before interest and tax
C Profit before tax
D Profit after tax

(2 marks)

78.4 In a company with a divisionalised structure, Division A transfers its output to Division B. Division A produces just one item, Component X. Division B makes and sells and end product that requires one unit of Component X.

	$ per unit of X
Marginal cost of production in Division A	8
Fixed overhead cost of production	3
Market price in the external market	16
Division B contribution from further processing Component X, before deducting the transfer cost	25

Division A is not working at full capacity, and can meet in full the external market demand and the demand from Division B for internal transfers.

What should be the minimum transfer price per unit and the maximum transfer price per unit for Component X in this situation?

A Minimum transfer price $8, maximum transfer price $16
B Minimum transfer price $8, maximum transfer price $25
C Minimum transfer price $11, maximum transfer price $16
D Minimum transfer price $11, maximum transfer price $25

(2 marks)

78.5 A hospital wishes to establish a performance measurement for its 'quality of care', and in particular its adherence to appointment times for patients receiving medical checks. Which one of the following performance measurements would be the most suitable for this purpose?

A Average length of appointments
B Average number of appointments per day
C Average number of days from making an appointment to the appointment date
D Average waiting time at the hospital

(2 marks)

78.6 Which one of the following is often used to protect an intranet from unauthorised access by an external hacker?

A Anti-virus software
B Data encryption
C Firewall
D Passwords

(2 marks)

78.7 A company that uses a balanced scorecard approach to performance measurement has recorded the following data for the previous financial year.

	Products made and sold for at least 2 years	*Products introduced to market within the previous two years = 'new products'*	*Total*
Number of products	16	4	
Annual sales	$3.0 million	$0.50 million	$3.50 million
Cost of sales	$2.4 million	$0.42 million	$2.82 million
Hours worked	27,500	4,500	
Research and development costs			$150,000

Which one of the following would be the most suitable measure of performance from the innovation and learning perspective in a balanced scorecard?

A Development cost per new product
B Sales revenue per new product
C Sales revenue from new products as a percentage of total revenue
D Sales revenue per hour worked on new products

(2 marks)

78.8 Which one of the following measures of performance for public sector services is a measure of efficiency?

A Number of patients treated per $1 spent on the state hospital service

B Percentage reduction in the spending budget of a government department compared with the previous year

C Proportion of reported crimes that are solved by the police service

D Proportion of students in a state-owned college achieving good pass grades in their examinations

(2 marks)

78.9 The following statements have been made about data and information.

(1) Automated systems for data capture are generally more reliable than data capture requiring input by individuals.

(2) As a general rule, secondary information is more expensive to collect than primary data.

Which of the above statements is/are true?

A 1 only
B 2 only
C Neither 1 nor 2
D Both 1 and 2

(2 marks)

78.10 When goods are transferred from one division in a company to another division, and there is an intermediate external market for the transferred item in which the goods could be sold, which of the following states the economic transfer pricing rule for what the maximum transfer price should be?

A Marginal cost of the transferring-out division minus any lost contribution of the transferring-out division from having to make the internal transfer

B The higher of the net marginal revenue for the transferring-in division and the external purchase price in the market for the intermediate product

C The lower of the net marginal revenue for the transferring-in division and the external purchase price in the market for the intermediate product

D None of the above

(2 marks)

(Total = 20 marks)

MCQ bank 3 — 36 mins

79.1 A company has a call centre to handle queries and complaints from customers. The company is concerned about the average length of calls and the time that it takes to deal with customers. As part of its balanced scorecard, it has set a target for reducing the average time per customer call.

A target for reducing the average time per call would relate to which one of the four balanced scorecard perspectives?

A Customer perspective
B Financial perspective
C Innovation and learning perspective
D Internal business (operational) perspective

(2 marks)

79.2 The following statements have been made about management information and management information systems.

(1) Management information is often produced from transaction processing systems.

(2) The data used in management information systems comes mainly from sources within the organisation and its operations.

Which of the above statements is/are true?

A 1 only
B 2 only
C Neither 1 nor 2
D Both 1 and 2

(2 marks)

79.3 The following statements have been made about operational control.

(1) Budgeting is commonly associated with decision making at the operational planning level within a management hierarchy.

(2) Operational control decisions in general are more narrowly focused and have a shorter time horizon than management control decisions.

Which of the above statements is/are true?

A 1 only
B 2 only
C Neither 1 nor 2
D Both 1 and 2

(2 marks)

79.4 Which one of the following terms is used to describe an information system that provides senior executives with online access to important information obtained from both internal and external sources?

A Executive information system
B Enterprise resource planning system
C Management information system
D Transaction processing system

(2 marks)

79.5 Data used by the management that has been obtained from an official government source is an example of:

A External primary data
B External secondary data
C Internal primary data
D Internal secondary data

(2 marks)

79.6 The following statements have been made about data and information.

(1) In-depth analysis of data on a database in order to identify undiscovered trends or patterns in the data is known as data mining.

(2) Large public databases are a major source of feedback for many commercial organisations.

Which of the above statements is/are true?

A 1 only
B 2 only
C Neither 1 nor 2
D Both 1 and 2

(2 marks)

79.7 In a balanced scorecard system of performance measurement, which one of the following is most likely to be used as a measure of performance from the customer perspective?

A Increase in size of product range
B Percentage of customers making repeat orders
C Number of orders won per sales representative
D Speed of processing an order

(2 marks)

79.8 The following statements have been made about performance measurements in not-for-profit organisations.

(1) Providing value for money (VFM) means providing a service that is cheap, efficient and effective.

(2) For the refuse collection department of a local government authority, the efficiency of operations can be measured by the proportion of collected refuse that is recycled.

Which of the above statements is/are true?

A 1 only
B 2 only
C Neither 1 nor 2
D Both 1 and 2

(2 marks)

79.9 In a company with a divisionalised structure, Division A transfers its output to Division B. Division A produces just one item, Component X. Division B makes and sells and end product that requires one unit of Component X.

	$ per unit of X
Marginal cost of production in Division A	8
Fixed overhead cost of production	3
Cost of selling in the external market	1
Market price in the external market	16
Division B contribution from further processing Component X, before deducting the transfer cost	25

Division A is working at full capacity.

What should be the minimum transfer price per unit of Component X in this situation?

A $8
B $12
C $13
D $15

(2 marks)

79.10 The following statements have been made about divisionalisation and performance measurement systems.

(1) Residual income as a measure of performance enables fair comparisons to be made between the performances of different divisions in the company.

(2) When a transfer price is based on cost because there is no external market for the transferred item, at least one of the divisional managers is likely to consider the transfer price as 'unfair'.

Which of the above statements is/are true?

A 1 only
B 2 only
C Neither 1 nor 2
D Both 1 and 2

(2 marks)

(Total = 20 marks)

MCQ bank 4 — 36 mins

80.1 Which one of the following aspects of performance is measured by the average time between receipt of an order from a customer and the time the goods are despatched?

A Quality
B Quantity
C Reliability
D Speed

(2 marks)

80.2 In the Fitzgerald and Moon model of performance measurement in services businesses, which one of the following dimensions of performance reflects past results or achievements rather than provides a guide or determinant for future performance?

A Competitiveness
B Flexibility
C Quality
D Resource utilisation

(2 marks)

80.3 Which one of the following is **not** usually a consequence of divisionalisation?

A Duplication of some activities and costs
B Goal congruence in decision making
C Faster decision making at operational level
D Reduction in head office control over operations

(2 marks)

80.4 At the beginning of 20X2, a division has capital employed, consisting of non-current assets of $2 million (at net book value) and working capital of $0.2 million. These are expected to earn a profit in 20X2 of $0.5 million, after depreciation of $0.4 million. A new machine will be installed at the beginning of 20X2. It will cost $0.8 million and will require an additional $0.1 million in working capital. It will add $0.35 million to divisional profits before deducting depreciation. This machine will have a four-year life and no residual value: depreciation is by the straight-line method. When calculating ROI, capital employed is taken at its mid-year value.

What is the expected ROI of the division in 20X2?

A 21.7%
B 23.2%
C 24.1%
D 26.0%

(2 marks)

80.5 The following statements have been made about the measurement of ROI and residual income.

(1) ROI is usually measured as divisional operating profit before deducting depreciation as a percentage of the division's capital employed.

(2) Residual income is calculated after deducting both depreciation on non-current assets and notional interest on the division's capital employed.

Which of the above statements is/are true?

A 1 only
B 2 only
C Neither 1 nor 2
D Both 1 and 2

(2 marks)

80.6 For which of the following reasons are controls needed over internally generated information?

(1) To prevent information overload
(2) To prevent unauthorised dissemination of information

A Reason (1) only
B Reason (2) only
C Neither reason
D Reasons (1) and (2)

(2 marks)

80.7 The following statements have been made about information systems.

(1) Feedback is information produced from a system that is used by management to take action to control further inputs to the system.

(2) Information for benchmarking purposes may be obtained from both internal and external sources.

Which of the above statements is/are true?

A 1 only
B 2 only
C Neither 1 nor 2
D Both 1 and 2

(2 marks)

80.8 The following statements have been made about transfer pricing.

(1) Transfer pricing is almost inevitably required when a business is structured as more than one division and some divisions provide goods or services to other divisions.

(2) Where a perfect external market price exists and unit variable costs and unit selling prices are constant, the opportunity cost of transfer will be external market price or external market price less savings in selling costs.

Which of the above statements is/are true?

A 1 only
B 2 only
C Neither 1 nor 2
D Both 1 and 2

(2 marks)

80.9 If the performance of a local fire service is judged in terms of its inputs rather than its outputs, which one of the following would be a suitable measure of performance?

A Average response times to call-outs
B Cost of the local fire service per member of the local population
C Number of emergency calls answered per month
D Average length of time between call-outs

(2 marks)

80.10 A typical balanced scorecard measures performance from four different perspectives. Which perspective is concerned with measuring 'What must we excel at?'

A Customer satisfaction perspective
B Financial success perspective
C Growth perspective
D Process efficiency perspective

(2 marks)

(Total = 20 marks)

MCQ bank 5 — 36 mins

81.1 The following statements have been made about performance measurement systems.

(1) When divisional assets are valued at net book value (carrying amount) and performance is measured by ROI or residual income, divisional managers may be encouraged to hold on to outdated plant and machinery.

(2) Key performance indicators (KPIs) are used to measure actual results against a target.

Which of the above statements is/are true?

A 1 only
B 2 only
C Neither 1 nor 2
D Both 1 and 2

(2 marks)

81.2 Which one of the following is **not** a correct statement of a feature of good performance measurements?

A They create an incentive to a manager to make a decision that is in the best interest of the organisation

B They measure only factors over which the manager responsible has control or influence

C They should be measurable in financial terms

D They should include long-term as well as short-term objectives

(2 marks)

81.3 The following statements have been made about data and information.

(1) The major problem with information overload is that managers may be given more information than they need to make their decisions.

(2) A major problem with external information is that it may be difficult to assess its reliability.

Which of the above statements is/are true?

A 1 only
B 2 only
C Neither 1 nor 2
D Both 1 and 2

(2 marks)

81.4 Liquidity is improved by:

A A shorter average receivables payment period and shorter average trade payables period
B A longer average receivables payment period and shorter average trade payables period
C A shorter average receivables payment period and longer average trade payables period
D A longer average receivables payment period and longer average trade payables period

(2 marks)

81.5 The following statements have been made about performance measurements.

(1) Non-financial performance measures are important because they can provide a good indication of future financial prospects.

(2) A problem with using multiple measures of performance, financial and non-financial, may be a lack of compatibility between the performance criteria for each measure.

Which of the above statements is/are true?

A 1 only
B 2 only
C Neither 1 nor 2
D Both 1 and 2

(2 marks)

81.6 A company has a divisionalised structure in which Division A transfers its output to Division B. There is no external market for the transferred item and cost will be used as the basis for setting a transfer price. Which one of the following will be the most appropriate basis for negotiating and agreeing a transfer price?

A Actual cost
B Actual cost plus a profit margin equal to a percentage of cost
C Standard cost
D Standard cost plus a profit margin equal to a percentage of cost

(2 marks)

81.7 A company has two Divisions, A and B. Division A manufactures a component which is transferred to Division B. Division B uses two units of the component from Division A in every item of finished product that it makes and sells. The transfer price is $43 per unit of the component.

	$ per unit
Selling price of finished product made in Division B	154
Variable production costs in Division B, excluding the cost of transfers from Division A	32
Variable selling costs, chargeable to the division	1
	33

Fixed costs	$160,000
External sales in units	7,000
Investment in the division	$500,000

The company uses 16% as its cost of capital.

What is the residual income of Division B for the period?

A $(23,000)
B $5,000
C $306,000
D $383,000

(2 marks)

81.8 An investment centre has prepared the following forecasts for the next financial year.

	$
Operating profit before depreciation	85,000
Depreciation	20,000
Net current assets at beginning of year	30,000
Carrying value of non-current assets at beginning of year	180,000

The centre manager is now considering whether to sell a machine that is included in these forecasts. The machine would add $2,500 to divisional profit next year after depreciation of $500. It has a carrying value of $6,000 and could be sold for this amount. He would use the proceeds from the sale plus additional cash from Head Office to purchase a new machine for $15,000. This new machine would add $5,200 to divisional profit next year after depreciation of $2,000.

What will be the expected return on investment (ROI) for the division next year, assuming that the manager acquires the new machine and that non-current assets are valued at the start-of-year carrying amount for the purpose of the ROI calculation.

A 30.9%
B 31.6%
C 35.8%
D 40.0%

(2 marks)

81.9 The following statements have been made about performance measurements in not-for-profit organisations.

(1) When a not-for-profit organisation has multiple objectives, it is very difficult to quantify the organisation's outputs.

(2) When a school service is measured on the basis of the success rate of students in examinations, there may be a temptation to manipulate the results in order to improve the reported performance.

Which of the above statements is/are true?

A 1 only
B 2 only
C Neither 1 nor 2
D Both 1 and 2

(2 marks)

81.10 The following statements have been made about information systems.

(1) Key features of enterprise resource planning systems are that they are IT systems that integrate the information requirements of different processes or functions within the organisation.

(2) All systems in which people work are open systems.

Which of the above statements is/are true?

A 1 only
B 2 only
C Neither 1 nor 2
D Both 1 and 2

(2 marks)

(Total = 20 marks)

82 ERP — 18 mins

Trendy manufactures a variety of clothing items which are sold through retailers, mainly in the domestic market. Most retailers are independent organisations, operating either as single outlets or as retail chains. Trendy has a small number of its own shops where it sells its own products exclusively.

In the past year or so, there has been a noticeable change in the buying habits of retailers. Whereas previously, retailers would often place a large order for items at the beginning of each season, they now make smaller orders throughout the season when they have established which items are selling well and which are less popular. Retailers are also expecting prompt deliveries when they place an order. The operations director of Trendy refers to this new retailer buying behaviour as 'just in time purchasing'.

The market for clothing is very competitive and retailers do not show much loyalty to their suppliers. Retailers buy what is available quickly at a good price and what will sell well. Occasionally, retailers may ask for a specially produced batch of items, subject to the items being available at a satisfactory price.

In order to maintain or increase market share, Trendy has a large sales force that travels round retail outlets and the central purchasing departments of large retail organisations. Trendy's sales staff receive a bonus based on the amount of sales they achieve.

Trendy has recently introduced an enterprise resource planning (ERP) system to coordinate the information systems of all the functions within the company, to replace the separate manufacturing, inventory, accounting and sales systems that were used previously. The CEO of Trendy believes that this will enable the company to be more effective and competitive. In addition, the CEO, who is a management accountant by training, believes that Trendy should use strategic management accounting methods to improve decision making, and he wants to establish an IT system for competitor analysis as a stage in the creation of a strategic information system.

Required

Explain how the introduction of an ERP system in Trendy should improve the competitiveness of the company.

(10 marks)

83 ICE **18 mins**

ICE is a private company which manufactures a range of packaging materials for customers in the fresh and frozen food industries. The company's chairman and founder has built up a vast network of contacts over a period of some 20 years and has always adopted a 'hands-on' management style, priding himself on the fact that he knows all his staff by name even though the company now has over 300 employees.

He is due to retire in about 18 months' time and the other members of the board are concerned that they will lose an incredible 'database' of knowledge.

Required

Describe how ICE could structure and implement formal methods and procedures for gathering information to monitor its external environment. **(10 marks)**

84 Biscuits and Cakes Part 1 (6/12 amended) **18 mins**

The Biscuits division (Division B) and the Cakes division (Division C) are two divisions of a large, manufacturing company. Whilst both divisions operate in almost identical markets, each division operates separately as an investment centre. Each month, operating statements must be prepared by each division and these are used as a basis for performance measurement for the divisions.

Last month, senior management decided to recharge head office costs to the divisions. Consequently, each division is now going to be required to deduct a share of head office costs in its operating statement before arriving at 'net profit', which is then used to calculate return on investment (ROI). Prior to this, ROI has been calculated using controllable profit only. The company's target ROI, however, remains unchanged at 20% per annum. For each of the last three months, Divisions B and C have maintained ROIs of 22% per annum and 23% per annum respectively, resulting in healthy bonuses being awarded to staff. The company has a cost of capital of 10%.

The budgeted operating statement for the month of July is shown below:

	B	*C*
	$'000	$'000
Sales revenue	1,300	1,500
Less variable costs	(700)	(800)
Contribution	600	700
Less controllable fixed costs	(134)	(228)
Controllable profit	466	472
Less apportionment of head office costs	(155)	(180)
Net profit	311	292
Divisional net assets	$23.2m	$22.6m

Required

(a) Calculate the expected annualised Return on Investment (ROI) using the new method as preferred by senior management, based on the above budgeted operating statements, for each of the divisions. **(2 marks)**

The divisional managing directors are unhappy about the results produced by your calculations in (a) and have heard that a performance measure called 'residual income' may provide more information.

(b) Calculate the annualised residual income (RI) for each of the divisions, based on the net profit figures for the month of July. **(2 marks)**

(c) Discuss the expected performance of each of the two divisions, using both ROI and RI, and making any additional calculations deemed necessary. Conclude as to whether, in your opinion, the two divisions have performed well. **(6 marks)**

(Total = 10 marks)

85 Biscuits and Cakes Part 2 (6/12 amended) **18 mins**

The Biscuits division (Division B) and the Cakes division (Division C) are two divisions of a large, manufacturing company. Whilst both divisions operate in almost identical markets, each division operates separately as an investment centre. Each month, operating statements must be prepared by each division and these are used as a basis for performance measurement for the divisions.

Last month, senior management decided to recharge head office costs to the divisions. Consequently, each division is now going to be required to deduct a share of head office costs in its operating statement before arriving at 'net profit', which is then used to calculate return on investment (ROI). Prior to this, ROI has been calculated using controllable profit only. The company's target ROI, however, remains unchanged at 20% per annum. For each of the last three months, Divisions B and C have maintained ROIs of 22% per annum and 23% per annum respectively, resulting in healthy bonuses being awarded to staff. The company has a cost of capital of 10%.

The budgeted operating statement for the month of July is shown below:

	B	*C*
	$'000	$'000
Sales revenue	1,300	1,500
Less variable costs	(700)	(800)
Contribution	600	700
Less controllable fixed costs	(134)	(228)
Controllable profit	466	472
Less apportionment of head office costs	(155)	(180)
Net profit	311	292
Divisional net assets	$23.2m	$22.6m

Division B has now been offered an immediate opportunity to invest in new machinery at a cost of $2.12 million.

The machinery is expected to have a useful economic life of four years, after which it could be sold for $200,000.

Division B's policy is to depreciate all of its machinery on a straight-line basis over the life of the asset. The machinery would be expected to expand Division B's production capacity, resulting in an 8.5% increase in contribution per month.

Required

(a) Recalculate Division B's expected annualised ROI and annualised RI, based on July's budgeted operating statement after adjusting for the investment. State whether the managing director will be making a decision that is in the best interests of the company as a whole if ROI is used as the basis of the decision. **(6 marks)**

(b) Explain any behavioural problems that will result if the company's senior management insist on using solely ROI, based on net profit rather than controllable profit, to assess divisional performance and reward staff. **(4 marks)**

(Total = 10 marks)

86 Brash Co (6/11 amended) **18 mins**

Brash Co is an electronics company specialising in the manufacture of home audio equipment. Historically, the company has used solely financial performance measures to assess the performance of the company as a whole. The company's Managing Director has recently heard of the 'balanced scorecard approach' and is keen to learn more.

Required

Describe the balanced scorecard approach to performance measurement. **(10 marks)**

87 Brace Co (6/11 amended) **18 mins**

Brace Co is a large software company specialising in the development of computer games and software products for commercial applications. Historically, the company has used solely financial performance measures to assess the performance of the company as a whole.

Brace Co is split into two divisions, A and B, each with their own cost and revenue streams. Each of the divisions is managed by a divisional manager who has the power to make all investment decisions within the division. The cost of capital for both divisions is 12%. Historically, investment decisions have been made by calculating the return on investment (ROI) of any opportunities and at present, the return on investment of each division is 16%.

A new manager who has recently been appointed in division A has argued that using residual income (RI) to make investment decisions would result in 'better goal congruence' throughout the company.

Each division is currently considering the following separate investments:

	Project for Division A	*Project for Division B*
Capital required for investment	$82.8 million	$40.6 million
Sales generated by investment	$44.6 million	$21.8 million
Net profit margin	28%	33%

The company is seeking to maximise shareholder wealth.

Required

Calculate both the return on investment and residual income of the new investment for each of the two divisions. Comment on these results, taking into consideration the manager's views about residual income. **(10 marks)**

88 Wash Co (12/12 amended) **18 mins**

Wash Co assembles and sells two types of washing machines – the Spin (S) and the Rinse (R). The company has two divisions: the assembly division, and the retail division.

The company's policy is to transfer the machines from the assembly division to the retail division at full cost plus 10%. This has resulted in internal transfer prices, when S and R are being transferred to the retail division, of $220.17 and $241.69 respectively. The retail division currently sells S to the general public for $320 per machine and R for $260 per machine. Assume it incurs no other costs except for the transfer price.

The retail division's manager is convinced that, if he could obtain R at a lower cost and therefore reduce the external selling price from $260 to $230 per unit, he could significantly increase sales of R, which would be beneficial to both divisions. He has questioned the fact that the overhead costs are allocated to the products on the current basis of labour hours; he thinks it should be done using activity based costing.

You have obtained the following information for the last month from the assembly division:

	Product S	*Product R*
Production and sales (units)	3,200	5,450
Materials cost	$117	$95
Labour cost (at $12 per hour)	$6	$9
Machine hours (per unit)	2	1
Total no. of production runs	30	12
Total no. of purchase orders	82	64
Total no. of deliveries to retail division	64	80

Overhead costs:	$
Machine set-up costs	306,435
Machine maintenance costs	415,105
Ordering costs	11,680
Delivery costs	144,400
Total	877,620

Required

(a) Using activity based costing to allocate the overheads, recalculate the transfer prices for S and R and comment on the view of the retail division manager.

Note. Round all workings to two decimal places. **(8 marks)**

(b) Calculate last month's profit for each division, showing it both for each product and in total, if activity based costing is used. **(2 marks)**

(Total = 10 marks)

89 PC (12/08 amended) 18 mins

Pace Company (PC) runs a large number of wholesale stores and is increasing the number of these stores all the time. It measures the performance of each store on the basis of a target return on investment (ROI) of 15%. Store managers get a bonus of 10% of their salary if their store's annual ROI exceeds the target each year. Once a store is built there is very little further capital expenditure until a full four years have passed.

PC has a store (store W) in the west of the country. Store W has historic financial data as follows over the past four years.

	20X5	*20X6*	*20X7*	*20X8*
Sales ($'000)	200	200	180	170
Gross profit ($'000)	80	70	63	51
Net profit ($'000)	13	14	10	8
Net assets at start of year ($'000)	100	80	60	40

The market in which PC operates has been growing steadily. Typically, PC's stores generate a 40% gross profit margin.

Required

(a) Discuss the past financial performance of store W using ROI and any other measure you feel appropriate and, using your findings, discuss whether the ROI correctly reflects Store W's actual performance. **(6 marks)**

(b) Explain how a manager in store W might have been able to manipulate the results so as to gain bonuses more frequently. **(4 marks)**

(Total = 10 marks)

90 Rotech Group (6/14 amended) 18 mins

The Rotech group comprises two companies, W Co and C Co.

W Co is a trading company with two divisions: The Design division, which designs wind turbines and supplies the designs to customers under licences and the Gearbox division, which manufactures gearboxes for the car industry.

C Co manufactures components for gearboxes. It sells the components globally and also supplies W Co with components for its Gearbox manufacturing division.

The financial results for the two companies for the year ended 31 May 20X4 are as follows:

	W Co		*C Co*
	Design division	*Gearbox division*	
	$'000	$'000	$'000
External sales	14,300	25,535	8,010
Sales to Gearbox division			7,550
			15,560
Cost of sales	(4,900)	(16,200)	(5,280)
Administration costs	(3,400)	(4,200)	(2,600)
Distribution costs	–	(1,260)	(670)
Operating profit	6,000	3,875	7,010
Capital employed	23,540	32,320	82,975

* Includes cost of components purchased from C Co.

Required

Discuss the performance of C Co and each division of W Co, calculating and using the following three performance measures:

(i) Return on capital employed (ROCE)
(ii) Asset turnover
(iii) Operating profit margin

Note. There are 4·5 marks available for calculations and 5·5 marks available for discussion. **(10 marks)**

91 Story **27 mins**

Story is a well-established, global publishing conglomerate. The corporation is structured to allow each country of operation to function as an autonomous business unit, that reports back to head office. The data from each business unit is entered onto the mainframe computer at head office. Each business unit can make use of any service offered by other business units and can also offer services to the other units. The services include translation into different languages, typesetting, printing, storage and so forth. In each country of operation there is at least one, and usually several, retail outlets.

The core business was traditionally based upon the provision of fictional stories for the mass market. For the past decade Story has diversified into publishing textbooks and technical literature. The organisation currently enjoys a good reputation in both areas of the business and global sales are increasing annually at a rate of 5% for fictional books and 2% for textbooks. Last year seven hundred million fictional works and twenty-five million textbooks were sold.

The corporate management team wish to increase the growth in sales of textbooks but realise that they cannot afford to allocate significant resources to this task as the market, and profit margin, for textbooks is very much smaller than for fiction. They also wish to improve the sales performance of the fictional books.

Story is currently having trouble in maintaining a corporate image in some countries of operation. For example, several business units may be unaware of additions to the product range. Another example is that a price change in a book is not simultaneously altered by all the business units leading to pricing discrepancies.

Some members of the corporate management team see possible advantages to upgrading the existing computer system to one that is fully networked. Other members are more sceptical and are reluctant to consider enhancing the system.

Required

(a) Discuss the issues involved in upgrading the existing information system and the proposed changes, with reference to both the wider business environment and the decision-making process. **(8 marks)**

(b) Explain what is meant by the terms **open systems** and **closed systems** as applied to systems theory. Identify, with justification and where possible, any examples of these from the information given in, or inferred from, the case study. **(7 marks)**

(Total = 15 marks)

92 Viga

27 mins

The Viga Drinks Company plc (Viga) has recently experienced several incidents that have called into question the adequacy of its procedures for protecting the confidentiality of sensitive information.

(1) The union representatives at one of the company's production centres called a strike because they received information that Viga's board had decided to close down the centre. This was not true. The board had discussed the possibility of merging two production centres, but had subsequently decided against the idea. Following assurances from the board that the production centre was not going to be closed, the strike was called off. Even so the directors were aware that information about their deliberations about the merger of the two centres must have been 'leaked'.

(2) In another incident, a member of the accounts department resigned from the company following disclosure of confidential information about his private life. This employee had recently reported a suspicion of fraud by a small group of managers. The board suspected that the identity of the whistle blower had been revealed, and the disclosure of the information about his private life was an act of retaliation or victimisation.

(3) In yet another incident, confidential information about the results of a health and safety inspection of the company's production centres by government health and safety inspectors had been given to the press, and had been reported as an 'exclusive' in a national newspaper.

(4) Most recently, within the past week, a railway company has returned a laptop computer that had been left on a train by Viga's company secretary. The laptop contained a lot of confidential information, including the company's draft budget for next year.

Viga's Chief Executive Officer (CEO) is seriously concerned by the breaches of confidentiality and secrecy. At the back of his mind is the thought that the commercial success of Viga is based on the success of a unique soft energy drink, the recipe for which is a closely guarded secret (and which has not been patented in order to protect its secrecy). The CEO is now wondering whether there is anyone in the company who might have access to the secret, and would be prepared to sell it to a rival drinks producer.

Required

(a) With reference to Viga, explain the reasons why confidential information may be improperly released, and the potential consequences for an organisation when this occurs. **(7 marks)**

(b) Recommend procedures that should be taken by Viga's senior management to ensure the security of highly confidential information. **(8 marks)**

(Total = 15 marks)

93 Lewisville

27 mins

Lewisville is a town with a population of 100,000 people. The town council of Lewisville operates a bus service which links all parts of the town with the town centre. The service is non-profit seeking and its mission statement is 'to provide efficient, reliable and affordable public transport to all the citizens of Lewisville'. Attempting to achieve this mission often involves operating services that would be considered uneconomic by private sector bus companies, due either to the small number of passengers travelling on some routes or the low fares charged. The majority of the town council members are happy with this situation as they wish to reduce traffic congestion and air pollution on Lewisville's roads by encouraging people to travel by bus rather than by car.

However, one member of the council has recently criticised the performance of the Lewisville bus service as compared to those operated by private sector bus companies in other towns. She has produced the following information:

Lewisville bus service

SUMMARISED INCOME AND EXPENDITURE ACCOUNT
YEAR ENDING 31 MARCH 20X6

	$'000	$'000
Passenger fares		1,200
Staff wages	600	
Fuel	300	
Depreciation	280	
		1,180
Surplus		20

SUMMARISED STATEMENT OF FINANCIAL POSITION AS AT
31 MARCH 20X6

	$'000	$'000
Non-current assets (net)		2,000
Current assets		
Inventory	240	
Cash	30	
	270	
Less creditors (suppliers) due within one year	60	
Net current assets		210
Total assets less liabilities		2,210
Ordinary share capital ($1 shares)		2,000
Reserves		210
		2,210

OPERATING STATISTICS FOR THE YEAR ENDED
31 MARCH 20X6

Total passengers carried	2,400,000 passengers
Total passenger miles travelled	4,320,000 passenger miles

Private sector bus companies industry average ratios

Year ended 31 March 20X6

Return on capital employed	10%
Return on sales (net margin)	30%
Asset turnover (revenue)	0.33 times
Average cost per passenger mile	37.4c

Required

(a) Assess the performance of the bus service for the year ended 31 March 20X6 using financial performance indicators calculated from the above information.

Note. Clearly state any assumptions and show all workings clearly. Your answer should be structured under the following main headings: Return on capital employed (ROCE); return on sales; asset turnover; average cost per passenger mile. **(12 marks)**

(b) Suggest two non-financial indicators that could be useful in measuring the performance of a bus service and explain why your chosen indicators are important. **(3 marks)**

(Total = 15 marks)

94 Heighway

27 mins

Heighway Co is a railway company. Heighway Co operates a passenger railway service and is responsible for the operation of services and the maintenance of track signalling equipment and other facilities such as stations. In recent years it has been criticised for providing a poor service to the travelling public in terms of punctuality, safety and the standard of facilities offered to passengers. In the last year Heighway Co has invested over $20 million in new carriages, station facilities and track maintenance programmes in an attempt to counter these criticisms. Summarised financial results for Heighway Co for the last two years are given below.

SUMMARISED INCOME STATEMENT FOR THE YEAR ENDED 31 DECEMBER

	20X3	*20X4*
	$ million	$ million
Sales revenue	180.0	185.0
Earnings before interest and tax	18.0	16.5
Interest	(3.2)	(4.7)
Tax	(4.4)	(3.5)
Earnings available to ordinary shareholders	10.4	8.3

SUMMARISED STATEMENT OF FINANCIAL POSITION AS AT 31 DECEMBER

	20X3		*20X4*	
	$m	$m	$m	$m
Non-current assets (net)		100.4		120.5
Current assets				
Inventory	5.3		5.9	
Receivables	2.1		2.4	
Cash	6.2		3.6	
		13.6		11.9
		114.0		132.4
Ordinary share capital ($1 shares)		25.0		25.0
Reserves		45.6		48.2
Amounts payable after more than one year				
8% Debenture 20X9		15.0		15.0
Bank loan		20.0		35.0
Payables due within one year		8.4		9.2
		114.0		132.4

Required

(a) Calculate the following ratios for Heighway Co for 20X3 and 20X4, clearly showing your workings.

(i) Return on capital employed (also known as return on investment) based upon closing capital employed
(ii) Net profit margin
(iii) Asset turnover
(iv) Current ratio **(4 marks)**

(b) Briefly comment on the financial performance of Heighway Co in 20X3 and 20X4 as revealed by the above ratios and suggest causes for any changes. **(8 marks)**

(c) Suggest **three** non-financial indicators that could be useful in measuring the performance of a passenger railway company and explain why your chosen indicators are important. **(3 marks)**

(Total = 15 marks)

95 Web Co (12/12 amended) **27 mins**

Web Co is an online retailer of fashion goods and uses a range of performance indicators to measure the performance of the business. The company's management have been increasingly concerned about the lack of sales growth over the last year and, in an attempt to resolve this, made the following changes right at the start of quarter 2:

Advertising: Web Co placed an advert on the webpage of a well-known online fashion magazine at a cost of $200,000. This had a direct link from the magazine's website to Web Co's online store.

Search engine: Web Co also engaged the services of a website consultant to ensure that, when certain key words are input by potential customers on to key search engines, such as Google and Yahoo, Web Co's website is listed on the first page of results. This makes it more likely that a customer will visit a company's website. The consultant's fee was $20,000.

Website availability: During quarter 1, there were a few problems with Web Co's website, meaning that it was not available to customers some of the time. Web Co was concerned that this was losing them sales and the IT department therefore made some changes to the website in an attempt to correct the problem.

As a **sales incentive**, a $10 discount was offered to all customers spending $100 or more at any one time.

The results for the last two quarters are shown below, quarter 2 being the most recent one. The results for quarter 1 reflect the period before the changes and incentive detailed above took place and are similar to the results of other quarters in the preceding year.

	Quarter 1	*Quarter 2*
Total sales revenue	$2,200,000	$2,750,000
Net profit margin	25%	16.7%
Total number of orders from customers	40,636	49,600
Total number of visits to website	101,589	141,714
Conversion rate – visitor to purchaser	40%	35%
The percentage of total visitors accessing website through magazine link	0	19.9%
Website availability	95%	95%
Number of customers spending more than $100 per visit	4,650	6,390

Required

Assess the performance of the business in Quarter 2 in relation to the changes and incentives that the company introduced at the beginning of this quarter. State clearly where any further information might be necessary, concluding as to whether the changes and incentives have been effective. **(15 marks)**

96 Bath Co (12/11 amended) **27 mins**

Bath Co is a company specialising in the manufacture and sale of baths. Each bath consists of a main unit plus a set of bath fittings. The company is split into two divisions, A and B. Division A manufactures the bath and Division B manufactures sets of bath fittings. Currently, all of Division A's sales are made externally. Division B, however, sells to Division A as well as to external customers. Both of the divisions are profit centres.

The following data is available for both divisions:

Division A	
Current selling price for each bath	$450
Costs per bath:	
Fittings from Division B	$75
Other materials from external suppliers	$200
Labour costs	$45
Annual fixed overheads	$7,440,000
Annual production and sales of baths (units)	80,000
Maximum annual market demand for baths (units)	80,000

Division B

Current external selling price per set of fittings	$80
Current price for sales to Division A	$75
Costs per set of fittings:	
Materials	$5
Labour costs	$15
Annual fixed overheads	$4,400,000
Maximum annual production and sales of sets of fittings (units) (including internal and external sales)	200,000
Maximum annual external demand for sets of fittings (units)	180,000
Maximum annual internal demand for sets of fittings (units)	80,000

The transfer price charged by Division B to Division A was negotiated some years ago between the previous divisional managers, who have now both been replaced by new managers. Head Office only allows Division A to purchase its fittings from Division B, although the new manager of Division A believes that he could obtain fittings of the same quality and appearance for $65 per set, if he was given the autonomy to purchase from outside the company. Division B makes no cost savings from supplying internally to Division A rather than selling externally.

Required

(a) Under the current transfer pricing system, prepare a profit statement showing the profit for each of the divisions and for Bath Co as a whole. Your sales and costs figures should be split into external sales and inter-divisional transfers, where appropriate. **(7 marks)**

(b) Head Office is considering changing the transfer pricing policy to ensure maximisation of company profits without demotivating either of the divisional managers. Division A will be given autonomy to buy from external suppliers and Division B to supply external customers in priority to supplying to Division A.

Calculate the maximum profit that could be earned by Bath Co if transfer pricing is optimised. **(8 marks)**

(Total = 15 marks)

97 Process Co (12/13 amended) 27 mins

Process Co has two divisions, A and B. Division A produces three types of chemicals: products L, M and S, using a common process. Each of the products can either be sold by Division A to the external market at split-off point (after the common process is complete) or can be transferred to Division B for individual further processing into products LX, MX and SX.

In November 20X1, which is a typical month, Division A's output was as follows:

Product	*Kg*
L	1,200
M	1,400
S	1,800

The market selling prices per kg for the products, both at split-off point and after further processing, are as follows:

	$		$
L	5.60	LX	6.70
M	6.50	MX	7.90
S	6.10	SX	6.80

The specific costs for each of the individual further processes are:

Variable cost of $0.50 per kg of LX
Variable cost of $0.70 per kg of MX
Variable cost of $0.80 per kg of SX

Further processing leads to a normal loss of 5% at the beginning of the process for each of the products being processed.

Required

(a) Calculate and conclude whether any of the products should be further processed in Division B in order to optimise the profit for the company as a whole. **(10 marks)**

It has been suggested that Division A should transfer products L and M to Division B for further processing, in order to optimise the profit of the company as a whole. Divisions A and B are both investment centres and all transfers from Division A to Division B would be made using the actual marginal cost. As a result, if Division A were to make the transfers as suggested, their divisional profits would be much lower than if it were to sell both products externally at split-off point. Division B's profits, however, would be much higher.

Required

(b) Discuss the issues arising from this suggested approach to transfer pricing. **(5 marks)**

(Total = 15 marks)

98 Hammer (6/10 amended) 27 mins

Hammer is a large garden equipment supplier with retail stores throughout Toolland. Many of the products it sells are bought in from outside suppliers but some are currently manufactured by Hammer's own manufacturing division 'Nail'.

The prices (a transfer price) that Nail charges to the retail stores are set by head office and have been the subject of some discussion. The current policy is for Nail to calculate the total variable cost of production and delivery and add 30% for profit. Nail argues that all costs should be taken into consideration, offering to reduce the mark-up on costs to 10% in this case. The retail stores are unhappy with the current pricing policy arguing that it results in prices that are often higher than comparable products available on the market.

Nail has provided the following information to enable a price comparison to be made of the two possible pricing policies for one of its products.

Garden shears

Steel: the shears have 0.4 kg of high quality steel in the final product. The manufacturing process loses 5% of all steel put in. Steel costs $4,000 per tonne (1 tonne = 1,000 kg)

Other materials: Other materials are bought in and have a list price of $3 per kg although Hammer secures a 10% volume discount on all purchases. The shears require 0.1kg of these materials.

The labour time to produce shears is 0.25 hours per unit and labour costs $10 per hour.

Variable overheads are absorbed at the rate of 150% of labour rates and fixed overheads are 80% of the variable overheads.

Delivery is made by an outsourced distributor that charges Nail $0.5 per garden shear for delivery.

Required

(a) Calculate the price that Nail would charge for the garden shears under the existing policy of variable cost plus 30%. **(4 marks)**

(b) Calculate the increase or decrease in price if the pricing policy switched to total cost plus 10%. **(3 marks)**

(c) Discuss whether or not including fixed costs in a transfer price is a sensible policy. **(4 marks)**

(d) Discuss whether the retail stores should be allowed to buy in from outside suppliers if the prices are cheaper than those charged by Nail. **(4 marks)**

(Total = 15 marks)

99 Woodside (6/07 amended) 27 mins

Woodside is a local charity dedicated to helping homeless people in a large city. The charity owns and manages a shelter that provides free overnight accommodation for up to 30 people, offers free meals each and every night of the year to homeless people who are unable to buy food, and runs a free advice centre to help homeless people find suitable housing and gain financial aid. Woodside depends entirely on public donations to finance its activities and had a fundraising target for the last year of $700,000. The budget for the last year was based on the following forecast activity levels and expected costs:

Free meals provision: 18,250 meals at $5 per meal
Overnight shelter: 10,000 bed-nights at $30 per night
Advice centre: 3,000 sessions at $20 per session
Campaigning and advertising: $150,000

The budgeted surplus (budgeted fundraising target less budgeted costs) was expected to be used to meet any unexpected costs. Included in the above figures are fixed costs of $5 per night for providing shelter and $5 per advice session representing fixed costs expected to be incurred by administration and maintaining the shelter. The number of free meals provided and the number of beds occupied each night depends on both the weather and the season of the year. The Woodside charity has three full-time staff and a large number of voluntary helpers.

The actual costs for the last year were as follows:

Free meals provision: 20,000 meals at a variable cost of $104,000
Overnight shelter: 8,760 bed-nights at a variable cost of $223,380
Advice centre: 3,500 sessions at a variable cost of $61,600
Campaigning and advertising: $165,000

The actual costs of the overnight shelter and the advice centre exclude the fixed costs of administration and maintenance, which were $83,000.

The actual amount of funds raised in the last year was $620,000.

Required

(a) Prepare an operating statement, reconciling budgeted surplus and actual shortfall. **(10 marks)**

(b) Discuss problems that may arise in the financial management and control of a not-for-profit organisation such as the Woodside charity. **(5 marks)**

(Total = 15 marks)

100 PAF Co (12/13 amended) 27 mins

Protect Against Fire Co (PAF Co) manufactures and sells fire safety equipment and also provides fire risk assessments and fire safety courses to businesses. It has been trading for many years in the country of Calana, where it is the market leader.

Five years ago, the directors of PAF Co established a similar operation in its neighbouring country, Sista, renting business premises at various locations across the country. The fire safety market in Sista has always been dominated by two other companies, and when PAF Co opened the Sista division, its plan was to become market leader there within five years. Division S left its prices for products and services unchanged in 20X3 rather than increasing them in line with its competitors.

Although the populations of both countries are similar, geographically, the country of Sista is twice as large as Calana and its customers are equally spread across the country. The products and services offered by the two divisions to their customers require skilled staff, demand for which is particularly high in Sista. Following the appointment of a new government in Sista at the end of 20X2, stricter fire safety regulations were immediately introduced for all companies. At the same time, the Government introduced a substantial tax on business property rents which landlords passed on to their tenants.

Summary statements of profit or loss for the two divisions for the two years ended 30 November 20X2 and 30 November 20X3 are shown below.

	Division S 20X3 $'000	*Division S* 20X2 $'000	*Division C* 20X3 $'000	*Division C* 20X2 $'000
Revenue	38,845	26,937	44,065	40,395
Material costs	(3,509)	(2,580)	(4,221)	(3,385)
Payroll costs	(10,260)	(6,030)	(8,820)	(7,700)
Property costs	(3,200)	(1,800)	(2,450)	(2,320)
Gross profit	21,876	16,527	28,574	26,954
Distribution and marketing costs	(10,522)	(7,602)	(7,098)	(5,998)
Administrative overheads	(7,024)	(6,598)	(12,012)	(11,974)
Operating profit	4,330	2,327	9,464	8,982
Employee numbers	380	241	420	385
Market share	30%	25%	55%	52%

Required

Using all the information above, assess the financial performance of Division S in the year ended 30 November 20X3. State clearly where further information might be required in order to make more reasoned conclusions about the division's performance.

Note. Up to 5 marks are available for calculations. **(15 marks)**

101 Ties Only Limited (12/07 amended) 27 mins

Ties Only Limited is a new business, selling high quality imported men's ties via the internet. The managers, who also own the company, are young and inexperienced but they are prepared to take risks. They are confident that importing quality ties and selling via a website will be successful and that the business will grow quickly. This is despite the well-recognised fact that selling clothing is a very competitive business.

They were prepared for a loss-making start and decided to pay themselves modest salaries (included in administration expenses in Table 1 below) and pay no dividends for the foreseeable future.

The owners are so convinced that growth will quickly follow that they have invested enough money in website server development to ensure that the server can handle the very high levels of predicted growth. All website development costs were written off as incurred in the internal management accounts that are shown below in Table 1.

Significant expenditure on marketing was incurred in the first two quarters to launch both the website and new products. It is not expected that marketing expenditure will continue to be as high in the future.

Customers can buy a variety of styles, patterns and colours of ties at different prices.

The business's trading results for the first two quarters of trade are shown below in Table 1.

Table 1

	Quarter 1		*Quarter 2*	
	$	$	$	$
Sales		420,000		680,000
Less cost of sales		(201,600)		(340,680)
Gross profit		218,400		339,320
Less expenses				
Website development	120,000		90,000	
Administration	100,500		150,640	
Distribution	20,763		33,320	
Launch marketing	60,000		40,800	
Other variable expenses	50,000		80,000	
Total expenses		(351,263)		(394,760)
Loss for quarter		(132,863)		(55,440)

Required

(a) Assess the financial performance of the business during its first two quarters using only the data in Table 1 above, and consider briefly whether the losses made by the business in the first two quarters are a true reflection of the likely future performance of the business. **(9 marks)**

The owners are well aware of the importance of non-financial indicators of success. A small number of measures are presented to management in a quarterly management report.

The data for the first two quarters management reports is shown below:

Table 2

	Quarter 1	*Quarter 2*
Number of ties sold	27,631	38,857
On time delivery	95%	89%
Sales returns	12%	18%
System downtime	2%	4%

The industry average for sales returns was 13%.

Required

(b) Comment on each of the non-financial data in Table 2 above taking into account, where appropriate, the industry averages provided, providing your assessment of the performance of the business. **(6 marks)**

(Total = 15 marks)

102 Squarize (6/13 amended) 27 mins

Squarize is a large company which, for many years, operated solely as a pay-TV broadcaster. However, five years ago, it started product bundling, offering broadband and telephone services to its pay-TV customers. Customers taking up the offer were then known in the business as 'bundle customers' and they had to take up both the broadband and telephone services together with the pay-TV service. Other customers were still able to subscribe to pay-TV alone but not to broadband and telephone services without the pay-TV service.

All contracts to customers of Squarize are for a minimum three-month period. The pay-TV box is sold to the customer at the beginning of the contract; however, the broadband and telephone equipment is only rented to them.

In the first few years after product bundling was introduced, the company saw a steady increase in profits. Then, Squarize saw its revenues and operating profits fall. Consequently, staff bonuses were not paid, and staff became dissatisfied. Several reasons were identified for the deterioration of results:

(1) In the economy as a whole, discretionary spending had been severely hit by rising unemployment and inflation. In a bid to save cash, many pay-TV customers were cancelling their contracts after the minimum three-month period as they were then able to still keep the pay-TV box. The box comes with a number of free channels, which the customer can still continue to receive free of charge, even after the cancellation of their contract.

(2) Some bundle customers found that the broadband service that they had subscribed to did not work. As a result, they were immediately cancelling their contracts for all services within the 14 day cancellation period permitted under the contracts.

In a response to the above problems and in an attempt to increase revenues and profits, Squarize made the following changes to the business:

(1) It made a strategic decision to withdraw the pay-TV-broadband-telephone (bundle) package from the market and, instead, offer each service as a standalone product.

(2) It guaranteed not to increase prices for a 12-month period for each of its three services.

(3) It investigated and resolved the problem with customers' broadband service.

It is now one year since the changes were made and the finance director wants to use a balanced scorecard to assess the extent to which the changes have been successful in improving the performance of the business.

Required

(a) For each perspective of the balanced scorecard, identify **one** goal (objective), together with a corresponding performance measure for each goal which could be used by the company to assess whether the changes have been successful. For each performance measure you select, give a brief explanation of why you have chosen it. **(11 marks)**

(b) Discuss how the company could reduce the problem of customers terminating their pay-TV service after only three months. **(4 marks)**

(Total = 15 marks)

103 Jump (6/10 amended) 27 mins

Jump has a network of sports clubs which is managed by local managers reporting to the main board. The local managers have a lot of autonomy and are able to vary employment contracts with staff and offer discounts for membership fees and personal training sessions. They also control their own maintenance budget but do not have control over large amounts of capital expenditure.

A local manager's performance and bonus is assessed relative to three targets. For every one of these three targets that is reached in an individual quarter, $400 is added to the manager's bonus, which is paid at the end of the year. The maximum bonus per year is therefore based on 12 targets (three targets in each of the four quarters of the year). Accordingly the maximum bonus that could be earned is 12 × $400 = $4,800, which represents 40% of the basic salary of a local manager. Jump has a 31 March year end.

The performance data for one of the sports clubs for the last four quarters is as follows.

	Qtr to 30 June 20X1	*Qtr to 30 September 20X1*	*Qtr to 31 December 20X1*	*Qtr to 31 March 20X2*
Number of members	3,000	3,200	3,300	3,400
Member visits	20,000	24,000	26,000	24,000
Personal training sessions booked	310	325	310	339
Staff days	450	480	470	480
Staff lateness days	20	28	28	20
Days in quarter	90	90	90	90

Agreed targets are:

(1) Staff must be on time over 95% of the time (no penalty is made when staff are absent from work).
(2) On average 60% of members must use the clubs' facilities regularly by visiting at least 12 times per quarter.
(3) On average 10% of members must book a personal training session each quarter.

Required

(a) Calculate the amount of bonus that the manager should expect to be paid for the latest financial year. **(6 marks)**

(b) Discuss to what extent the targets set are controllable by the local manager (you are required to make a case for both sides of the argument). **(9 marks)**

(Total = 15 marks)

104 The Accountancy Teaching Co (12/10 amended) 27 mins

The Accountancy Teaching Co (AT Co) is a company specialising in the provision of accountancy tuition courses in the private sector. It makes up its accounts to 30 November each year. In the year ending 30 November 20X1, it held 60% of market share. However, over the last twelve months, the accountancy tuition market in general has faced a 20% decline in demand for accountancy training leading to smaller class sizes on courses. In 20X1 and before, AT Co suffered from an ongoing problem with staff retention, which had a knock-on effect on the quality of service provided to students. Following the completion of developments that have been ongoing for some time, in 20X2 the company was able to offer a far-improved service to students. The developments included:

- A new dedicated 24 hour student helpline.
- An interactive website providing instant support to students.
- A new training programme for staff.
- An electronic student enrolment system.
- An electronic marking system for the marking of students' progress tests. The costs of marking electronically were expected to be $4 million less in 20X2 than marking on paper. Marking expenditure is always included in cost of sales.

Extracts from the management accounts for 20X1 and 20X2 are shown below:

	20X1		*20X2*	
	$'000	$'000	$'000	$'000
Turnover		72,025		66,028
Cost of sales		(52,078)		(42,056)
Gross profit		19,947		23,972
Indirect expenses:				
Marketing	3,291		4,678	
Property	6,702		6,690	
Staff training	1,287		3,396	
Interactive website running costs	–		3,270	
Student helpline running costs	–		2,872	
Enrolment costs	5,032		960	
Total indirect expenses		(16,312)		(21,866)
Net operating profit		3,635		2,106

On 1 December 20X1, management asked all 'freelance lecturers' to reduce their fees by at least 10% with immediate effect ('freelance lecturers' are not employees of the company but are used to teach students when there are not enough of AT Co's own lecturers to meet tuition needs). All employees were also told that they would not receive a pay rise for at least one year. Total lecture staff costs (including freelance lecturers) were $41.663 million in 20X1 and were included in cost of sales, as is always the case. Freelance lecturer costs represented 35% of these total lecture staff costs. In 20X2 freelance lecture costs were $12.394 million. No reduction was made to course prices in the year and the mix of trainees studying for the different qualifications remained the same. The same type and number of courses were run in both 20X1 and 20X2 and the percentage of these courses that was run by freelance lecturers as opposed to employed staff also remained the same.

Due to the nature of the business, non-financial performance indicators are also used to assess performance, as detailed below.

	20X1	*20X2*
Percentage of students transferring to AT Co from another training provider	8%	20%
Number of late enrolments due to staff error	297	106
Percentage of students passing exams first time	48%	66%
Labour turnover	32%	10%
Number of student complaints	315	84
Average number of employees	1,080	1,081

Required

Assess the performance of the business in 20X2 using both financial performance indicators calculated from the above information **and** the non-financial performance indicators provided.

Note. Clearly state any assumptions and show all workings clearly. Your answer should be structured around the following main headings: turnover; cost of sales; gross profit; indirect expenses; net operating profit. However, in discussing each of these areas you should also refer to the non-financial performance indicators, where relevant.

(15 marks)

105 Bridgewater Co (6/08 amended) — 27 mins

Bridgewater Co provides training courses for many of the mainstream software packages on the market.

The business has many divisions within Waterland, the one country in which it operates. The senior managers of Bridgewater Co have very clear objectives for the divisions and these are communicated to divisional managers on appointment and subsequently in quarterly and annual reviews. These are:

- Each quarter, sales should grow and annual sales should exceed budget
- Trainer (lecture staff) costs should not exceed $180 per teaching day
- Room hire costs should not exceed $90 per teaching day
- Each division should meet its budget for profit per quarter and annually

It is known that managers will be promoted based on their ability to meet these targets. A member of the senior management is to retire after quarter 2 of the current financial year, which has just begun. The divisional managers anticipate that one of them may be promoted at the beginning of quarter 3 if their performance is good enough.

The manager of the Northwest division is concerned that his chances of promotion could be damaged by the expected performance of his division. He is a firm believer in quality and he thinks that if a business gets this right, growth and success will eventually follow.

The current quarterly forecasts, along with the original budgeted profit for the Northwest division, are as follows:

	Q1	*Q2*	*Q3*	*Q4*	*Total*
	$'000	$'000	$'000	$'000	$'000
Sales	40.0	36.0	50.0	60.0	186.0
Less:					
Trainers	8.0	7.2	10.0	12.0	37.2
Room hire	4.0	3.6	5.0	6.0	18.6
Staff training	1.0	1.0	1.0	1.0	4.0
Other costs	3.0	1.7	6.0	7.0	17.7
Forecast net profit	24.0	22.5	28.0	34.0	108.5
Original budgeted profit	25.0	26.0	27.0	28.0	106.0
Annual sales budget					180.0
Teaching days	40	36	50	60	

Required

(a) Assess the financial performance of the Northwest division against its targets and reach a conclusion as to the promotion prospects of the divisional manager. **(7 marks)**

The manager of the Northwest division has been considering a few steps to improve the performance of his division.

Software upgrade

A new important software programme has recently been launched for which there could be a market for training courses. Demonstration programs can be bought for $1,800 in quarter 1. Staff training would be needed, costing $500 in each of quarters 1 and 2 but in quarters 3 and 4 extra courses could be offered selling this training. Assuming similar class sizes and the usual sales prices, extra sales revenue amounting to 20% of normal sales are expected (measured before the voucher promotion above). The manager is keen to run these courses at the same tutorial and room standards as he normally provides. Software expenditure is written off in the income statement as incurred.

Delaying payments to trainers

The manager is considering delaying payment to the trainers. He thinks that, since his commitment to quality could cause him to miss out on a well deserved promotion, the trainers owe him a favour. He intends to delay payment on 50% of all invoices received from the trainers in the first two quarters, paying them one month later than is usual.

Required

(b) Revise the forecasts to take account of both of the proposed changes. **(5 marks)**

(c) Comment on each of the proposed steps and reach a conclusion as to whether, if both the proposals were taken together, the manager will improve his chances of promotion. **(3 marks)**

(Total = 15 marks)

106 Oliver's Salon (6/09 amended) 27 mins

Oliver is the owner and manager of Oliver's Salon which is a quality hairdresser that experiences high levels of competition. The salon traditionally provided a range of hair services to female clients only, including cuts, colouring and straightening.

A year ago, at the start of his 20X9 financial year, Oliver decided to expand his operations to include the hairdressing needs of male clients. Male hairdressing prices are lower, the work simpler (mainly hair cuts only) and so the time taken per male client is much less.

The prices for the female clients were not increased during the whole of 20X8 and 20X9 and the mix of services provided for female clients in the two years was the same.

The latest financial results are as follows:

	20X8		*20X9*	
	$	$	$	$
Sales		200,000		238,500
Less cost of sales:				
Hairdressing staff costs	65,000		91,000	
Hair products – female	29,000		27,000	
Hair products – male			8,000	
		94,000		126,000
Gross profit		106,000		112,500
Less expenses:				
Rent	10,000		10,000	
Administration salaries	9,000		9,500	
Electricity	7,000		8,000	
Advertising	2,000		5,000	
Total expenses		28,000		32,500
Profit		78,000		80,000

Oliver is disappointed with his financial results. He thinks the salon is much busier than a year ago and was expecting more profit. He has noted the following extra information:

Some female clients complained about the change in atmosphere following the introduction of male services, which created tension in the salon.

Two new staff were recruited at the start of 20X9. The first was a junior hairdresser to support the specialist hairdressers for the female clients. She was appointed on a salary of $9,000 per annum. The second new staff member was a specialist hairdresser for the male clients. There were no increases in pay for existing staff at the start of 20X9 after a big rise at the start of 20X8 which was designed to cover two years' worth of increases.

Oliver introduced some non-financial measures of success two years ago.

	20X8	20X9
Number of complaints	12	46
Number of male client visits	0	3,425
Number of female client visits	8,000	6,800
Number of specialist hairdressers for female clients	4	5
Number of specialist hairdressers for male clients	0	1

Required

(a) Assess the financial performance of the salon using the data above. **(10 marks)**

(b) Analyse and comment on the non-financial performance of Oliver's business, under the headings of quality and resource utilisation. **(5 marks)**

(Total = 15 marks)

Answers

Question 1

1.1 B (Syllabus area A1(c))

ABC is a method of absorption costing that uses cost drivers to calculate absorption rates per unit of overhead activity, and then apportion overhead costs to products. It is not a technique for identifying variable overhead costs.

ABC can be used as a basis for preparing budgets. This approach to budgeting is called activity based budgeting (ABB).

1.2 D (Syllabus area A4(b))

Reducing material costs or increasing the sales price will increase throughput per machine hour. Reducing factory costs will reduce the factory cost per machine hour. These will increase the TA ratio.

1.3 D (Syllabus area A3(c))

Life cycle costing can be used for products with a short life cycle, and is particularly useful where a large proportion of total costs are incurred during the research design and development phase of the product life. However life cycle costing can also be appropriate for products with a long life cycle, where disposal costs or clean-up costs will be very high (such as a nuclear power station).

Product life cycle costing looks at costs over the entire life of a product whereas budgetary control systems focus on individual financial years. The two costing systems can be operated by a company, but life cycle costing cannot easily be made part of the budgeting and budgetary control system.

1.4 A (Syllabus area A4(b))

The return per factory hour is measured using the bottleneck resource as a measure of factory hours.

Return = Throughput

Return per machine hour = $(15 – 6)/0.10 hours = $90

1.5 D (Syllabus area A2(a))

In order to identify the desirable features for a new product and set a target sales price, it is necessary to look first at what competitors are offering in the market.

The biggest and most effective cost savings are achieved at the product design stage, before production begins. When production begins it becomes more difficult to make changes in order to reduce costs.

1.6 B (Syllabus area A2(b))

Target costing can be used for an innovative new product, provided that a target selling price is first identified. A target cost may be exceeded during the growth phase of the life cycle for a new product, but the target cost gap should be closed by the time that the product reaches the maturity phase of its life cycle.

1.7 A (Syllabus area A2(a))

Target profit (25% of cost = 20% of sales price) = $2
Target cost $10 – $2 = $8
Target cost gap = $8.40 – $8 = $0.40

1.8 D (Syllabus area A5(b))

With life cycle costing, the expected costs of clean-up and decontamination at the end of the life of a project or product are taken into consideration at the initial design stage. Decisions can then be taken from the outset that will reduce these costs at the end of the projected product's life.

1.9 D (Syllabus area A4(b))

Production capacity is 30 TRLs per week on Machine Z and 40 × 85% = 34 TRLs per week on Machine X. Machine Z is therefore a bottleneck resource and there are 1,920 production hours per year (= 40 × 48)

Throughput per unit of TRL = $2,000 – $800 = $1,200
Machine Z hours per unit of TRL = 40 hours per week/30 units per week = 1.3333 hours
Throughput per Machine Z hour = $1,200/1.3333 = $900
Factory costs per year = $264,000 + $834,000 = $1,098,000
Factory costs per Machine Z hour = $1,098,000/1,920 = $571.875
Throughput accounting ratio = $900/$571.875 = 1.574

1.10 B (Syllabus area A4(a))

The throughput concept is that inventories should be kept as close to zero as possible, because items held as inventory do not provide any value. Throughput accounting is best suited to a just-in-time purchasing and production environment.

The assumption is that labour and other factory costs are fixed in the short term, and throughput can be measured as the sales revenue from produced items less their materials cost.

Question 2

2.1 B (Syllabus area A1(a))

Implementation of ABC is likely to be cost effective when variable production costs are a low proportion of total production costs and overhead costs, traditionally assumed to be fixed costs, are a large proportion of total production costs.

At a unit level, the cost driver for production-related overheads is likely to be direct labour hours or machine hours.

2.2 B (Syllabus area A4(b))

Throughput per unit = $(18 – 8) = $10
Throughput per machine hour = $10/0.3 hours = $33.3
Factory cost per machine hour = $(4 + 2)/ 0.3 hours = $20
Throughput accounting ratio = $33.3/$20 = 1.67

2.3 C (Syllabus area A4(a))

The aim should be to improve the performance of the binding constraint. This can be done by achieving more output per unit of binding resource (improving efficiency) or obtaining more of the resource that is the binding constraint. By increasing output through the binding constraint, a point will eventually be reached where it ceases to be the binding constraint, and another resource becomes the binding constraint.

2.4 C (Syllabus area A5(a))

A company may incur costs for contamination of the environment, but this cost should not be included within budgeted (and so 'acceptable') environmental costs.

2.5 D (Syllabus area A3(a))

Planning for costs is a forward-looking exercise. Control involves monitoring actual costs. Life cycle costs cover the full expected life of a product, which may be several years. Because of the long time scale that may be involved, monitoring actual life cycle costs is impracticable. Most of the life cycle costs for a product are determined by decisions taken in the early stage of a product's life cycle, particularly when the product is designed and the method of producing it is decided.

2.6 D (Syllabus area A1(c))

It is a mistake to associate activity based costs with the variable costs of an activity. Some of the costs may be variable in the short run, but others are not. So ABC costs should not be treated as relevant costs for the purpose of short-term decision making. It is more appropriate to think of ABC as a form of absorption costing, where overheads are allocated to activities and products on a more meaningful basis than with traditional absorption costing.

2.7 A (Syllabus area A5(a))

Costs of wasted materials include costs of inefficiencies in the production process, such as waste and emissions. Waste has a material cost, but also associated labour costs and other overhead costs.

2.8 D (Syllabus area A4(c))

The theory of constraints is based on the view that the focus should be on elevating a bottleneck resource to the level where it ceases to be a bottleneck, and at this time a new bottleneck will 'take over'. The throughput accounting ratio is the ratio of return per factory hour divided by cost per factory hour. If this ratio is less than 1, the commercial viability of the product should be questioned.

2.9 A (Syllabus area A5(b))

'Input' costs consist of material costs, waste management costs, energy costs and system costs (labour and overhead costs). Output costs are allocated between positive products (good finished output) and negative product costs (cost of waste and emissions).

2.10 C (Syllabus area A4(c))

Throughput is sales revenue minus material costs. Higher labour costs will not affect throughput. Only measures that increase output capacity of the bottleneck resource might increase throughput. So measure (3) will increase total throughput, but it is only worthwhile if the increase in throughput exceeds the increased factory cost of $4 per hour worked of Grade A labour time.

Question 3

3.1 D (Syllabus area A1(c))

Some overhead costs are usually absorbed on an arbitrary basis, such as a rate per direct labour hour, because they are not associated with any specific activity.

The costs of any management information system may exceed the benefits obtained: in such cases there is no value in establishing and operating such a system. This applies to any cost and management accounting system, not just ABC.

3.2 C (Syllabus area A2(c))

Target costing may take product development costs into consideration, but recovery of product design and development costs is associated more with life cycle costing. Even with life cycle costing, recovery of design and development costs is not ensured: much depends on whether customers will buy enough of the product at the target price.

In target costing, a cost gap is the difference between the current estimate of the cost per unit of the product and the target cost that the entity wants to achieve.

3.3 C (Syllabus area A3(c))

Financial returns can be improved over the life cycle of a product by minimising the breakeven time, minimising the time to get a new product to market and maximising the length of the product life cycle.

3.4 B (Syllabus area A5(a))

Environmental management accounting measures physical quantities as well as monetary amounts. Management accounting is concerned with providing information to management, not with external reporting to shareholders.

3.5 D (Syllabus area A5(a))

A system of environmental management accounting provides environmental information for internal use by management, but not for external reporting. It is distinct from environmental accounting, which is concerned with external reporting (as well as internal reporting). Environmental management accounting systems typically make use of life cycle costing, given that there may be substantial clean-up and disposal costs at the end of the life of an activity or operation.

3.6 B (Syllabus area A4(a))

Output from a binding constraint should be used immediately, not built up as inventory, because it is the factor that constrains output and sales. Some inventory may build up before the binding constraint, but the general principle in throughput accounting is that any inventory is undesirable.

3.7 A (Syllabus area A4(b))

Throughput per unit of Product X = $(40 – 10) = $30
Throughput per bottleneck hour = $30/0.01 hours = $3,000
Factory costs per year = $2,920,000 + (50,000 × $12) = $3,520,000
Factory cost per bottleneck hour = $3,520,000/4,000 hours = $880
Throughput accounting ratio = $3,000/$880 = 3.41

3.8 D (Syllabus area A5(b))

In MFCA, a distinction is made between good finished output (positive output) and waste and emissions (negative output). Both types of output are given a cost. Performance can be improved by finding ways to reduce the amount of negative output – and so achieve the same amount of output with less input materials.

3.9 D (Syllabus area A2(b))

For services that have a large fixed cost based, other methods of cost control may be more appropriate, such as activity based management, and a key to reducing costs is often increasing sales volumes rather than reducing expenditures. To achieve a target cost, one approach is to remove design features from a product specification that do not add value for customers (so do not affect the price that customers are willing to pay).

3.10 D (Syllabus area A4(d))

	A	*B*	*C*	*D*
Maximum sales demand	1,000	500	2,000	1,000
Selling price per unit	$15	$21	$18	$25
Material cost per unit	$6	$10	$9	$16
Throughput per unit	$9	$11	$9	$9
Machine hours per unit	0.1	0.2	0.3	0.2
Throughput per machine hour	$90	$55	$30	$45
Priority for manufacture	1st	2nd	4th	3rd

In the 750 hours available, the company should make 1,000 units of A (100 hours), then 500 units of B (100 hours), then 1,000 units of D (200 hours) leaving 350 hours available to make 1,166 units of Product C.

Question 4

4.1 B (Syllabus area A1 (a))

Implementation of ABC is likely to be cost effective when variable production costs are a low proportion of total production costs and overhead costs, traditionally assumed to be fixed costs, are a large proportion of total production costs.

At a unit level, the cost driver for production-related overheads is likely to be direct labour hours or machine hours.

4.2 D (Syllabus area A1 (c))

It is a mistake to associate activity based costs with the variable costs of an activity. Some of the costs may be variable in the short run, but others are not. So ABC costs should not be treated as relevant costs for the purpose of short-term decision making. It is more appropriate to think of ABC as a form of absorption costing, where overheads are allocated to activities and products on a more meaningful basis than with traditional absorption costing.

4.3 A (Syllabus area A2 (a))

If there is a target cost gap that cannot be eliminated, management may consider whether or not to continue with the product, since it will not be achieving the required profit margin. However, a decision to discontinue a product on whether to continue making it may not be based on target costs or profit margins alone.

4.4 D (Syllabus area A3 (b))

Breakeven time is the time from the initial product concept to the time that operating profits have covered the initial investment costs.

Month after launch	*Operating profit*	*Cumulative return*
	$	$
0	–	(800,000)
1	120,000	(680,000)
2	180,000	(500,000)
3	240,000	(260,000)
4	300,000	40,000

Breakeven is in the fourth month after launch. Allowing for the 8 months from concept to market launch, the breakeven time is 12 months.

4.5 A (Syllabus area A4 (a))

The production capacity of a bottleneck resource should determine the production schedule for the organisation as a whole. This means inevitably that there will be idle time in other parts of production where capacity is greater.

4.6 B (Syllabus area A1 (a))

The cost driver for quality inspection costs is likely to be either the number of units produced or the number of batches produced, depending on whether quality inspection is linked to batches produced or total production output. The batch size is not a factor that drives total inspection costs.

4.7 D (Syllabus area A2 (c))

Cost reduction measures may reduce the perceived value of a product to customers, so that the target selling price becomes unachievable for the sales volume required. The projected cost of a new product may be reduced by simplifying the design (such as using more standard components, fewer components in total and removing design features that do not add value), but simplification of the design should not reduce the value of the product for customers.

4.8 C (Syllabus area A3 (c))

A product is usually most profitable during the maturity phase of its life cycle. Life cycle costing is not particularly useful for deciding the selling price for a product, because the appropriate selling price changes over the life of a product.

4.9 C (Syllabus area A4 (a))

In throughput accounting, all inventory, including work in progress and finished goods, should be valued at the cost of their materials. They should not include any other costs (labour or overhead costs). The aim should not be to maximise the use of all available resources, because this will simply create unwanted inventory. The aim should be to maximise the use of the bottleneck resource and efficiency is achieved by meeting production schedules and delivery dates to customers.

4.10 D (Syllabus area A3 (b))

	$
Variable costs	
Year 1: $(30 + 6 + 4) × 25,000	1,000,000
Year 2: $(25 + 5 + 3) × 100,000	3,300,000
Year 3: $(20 + 4 + 2) × 75,000	1,950,000
R&D costs	940,000
Other fixed costs	3,000,000
Total life cycle costs	10,190,000
Total units made and sold	200,000
Average life cycle cost per unit	$50.95

Question 5

5.1 C (Syllabus area A1 (a))

Some costs of activities may vary with the volume of the activity, but other costs of the activity will be fixed costs. A cost driver is not the cost itself; it is a measure of the volume or quantity of an activity.

5.2 A (Syllabus area A2 (b))

Overhead costs are usually a large proportion of total costs; therefore it is important to have reliable estimates of sales demand at a given target sales price in order to establish a target cost. Target costing is dependent on identifying a target selling price for an item, so it is not appropriate for costing services provided free of charge. Call centre costs, for example, should be managed using other methods of cost control.

5.3 D (Syllabus area A4 (a))

By looking at the costs over the entire life cycle of a product, and comparing these with expected sales revenues, a decision can be taken at an early stage, before too much cost has been committed, about whether to go ahead with developing a new product. Life cycle costing also helps management to consider the merits of investing more money at the design stage for a new product if this will reduce operating costs over the product life cycle.

5.4 A (Syllabus area A3 (c))

With product life cycle costing, an aim should be to ensure that initial development costs do not exceed expected development costs. This means that new product development may be treated as a project, and the aim of project management is to produce the product for market to specification, on time and within the budgeted cost.

Customer life cycles are not the same as product life cycles. Customers may buy many different products from a company over their time as customers of the company. Some customers may even stay with a company (such as a bank) for life.

5.5 D (Syllabus area A3 (b))

	Year 1	*Year 2*	*Year 3*	*Year 4*	*Total*
	$'000	$'000	$'000	$'000	$'000
R&D costs	900	300			1,200
Marketing	300	300	100	100	800
Production	400	400	750	300	1,850
Customer services	100	150	250	50	550
Disposal				200	200
Total					4,600
Units					50,000
Life cycle cost per unit					$92.00

5.6 D (Syllabus area A4 (a))

Factory labour costs are always treated as a part of the factory cost/conversion cost of a product. Throughput accounting does not make a distinction between direct and indirect costs. It is also assumed that labour costs are a fixed cost, so if machine time is the bottleneck resource, nothing is gained by improving labour efficiency, because this will not increase throughput.

5.7 D (Syllabus area A4 (a))

A binding constraint is anything that restricts production and sales. Limited sales force capacity, for example, may act as a binding constraint on selling. When the bottleneck resource is a production resource such as machine time, production must be restricted to the capacity of this resource, to prevent unwanted inventory from accumulating through the production process. However the bottleneck resource should be fully utilised so as to maximise throughput and profit.

5.8 B (Syllabus area A5 (a))

The US Environment Protection Agency in 1998 suggested classifying environmental costs into four types: conventional costs, hidden costs (costs hidden because they are included in general overheads and not identified separately), contingent costs and image and relationship costs.

5.9 C (Syllabus area A2 (c))

Esteem is the status that the owner/customer attributes to possession of the product. Esteem may be affected by the product quality, but it is also possible that extra quality in a product does not add to its perceived value in the view of the customer.

5.10 C (Syllabus area A1 (c))

ABC can be used for cost-plus pricing. Traditional absorption costing tends to allocate insufficient overhead costs to low-volume products that use up a disproportionate amount of time for order handling, production runs and set-ups.

6 Linacre Co

Text references. Activity based costing is covered in Chapter 2a.

Top tips. This question on activity based costing (ABC) requires you to calculate cost pools, calculate a product cost based on your ABC cost.

Easy marks. The question is split into two smaller calculation elements that will gain you marks for method as well as the correct answer.

Examiner's comments. This was a very popular question and most candidates gained full marks in part (a). Most answers to part (b) contained errors of calculation or omission.

Marking scheme

			Marks
(a)	ABC recovery rates		2
(b)	Cost drivers for Product ZT3	1	
	ABC overheads for Product ZT3	2	
	General overheads for Product ZT3	1	
	Total overhead per unit	1	
	Direct labour cost	1	
	Standard total unit cost	1	
	Standard selling price	1	8
			10

(a) **ABC recovery rates for each cost pool**

Cost Pool	Cost ($)	Cost driver	Number of drivers	ABC recovery rate ($)
Production set-ups	105,000	Set-ups	300	350 per set-up
Product testing	300,000	Tests	1,500	200 per test
Component supply and storage	25,000	Component orders	500	50 per order
Customer orders and delivery	112,500	Customer orders	1,000	112.50 per order

(b) **Total unit cost and selling price for Product ZT3**

Cost	*Working*	*$/unit*	
Component cost		1.00	Unit cost as stated
Direct labour	2	1.30	
General O/H	3	0.50	
Overheads	4	3.33	
Total unit cost		6.13	
Mark-up		2.45	At 40% of total unit cost
Selling price		8.58	

Workings

1 **Orders**. 100 orders × 60 units + 60 orders × 50 units = 9,000 units

2 10 minutes per unit at $7.80 per hour = 10/60 × 7.80 = $1.30 per unit

3 $900,000/300,000 = $3/direct labour hour

9,000/6 or 1,500 direct labour hours spent on manufacture (10 minutes per unit)

1,500 hours/9,000 units × $3/unit = $0.50/unit

4 **Set-ups**. 10 runs × 900 units each. So $350 × 10 annual cost = $3,500. Divide by 9,000 units gives $0.39/unit.

Product test. 4 tests per run × 10 runs = 40 tests. At $200/test = $8,000 annual cost. Divide by 9,000 units gives $0.89/unit.

Component supply. 1 order per run × 10 runs = 10 orders. At $50/order = $500 annual cost. Divide by 9,000 units gives $0.056/unit.

Customer supply. 160 orders × $112.50/order = $18,000 annual cost. Divide by 9,000 units gives $2/unit.

Total overhead costs from cost pools.

This is $(0.39 + 0.89 + 0.056 + 2) = $3.33/unit.

7 Jola Publishing Co

Text references. Activity based costing is covered in Chapter 2a.

Top tips. Read the requirements very carefully and make sure you answer the specific requirements of the question (see the examiner's comments below).

Easy marks. There are not necessarily any easy marks in this question ,which calls for a good understanding of ABC and how it differs from traditional absorption costing. To earn marks however, it is essential to show that you understand the question, and you should try to answer it specifically rather than just write around the general subject of ABC.

Examiner's comments. Part (a) produced some good answers, however many completely misread the requirement and gave a text book explanation of the process involved in ABC. This gained very few marks. Vague references to 'activities' without referring to the specific activities in the question gained only a few marks. The examiner wanted candidates to explain why these products costs had changed following the introduction of ABC.

Part (b) also produced many good answers. It asked for implementation problems not merely 'issues' and so marks were lost through poor focus again. The fact that ABC might result in a price change is an issue but not necessarily a problem. The fact that subsequent to a price change customers could complain is a problem.

Marking scheme

			Marks
(a)	Comment on property costs	2	
	Comment on quality control	2	
	Comment on production set up cost	2	
	Comment on overall effect	1	
			7
(b)	For each explanation: 1.5 marks		3
			10

(a) **Overall effect**

The change in overheads following re-allocation is not particularly significant overall. CB has only absorbed \$0.05 more overhead which is 2% ($0.05/2.40 \times 100$) and the overheads for TJ have fallen by 8% ($0.3/4.00 \times 100$).

Property costs

The **largest overhead** is property costs which comprise 75% of total overhead. The activity driver for property costs is **machine hours** and this is also the basis used for absorption costing. This explains why the overall overhead change is not significant.

Quality control

Quality control comprises 23% of total overhead so is important. The activity driver for quality control is **number of inspections** and this will have a significant effect on the way overheads are allocated using ABC.

CB takes **fewer machine hours** to produce than TJ as it is a shorter book. It does however go through **frequent quality checks** so under ABC, will incur **much more** of the quality control overhead than TJ which has only a small number of inspections.

Production set-up costs

Production set-up costs comprise only 2% of total overhead so a change in overhead allocation will **not have a significant effect**.

However, the treatment of the overheads will be **very different** under ABC. CB is produced in four long production runs, whereas TJ is produced monthly in 12 production runs. Each production run incurs a set-up cost so TJ will incur a much higher proportion of these costs than if traditional absorption costing is used.

(b) **Implementation problems**

Lack of data

ABC requires **detailed accounting records** which may not be available in the business. Information is required on cost pools and cost drivers. This information is usually time consuming to derive and there may be resistance from employees.

Identifying cost drivers

It can be very difficult to identify a **single cost driver** which explains the behaviour of all items in its associated pool. For example, the property costs for this company could be driven by a number of different activities.

Lack of understanding

ABC is a **complex, time consuming technique** which will not necessarily be sufficiently understood and accepted by managers to enable them to provide **meaningful product costs** or extra information.

There can be an incorrect belief that ABC can solve all an organisation's problems but **costs of implementation** may **exceed the benefits.**

8 The Gadget Co

Text reference. Activity based costing is covered in Chapter 2a.

Top tips. Part (a) requires methodical, clear calculations. Show all your workings to maximise your score. In part (b) you should compare the costs per unit with absorption costing and with ABC and then comment on what they mean for The Gadget Co.

Easy marks. There are easy marks to be gained in part (a), but remember to present your workings and calculations clearly.

Examiner's comments. Part (a) produced more mixed results. Perhaps the most surprising outcome was that nearly all candidates mixed up the driver for machine set ups (which should have been the 36 machine set ups) with the driver for machine running costs (which should have been 32,100 machine hours). I'm not quite sure why there was such an incidence of error here, but fortunately most candidates went on to complete the calculations correctly and earn the appropriate follow-on marks.

Answers to part (b) were very poor. The requirement was very specific about what should be talked about – how ABC may help the company to improve profitability in relation to improving the profitability of this company, not in general. Candidates were expected to say that because, for example, 'product A required more set ups than products B and C, the set up costs were higher, meaning that A's profitability was far lower under ABC. The company could use this to identify how cost savings could then be made, by reducing the number of set ups. Alternatively, the company could consider whether it could charge a higher price for product A, thus improving profit by pushing up revenues'. The biggest problem with answers to part (b) was that candidates did not read it properly and simply started taking about the benefits of ABC in general. They scored poorly for this.

Marking scheme

			Marks
(a)	Cost under ABC:		
	Correct cost driver rates (0.5 for each rate)	2	
	Correct overhead unit cost for A	1	
	Correct overhead unit cost for B	1	
	Correct overhead unit cost for C	1	
	Correct cost per unit under ABC	1	
			6
(b)	Using ABC to improve profitability:		
	Up to 2 marks each for commenting on Products A and C. Up to 1 mark for commenting on Product B		max 4
			10

(a) **Cost per unit using activity based costing**

ABC recovery rates for each cost pool

Cost pool	*Cost ($)*	*Cost driver*	*Number of drivers*	*ABC recovery rate*
Machine set up costs	26,550	Production runs	36 (16 + 12 + 8)	$737.50 per set up
Machine running costs	66,400	Machine hours	32,100 (7,500 + 8,400 +16,200)	$2.07 per hour
Procurement costs	48,000	Purchase orders	94 (24 + 28 + 42)	$510.64 per order
Delivery costs	54,320	Deliveries	140 (48 + 30 + 62)	$388 per delivery
	195,270			

Total overheads by product and per unit

	Product A		*Product B*		*Product C*	
Overhead	*Activity*	*Cost*	*Activity*	*Cost*	*Activity*	*Cost*
		$		$		$
Machine set-ups	16	11,800	12	8,850	8	5,900
Machine running	7,500	15,525	8,400	17,388	16,200	33,534
Procurement	24	12,255	28	14,298	42	21,447
Delivery	48	18,624	30	11,640	62	24,056
Total o'hd cost		58,204		52,176		84,937
Units produced		15,000		12,000		18,000
Overhead cost per unit		$3.88		$4.35		$4.72

Total cost per unit

	A	*B*	*C*
	$	$	$
Materials	2.40	3.60	4.80
Labour	1.48	2.22	2.96
Overheads	3.88	4.35	4.72
	7.76	10.17	12.48

(b) **How activity based costing can improve product profitability**

Product A

The cost of product A under an ABC system is $7.76. This is 16% higher than the costs under traditional absorption costing ($6.71) and is significant given that The Gadget Co sells product A for $7.50.

Product A therefore makes a loss under ABC. Management may consider increasing the selling price of product A as well as investigating ways to reduce the costs associated with the product. Machine product costs for product A are higher than the other products due to the number of production runs. Management should investigate whether it is possible to reduce the number of production runs associated with the product.

Product B

The cost of product B is $0.10 higher under ABC. This difference is minimal and the product makes a healthy profit under both methods, given its selling price of $12.

Product C

Product C appears to be loss making under the traditional costing system with costs totalling $13.42 in comparison to the selling price of $13.00, yielding a loss of $0.42 per unit. In contrast, the product is profitable under ABC with costs totalling $12.48 per unit. Management may therefore wish to consider putting more emphasis on to sales of Product C rather than the less profitable Product A.

9 Duff Co

Text references. Activity based costing is covered in Chapter 2a.

Top tips. This question on activity based costing (ABC) requires you to calculate cost driver rates, and calculate a product cost for three products based on your ABC cost.

Examiner's comments. On the whole this was very well answered, where mistakes were made, they generally arose from misreading the information in the question.

Marking scheme

		Marks
Activity based cost		
Correct cost driver rates	4.5	
Overhead unit cost for X	1	
Overhead unit cost for Y	1	
Overhead unit cost for Z	1	
Adding labour and materials costs	1	
Total cost for X	0.5	
Total cost for Y	0.5	
Total cost for Z	0.5	10

ABC recovery rates for each cost pool

Cost pool	*Cost ($)*	*Cost driver*	*Number of drivers*	*ABC recovery rate*
Machine set up costs	280,000	Number of batches	115 (40 + 20 + 55) (W1)	$2,434.78 per set up
Machine ordering costs	316,000	Number of purchase orders	480 (160 + 100 + 220) (W2)	$658.33 per order
Machine running costs	420,000	Machine hours	80,800 (30,000 + 20,000 + 30,800)	$5.20 per hour
General facilities cost	361,400	Machine hours	80,800 (30,000 + 20,000 + 30,800)	$4.47 per hour
	1,377,400			

Total overheads by product and per unit

	Product X		*Product Y*		*Product Z*	
Overhead	*Activity*	*Cost*	*Activity*	*Cost*	*Activity*	*Cost*
		$		$		$
Machine set-ups	40	97,391	20	48,696	55	133,913
Material ordering costs	160	105,333	100	65,833	220	144,834
Machine running costs	30,000	156,000	20,000	104,000	30,800	160,160
General facility costs	30,000	134,100	20,000	89,400	30,800	137,676
Total o'hd cost		492,824		307,929		576,583
Units produced		20,000		16,000		22,000
Overhead cost per unit		$24.64		$19.25		$26.21

Total cost per unit

	X	*Y*	*Z*
	$	$	$
Materials	25	28	22
Labour	30	36	24
Overheads	24.64	19.25	26.21
	79.64	83.25	72.21

Workings

1 *Number of batches*:

X 20,000 units ÷ 500 (batch size) = 40
Y 16,000 units ÷ 800 (batch size) = 20
Z 22,000 units ÷ 400 (batch size) = 55

2 *Number of purchase orders*:

X 40 batches (from W1) × 4 (number of purchase orders per batch) = 160
Y 20 batches (from W1) × 5 (number of purchase orders per batch) = 100
Z 55 batches (from W1) × 4 (number of purchase orders per batch) = 220

10 Target costing

Text reference. Target costing is covered in Chapter 2b.

Top tips. This question is adapted from the first two parts of a question in the June 2012 examination. Both parts are a simple knowledge test.

Easy marks. Answers to each part of the question could come straight from your Study Text!

Examiner's comments. Requirements (a) and (b) were generally well answered, with many candidates scoring full marks.

Marking scheme

			Marks
(a)	Steps:		
	Develop product	1	
	Set target price	1	
	Set profit margin	1	
	Set target cost	1	
	Close gap	1	
	Value engineering	1	
	Negotiate	1	
			max 6
(b)	Characteristics:		
	Spontaneity	1	
	Heterogeneity	1	
	Inseparability	1	
	Perishability	1	
	Other	1	
			max 4
			10

(a) **Steps involved in developing a target price and target cost in a manufacturing company**

Step 1 Determine a product specification of which an adequate sales volume is estimated.

Step 2 Set a selling price at which the organisation will be able to achieve a desired market share.

Step 3 Estimate the required profit based on return on sales or return on investment.

Step 4 Calculate the target cost = estimated selling price – target profit.

Step 5 Compile an estimated cost for the product based on the anticipated design specification and current cost levels.

Step 6 Calculate target cost gap = estimated cost – target cost.

Step 7 Make efforts to close the gap. This is more likely to be successful if efforts are made to 'design out' costs prior to production, rather than to 'control out' costs during the production phase.

Step 8 Negotiate with the customer before making the decision about whether to go ahead with the project.

(b) **Key characteristics of services**

Intangibility refers to the lack of substance which is involved with service delivery. Unlike goods (physical products such as confectionery), there is no substantial material or physical aspects to a service: no taste, feel, visible presence and so on. For example, if you go to the theatre, you cannot take the 'play' with you.

Inseparability/simultaneity. Many services are created at the same time as they are consumed. (Think of dental treatment.) No service exists until it is actually being experienced/consumed by the person who has bought it.

Variability/heterogeneity. Many services face the problem of maintaining consistency in the standard of output. It may be hard to attain precise standardisation of the service offered, but customers expect it (such as with fast food).

Many services are non-standard, which makes it difficult to establish a standard target cost.

Perishability. Services are innately perishable. The services of a beautician are purchased for a period of time.

No transfer of ownership. Services do not result in the transfer of property. The purchase of a service only confers on the customer access to or a right to use a facility.

Note. Only four key characteristics were required.

11 UHS

Text reference. Target costing is covered in Chapter 2b.

Top tips. This question was 10 marks of a longer question in the June 2012 examination paper. Make sure you answer the requirement in part (a) – the question asks you how the trust could **'derive'** the target cost, not how it could try to **'achieve'** it. Common sense answers to part (b) will score well – consider the level of government control, medical regulations and the overall aims and objectives of the trust.

Easy marks. There could be easy marks to obtain in part (b), where you can use your common sense to think of some ideas to put forward in your answer.

Examiner's comments. Part (a) was quite demanding as candidates were required to derive target costs for different services. Good answers reflected the fact that, in part (i), the target cost might simply be the pre-set tariff and in part (ii), it could simply be the price that has historically been charged.

Part (b), on the difficulties the trust might find in using target costing, attracted some really good, common sense answers and many candidates scored full marks.

Marking scheme

		Marks
(a)	Deriving target costs:	
	(i) Scheme target costs	2
	(ii) Other services' target costs	2
(b)	Difficulties:	
	Two marks per difficulty explained	6
		10

(a) **Deriving target costs**

(i) **For services under the 'payment by results' scheme**

The Trust could set the target cost at the pre-set tariff that it currently receives as fee income for each service. There is no need to deduct any profit margin from the tariff as the Trust is a not-for-profit organisation. The fact that costs sometimes exceed this pre-set tariff could cause problems (discussed in part (b) to this question).

(ii) **For transplant and heart operations**

The Trust currently receives payment based on the actual costs incurred in providing the operations. The target cost could be based on the average cost of providing these services in the past. Alternatively the target cost could be set at the minimum cost that the Trust has managed to provide the services for in the past. This approach would encourage cost savings but quality should not be overlooked.

(b) **Difficulties for the Sickham UHS Trust in using target costing**

Correct target cost

The Trust may find it difficult to decide on the correct target cost for some current services. Whilst the obvious target cost for pre-set tariff services is the pre-set tariff, the Trust knows that some services can be provided for significantly less than this and that some services cannot be provided at this price at all. A target cost which is easily met will not encourage **cost savings** and one which is unachievable is likely to demotivate staff.

The target cost should be set at a level which is both **achievable** but **feasible**.

Defining services

All services need to be **clearly defined** if the correct target cost is to be selected. This could prove difficult for services not covered by the pre-set tariff.

Existing costing systems

The current costing systems at the Trust are poor. For target costing to be effective costs need to be **analysed** in depth and overhead costs need to be **allocated** to services on a fair and consistent basis. This may not be possible.

Target costing for new services

The Trust may find it difficult to establish target costs for **new services** where there is no **comparative data** available, unless other hospitals have already provided the service(s) and are willing to share such information.

Note. Only three difficulties were required.

12 Edward Limited

Text reference. Target costing is covered in Chapter 2b.

Top tips. In computation questions, it is important to show your workings clearly and state any assumptions that you make. Note the examiner's comment about the high-low method: it is examinable. Remember that when you have calculated the expected cost per unit, you need to measure the target cost gap – the gap between the current expected cost and the target cost.

When you are told that the target profit margin is 20%, this means the profit/sales ratio is 20%. If you are told that the mark-up is 20%, this means that the profit margin is 20% on cost. In this question the profit margin is 20%.

Easy marks. There are easy marks to be obtained by calculating the expected cost per unit.

Examiner's comments. A substantial number of candidates had very little idea of what target costing is. The benefits of target costing was not well done. The examiner wants to know why something is done as well as how it is done.

High-low was poorly done by large numbers of candidates. This must be revised as it is likely to be examined again. Allowances for waste and idle time were often incorrectly done and this is an area that will be revisited so students must learn the correct method.

Marking scheme

	Marks
Component 1	1.0
Component 2	2.0
Assembly labour	2.0
High low calculation	2.0
Variable production overhead per unit	0.5
Fixed production o'hd absorption rate calculation	0.5
Fixed production overhead	0.5
Expected cost	0.5
Cost gap identified	1.0
	10

Production overheads

Using the high-low method:

$$\text{Variable cost per hour} = \frac{700{,}000 - 620{,}000}{23{,}000 - 19{,}000} = \frac{80{,}000}{4{,}000} = \$20$$

Fixed costs = 620,000 – (19,000 × $20) = $240,000

Annual fixed production overhead = $240,000 × 12 = $2,880,000

Absorption rate = $2,880,000/240,000 = $12 per hour

Expected cost per unit

		$ per unit
Component 1	\$4.10 + (\$2,400/4,000)	4.70
Component 2	25/100 × \$0.50 × 100/98	0.13
Other material		8.10
Assembly labour	30/60 × \$12.60 × 100/90	7.00
Variable production overhead	30/60 × \$20	10.00
Fixed production overhead	30/60 × \$12	6.00
Total cost		35.93
Target cost	\$44 × 80%	(35.20)
Cost gap		0.73

13 Fit Co

Text reference. Life cycle costing is covered in Chapter 2c.

Top tips. Part (a) requires you to calculate the life cycle cost **per unit**. Do not forget to divide the total life cycle cost by the number of units.

Easy marks. There should be fairly easy marks to be obtained in part (a), putting together the life cycle costs for the product. You should also be able to score well in part (b) by briefly discussing the implications of life cycle costing on pricing, performance management and decision making.

Examiner's comments. Part (a) was relatively straightforward.

Marking scheme

			Marks
(a)	Life cycle cost:		
	R&D costs	0.5	
	Product design costs	0.5	
	Marketing costs	0.5	
	Fixed production costs	0.5	
	Fixed distribution costs	0.5	
	Fixed selling costs	0.5	
	Administration costs	0.5	
	Variable selling costs	0.5	
	Variable manufacturing costs	0.5	
	Variable distribution costs	0.5	
	Total costs	0.5	
	Cost per unit (correct figure)	0.5	
			6
(b)	Per valid point made – 1.5 marks per point		max 4
			10

(a) **Life cycle cost per unit**

	$
R&D costs	160,000
Product design costs	800,000
Marketing costs	3,950,000
Fixed production costs	1,940,000
Fixed distribution costs	240,000
Fixed selling costs	360,000
Administration costs	2,600,000
Variable manufacturing costs (W1)	12,400,000
Variable distribution costs (W2)	1,300,000
Variable selling costs (W3)	940,000
Total life cycle cost	24,690,000

Life cycle cost per unit = $24,690,000/300,000 units = $82.30

Workings

1 *Variable manufacturing costs*

(100,000 units × $40) + (200,000 units × $42) = $12,400,000

2 *Variable distribution costs*

(100,000 units × $4) + (200,000 units × $4.50) = $1,300,000

3 *Variable selling costs*

(100,000 units × $3) + (200,000 units × $3.20) = $940,000

(b) **The benefits of life cycle costing**

Life cycle costing **tracks and accumulates actual costs and revenues** attributable to each product over the entire product life cycle.

The total profitability of any given product can be determined, meaning that **prices can be set** with better knowledge of the **true costs**.

Life cycle costing shows **all costs** relating to a product rather than costs relating to a single period, thus providing more **accurate information for decision making**.

The costs of researching, developing and designing products are also taken into account. This will allow for more accurate analysis when **measuring the performance** of new products.

14 Cam Co

Text reference. Life cycle costing is covered in Chapter 2c of the BPP Study Text.

Top tips. This question may look daunting at first glance, given the volume of information provided and the marks available. Focus on each calculation in turn (direct material cost, then direct labour cost using the learning curve). Remember to show and label all of your workings to maximise your score.

Easy marks. Even if you struggle with the learning curve calculations, the cost of the revised material cost should be fairly straightforward.

Examiner's comments. The requirement read 'recalculate the estimated lifetime cost per unit for the webcam …' Candidates had to make numerous adjustments to the costings provided in the question to reflect the learning curve effect and other factors that would result in cost savings. It was good to see that most candidates were able to handle the fact that the company in the scenario was using life cycle costing to work out the target costs for its products. Most answers reflected the fact that the total labour cost therefore had to be worked out in two parts: one cost for the first 100 units and then another cost for the remaining 49,900 units, the latter being based on the incremental time it had taken to produce the 100th unit. It was good to see that candidates identified this and gave the question a good attempt.

Marking scheme

	Marks
Revised lifetime cost:	
Direct material cost	2.5
Direct labour cost:	
Cumulative average time per unit for 100 units	1.0
Cumulative total time for 100 units	0.5
Cumulative average time per unit for 99 units	1.0
Cumulative total time for 99 units	0.5
Incremental time for 100th unit	1.0
Total time for 49,900 units	0.5
Total time for 50,000 units	0.5
Total labour cost for 50,000 units	0.5
Average labour cost per unit	1.0
Total cost	1.0
	10.0

Revised target cost

	$	$
Manufacturing cost		
Direct material (W1)	21.60	
Direct labour (W2)	10.98	
Machine costs	24.00	
Quality control costs	10.00	
		66.58
Non-manufacturing costs		60.00
Total cost (less than the target cost of $130)		126.58

Workings

1 *Direct material cost*

Parts to be replaced by standard parts = $40 × 80% = $32
New cost of standard parts at 45% (100% – 55%) = $14.40

Unique irreplaceable parts (original cost) = $40 × 20% = $8
New cost = $8 × 90% = $7.20

Revised direct material cost = $14.40 + $7.20 = $21.60

2 *Direct labour*

$Y = ax^b$

b = – 0.152 (given in question)

The question states that a learning curve of 90% is expected to occur until the 100th unit has been completed.

Total labour time for first 100 units
x = 100
The question states that the first unit is expected to take 45 minutes (a = 45)

$Y = 45 \times 100^{-0.152}$

= 45 × (1/2.0137)
= 22.3469 minutes

Therefore, labour time for 100 units = 22.3469 × 100 = 2,234.69 minutes

Labour time for the 100th unit

Time for 99 units

$Y = 45 \times 99^{-0.152}$
$= 45 \times (1/2.01065)$
$= 22.38082$ minutes

Therefore, labour time for 99 units = 22.38082 × 99 = 2,215.70 minutes

Therefore, time for 100th unit = 2,234.69 – 2,215.70 = 18.99 minutes, say 19 minutes

Labour time for remaining 49,900 units × 19 = 948,100 minutes
Total labour time for 50,000 units = 2,234.69 + 948,100 = 950,334.69 minutes

Therefore, total labour cost = (950,334.69/60) × $34.67 per hour = $549,135
Average labour cost per unit = $549,135/50,000 = $10.98

15 Sapu

Text references. Activity based costing is covered in Chapter 2a, and target costing in Chapter 2b.

Top tips. The calculations required in this question should be straightforward. Note that 40% of the marks available are for a written answer in part (b). This is to be expected in your exam, so make sure you can answer the written parts as well as do the calculations.

Easy marks. Having made the comment above, there should be easy marks to be obtained by doing the ABC calculations.

Marking scheme

			Marks
(a)	Materials-related overhead cost per cost driver unit	2	
	Labour-related overhead cost per cost unit	2	
	Unit costs for each product with ABC	2	
			6
(b)	Marks per relevant point: 2 marks	max	4
			10

(a) **ABC approach**

	A	B
	$	$
Direct material cost per unit	16.00	30.00
Direct labour cost per unit	8.00	10.00
Variable overhead cost per unit (see Workings)	71.68	14.17
	95.68	54.17

Workings

Material-related overheads

		Bulk
Number of cost drivers		$'000
(product A)	4 × 5,000	20
(product B)	1 × 10,000	10
(other products)	1.5 × 40,000	60
		90

∴ Overhead per cost driver = \$600,000 ÷ 90,000
= \$6.67

Labour-related overheads

		Labour operations
Number of cost drivers		\$'000
Product A	6 × 5,000	30
Product B	1 × 10,000	10
Other products	2 × 40,000	80
		120

∴ Overhead per cost driver = \$900,000 ÷ 120,000 = \$7.50

Variable overhead per unit

	A	*B*
	\$	\$
Material related: \$6.67 × 4/1	26.68	6.67
Labour related: \$7.50 × 6/1	45.00	7.50
	71.68	14.17

(b) **Target costing** is a term that has been defined in a number of ways. The essence of the concept is that a **product should cost less than the price that can be obtained for it in the market**.

Targets for reductions in the high rate of both material bulk and labour operations cost drivers for product A would, if achieved, produce a considerable reduction in the unit cost of product A. This may mean redesigning the product entirely or simply reorganising production methods. Such changes may, of course, also reduce the level of direct material and direct labour costs.

ABC can be combined usefully with target costing if it is felt that overheads are the main area in which costs can be reduced. Activity analysis identifies the factors that cause overheads to be incurred and so draws attention to the factors that need to be more closely controlled.

16 Environmental

Text references. Environmental management accounting is covered in Chapter 2e.

Top tips. Both parts of the question are relatively straightforward, but you need to have studied environmental management accounting and test your knowledge on environmental systems and environmental costs.

Easy marks. There are fairly easy marks to be obtained here, but only if you have studied and learned the topic.

Marking scheme

			Marks
(a)	For each valid point: 1 mark		max 5
(b)	Difference between internalised environmental costs and externalised environmental impacts	1	
	For each example provided: 1 mark	4	
			5
			10

(a) There are a number of key features to any environmental management system.

Each environmental management system should contain an **environmental policy statement**. This can be developed through review of environmental impacts of materials, issues and products and of business issues arising.

Effective systems should take steps to ensure **regulatory compliance**. Environmental **audits** will help to confirm current legal requirements are being fulfilled as well as ensuring that the business is up-to-date with practical implications of likely **changes in legislation**.

Realistic and measurable **targets** should be set. Targets should be **quantified** within a specified time period. For example, reducing carbon dioxide emissions by X% within a 12 month period.

An effective system should be established to **account for environmental costs**. Key features include budgeting, forecasting, a clear structure of responsibilities as well as the establishment of an environmentally-friendly **culture** and performance appraisal process.

The business should make a **public declaration** of environmental standards that are met such as the ISO standards. This could lead to the business establishing a competitive advantage over competitors.

(b) **Internalised environmental costs**

Internalised environmental costs are **incurred within the organisation.** They can be identified from the accounting records, can be **quantified and valued in monetary terms** and can often be traced to individual products and services, perhaps using an activity based costing system.

Two examples of internalised environmental costs are the cost of environmental certification and waste disposal costs.

Externalised environmental impacts

Externalised environmental impacts are the **effects that the organisation's activities have on the external environment.** Not all externalised environmental impacts result in the organisation itself incurring a cost that can be quantified and recorded in the costing system. However, environmental costing is concerned with monitoring an organisation's external environmental impact, even if not all impacts can be quantified in financial terms. Such impacts might also be **traced to individual products and services** to assess the effect on the external environment of the manufacturing of specific products and the provision of individual services. As part of its environmental costing, the organisation might **develop measures** to ensure that external standards concerning the impact of the organisation on the external environment are adhered to.

Two examples of externalised environmental impacts are carbon emissions and resource consumption.

17 Yam Co

Text references. Throughput accounting is covered in Chapter 2d.

Top tips. In part (a), to save time, you don't need to calculate the output capacity of each process. If you can see that the processing time for the pressing process is the slowest, so then just need to explain why this creates a bottleneck.

Easy marks. The calculations in part (a) should provide easy marks, provided you have learnt how to calculate a throughput accounting ratio. Three good, common sense points should earn you easy marks in Part (b).

Examiner's comments. It was clear that many candidates had poor knowledge of throughput accounting. Few could properly identify the bottleneck process and many used total hours per product as their guide to a wrong answer.

In the throughput calculations many included labour in the calculation of contribution, whereas its exclusion is more normal. Labour is properly treated as a fixed cost and yet many did not include it in the overheads part of the calculations.

Most candidates could give some reasonable suggestions on how to improve a TPAR, however not enough scored the easy marks on offer.

Marking scheme

			Marks
(a)	Identification of bottleneck	2	
	Throughput per product	1	
	Throughput per bottleneck hour for each product	2	
	Factory (fixed) cost per bottleneck hour	1	
	TPAR for each product	1	
			7
(b)	Increase speed of bottleneck	1	
	Increase selling prices – difficult to do	1	
	Reduce material prices	1	
	Reduce level of fixed costs	1	
	Maximum		max 3
			10

(a) **Output capacity for each process**

Total processing hours for the factory = 225,000

	Product A	*Product B*	*Product C*
	Metres	Metres	Metres
Pressing	225,000/0.50 = 450,000	225,000/0.50 = 450,000	225,000/0.40 = 562,500
Stretching	225,000/0.25 = 900,000	225,000/0.40 = 562,500	225,000/0.25 = 900,000
Rolling	225,000/0.40 = 562,500	225,000/0.25 = 900,000	225,000/0.25 = 900,000

The **bottleneck process** is **pressing** which has a lower output capacity for all three processes.

Throughput accounting ratios

TPAR = Return per factory hour/total conversion cost per factory hour

Conversion cost = Labour costs + factory costs
= (225,000 hours × $10) + $18,000,000
= $20,250,000

Conversion cost per factory hour = $20,250,000/225,000 hours
= $90

Return per factory hour = Sales – direct costs/usage of bottleneck resource in hours

	Product A	*Product B*	*Product C*
	$	$	$
Selling price per metre	70.00	60.00	27.00
Raw material cost per metre	3.00	2.50	1.80
Throughput per metre	67.00	57.50	25.20
Usage of bottleneck resource in hours	0.50	0.50	0.40
Throughput per factory hour	134.00	115.00	63.00
Conversion cost per factory hour	90.00	90.00	90.00
TPAR	1.49	1.28	0.70

(b) **How to improve the TPAR of Product C**

For the three marks available, your answer should identify three of the four points shown in bold lettering. The rest of the text is provided as an explanation of the answer, and is not required in the actual answer to part (b).

Increase the selling price

Product C has the **lowest selling price** of the three products and Yam carries **very little inventory** so is presumably selling all that it produces. This could mean that there is potential to increase the selling price and therefore the TPAR.

However, Yam faces **tough price competition** in a mature world market so a price increase could simply result in lower sales.

Increase the speed of the pressing process

The pressing process has been identified as a bottleneck so if this process is **speeded up**, throughput would increase. This could be achieved by increasing the productivity of the workforce, perhaps through **workflow optimisation** or more **training**. Alternatively, greater **automation** of the process may increase the speed but this could require investment in new machinery. This will only work if the extra output of all three products can be sold.

Reduce factory costs

The factory costs should be investigated to determine if there is any way to make cost savings. A **detailed budget** and **variance analysis** would help with this process. Some aspects could be **outsourced** or **alternative cheaper suppliers** identified.

Reduce material costs

There may be opportunities to buy the metal raw material from **cheaper, alternative suppliers**. The danger with this is a fall in **quality** which would impact on the quality of the final products and/or increase the risk of breakdown in production. **Bulk buying** could result in discounted raw material prices but the cost of **holding inventory** may outweigh the cost benefit.

18 Thin Co

Text references. Throughput accounting is covered in Chapter 2d.

Top tips. In this question, throughput accounting is tested in a service centre context rather than the usual traditional manufacturing context. Do not let this confuse you – the question states that hospital costs are 'comparable to factory costs in a traditional manufacturing environment'.

Easy marks. There are some easy marks in the calculations in part (a), but the question is quite challenging.

Examiner's comments. Answers to part (a) were very mixed. There were quite a few totally correct ones and most candidates managed to score some of the five marks. More problematic was part (b). Calculating the optimum product mix is simple key factor analysis, regardless of whether the calculations are based on maximising throughput, as in this case, or maximising contribution. It is a technique which all trainee accountants should be familiar with. Clearly, not much revision of this area had taken place because answers were fairly poor.

Marking scheme

			Marks
(a)	Throughput accounting ratio:		
	Fixed cost per hour	2	
	Throughput return per hour (procedure C)	2	
	Throughput accounting ratio (procedure C)	1	
			5
(b)	Optimum production plan:		
	Ranking	1.0	
	Optimum number of A	0.5	
	Optimum number of B	0.5	
	Optimum number of C	1.0	
	Total throughput	1.0	
	Less cost	0.5	
	Profit	0.5	
			5
			10

(a) **Throughput accounting ratio, procedure C**

In the context of a hospital, the TAR will be throughput per hospital hour/fixed cost per hospital hour.

Performance measures in throughput accounting are based around the concept that only **direct materials** are regarded as **variable costs**. All other costs are treated as fixed costs.

Fixed cost per hospital hour

Total hospital costs are therefore all **salaries** plus **general overheads**.
\$45,000 + \$38,000 + \$75,000 + \$90,000 + \$50,000 + \$250,000 = \$548,000

The question states that surgeon's hours have been correctly identified as the bottleneck resource. 40 hours × 47 weeks = 1,880 hours.

Total fixed cost per hospital hour = \$548,000 / 1,880 hours = \$291.49

Throughput return per hospital hour

Throughput return per hospital hour = (Sales – Direct material costs) / Usage of bottleneck resource in hours

	\$ *per procedure C*
Selling price	4,250.00
Materials cost:	
Injection	(1,000.00)
Anaesthetic	(45.00)
Dressings	(5.60)
Throughput per procedure (unit)	3,199.40
Time on bottleneck resource (surgeon's hours)	1.25 hrs
Return per hour (\$)	2,559.52

TAR = \$2,559.52 / \$291.49 = 8.78

(b) **Optimum production plan**

In a throughput environment, **production priority** must be given to the products best able to generate throughput. That is those products (in this case procedures) that **maximise throughput per unit of bottleneck resource**.

Step 1 **Rank products**

	A	*B*	*C*
TAR	8.96	9.11	8.78
Ranking	2nd	1st	3rd

Step 2 **Allocate resources to arrive at optimum production plan**

The optimum product (procedure) mix per annum is as follows.

Procedure	*Number*	*Surgeon hours per procedure*	*Total hours*	*Throughput per hour*	*Total throughput*
				$	$
B	800	1	800	2,654.40	2,123,520.00
A	600	0.75	450	2,612.53	1,175,638.50
C	504*	1.25	630	2,559.52	1,612,497.60
			1,880		4,911,656.10

* Balancing number of procedure C (630 hours remaining/1.25 hours per procedure).

Total profit per annum is as follows.

	$
Throughput	4,911,656.10
Less total costs	(548,000.00)
Profit	4,363,656.10

19 Solar Systems

Text reference. Throughput accounting is covered in Chapter 2d of the BPP Study Text.

Top tips. As long as you know how to calculate a throughput accounting ratio, part (a) should be fairly straightforward. The main complication is in calculating the number of Machine M hours per year in order to calculate the factory cost of a Machine M hour. You are given a 13-hour day, which is reduced to 12 hours by a one-hour lunch break, and there is 10% lost time due to maintenance and staff absenteeism. If you think carefully, you should see that the required number of hours is the effective Machine M hours per year.

The answer to part (b) calls for two ideas on how to increase production capacity. Make clear in your answer that the aim should be to increase production on the bottleneck capacity – Machine M operational time. The question gives some good hints about possible answers.

Easy marks. You should be able to earn marks by calculating throughput per Machine M hour for each product, even if you have difficulty with the factory cost per Machine M hour. Ideas for part (b) – increasing productive time on Machine M – should be fairly easy to identify, given the information in the question.

Marking scheme

			Marks
(a)	Throughput per Machine M hour for each product	1	
	Factory cost per machine hour	2	
	Throughput accounting ratio for each product	1	
	Brief analysis of results	2	
			6
(b)	Comment on need to increase production capacity for bottleneck resource	1	
	For each method of increasing production capacity: 1.5 marks	3	
			4
			10

(a) Time on Machine M is a bottleneck resource

Operating hours per year: 50 weeks × 5 days per week × 12 hours per day = 3,000 hours

However Machine M operates for only 90% of this time: 2,700 hours

Factory cost per Machine M hour = $12 million/2,700 = $4,444.44

	Large panels	*Small panels*
	$	$
Selling price per unit	12,600	3,800
Material costs per unit	4,300	1,160
Throughput per unit	8,300	2,640
Machine M hours per unit	1.4	0.6
Throughput per Machine M hour	$5,928.57	$4,400.00
Factory cost per Machine M hour	$4,444.44	$4,444.44
Throughput accounting ratio	1.33	0.99
Priority for manufacture and sales	1st	2nd

This shows that in order to maximise profit, given that Machine M is a bottleneck resource, the company should give priority to manufacturing and selling large panels.

The throughput accounting ratio for small panels is less than 1.0, indicating that the contribution or throughput from small panels is insufficient to cover factory costs. Unless this ratio can be increased above 1.0, it is questionable whether small panels should be produced in the long term.

However for the next two years, the company is committed to producing at least 1,000 small panels each year, with no increase in the selling price.

(b) From the information available in the question, production capacity will only be increased by increasing the production capacity on Machine M – the bottleneck resource – up to a level where it ceases to be a bottleneck. Production capacity on Machine M could be improved in the following ways, without the purchase of additional machinery.

(i) Work longer hours each week (or possibly more weeks each year).

(ii) Reduce time lost due to maintenance by carrying out maintenance outside normal working hours.

(iii) Train more skilled workers so that time lost through absenteeism is reduced. This may be achieved by training employees to work on all three types of machine, so that they can be switched between machines to meet production requirements.

(Only two suggestions are required for your solution.)

20 Corrie

Text references. Throughput accounting is covered in Chapter 2d.

Top tips. This is a straightforward question including both a numerical and a discursive part as can be expected in your exam. You need to learn how to calculate the throughput accounting ratio and be prepared to discuss its implications.

Easy marks. There should be easy marks to obtain from calculating the throughput accounting ratios and identifying some of the points for part (b) of the question.

Marking scheme

			Marks
(a)	Throughput per hour for each product	1.5	
	Factory cost per hour	1.0	
	Throughput accounting ratios for each product	1.5	
			4
(b)	Advice		2
(c)	Actions		
	Sales price increase	1.0	
	Material cost reduction	1.0	
	Reduction in factory costs	1.0	
	Improving output capacity on bottleneck resource	1.0	
			4
			10

(a) **TA ratio** = throughput per factory hour/conversion cost per factory hour

Conversion cost per process alpha hour = $720,000/8 = $90,000

Product	*Throughput per hour*	*Cost per hour*	*TA ratio*
X	$80 × (60 ÷ 0.05 mins) = $96,000	$90,000	1.07
Y	$80 × (60 ÷ 0.04 mins) = $120,000	$90,000	1.33
Z	$200 × (60 ÷ 0.10 mins) = $120,000	$90,000	1.33

(b) An attempt should be made to **remove the restriction on output** caused by process alpha's capacity. This will probably result in another bottleneck emerging elsewhere.

The extra capacity required to remove the restriction could be obtained by **working overtime**, making **process improvements** or **product specification** changes.

Until the volume of throughput can be increased, output should be concentrated upon products Y and Z (the highest TA ratios: both have the same ratio), unless there are good marketing reasons for continuing the current production mix.

(c) Actions that could be considered to improve the TA ratio are as follows.

(1) **Increase the selling price** of the product. This will increase the throughput per process alpha hour.

(2) **Reduce the material cost** per unit of the product. This will also increase the throughput per process alpha hour.

(3) Reduce the total expenditure on **factory conversion costs**. This would reduce the factory conversion cost per process alpha hour.

(4) Change the **working practices** on the bottleneck resource, to increase the number of hours of capacity available. This should be achieved without extra factory conversion cost being incurred, perhaps by altering the method of setting up the machine, to improve productivity. This action would have no effect on the throughput per hour but would reduce the factory conversion cost per hour. This would increase the TA ratio.

Question 21

21.1 B (Syllabus area B4(g))

Penetration pricing, by encouraging more customers to buy the product at an early stage in its life cycle, should shorten the length of the initial stage of the life cycle. As demand picks up, the product will enter into its growth stage more quickly.

21.2 B (Syllabus area B6(b))

Expected values are used to support a risk-neutral attitude to decision making. A risk-neutral decision maker will ignore the range of possible outcomes (and the size of this range) and is concerned only with the expected value of outcomes.

Expected values are more valuable as a guide to decision making where they refer to outcomes which will occur many times over, because the actual outcome, on average, should be close to the EV. In contrast, the expansion decision is a **one-off decision**, the actual outcome may not be very close to the expected value.

21.3 C (Syllabus area B1(a))

An opportunity cost is the benefit forgone taking one course of action instead of the next most profitable course of action.

The effect of business decisions on profit or cost is an important factor in decision making, but non-financial factors should also be taken into consideration.

21.4 A (Syllabus area B6(f))

Data can be either primary (collected at first hand from a sample of respondents), or secondary (collected from previous surveys, other published facts and opinions, or from experts). Secondary research is also known as desk research. Market research obtains primary data.

Market research may obtain qualitative data about a market, such as the preferences and attitudes of customers or potential customers. Research may also provide quantitative information, for example about numbers or frequencies of purchases by respondents.

21.5 A (Syllabus area B2(b))

Breakeven point = Fixed costs/ C/S ratio = \$1,232,000/0.56 = \$2,200,000.

Margin of safety = (\$3,000,000 – \$2,200,000)/\$3,000,000 = 26.7%.

The margin of safety is expressed as a percentage of the budgeted sales volume, not the breakeven sales volume.

21.6 C (Syllabus area B1(b))

	\$	\$
Sales (480,000 × 1.15 × 0.97)		535,440
Direct materials (140,000 × 1.15 × 0.98)	157,780	
Direct labour: 110,000 + (110,000 × 0.15 × 1.50)	134,750	
Variable overheads (50,000 × 1.15)	57,500	
Fixed overheads	132,000	
Total costs		482,030
Profit		53,410

21.7 C (Syllabus area B3(c))

Sales price (for maximising revenue) or sales price minus variable cost (for maximising contribution) affects the objective function rather than constraints. If a constraint is $0.04x + 0.03y \leq 2,400$, the boundary line for the constraint can be drawn on a graph by joining up the points y = 0, x = 2,400/0.04 = 60,000 and x = 0, y = 2,400/0.03 = 80,000 with a straight line.

21.8 C (Syllabus area B4(a))

For example, the demand for cars and petrol is likely to fall if the cost of travel by train (a substitute) falls; but the demand for cars is likely to increase if the price of petrol (a complement) falls.

21.9 D (Syllabus area B1(b))

Contribution per hour is after deducting labour and variable overhead costs, so these are relevant costs. (Alternatively, the contribution forgone is $15 + 12 + $2 per hour.)

	$
Cost of labour (10 hours × $12)	120
Cost of variable overhead (at $2)	20
Contribution forgone (at $15)	150
Relevant cost total	290

21.10 B (Syllabus area B5(b))

Component	A	B	C
Extra cost of external purchase	$20	$8	$24
Machine hours per unit	9	5	12
Extra cost of purchase, per hour saved	$2.22	$1.60	$2.00
Priority for in-house manufacture	1st	3rd	2nd

	Machine hours	*Variable cost*
		$
Make A 3,000 units	27,000	135,000
Make C (balance, 2,750 units)	33,000	154,000
	60,000	289,000
Buy 250 C at $80		20,000
Buy 3,000 B at $78		234,000
		543,000

Question 22

22.1 A (Syllabus area B4(f))

When P = 24 – 0.004Q, the marginal revenue MR = 24 – 0.008Q (from the formula sheet).

Total sales revenue increases when the price is increased as long as the marginal revenue is a positive value.

MR starts to go into negative values when sales demand exceeds the quantity where:

24 – 0.008Q = 0

Q = 3,000

At this demand quantity, the sales price is P = 24 – 0.004 (3,000) = $12.

The company can raise the sales price by $2 to $12 per unit in order to increase sales revenue, but at higher prices total sales revenue will fall.

(Check: If P = $12 and Q = 3,000, total weekly revenue = $3,600. This is $100 per week more than the revenue from selling 3,500 units at $10 each.)

22.2 C (Syllabus area B4(g))

Market skimming is an appropriate pricing policy when a product is expected to have only a short life cycle; prices need to be set at a high level in order to recover development costs quickly and maximise short-term profit.

The protection of a patent creates a barrier to entry to the market for competitors and enables the holder of the patent to charge higher prices than would otherwise be possible. When demand is unknown it is probably safer to charge a higher price, to improve the chance of recovering development costs and making a profit.

22.3 D (Syllabus area B1(a))

These are fundamental statements about relevant costing.

22.4 B (Syllabus area B2(b))

Current position: Breakeven point = $840,000/0.60 = $1,400,000
Margin of safety = $(1,600,000 – 1,400,000)/$1,600,000 = 12.5%

With the change in production method, variable costs will fall from 40% of sales to 36% of sales, giving a C/S ratio of 64%. Fixed costs will be $1,008,000.

New breakeven point $1,008,000/0.64 = $1,575,000 (= higher)
New margin of safety = $(1,600,000 – 1,575,000)/$1,600,000 = 1.56% (= lower)

22.5 D (Syllabus area B3(d))

The shadow price of Material X is $6, so buying additional quantities at a price $4 above its normal variable cost would add $2 to profit for each kilogram of material bought and used. (However, this applies only as long as the shadow price of Material Q remains at $6 per kg). The shadow price of skilled labour Y is $0, which means that available amounts of time are not fully utilised. There is no requirement to work overtime.

22.6 A (Syllabus area B2(d))

A multi-product profit-volume chart can be drawn that shows the contribution of each product to the budgeted sales volume and budgeted contribution, but not to the breakeven sales volume.

22.7 B (Syllabus area B4(g))

Charging prices at full cost plus a fixed margin for profit will not necessarily ensure that the business will make a profit in each period. Profitability will also depend at working at or close to budgeted capacity; otherwise there could be substantial 'losses' from under-absorbed overheads.

The allocation and apportionment of overheads between products can be fairly arbitrary in nature, with the result that some products have a high overhead cost and others a low overhead cost. This will affect prices and, depending on market conditions, could result in prices that are too high to attract customers, or too low (so that demand may exceed output).

22.8 C (Syllabus area B1(b))

	$
Direct materials	400
Skilled labour (15 hours at $8)	120
Variable production overhead (at $2 per hour)	30
Opportunity cost: contribution forgone ($25 per hour)	375
Minimum price	925

22.9 C (Syllabus area B6(d))

	Weekly contribution			
	Price P1	*Price P2*	*Price P3*	*Price P4*
	$	$	$	$
Best possible	30,000	31,500	32,000	31,500
Most likely	24,000	26,250	28,000	27,000
Worst possible	18,000	17,500	16,000	13,500

The maximax decision rule is to select the price offering the maximum possible benefit, which is P3. This will provide the biggest weekly contribution, provided that the best possible sales demand is achieved.

22.10 C (Syllabus area B3(c))

The optimal solution cannot be at Point A, because Point B (same units of Y, more units of X) is clearly more profitable.

At point B

y = 20,000, and
3x + 4.8y = 120,000; therefore x = 8,000
Total contribution = (20,000 × \$30) + (8,000 × \$20) = \$760,000

At Point D

x = 30,000, and
5x + 4y = 160,000; therefore y = 2,500
Total contribution = (2,500 × \$30) + (30,000 × \$20) = \$675,000

At Point C

(1)	5x + 4y	=	160,000
(2)	3x + 4.8y	=	120,000
Multiply (1) by 3			
(3)	15x + 12y	=	480,000
Multiply (2) by 5			
(4)	15x + 24y	=	600,000
Subtract (3) from (4)	12y	=	120,000
	y	=	10,000
Therefore	x	=	24,000

Total contribution = (10,000 × \$30) + (24,000 × \$20) = \$780,000

Contribution maximised at Point C

Question 23

23.1 B (Syllabus area B6(e))

The decision options are given expected values, not the various different possible outcomes from each decision option. Each possible outcome is given a value, but not an expected value (EV).

23.2 A (Syllabus area B4(b))

In circumstances of inelastic demand, prices should be increased because revenues will increase and total costs will reduce (because quantities sold will reduce).

Price elasticity of demand is measured as the amount of change in quantity demanded (measured as a percentage of the current sales volume) divided by the amount of change in sales price (measured as a percentage of the current sales price)

$$\frac{\text{The change in quantity demanded, as a \% of demand}}{\text{The change in price, as a \% of the price}}$$

23.3 B (Syllabus area B4(g))

A price in excess of full cost per unit will not necessarily ensure that a company will cover all its costs and make a profit. Making a profit with cost plus pricing also depends on working at a sufficient capacity level, so that all fixed costs are covered by sales revenue.

Cost plus pricing is an appropriate pricing strategy when there is no comparable market price for the product or service.

23.4 D (Syllabus area B2(b))

When sales revenue is \$1.5 million, total contribution is 45% × \$1.5 million = \$675,000.

This leaves a further \$625,000 of fixed costs to cover. To achieve breakeven, sales in excess of \$1.5 million need to be \$625,000/0.48 = \$1.302 million.

Total sales to achieve breakeven = \$1.5 million + \$1.302 million = \$2.802 million.

23.5 D (Syllabus area B3(c))

Statement (1) is a simple definition of slack for a production resource. When there is a minimum sales constraint for a product, surplus will occur when the quantity of production and sales for the product in the optimal solution exceeds the minimum sales requirement in the constraint.

23.6 A (Syllabus area B5(b))

Total labour hours required to meet sales budget: (10,000 + 6,250 + 15,000 + 10,000) = 41,250.

Direct labour hours are therefore a limiting factor on production.

Product	*W*	*X*	*Y*	*Z*
Contribution per unit	\$3.5	\$2.0	\$1.8	\$4.0
Direct labour hours per unit	0.5	0.25	0.3	0.8
Contribution per direct labour hour	\$7	\$8	\$6	\$5
Priority for manufacture and sales	2nd	1st	3rd	4th

So make and sell 25,000 units of X (6,250 hours), 20,000 units of W (10,000 hours) and 25,833.33 units of Y with the remaining 7,750 hours available.

23.7 D (Syllabus area B6(c))

Sensitivity analysis can be used to identify how much the outcome from a situation or decision would be different if the value of an input variable changes. In this way, the input variables that are most critical to the situation or decision can be identified. Sensitivity analysis can also be described as assessing how projected performance or outcome will be affected by changes in the assumptions that have been used.

23.8 C (Syllabus area B4(d))

For every \$1 change in price, the quantity demanded will change by 4,000/10 = 400 units
When demand Q = 0, the price will be: 180 + (50,000/400) = 305
Demand curve P = 305 – (1/400) × Q = 305 – 0.0025Q
Total revenue = 305Q – 0.0025Q^2
Marginal revenue = 305 – 0.005Q
Marginal cost = 125
Profit maximised when 305 – 0.005Q = 125, Q = 36,000
P = 305 – (0.0025 × 36,000) = \$215

23.9 D (Syllabus area B1(b))

		\$
Material W	500 kg × \$8	4,000
Material X	(300 kg × \$3) + (200 kg × \$7)	2,300
Material Y	500 kg × \$11	5,500
Material Z	Higher of (100 × \$12) and (150 × \$9)	1,350
		13,150

23.10 C (Syllabus area B6(c))

	Prob	*Price P1*		*Price P2*		*Price P3*		*Price P4*	
		Cont'n	*EV*	*Cont'n*	*EV*	*Cont'n*	*EV*	*Cont'n*	*EV*
		\$	\$	\$	\$	\$	\$	\$	\$
Best	0.2	30,000	6,000	31,500	6,300	32,000	6,400	31,500	6,300
Most likely	0.5	24,000	12,000	26,250	13,125	28,000	14,000	27,000	13,500
Worst	0.3	18,000	5,400	17,500	5,250	16,000	4,800	13,500	4,050
Total EV			23,400		24,675		25,200		23,850

Question 24

24.1 A (Syllabus area B6(b))

Expected value is a more reliable guide to the outcome from a situation that will occur many times over than for an outcome that will happen only once. A risk-averse decision maker makes decisions on the basis that the worst outcome will occur, but no one can avoid risk entirely in decision making.

24.2 A (Syllabus area B4(g))

Price discrimination involves charging different prices in two or more different markets. This is only effective when the markets can be kept entirely separate – such as charging different prices for different age groups (children and old age pensioners), or charging a different price for a product or service at different times of the day or week.

24.3 D (Syllabus area B6(f))

EV of Project 1 = (0.1 × 70,000) + (0.4 × 10,000) – (0.5 × 7,000) = \$7,500
EV of Project 2 = (0.1 × 25,000) + (0.4 × 12,000) + (0.5 × 5,000) = \$9,800
EV of Project 3 = (0.1 × 50,000) + (0.4 × 20,000) – (0.5 × 6,000) = \$10,000

Project 3 would be chosen on the basis of EV without perfect information. With perfect information, this decision would be changed to Project 1 if market research indicates strong demand and Project 2 if market research indicates weak demand.

EV with perfect information: (0.1 × 70,000) + (0.4 × 20,000) + (0.5 × 5,000) = \$17,500

Value of perfect information = \$(17,500 – 10,000) = \$7,500 – ignoring the cost of obtaining the information.

24.4 A (Syllabus area B5(d))

	FP1	*FP2*	*Total*
Input to further processing (kg)	5,500	4,000	
Finished output (kg)	4,950	3,800	
	\$	\$	\$
Revenue from sales of FP1/FP2	44,550	34,200	
Relevant further processing costs	(11,000)	(12,000)	
Revenue from sales of CP1/CP2	(33,000)	(20,000)	
	550	2,200	2,750

24.5 D (Syllabus area B4(d))

For every \$1 increase in price, demand will fall by 10,000 × (1/5) = 2,000 units
Demand will be 0 when the price is \$120 + \$(200,000/2,000) = \$220
The demand curve P = 220 – (1/2,000) × Q = 220 – 0.0005Q
Total revenue = (220 – 0.0005Q) × Q = 220Q – $0.0005Q^2$
Marginal revenue MR = 220 – 0.001Q
Revenue is maximised when marginal revenue = 0
220 – 0.001Q = 0; therefore Q = 220/0.001 = 220,000 units, and P = 220 – (220,000 × 0.0005) = 110

24.6 C (Syllabus area B2(c))

Breakeven sales = \$(2.4 million – 400,000) = \$2,000,000

Contribution at this level of sales = \$360,000. Therefore contribution/sales ratio = 360,000/2,000,000 = 18%

Variable costs = 82% of sales. At a sales level of \$2.4 million, variable costs = 82% × \$2.4 million = \$1.968 million

24.7 D (Syllabus area B4(g))

For products produced or services provided in large volumes, there may be an optimal (profit-maximising) combination of price and sales demand. Cost plus pricing ignores sales demand at different price levels, and assumes that output (and sales) will be a budgeted or normal capacity.

Full cost depends on the methods of overhead apportionment and absorption that are used. If overheads are apportioned on an 'unfair' basis, some products will be given a cost that is too high and others will be given a cost that is too low. This will probably affect the sales demand and profitability of each product.

24.8 B (Syllabus area B6(e))

Decision trees are used primarily to show decision options and decision outcomes in order to identify the decision option with the most favourable expected value. They cannot easily be used to show minimax regret values.

Decision trees may omit some possible decision options, or may simplify the possible outcomes. For example, a decision tree may show possible outcomes as 'sales demand 10,000' and 'sales demand 3,000' whereas a variety of outcomes between these two figures for sales demand may be possible. The decision tree is therefore likely to be a simplification of reality.

24.9 A (Syllabus area B4(b))

If demand is price-inelastic, a reduction in price will result in a fall in total sales revenue. At the lower price, there will be some increase in sales demand, so total costs will increase. With falling revenue and increasing costs, profits will fall.

24.10 A (Syllabus area B3(d))

If one extra direct labour hour is available, the optimal solution will change to the point where:

(1): sales demand for X	x	=	10,000
(2): direct labour	5x + 4y	=	60,001
Multiply (1) by 5			
(3)	5x	=	50,000
Subtract (3) from (2)	4y	=	10,001
	y	=	2,500.25

Total contribution = $(10,000 × $8) + $(2,500.25 × $6) = $80,000 + $15,001.15 = $95,001.5

Total contribution in original solution = $(10,000 × $8) + $(2,500 × $6) = $95,000

The shadow price per direct labour hour is therefore $1.50

The solution is changing because each additional labour hour allows the company to produce an additional 0.25 units of Product Y, to increase total contribution by $1.50.

This shadow price will cease to apply when the direct labour hours constraint is replaced in the optimal solution by the sales demand for Product Y constraint. At this level of output, total labour hours would be (10,000 units of X at 5 hours) + (12,000 units of Y at 4 hours) = 98,000 hours.

The shadow price of $1.50 per hour therefore applies for an additional 38,000 hours above the current limit.

Question 25

25.1 A (Syllabus area B4(g))

Marginal cost plus pricing, with prices determined by a fixed mark-up on marginal cost, does not allow for market conditions and in this respect is no different from full cost plus pricing. Marginal cost plus pricing is used widely in retailing, but retailers continually alter the size of the mark-up in response to customer demand. They do not charge a fixed mark-up.

25.2 A (Syllabus area B5(b))

Product	*W*	*X*	*Y*	*Z*
Extra cost of external purchase	$1	$2.1	$2	$1
Direct labour hours per unit	0.1	0.3	0.25	0.2
Extra cost per hour saved by purchasing	$10	$7	$8	$5
Priority for external purchasing	4th	2nd	3rd	1st
Priority for making in-house	1st	3rd	2nd	4th

25.3 D (Syllabus area B3(c))

Cost minimisation problems can be solved using linear programming. The feasible region on a graph is shaped by the constraints that may determine the optimal solution.

25.4 C (Syllabus area B3(d))

If one extra direct labour hour is available, the optimal solution will change to the point where:

(1): direct labour hours	2x + 4y	=	10,001
(2): materials	4x + 2y	=	14,000
Multiply (1) by 2			
(3)	4x + 8y	=	20,002
Subtract (2) from (3)	6y	=	6,002
	y	=	1,000.333
Substitute in (2)	4x + 2,000.667	=	14,000
	x	=	2,999.8333

Total contribution = $(2,999.833 × $12) + $(1,000.333 × $18) = $35,998 + $18,006 = $54,004

Total contribution in original solution = $(3,000 × $12) + $(1,000 × $18) = $54,000

The shadow price per direct labour hour is therefore $54,004 - $54,000 = $4

25.5 B (Syllabus area B2(b))

	$
Total cost at sales of $6.8 million	6,560,000
Deduct step increase in fixed costs	(400,000)
Total cost excluding step cost increase	6,160,000
Total cost at sales of $5.2 million	5,440,000
Therefore variable cost of sales of $1.6 million	720,000

Variable cost = 720,000/1,600,000 = 45% of sales. Contribution/sales ratio is 55%.

	$
Total cost at sales of $6.8 million	6,560,000
Variable cost (45%)	(3,060,000)
Fixed cost	3,500,000

If fixed costs are $3.5 million at the higher sales level and so $3.1 million at the lower sales level.

When fixed costs are $3.1 million, breakeven sales = $3.1 million/0.55 = $5.636 million

When fixed costs are $3.5 million, breakeven sales = $3.5 million/0.55 = $6.363 million

25.6 B (Syllabus area B1(c))

The question provides a definition of opportunity cost. An opportunity cost is a relevant cost for the purpose of decision making, but the definition in the question is too narrow to fit the term 'relevant cost'.

25.7 C (Syllabus area B1(b))

	$
Additional purchases (5 tonnes × $50)	250
Relevant cost of material M already held: higher of $126 and (3 × $35)	126
Relevant cost total	376

25.8 A (Syllabus area B6(d))

	Weekly contribution			
	Price P1	*Price P2*	*Price P3*	*Price P4*
	$	$	$	$
Best possible	30,000	31,500	32,000	31,500
Most likely	24,000	26,250	28,000	27,000
Worst possible	18,000	17,500	16,000	13,500

The maximin decision rule is to select the price offering the maximum possible benefit under the worst of circumstances. (It is similar to the minimax rule for decisions on minimising cost.) Price P1 will provide the biggest weekly contribution under the worst of circumstances, which is a contribution of $18,000 if the worst possible demand occurs. Only the bottom line of the above table needs to be calculated for your answer. The full table is shown here for the sake of completeness.

25.9 C (Syllabus area B6(a))

A unique feature of simulation modelling using the Monte Carlo method is the use of random numbers to determine the value of input variables to the model.

25.10 D (Syllabus area B6(e))

EV of Choice 1 = $9,500
EV of Choice 2 = (0.3 × 14,000) + (0.3 × 10,000) + (0.4 × 5,000) = $9,200
EV of Choice 3 = (0.4 × 10,000) + (0.6 × 9,000) = $9,400
EV of Choice 4 = (0.7 × 8,000) + (0.3 × 14,000) = $9,800

Question 26

26.1 B (Syllabus area B6(b))

The 'What if' refers to the type of question used in sensitivity analysis. For example, what if the volume of sales is 10% less than expected? What if variable unit costs are 5% more than expected?

26.2 A (Syllabus area B4(b))

Advertising and sales promotion may persuade customers to pay more for a product, and so may make demand more inelastic in response to price changes. When demand is very inelastic with regard to the sales price, elasticity may be increased to some extent by means of advertising and sales promotion.

26.3 B (Syllabus area B5(b))

Material	*W*	*X*	*Y*	*Z*
	$	$	$	$
Extra cost per unit of external purchase	1	6	3	2
Total extra cost of external purchase	4,000	12,000	9,000	8,000
Fixed costs saved by not making in-house	(5,000)	(8,000)	(6,000)	(7,000)
Difference	(1,000)	4,000	3,000	1,000

It would save $1,000 in cash to buy Material W externally. If full production can be achieved for the other materials, only W would be purchased externally. However, there is insufficient capacity to produce all three materials in-house.

Only 8,000 units can be produced in-house. If all the requirement for W is purchased externally (4,000 units), at least 1,000 units of X, Y or Z must be purchased externally too. The additional cost of buying Z externally is the least of these three.

If in-house production of Material Z is reduced to 3,000 units, the additional cost of external purchase would be only $6,000, so that $1,000 would be saved by purchasing all of Z externally.

26.4 B (Syllabus area B6(d))

	Weekly contribution			
	Price P1	*Price P2*	*Price P3*	*Price P4*
	$	$	$	$
Best possible	30,000	31,500	32,000	31,500
Most likely	24,000	26,250	28,000	27,000
Worst possible	18,000	17,500	16,000	13,500

	Regret			
	Price P1	*Price P2*	*Price P3*	*Price P4*
	$	$	$	$
Best possible	2,000	500	0	500
Most likely	4,000	1,750	0	1,000
Worst possible	0	500	2,000	4,500
Maximum regret	4,000	1,750	2,000	4,500

The maximum regret is minimised by selecting Price P2

26.5 A (Syllabus area B6(f))

EV of Project 1 = (0.2 × 80,000) + (0.4 × 50,000) – (0.4 × 5,000) = $34,000

EV of Project 2 = (0.2 × 60,000) + (0.4 × 25,000) + (0.4 × 10,000) = $26,000

Project 1 would be chosen on the basis if EV without perfect information. With perfect information, this decision would be changed to Project 2 if market research indicates weak demand.

EV with perfect information: (0.2 × 80,000) + (0.4 × 50,000) + (0.4 × 10,000) = $40,000

Value of perfect information = $(40,000 – 34,000) – $4,500 cost = $1,500

26.6 C (Syllabus area B3(d))

The shadow price of a limiting resource is the amount above the normal variable cost that will be added to the objective function (total contribution) if one extra unit of the resource is made available. This means that the company would increase contribution by paying up to $(8 + 4.50) = $12.50 per hour for additional labour time. However, it would not pay exactly $12.50, as this would leave it no better and no worse off than if it did not have the extra labour hour.

26.7 A (Syllabus area B2(d))

Weighted average sales price per unit = [(20 × 2) + (18 × 3) + (24 × 5)]/((2 + 3 + 5) = $21.40
Weighted average variable cost per unit = [(11 × 2) + (12 × 3) + (18 × 5)]/((2 + 3 + 5) = $14.80
Therefore weighted average contribution per unit = $(21.40 – 14.80) = $6.60
Weighted average C/S ratio = 6.60/21.40 = 0.3084112

Sales required to achieve target contribution of $1.6 million = $1.6 million/0.3084112 = $5.188 million.

26.8 D (Syllabus area B4(f))

An increase in price of $25 will result in a fall in demand quantity by 6,250 units. Each $1 change in price therefore results in a change in demand by 6,250/25 = 250 units.

Demand Q will be 0 when the price P is $145 + $(5,000/250) $165
Demand function = 165 – Q/250 = 165 – 0.004Q
Marginal revenue = 165 – 0.008Q

Profit is maximised when marginal revenue equals marginal cost:

When 27 = 165 – 0.008Q, so Q = 138/0.008 = 17,250

Price = 165 – (17,250/250) = $96

26.9 A (Syllabus area B4(b))

When the price elasticity of demand is elastic, a reduction in price by x% will increase the quantity demanded by more than x% and as a result total sales revenue will increase. Without knowing about marginal costs, it is not possible to determine whether profits would increase or fall.

26.10 C (Syllabus area B2(b))

Product	*A*	*B*	*C*	*Total*
	$'000	$'000	$'000	$'000
Sales revenue	360	720	200	1,280
Variable costs	90	240	110	440
Contribution	270	480	90	840
Fixed costs	180	360	60	600

Contribution/sales ratio = 840/1,280 = 0.65625

Breakeven point in sales revenue = $600,000/0.65625 = $914,286

With CVP analysis for a company that sells several products, a fixed sales mix has to be assumed.

27 Devine Desserts

Text references. CVP analysis is covered in Chapter 3.

Top tips. There are ten marks available for this question, so think carefully about everything you could comment about. Make sure that you understand the significance of points A, B, C and D on the graph before you start writing an answer.

Easy marks. You can earn marks by explaining the aspects of the diagram that you understand. Don't worry if you can't identify everything to comment about.

Marking scheme

		Marks
For comments on:		
Fixed costs at zero activity	1.0	
Step fixed costs	1.5	
Variable costs and variations in unit variable costs	2.0	
Sales revenue and change in the sales price	1.5	
Maximum profit	1.0	
Output and sales level A	1.0	
Output and sales level B	1.0	
Output and sales level C	1.0	
Output and sales level D	1.0	
Marks available	11.0	
Maximum mark		10

The diagram shows the monetary values of costs and revenues over a range of activity levels.

The diagram shows that significant fixed costs are incurred at an activity level of zero. Examples of such costs are rent and rates on business premises that need to be paid regardless of the level of sales.

Fixed costs increase significantly at certain activity levels (at points B and D in the diagram). This is an example of **a stepped fixed cost**. Managers should be made aware of these activity levels, otherwise there is a risk that an order may be accepted which significantly increases costs for a small additional amount of revenue.

Variable costs are proportional to the level of activity and may include the costs such as raw ingredients and the packaging for the desserts. The diagram shows that the variable costs are constant per unit of activity up to activity level B as the gradient of the line is constant throughout this activity range. Between activity levels B and D the variable costs are constant per unit, but the unit cost is lower than that up to point B possibly due to **economies of scale** and **learning effects**. However, above activity level D it can be seen that the gradient of the line increases. This represents a higher unit cost for these units.

Total costs are the sum of the fixed costs and variable costs.

Sales revenue up to point C on the diagram is constant, implying that the selling price per unit is constant. Above point C, sales revenue continues to increase but at a slower rate. This shows that in order to sell a volume higher than activity level C the price per unit must be reduced.

Profits are maximised where the vertical distance between the sales revenue and total cost lines is greatest.

Activity level A is the breakeven point where **total revenue is equal to total costs** yielding a profit of zero. At activity levels beyond point A, the company makes a profit but activity levels below point A yield a loss.

Activity level B has already been explained as the point at which the fixed costs and total costs increase due to the step effect. It can be seen that this has a significant effect on the profit being earned.

Activity level C shows the point at which reductions in selling price are required in order to increase the volume of sales being achieved. Beyond this point the slopes of the total cost and sales revenue lines show that total costs are rising faster than total revenues and thus **profits are falling**.

Activity level D shows the impact of the next step in the fixed costs which has a similar effect on profit as that indicated in relation to activity point B above.

28 Cut and Stitch

Text references. Linear programming is covered in Chapter 4.

Top tips. Remember to show all your workings in part (a) to maximise your score.

Easy marks. There are four marks available for calculating the optimal production mix and related contribution in part (a).

Examiner's comments. Part (a) should have been really well answered and I think the reason why it wasn't is because candidates did not expect to be given the optimal production point in a question. They expected to have to find it themselves. Because of this, they didn't read the question properly and many candidates performed lots of calculations trying to find the optimal production point! A good attempt at part (a) would have been to solve the two simultaneous equations for the critical constraints at point B, in order to arrive at the optimum quantity of W and L to be produced. Then, these numbers needed to be put into the objective function in order to find contribution. It is essential to show all workings. Where workings are not shown, full marks cannot be given.

Most answers to part (b) were poor and this is clearly an area that needs to be revisited. A common error was finding a total shadow price of $14 for fabric and tailor time jointly, rather than calculating them separately. Such answers scored poorly.

Marking scheme

			Marks
(a)	Optimal point calculation	3	
	Contribution	1	
			4
(b)	For each shadow price	3	
			6
			10

(a) **The optimal production mix can be found by solving the constraint equations for F and T**

7W + 5L = 3,500 (1)
2W + 2L = 1,200 (2)

Multiply the second equation by 2.5 to yield a common value for L in each equation

7W + 5L = 3,500 (1)
5W + 5L = 3,000 (3)
2W = 500 (1) – (3)
W = 250

Substitute W = 250 into the fabric equation to calculate L

2 x 250 + 2L = 1,200
2L = 700
L = 350

Calculate the related contribution to the optimal production mix

C = 48W + 40L
C = (48 × 250) + (40 × 350)
C = 26,000

The contribution gained is $26,000

(b) **The shadow prices can be found by adding one unit to each constraint in turn**

Shadow price of T

7W + 5L = 3,501 (1)
2W + 2L = 1,200 (2)

Multiply the second equation by 2.5 to yield a common value for L in each equation

7W + 5L = 3,501 (1)
5W + 5L = 3,000 (3)
2W = 501 (1) – (3)
W = 250.5

Substitute W = 250.5 into the fabric equation to calculate L

(2 × 250.5) + 2L = 1,200
2L = 1,200 – 501
L = 349.5

Contribution earned at this point would be = (48 × 250.5) + (40 × 349.5) = 26,004 (increase of $4).

The shadow price of T is $4 per hour.

Shadow price of F

7W + 5L = 3,500
2W + 2L = 1,201

Multiply the second equation by 2.5 to yield a common value for L in each equation

7W + 5L = 3,500.0
5W + 5L = 3,002.5
2W = 497.5
W = 248.75

Substitute W = 248.75 into the fabric equation to calculate L

(2 × 248.75) + 2L = 1,201
2L = 1,201 – 497.5
L = 351.75

Contribution earned at this point would be = (48 × 248.75) + (40 × 351.75) = 26,010 (increase of $10).

The shadow price of F is $10 per metre.

29 RB Co

Text reference. Pricing is covered in Chapter 5.

Top tips. In part (a) make sure you relate your discussion to the specific circumstances of RB Co rather than just providing a general explanation of cost-plus pricing.

In part (b) the problem is deciding on the alternative pricing strategies to suggest. You may have included target pricing, for example.

Part (c) is a straightforward use of the demand curve formula which you will be given in the exam.

Easy marks. You may choose to answer part (c) first, if you are familiar with the formula.

Marking scheme

			Marks
(a)	Identify cost plus as the pricing strategy	1	
	Disadvantages of cost plus pricing, maximum	2	
	Advantage of cost plus pricing	1	
			4
(b)	Discussion of a first alternative pricing strategy	2	
	Discussion of a second alternative pricing strategy	2	
			4
(c)	Demand equation formula		2
			10

(a) **Managing director's pricing strategy**

The managing director has adopted what is known as a **full cost plus** pricing strategy, which means that a profit margin (in this case, of 50%) is added to the budgeted full cost of the product.

Disadvantages of this pricing strategy

Its **focus** is **internal** – internal costs and internal targets. It therefore takes **no account of the market conditions** faced by RB Co, which is why the company's selling price bears little resemblance to those of competitors. By adopting a fixed mark-up, **it does not allow the company to react to competitors'** pricing decisions.

Absorption bases used when calculating the full cost are **decided arbitrarily. Depending on the absorption basis** used in the calculation of total cost, the strategy can **produce different selling prices**.

Advantages of this pricing strategy

It is **quick**, **cheap** and relatively **easy** to apply. Pricing can therefore be delegated to more junior management if necessary.

The **costs of collecting market information** on demand and competitor activity are **avoided**.

(b) **Alternative pricing strategies**

(1) **Market penetration pricing**

Market penetration pricing is a policy of **low prices** when a product is first launched in order to achieve **high sales volumes** and hence gain a **significant market share**. If RB Co had adopted this strategy it might have discouraged competitors from entering the market.

(2) **Market skimming**

This pricing strategy involves charging **high prices** when a product is first launched and **spending heavily on advertising and promotion** to obtain sales so as to exploit any price insensitivity in the market. Such an approach would have been particularly suitable for RB's circumstances: demand for the software would have been relatively inelastic, customers being prepared to pay high prices for the software given its novelty appeal. As the product moves into later stages of its life cycle, prices can be reduced in order to remain competitive.

(c) When demand is linear the equation for the demand curve is:

P = a – bQ

where P = the price

Q = the quantity demanded

a = the price at which demand would be nil

$$b = \frac{\text{Change in price}}{\text{Change in quantity}}$$

a = $750

b = $10/1,000

= 0.01

∴ P = 750 – 0.01Q

30 Heat Co

Text references. The demand equation, the profit-maximising price/output level and pricing strategies are covered in Chapter 5. The learning curve is covered in Chapter 9.

Top tips. Set out your workings in part (a) in stages to maximise your score. Do not forget to exclude the fixed overheads relating to the air conditioning unit in part (b) – the question asks you to calculate the marginal cost for each unit.

Easy marks. There are no easy marks in this question unless you can construct the demand function in part (a).

Examiner's comments. The requirement to calculate the optimum price and quantity in part (a) was new to the syllabus in June 2011 and about half of candidates seemed not to have revised it and could not attempt it. It was really pleasing to see some good attempts at part (b) which tested the ability to adjust the labour cost for the learning effect.

Marking scheme

			Marks
(a)	Establish demand function:		
	Find 'b'	1	
	Find 'a'	1	
			2
(b)	Find MC:		
	Average cost of 100	1	
	Total cost of 100	1	
	Average cost of 99	1	
	Total cost of 99	1	
	Difference	1	
	Correct total MC excluding fixed cost	1	
			6
(c)	Establish MR function and equate MC and MR to find Q	1	
	Find optimum price	1	
			2
			10

(a) **Profit**

Apply the demand equation to calculate the optimum price:

P = a – bQ

Where P = the price

Q = the quantity demanded

a = the price at which demand would be nil

$$b = \frac{\text{Change in price}}{\text{Change in quantity}}$$

Establish the demand function (equation)

Step 1 **Calculate 'b'**

$$b = \frac{\text{Change in price}}{\text{Change in quantity}} = \$15/1{,}000 = 0.015$$

Step 2 **Substitute the known value for 'b' into the demand function to find 'a'**

We know that if the company set the price at $735, demand would be 1,000 units.

735 = a – 0.015Q

735 = a – (0.015 × 1,000)

735 = a – 15

735 + 15 = a

a = 750

The demand function is therefore P = 750 – 0.015Q

(b) **Establish marginal cost**

Labour time is calculated using the learning curve formula and then converted to cost.

$Y = ax^b$

Where Y = the cumulative average time per unit to produce x units

x = the cumulative number of units

a = the time taken for the first unit of output

b = the index of learning (logLR/log2)

The labour cost for 100 units:

We are told that b = –0.0740005. We are also told that a = 1.5 (the first air conditioning unit took 1.5 hours to make).

x = 100

$Y = 1.5 \times 100^{-0.0740005}$

Y = 1.0668178

Therefore cost per unit = 1.0668178 × $8 = $8.5345

Total cost for 100 units = $8.5345 × 100 = $853.45

Similarly, the labour cost for 99 units (x = 99):

$Y = 1.5 \times 99^{-0.0740005}$

Y = 1.0676115

Therefore cost per unit = 1.0676115 × $8 = $8.5409

Total cost for 99 units = $8.5409 × 99 = $845.55

Therefore cost of 100th unit = \$853.45 – \$845.55 = \$7.90

Total marginal cost = \$42 (direct materials) + \$7.90 = \$49.90

Fixed overheads are ignored as they are not part of the marginal cost.

(c) **Find profit**

Step 1 **Establish the marginal revenue function (equation)**

MR = a – 2bQ

Using the values of 'a' and 'b' from part (i):

MR = 750 – 0.03Q

Step 2 **Equate MC and MR to find Q (quantity demanded)**

MC = MR

49.90 = 750 – 0.03Q

0.03Q = 750 – 49.90

0.03Q = 700.10

Q = 700.10/0.03

Q = 23,337

Step 3 **Find optimum price**

P = a – bQ

P = 750 – (0.015 × 23,337)

P = \$399.95

31 Metallica Ltd

Text references. Limiting factor analysis is revised in Chapter 4.

Top tips. This question requires you to use brought-forward knowledge to calculate the contribution per unit of the limiting factor. Use a clear layout to show how you arrived at your conclusions.

Easy marks. There are some straightforward calculations in the question. Do what you can in the time available.

Marking scheme

			Marks
(a)	Calculation of contribution per unit	2	
	Calculation of contribution per m^2 and ranking	2	
	Production plan	3	
			7
(b)	1 mark per factor		3
			10

(a) The most profitable course of action can be determined by ranking the products and components according to **contribution per unit of the limiting factor**. Direct material M1 is the limiting factor in this case, therefore the highest rank will be given to the product/component with the greatest contribution per m^2 of this material.

	Product P4	*Product P6*	*Component C3*	*Component C5*
	$	$	$	$
Selling price	125	175	–	–
Opportunity cost			75	95
Direct materials:				
M1	15	10	5	10
M2	10	20	15	20
Direct labour	20	30	16	10
Variable overhead	10	15	8	5
Total direct costs	55	75	44	45
Contribution/unit	70	100	31	50
m^2 of M1/unit	0.75	0.5	0.25	0.5
Contribution/m^2	$93.33	$200	$124	$100
Ranking	4	1	2	3

Optimal production schedule

		Material available
		m^2
Total available		1,000
Produce:	1,500 units of P6	750
		250
	500 units of C3	125
		125
	125/0.5 per unit = 250 units of C5	125
		NIL

Optimal production plan is therefore:

P4	No units
P6	1,500 units
C3	125 units
C5	250 units

(b) **Other factors to be considered** (only three are required).

- Will the non-production of P4 have an effect on the sales of other products?
- What is the likelihood of the price of Material M1 remaining at $20 per m^2?
- Is there a possibility of replacing Material M1 with another material that is in more plentiful supply?
- What are the future prospects for product P4? Should production be terminated completely? Would this affect the company's overall market position?

32 Ennerdale

Text references. Short-term decisions are covered in Chapter 6.

Top tips. Part (a) deals with a price for a one-off contract. Therefore it is important to look at the quantities needed for that contract, when calculating the relevant costs. When looking at labour costs, remember that there is a shortage of skilled labour which must be built into the cost.

In part (b) remember to only look at the incremental revenues and costs after the common process.

Marking scheme

			Marks
(a)	Relevant cost Material K	2	
	Relevant cost Material L	1	
	Relevant cost skilled labour	2	
			5
(b)	Financial viability of the common process	1	
	Net incremental revenue from further processing each product	3	
	Conclusion/recommendation	1	
			5
			10

(a) (i) **Relevant cost – Material K**

Since the material is regularly used by the company, the relevant cost of material K is the current price of the material.

Cost last month $= \dfrac{\$19{,}600}{2{,}000\,\text{kg}}$

$= \$9.80$

Revised cost (+5%) $= \$9.80 \times 1.05$

$= \$10.29$

$\therefore$ Relevant cost of Material K $= 3{,}000\text{ kg} \times \$10.29$ per kg

$= \$30{,}870$

Relevant cost – Material L

Since the material is **not** required for normal production, the relevant cost of this material is its net realisable value if it were sold.

$\therefore$ Relevant cost of Material L $= 200\text{ kg} \times \$11$ per kg

$= \$2{,}200$

(ii) **Relevant cost – skilled labour**

Skilled labour is in short supply and therefore the relevant cost of this labour will include both the actual cost and the opportunity cost of the labour employed.

	$
Cost of skilled labour (800 hours × $9.50)	7,600
Opportunity cost of skilled labour (see working)	8,000
Relevant cost – skilled labour	15,600

Working

Skilled labour cost per unit of Product P = $38

Cost per skilled labour hour = $9.50

$\therefore$ Number of hours required per unit of Product P $= \dfrac{\$38}{\$9.50}$

$= 4$ hours

Contribution per unit of Product P $= \$40$

$\therefore$ Contribution per skilled labour hour $= \dfrac{\$40}{4\text{ hours}}$

$= \$10$ per hour

∴ Opportunity cost of skilled labour	= 800 hours × \$10 per hour
	= \$8,000

(b) **Financial viability of the common process**

Product	*Selling price after common process*	*Litres*	*Total revenue*
	\$/litre		\$
M	6.25	25,000	156,250
N	5.20	15,000	78,000
P	6.80	45,000	306,000
			540,250
Less costs at end of common process			(480,000)
Net revenue at the end of the common process			60,250

Therefore the common process is viable as net revenue is positive.

Optimal processing plan for each product

Product	*Further revenues*	*Further costs*	*Incremental net revenue from further processing*
	\$	\$	\$
M	\$2.15 × 25,000 = 53,750	\$1.75 × 25,000 = 43,750	10,000
N	\$1.25 × 15,000 = 18,750	\$0.95 × 15,000 = 14,250	4,500
P	\$0.65 × 45,000 = 29,250	\$0.85 × 45,000 = 38,250	(9,000)

Therefore products M and N make additional profit and so should be processed further.

Product P should not be processed beyond the common stage as net revenue is negative.

33 Hair

Text reference. Cost volume profit (CVP) analysis is covered in Chapter 3.

Top tips. Show all your workings to parts (a) and (b), and round all workings to two decimal places as requested in the question.

Note that part (c) asks you to draw a multi-product PV chart showing (i) the products in order of C/S ratio **and** (ii) assuming the products are sold in a constant mix. Clearly label each line on your PV chart.

Easy marks. There are easy marks available for calculating the weighted average C/S ratio and the break-even sales revenue in parts (a) and (b).

Examiner's comments. In part (a) the majority of candidates were able to calculate the unit contributions, which is obviously a very basic F2 skill. However, many students seemed unclear where to go from here. The most common error was that candidates then simply added together the three unit contributions, added together the three unit selling prices, and divided the former by the latter, giving a contribution to sales ratio of 36.9%. The problem with this calculation is that it does not take into account the relative sales volume of each product and it is not therefore a weighted average contribution to sales ratio but rather just an average contribution to sales ratio.

Part (c) examined break-even charts. This was poorly answered by the majority of candidates with very few scoring full marks. There seemed to be two main problems. Firstly, there seemed to be a lack of knowledge about what a break-even chart looked like. Many candidates drew profit-volume charts, which are different. Secondly, in order to plot the lines, candidates needed to do some preliminary calculations for cumulative profit and revenue. Many missed this point and were therefore unable to plot the lines.

Marking scheme

			Marks
(a)	Weighted average C/S ratio:		
	Individual contributions	1	
	Total sales revenue	1	
	Total contribution	1	
	Ratio	1	
			4
(b)	Break-even revenue		2
(c)	PV chart:		
	Individual CS ratios	1.5	
	Ranking	1.0	
	Workings for chart	2.0	
	Chart:		
	Labelling	0.5	
	Plotting each of six points	4.0	
			9
			15

(a) **Weighted average contribution to sales (C/S) ratio for Hair Co**

Weighted average C/S ratio = (Total contribution / Total sales revenue) × 100%

	C	*S*	*D*	*Total*
	$	$	$	
Selling price	110	160	120	
Material	(20)	(50)	(42)	
Labour	(30)	(54)	(50)	
	60	56	28	
Sales units	20,000	22,000	26,000	
Total sales revenue	$2,200,000	$3,520,000	$3,120,000	$8,840,000
Total contribution	$1,200,000	$1,232,000	$728,000	$3,160,000

Weighted average C/S ratio = ($3,160,000/$8,840,000) × 100%

= 35.75%

(b) **Break-even sales revenue**

Break-even sales revenue = Fixed costs / C/S ratio

= $640,000 / 35.75%

= $1,790,209.79

(c) **PV chart**

Calculate the individual C/S ratio for each product and rank them (highest C/S ratio first).

	C	*S*	*D*
	$	$	$
Contribution	60	56	28
Selling price	110	160	120
C/S ratio	0.55	0.35	0.23
Ranking	1	2	3

	Revenue	*Cumulative revenue* (x axis coordinate)	*Profit*	*Cumulative profit* (y axis)
	$	$	$	$
0	0	0	(640,000)	(640,000)
Make C	2,200,000	2,200,000	1,200,000	560,000
Make S	3,520,000	5,720,000	1,232,000	1,792,000
Make D	3,120,000	8,840,000	728,000	2,520,000

Note. **Refer to P/V chart on next page.**

The **solid line** shows the **cumulative profit/loss** and the **cumulative sales** as each product's sales and contribution are in turn added to the sales mix (in order of **C/S ratio**).

The **dotted line** which joins the two ends of this solid line indicates the **average profit** which will be earned from sales of the three products in this mix.

P/V chart for Hair Co – part (c)

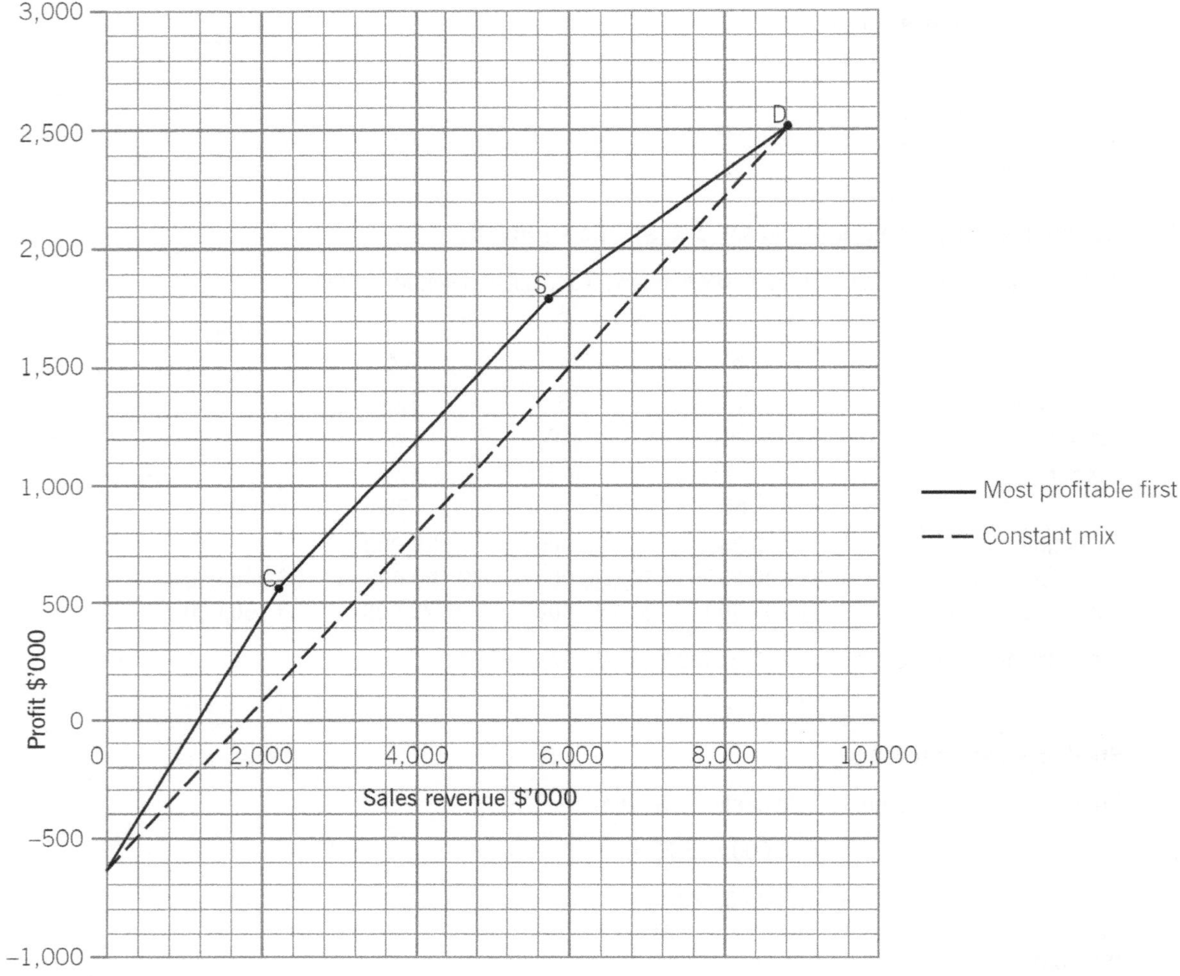

34 Higgins Co

Text references. Linear programming is covered in Chapter 4.

Top tips. The biggest problem with this question is time management. There is a lot to do in the time allowed.

Make sure all calculations and the graph are neatly laid out and easy for the marker to read.

For part (b), remember that the dual price is zero for any constraining factor for which there is slack (ie the factor is not acting as an actual constraint).

Easy marks. Part (a) should be straightforward. Do as much as you can in the time you allocate. In part (b) you should be able to give a good definition of dual price.

Examiner's comments. This question was in the main reasonably well done. Some common errors were made though in the construction of the basic model including ignoring the demand (external) constraints completely and missing out the non-negativity constraints. Some candidates did not fully understand what a shadow prices was and fewer still how to calculate it.

Marking scheme

			Marks
(a)	Defining ash constraint	1.0	
	Defining craftsmen constraint	1.0	
	Demand constraints for pool and snooker cues – pool cue	0.5	
	Non-negativity constraints	0.5	
	Correctly drawn diagram		
	Labels and title	0.5	
	Ash constraint line	0.5	
	Craftsmen constraint line	0.5	
	Pool cues sales demand line and snooker cues sales demand line	0.5	
	Identified feasible region	0.5	
	Iso-contribution line	1.0	
	Identified optimal point	0.5	
	Solve at optimal point for units of each product	2.0	
	Calculation of contribution	1.0	
			10
(b)	Explanation of a shadow price	2	
	Ash shadow price	1	
	Craftsmen shadow price	2	
			5
			15

(a) **Define variables**

Let **P** = number of pool cues sold per period
S = number of snooker cues sold per period

Establish constraints

Craftsmen	$0.5P + 0.75S \leq 12{,}000$
Ash	$0.27P + 0.27S \leq 5{,}400$
Demand for pool cues	$P \leq 15{,}000$
Demand for snooker cues	$S \leq 12{,}000$

Objective function

The objective is to maximise contribution (C):

C = 20P + 40S

Construct an iso-contribution line

C = 20P + 40S

Say 20P + 40S = 80 (where 80 = 20 × 40 / 10*), then:

If P = 0, S = 2

If S = 0, P = 4

* Divided by 10 to enable line to be plotted on graph.

Linear programming graph

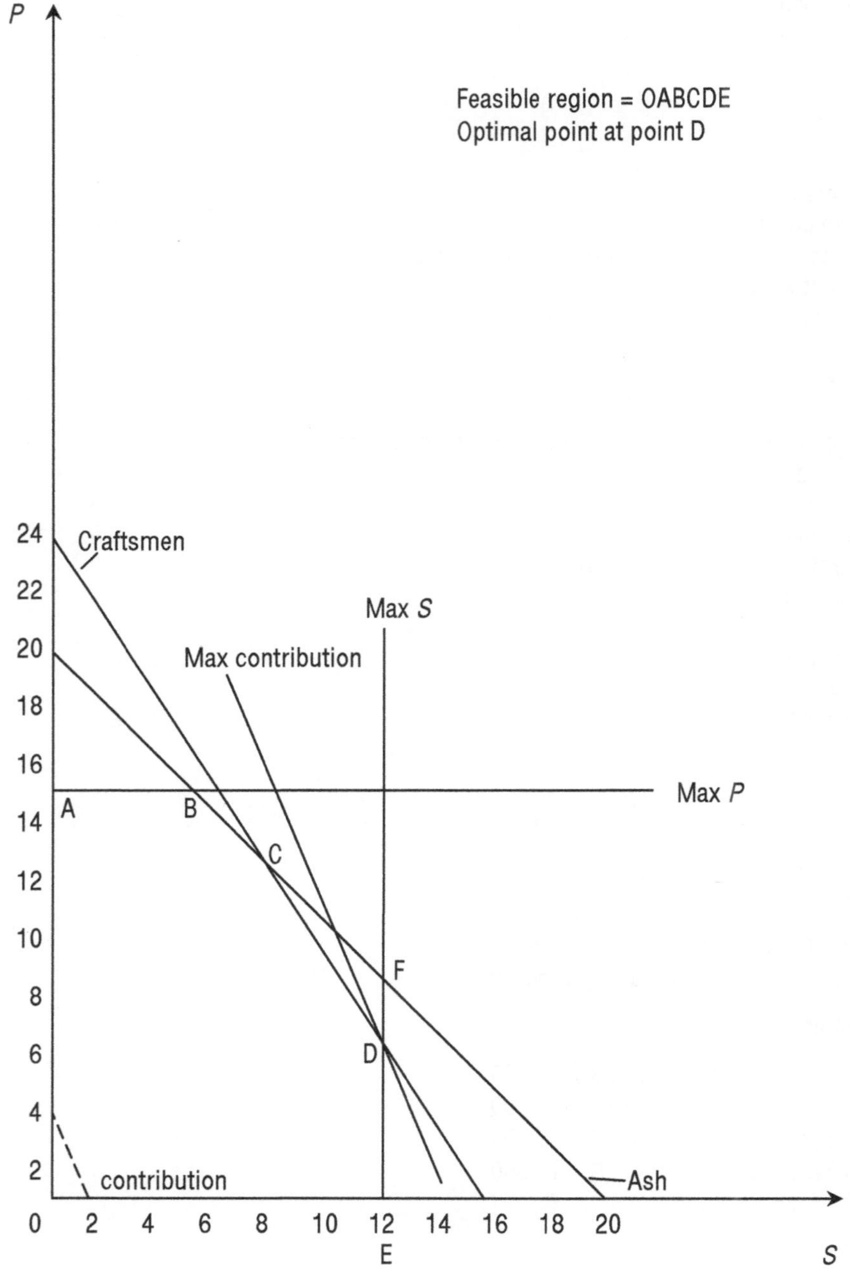

The **feasible region** is the area inside OABCDE.

The iso-contribution line is the dotted line which can be pushed outwards to increase the contribution gained. This gives a maximum contribution at **point D** where the craftsmen constraint line meets the maximum demand for S constraint line.

Solving at point D

Maximum demand S = 12,000 (1)
Craftsmen 0·5P + 0·75S = 12,000 (2)
Substituting S = 12,000 in equation (2)
0.5P + (0.75 × 12,000) = 12,000
0.5P + 9,000 = 12,000
0.5P = 3,000
P = 6,000

Therefore the maximum contribution is earned when 6,000 pool cues and 12,000 snooker cues are made and sold in a three month period.

The **contribution** earned	= ($20 × 6,000) + ($40 × 12,000)
	= $(120,000 + 480,000)
	= $600,000

Alternative solution

Instead of using an iso-contribution line, the contribution at each inter-section of the feasible region can be calculated and the point with the largest contribution chosen.

Point B

Maximum demand	P = 15,000 (1)
Ash	0.27P + 0.27S = 5,400 (2)
Substituting	P = 15,000 in equation (2)
	(0.27 × 15,000) + 0.27S = 5,400
	4,050 + 0.27S = 5,400
	0.27S = 1,350
	S = 5,000
Contribution earned	= (20 × 15,000) + (40 × 5,000)
	= 300,000 + 200,000
	= $500,000

Point C

Ash	0.27P + 0.27S = 5,400 (1)
Craftsmen	0·5P + 0·75S = 12,000 (2)
	(1) × 0.5
	0.135P + 0.135S = 2,700 (3)
	(2) × 0.27
	0.135P + 0.2025S = 3,240 (4)
	(4) – (3)
	0.0675S = 540
	S = 8,000

Substituting in (1)

$$0.27P + (0.27 \times 8{,}000) = 5{,}400$$

$$0.27P = 5{,}400 - 2{,}160$$

$$P = 12{,}000$$

Contribution earned $= (20 \times 12{,}000) + (40 \times 8{,}000)$

$= 240{,}000 + 320{,}000$

$= \$560{,}000$

Point D

Contribution = $600,000 (already calculated above)

(b) **Shadow price**

The shadow price is the **extra contribution** or profit that may be earned if one more unit of a **binding resource** or **limiting factor** becomes available.

It can be used to inform managers of the **maximum price** that should be paid for more of a scarce resource over and above the basic rate. The shadow price of a constraint that is not binding at the optimal solution is zero.

Calculation of shadow prices

At the optimal solution, P = 6,000 and S = 12,000

Contribution = $600,000

Ash

$0.27P + 0.27S = 5{,}400$

$(0.27 \times 6{,}000) + (0.27 \times 12{,}000) = 4{,}860 < 5{,}400$

There is **slack**, so ash is not a binding constraint and there is no shadow price.

Craftsmen

$0.5P + 0.75S = 12{,}000$

$(0.5 \times 6{,}000) + (0.75 \times 12{,}000) = 12{,}000$ = availability

The constraint is **binding.** If one more hour of labour was available, the new optimal product mix would be at the intersection of the lines:

Maximum demand $S = 12{,}000$ (1)

Craftsmen $0.5P + 0.75S = 12{,}001$ (2)

Substituting $S = 12{,}000$ in equation (2)

$$0.5P + (0.75 \times 12{,}000) = 12{,}001$$
$$0.5P + 9{,}000 = 12{,}001$$
$$0.5P = 3{,}001$$
$$P = 6{,}002$$

The contribution earned $= (20 \times 6{,}002) + (40 \times 12{,}000)$
$= 120{,}040 + 480{,}000$
$= \$600{,}040$

The **shadow price** of one hour of craftsman's time is the extra contribution generated which is **$40.**

35 The Cosmetic Co

Text reference. Graphical linear programming is covered in Chapter 4.

Top tips. Perhaps the biggest challenge in this question is time management. There is a lot to do in the time allowed.

Use the step by step approach in part (a), clearly labelling your workings to make it easy for the marker to follow. Make sure your read the question scenario very carefully as it is easy to miss an element.

Easy marks. There are plenty of easy marks available throughout for establishing the constraints and clearly drawing and labelling each line on the graph.

Examiner's comments. Much of this question could have been examined at F2. Why then, was it in the F5 paper? It is becoming more and more apparent that the assumed F2 knowledge for F5 simply isn't there and it is therefore necessary to make candidates realise that it is examinable under F5 and that, if they don't know the subject matter, they need to go away and study it!

Candidates who had revised this area made a decent attempt at this question, with many of them scoring full marks in part (a) at least. It is important, when answering a linear programming question like this, to set out your workings clearly, with a logical progression in steps from defining the variables and constraints, through to drawing the graph and finding the solution. This makes it easier to mark. The recommended approach is to use the iso-contribution line to find the optimum solution; it is the quickest way to do it. Candidates weren't penalised if they used the simultaneous equations method, because they were not told which method to use, but they penalised themselves because it took them longer to do it.

It is essential to show all of your workings. So, for example, the iso-contribution line needs to be worked out and then drawn onto the graph. If you didn't show how you worked it out, you stood to lose some marks.

Where you are asked to work to two decimal places, you should do it. In this question, it was necessary in order to keep a level of accuracy required to answer part (b) as well. Whilst we gave follow on marks for part (b) wherever possible, if fundamental mistakes had been made in part (a) so that, for example, there was no slack for amino acids, it was hard to award marks.

Marking scheme

			Marks
(a)	Objective function	0.5	
	Defining silk powder constraint	0.5	
	Defining silk amino constraint	0.5	
	Defining skilled labour constraint	0.5	
	Demand constraint	0.5	
	Non-negativity constraints	0.5	
	Correctly drawn diagram		
	Labels and title	0.5	
	Silk powder constraint line	0.5	
	Silk amino constraint line	0.5	
	Skilled labour constraint line	0.5	
	Sales demand constraint line	0.5	
	Iso-contribution line	1.0	
	Identified optimal point	0.5	
	Solve at optimal point for units of each product	2.0	
	Calculation of contribution	1.0	
			10
(b)	Shadow price calculation	2	
	Slack calculation	3	
			5
			15

(a) **Define variables**

Let x = number of jars of face cream to be produced
Let y = number of bottles of body lotion to be produced
Let C = contribution

Establish objective function

The objective is to maximise contribution (C)
Face cream contribution (x) = $9.00 per unit
Body lotion contribution (y) = $8.00 per unit
Maximise C = 9x + 8y, subject to the constraints below.

Establish constraints

Silk powder:	$3x + 2y \leq 5,000$
Silk amino acids:	$1x + 0.5y \leq 1,600$
Skilled labour:	$4x + 5y \leq 9,600$
Non-negativity constraints:	$x, y \geq 0$
Maximum demand for body lotion:	$y \leq 2,000$

Establish coordinates to plot lines representing the inequalities

Silk powder:	$3x + 2y \leq 5,000$ If x = 0, y = 2,500 If y = 0, x = 1,666.7
Silk amino acids:	$1x + 0.5y \leq 1,600$ If x = 0, y = 3,200 If y = 0, x = 1,600
Skilled labour:	$4x + 5y \leq 9,600$ If x = 0, y = 1,920 If y = 0, x = 2,400

Also plot the line y = 2,000 (maximum weekly demand for body lotion).

Draw the graph

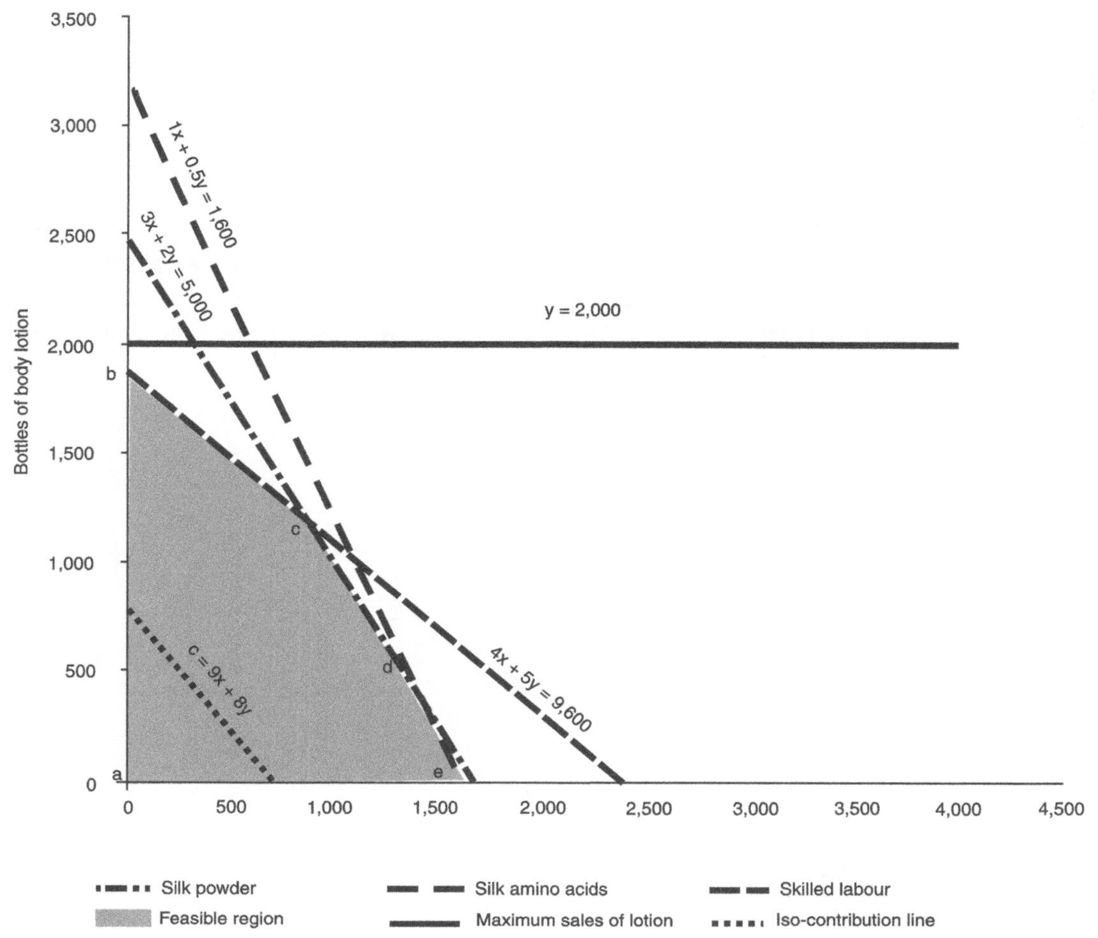

Find the optimal solution using an iso-contribution line

C = 9x + 8y

If C = (8 × 800) = 6,400, then:

If y = 0, 9x = 6,400

Therefore x = 711.11

By moving the iso-contribution line out across the graph, it is clear that the optimal solution lies as point C, the intersection of the constraints for skilled labour and silk powder.

Solving the simultaneous equations for these constraints:
4x + 5y = 9,600 × 3
3x + 2y = 5,000 × 4

12x + 15y = 28,800 (1)
12x + 8y = 20,000 (2)
Subtract (2) from (1):
7y = 8,800
y = 1,257.14

If y = 1,257.14 and;
4x + 5y = 9,600

The 5 × 1,257.14 + 4x = 9,600

Therefore x = 828.58

The **optimal solution** is therefore to make 828.58 jars of face cream and 1,257.14 bottles of body lotion.

Maximum profit

		$
Contribution		
Face cream:	828.58 units × unit contribution of $9.00	7,457.22
Body lotion:	1,257.14 units × unit contribution of $8.00	10,057.12
		17,514.34

(b) **Shadow price for silk powder**

The shadow price for silk powder can be found by solving the two simultaneous equations that intersect at point C on the graph in part (a). The **shadow price** is the **increase in value which would be created by having one additional unit** of limiting factor. For this reason, we must add one more hour to the equation for silk powder.

$4x + 5y = 9{,}600 \quad \times 3$
$3x + 2y = 5{,}001 \quad \times 4$

$12x + 15y = 28{,}800 \quad (1)$
$12x + 8y = 20{,}004 \quad (2)$

Subtract (2) from (1):
$7y = 8{,}796$
$y = 1{,}256.57$

$3x + (2 \times 1{,}256.57) = 5{,}001$
$x = 829.29$

$C = (9 \times 829.29) + (8 \times 1{,}256.57) = \$17{,}516.17$

Original contribution = $17,514.34

The **shadow price for silk powder** is therefore $1.83 per gram.

Slack for amino acids

Each unit of face cream requires 1 gram of silk amino acids and each unit of body lotion requires 0.5 grams of amino acids.

$(828.58 \times 1) + (0.5 \times 1{,}257.14) = 1{,}457.15$ grams used

Grams available = 1,600 grams

Therefore slack = 142.85 grams

36 LD Co

Text references. Linear programming is covered in Chapter 4.

Top tips. Follow the step-by step process in this question, clearly labelling your workings and it should be straightforward. Make sure you read all parts of the question very carefully as it is easy to miss an essential element.

You may not like drawing graphs. Unfortunately, without drawing the graph, you can't easily calculate the profit-maximising output levels, and this will restrict your ability to answer part (b).

Easy marks. Being able to explain the meaning of slack, surplus and shadow process should provide easy marks even you make a mistake in the calculations.

Marking scheme

		Marks
(a) (i) Objective function	1.0	
Constraints for cleaning materials, direct labour and machine time	1.5	
Minimum sales constraints for each product	1.0	
Maximum sales constraints for each product	0.5	
		4
(ii) Constraint lines for cleaning materials, direct labour and machine time	3.0	
Constraint lines for maximum and minimum sales demand quantities	1.0	
Iso-contribution line	1.0	
Identify contribution-maximising output	1.0	
Calculate maximum profit	1.0	
		7
(b) General definition of dual price	1.0	
Calculation of dual price	2.0	
Interpretation of calculated dual price	1.0	
		4
		15

(a) (i) **Define variables**

Let L = number of laundry services provided

Let D = number of dry cleaning services provided

Establish objective function

Fixed costs will be the same irrespective of the optimal mix and so the objective is to maximise contribution (C).

Laundry contribution = \$5.60 – \$(2 + 1.2 + 0.5)

= \$1.90

Dry cleaning contribution = \$13.20 – \$(3 + 2 + 1.5)

= \$6.70

Maximise C = 1.9L + 6.7D, subject to the constraints below.

Establish constraints

Cleaning materials: $^{2}/_{10}L + ^{3}/_{10}D \leq 5{,}000$

$0.2L + 0.3D \leq 5{,}000$

Direct labour: $^{1.2}/_{6}L + ^{2}/_{6}D \leq 6{,}000$

$0.2L + 0.333D \leq 6{,}000$

Machine time: $^{0.5}/_{3}L + ^{1.5}/_{3}D \leq 5{,}000$

$0.167L + 0.5D \leq 5{,}000$

Maximum and minimum services (for contract): $L \leq 14{,}000$

$L \geq 1{,}200$

$D \geq 2{,}000$

$D \leq 9{,}975$

(ii) Establish coordinates to plot lines representing the inequalities.

Cleaning materials: If L = 0, D = 16,667

If D = 0, L = 25,000

Direct labour: If L = 0, D = 18,000

If D = 0, L = 30,000

Variable machine cost: If L = 0, D = 10,000

If D = 0, L = 30,000

Also plot the lines L = 1,200, D = 2,000, L = 14,000 and D = 9,975

Construct an iso-contribution line

C = 1.9L + 6.7D

If C = (1.9 × 6.7 × 1,000) = 12,730, then:

if L = 6,700, D = 0

if D = 1,900, L = 0

Draw the graph

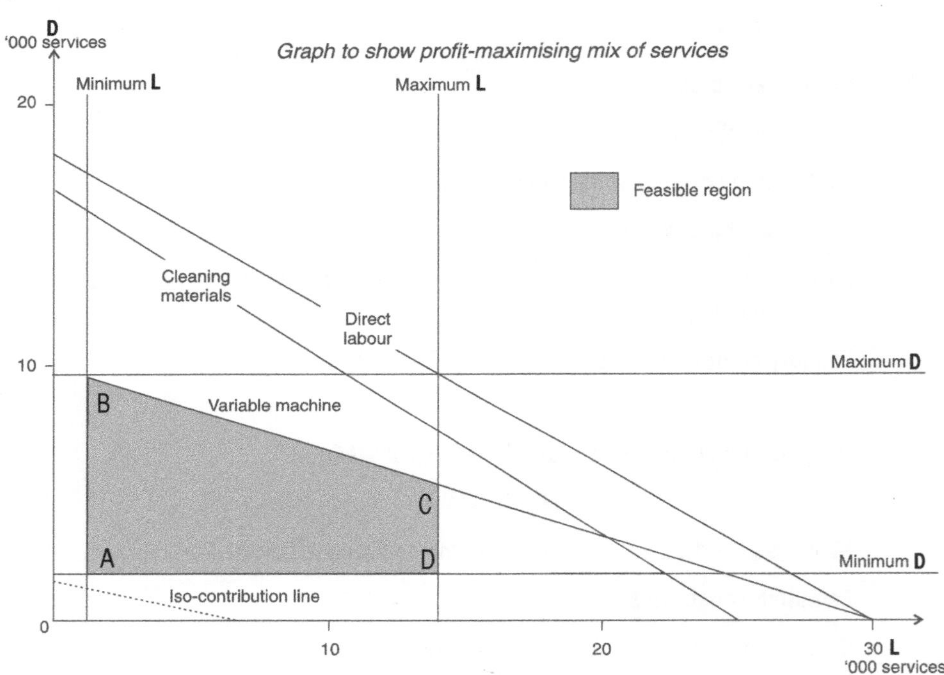

The **feasible region** is the area inside area ABCD.

Find the optimal solution

By moving the iso-contribution line out across the graph, it is clear that the optimal solution lies at the intersection of lines representing the constraints for minimum number of laundry services and machine hours.

∴ Optimal solution occurs when:

L = 1,200 and 0.167L + 0.5D = 5,000

If L = 1,200, then D = (5,000 – 200) × 2 = 9,600

The **optimal solution** is to carry out 1,200 laundry services and 9,600 dry cleaning services.

Maximum profit

		$
Contribution		
Laundry:	1,200 × unit contribution of $1.90	2,280
Dry cleaning:	9,600 × unit contribution of $6.70	64,320
		66,600
Less fixed costs (32,825/12)		2,735
		63,865

(b) The **shadow price** or dual price of a limiting factor is the increase in value which would be created by having one additional unit of the limiting factor at the original cost. For this company under these conditions, machine hours are a binding constraint and a limiting factor so we can calculate how much extra contribution will be obtained if one extra hour of machine time becomes available.

The machine hours constraint will now be $0.167L + 0.5D \leq 5{,}001$ and the optimal point will be where this line crosses the line representing $L \geq 1{,}200$.

If L = 1,200

$(0.167 \times 1{,}200) + 0.5D = 5{,}001$

$0.5D = 5{,}001 - 200$

$0.5D = 4{,}801$

$D = 4{,}801 \times 2 = 9{,}602$

Contribution at this point = (1,200 × $1.90) + (9,602 × $6.70) = $66,613.40

The shadow price is the price over and above the usual price that LD Co would pay for a machine hour. This is calculated as $(66,613.40 – 66,600) = $13.40. This means that the price they would be prepared to pay is $13.40 + $3 = $16.40.

This means that extra machine time could be rented, for example, provided the **extra cost** is less than $13.40 per hour.

37 Tablet Co

Text references. Linear programming is covered in Chapter 4.

Top tips. Follow the step-by step process in this question, clearly labelling your workings and it should be straightforward. Make sure you read all parts of the question very carefully as it is easy to miss an essential element.

Examiner's comments. There were good attempts to answer this question in general, however, there are a number of points to bear in mind. It doesn't matter whether a candidate works in hours or minutes, as long as a consistent approach is adopted. Always state clearly what the optimum point is. This makes it easy to award follow on marks where there has been an error.

Marking scheme

		Marks
Optimum production plan		
Defining the variables	0.5	
Stating the objective function	0.5	
Constraints for build time, program time and test time (0.5 marks each)	1.5	
Non-negativity constraints	0.5	
Sales constraint x, and y (0.5 marks each)	1	
Iso-contribution line	1	

		Marks
The graph:		
Labels	0.5	
Lines: Build time, program time, test (0.5 marks each)	1.5	
Demand lines: x, y (0.5 marks each)	1	
Iso-contribution line	0.5	
Feasible region identified and labelled/shaded	1	
Optimum point identified	1	
Equations solved at optimum point	3	
Total contribution	1	
Total profit	0.5	
		15

Step 1: **Define variables**

Let x = number of units of Xeno to be produced

Let y = number of units of Yong to be produced

State objective function

Fixed costs will be the same irrespective of the optimal mix and so the objective is to maximise contribution (C).

Maximise C = 30x + 40y, subject to the constraints below.

State constraints

Build time:	$24x + 20y \leq 1,800,000$
Program time:	$16x + 14y \leq 1,680,000$
Test time:	$10x + 4y \leq 720,000$

Non-negativity constraints:

$x, y \geq 0$

Sales constraints

$x \leq 85,000$

$y \leq 66,000$

Establish coordinates to plot lines representing the inequalities.

Build time:	If x = 0, y = 1,800,000/20 = 90,000
	If y = 0, x = 1,800,000/24 = 75,000
Program time:	If x = 0, y = 1,680,000/14 = 120,000
	If y = 0, x = 1,680,000/16 = 105,000
Test time:	If x = 0, y = 720,000/4 = 180,000
	If y = 0, x = 720,000/10 = 72,000

Construct an iso-contribution line

If y = 40,000, C = 40,000 × \$40 = \$1,600,000

If C = \$1,6000,000 and y = 0, x = \$1,600,000/\$30 = 53,333.33

Draw the graph

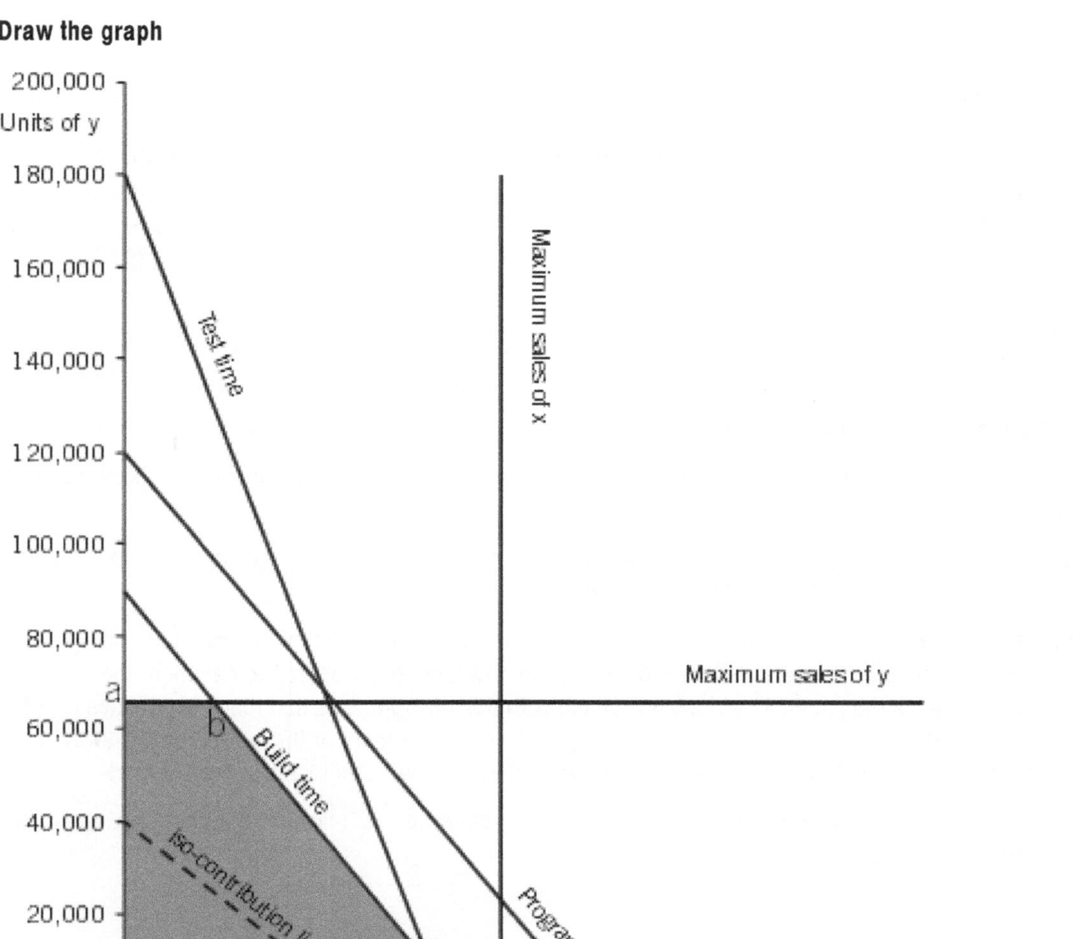

The **feasible region** is the area inside area ABCD.

Find the optimal solution

By moving the iso-contribution line out across the graph, it is clear that the optimal solution lies at point b, the intersection of lines representing the constraints for maximum sales of y, and build time.

∴ Optimal solution occurs when:

y = 66,000 and 24x + 30y = 1,800,000

24x + (20 × 66,000) = 1,800,000

24 + 1,320,000 = 1,800,000

24x = 480,000

x = 20,000

C = 30x + 40y

Maximum profit

	$
Contribution	
X: 20,000 units × unit contribution of $30	600,000
Y: 66,000 units × unit contribution of $40	2,640,000
	3,240,000
Less fixed costs (650,000 × 3)	1,950,000
	1,290,000

38 T Co

Text reference. Relevant costing is covered in Chapter 6.

Top tips. Show all your workings and make sure that you explain **why** each cost is included or excluded from the cost statement.

Easy marks. There are easy marks available by taking some of the items of cost and identifying the relevant cost for the item. Remember however to provide good explanations.

Examiner's comments. This was a nice, straightforward relevant costing question, which should have been well-answered by most people. This was definitely not the case, however, and it proved to be one of the most poorly answered questions on the paper. The biggest problem with this question was that many candidates clearly don't understand relevant costing, so they simply couldn't get either the numbers or the words right anyway. Out of all the scripts that I personally looked at, and this was a lot, I only saw two candidates score full marks.

Many candidates just wrote down that a cost was included because it was 'relevant' but didn't say why. This is not an explanation and didn't score marks.

Marking scheme

	Marks
Costing statement:	
Lunch	1
Engineer costs	4
Technical adviser	1
Site visits	1
Training costs	1
Handsets	2
Control system	3
Cable	1
Minimum price	1
	15

Cost statement for T Co

	Note	$
Demonstration and complimentary lunch	1	Nil
Engineers	2	500
Technical adviser	3	480
Site inspector visits	4	Nil
Training costs	5	125
Telephone handsets	6	2,184
Computerised control system	7	7,600
Cable costs	8	1,300
Minimum price		12,189

(1) **Demonstration and complimentary lunch**

The salesman has already been to visit Push Co to demonstrate the new system. The associated costs are sunk costs (they have already been incurred) and are therefore excluded from the cost statement.

Relevant cost = $0

(2) **Engineers**

One of the three engineers has spare capacity to complete the installation and his/her salary will be paid regardless of whether they work on the contract for Push Co. The relevant cost is therefore $Nil.

The other two engineers are currently fully utilised and earn a contribution of $5 per hour each on Contract X. The engineers could be temporarily taken off of Contract X to work on the contract for Push Co. Work on Contract X would recommence in one week's time when there is no other scheduled work for the engineers.

Delaying the work on Contract X would result in T Co missing the contractual completion deadline and having to pay a one-off penalty of $500.

Relevant cost = $500

(3) **Technical adviser**

The technical adviser is working at full capacity so would need to work 8 hours overtime on the contract for Push Co. All overtime is paid at a premium of 50% above his usual hourly rate of $40 ($40 × 1.5 = $60).

Relevant cost = $60 × 8 hours = $480

(4) **Site inspector visits**

The site inspector is an independent contractor who is not employed by T Co and charges Push Co directly for the work. Since the site engineer charges Push, the relevant cost for T Co is nil.

Relevant cost = $Nil

(5) **Training costs**

The system trainer is paid a monthly salary of $1,500. This is not a relevant cost, as it is not incremental. The trainer is also paid $125 commission for each day spent delivering training at a client's site. This cost will arise as a direct result of the decision and is therefore included.

Relevant cost = $125 per day × 1 day = $125

(6) **Handsets**

120 handsets would need to be supplied to Push Co. Though 80 handsets are already in inventory, the handsets are frequently requested by T Co's customers and so would need to be replaced if supplied to Push Co. The current cost of a handset is $18.20.

Relevant cost = $18.20 × 120 handsets = $2,184

(7) **Computerised control system**

The current market price of Swipe 2 is $10,800.

The original cost of Swipe 1 ($5,400) is a sunk cost and not relevant to the decision.

The current market price of Swipe 1 ($5,450) is also not relevant to the decision as T Co has no intention of replacing Swipe 1.

The company could sell Swipe 1 for $3,000 if it does not use it for this contract. This represents an opportunity cost.

In addition to the $3,000, Swipe 1 could be modified at a cost of $4,600, bringing the total cost of converting Swipe 1 to $7,600.

The total cost of converting Swipe 1 ($7,600) is significantly less than purchasing Swipe 2 ($10,800). It is assumed that the company would choose the cheaper option.

Relevant cost = $7,600

(8) **Cable costs**

1,000 metres of cable is required. Although T Co has 200 metres of cable in inventory, it is used frequently and so would need to be replaced. All 1,000 metres should be valued at the current market rate ($1.30 per metre). The original purchase cost of $1.20 per metre is a sunk cost and is not relevant to the decision.

Relevant cost = 1,000 metres × $1.30 per metre = $1,300

39 Robber Co

Text reference. Make/buy decisions and relevant costs are covered in Chapter 6.

Top tips. This question tests relevant costing within a 'make or buy context'. There are a number of calculations required for both parts (a) and (b) so present your answer clearly and show all of your workings to maximise your score.

Easy marks. There should be easy marks available for recognising the relevant costs.

Examiner's comments. It was pleasing to see many candidates making a decent attempt at part (a). In the suggested solution, the $4,000 and $6,000 machine costs are treated as **specific** fixed costs and are therefore included in the relevant cost of manufacturing in-house, together with the depreciation. However, it is acceptable to assume these costs to be **general** fixed costs and therefore exclude them for their manufacture cost together with the depreciation.

Part (b) produced weaker answers but many candidates were at least able to work out the shortage of hours and the number of units that needed to be bought in (without going through the process of ranking the two components), for which they could earn nearly half of the total marks available.

Marking scheme

			Marks
(a)	Incremental cost of buying in:		
	Direct materials	0.5	
	Direct labour	0.5	
	Heat and light	0.5	
	Set-up costs	3.0	
	Depreciation and insurance	1.0	
	Total cost of making	0.5	
	Total cost of buying	0.5	
	Saving	0.5	
	Conclusion	1.0	
			8
	Method 2:		
	Direct materials	0.5	
	Direct labour	0.5	
	Heat and power	0.5	
	Avoidable fixed costs	0.5	
	Activity related costs	3.0	
	Avoidable depreciation and insurance	0.5	
	Total relevant manufacturing costs	0.5	
	Relevant cost per unit	0.5	
	Incremental cost of buying in	0.5	
	Conclusion	1.0	
			8

			Marks
(b)	If 100,000 control panels made:		
	Variable cost of making per unit	1.0	
	Saving from making	1.0	
	Saving per labour hour	1.0	
	Ranking	1.0	
	Make 100,000 keypads	1.0	
	Make 66,666 display screens	1.0	
	Buy 33,334 display screens	1.0	
			7
			15

(a) **Incremental costs of making in-house compared to cost of buying**

	Keypads (K)	*Display screens (D)*
	$	$
Variable costs		
Materials:		
K = ($160k × 6/12) + ($160k × 1.05 × 6/12) : D = ($116k × 1.02)	164,000	118,320
Direct labour	40,000	60,000
Machine set-up costs:		
K = ($26k – $4k) × 500/400 : D = ($30k – $6k) × 500/400	27,500	30,000
	231,500	208,320
Attributable fixed costs		
Heat and power: K = ($64k – $20k) : D = ($88k – $30k)	44,000	58,000
Fixed machine costs	4,000	6,000
Depreciation and insurance: K = ($84k × 40%) : D = ($96k × 40%)	33,600	38,400
	81,600	102,400
Total incremental costs of making in-house	313,100	310,720
Cost of buying: K = (80,000 × $4.10) : D = (80,000 × $4.30)	328,000	344,000
Total saving from making	14,900	33,280

Robber Co should therefore make all of the keypads and display screens in-house.

Note. The above calculations assume that the fixed set-up costs only arise if production takes place.

Alternative approach (Relevant costs)

	Keypads (K)	*Display screens (D)*
	$	$
Direct materials:		
K = ($160k / 2) + ($160k / 2 × 1.05) : D = $116k × 1.02	164,000	118,320
Direct labour	40,000	60,000
Heat and power		
K = $64K – (50% × $40K) : D = $88k – (50% × $60k)	44,000	58,000
Machine set-up costs:		
Avoidable fixed costs	4,000	6,000
Activity related costs (W1)	27,500	30,000
Avoidable depreciation and insurance costs:		
K = ($84k × 40%) : D = ($96k × 40%)	33,600	38,400
Total relevant manufacturing costs	313,100	310,720
Relevant cost per unit	3.91375	3.884
Cost per unit of buying in	4.10	4.30
Incremental cost of buying in	0.18625	0.416

As each of the components is cheaper to make in-house than to buy in, the company should continue to manufacture both products in-house.

Working

Current no. of batches produced = 80,000 / 500 = 160
New no. of batches produced = 80,000 / 400 = 200
Current cost per batch for keypads = ($26,000 – $4,000) / 160 = $137.50
Therefore new activity related batch cost = 200 × $137.50 = $27,500
Current cost per batch for display screens = ($30,000 – $6,000) / 160 = $150
Therefore new activity related batch cost = 200 × $150 = $30,000

(b) **Note.** Attributable fixed costs are not included in the following calculation. Attributable fixed costs remain unaltered irrespective of the level of production of keypads and display screens, because as soon as one unit of either is made, the costs rise. We know that we will make at least one unit of each component as both are cheaper to make than buy. They are therefore an irrelevant common cost.

Plan to minimise costs

	Keypads (K)	*Display screens (D)*
	$	$
Buy-in price	4.10	4.30
Variable cost of making:		
K = ($231,500 / 80,000): D = ($208,320 / 80,000)	2.89	2.60
Saving from making (per unit)	1.21	1.70
Labour hours per unit	0.50	0.75
Saving from making (per unit of limiting factor)	2.42	2.27
Priority for making	1	2

Total labour hours available = 100,000 hours

Make maximum keypads, ie 100,000 using 50,000 labour hours (100,000 × 0.5 hours per unit)

Use remaining 50,000 labour hours to make 66,666 display screens (50,000 / 0.75 hours per unit)

Therefore buy in 33,334 display screens (100,000 – 66,666).

40 Stay Clean

Text reference. Short-term decisions are covered in Chapter 6 and pricing strategies in Chapter 5.

Top tips. This is a long scenario and may initially look daunting. However a step-by-step logical approach will gain marks throughout part (a), even if you get stuck on some of the trickier parts such as material discounts.

Make sure you leave enough time for part (b) which calls for straightforward explanations.

Easy marks. There are easy marks available in part (a) for some of the calculations.

Examiner's comments. In part (a) most candidates adopted the approach of doing two calculations: one considered the financial position if the production of TDs ceased immediately; the other considered the position if production stopped in twelve months. This approach was absolutely fine as long as candidates didn't include figures as costs in one calculation and then as savings in the other.

As regards the pricing strategies in part (b) the only really suitable strategies were to introduce complementary/product line pricing or to simply increase the price to cover costs. Many candidates suggested 'penetration pricing' or market skimming', which is inappropriate given that TD was not a new product.

Marking scheme

			Marks
(a)	Lost revenue and saved labour cost	2	
	Lost contribution from other products	2	
	Redundancy and recruitment cost	2	
	Supplier payments	3	
	Sublet income	1	
	Supervisor	1	
			11
(b)	Complementary pricing	2	
	Product line pricing	2	
	Other valid suggestions	2	
		max	4
			15

(a) **Ceasing production now**

TD saved contribution

All sales of the TD will be lost for the next 12 months, this will result in contribution saved of 1,200 units × ($10) = $12,000

DW and WM lost contribution

Lost contribution = 5% × ((5,000 units × $80) + (6,000 units × $170)) = $71,000

Labour

If TD is ceased now:

	$
Redundancy cost	(6,000)
Retraining saved	3,500
Recruitment cost	(1,200)
Total cost	(3,700)

Lost discount

	DW	*WM*	*TD*	*Net cost*	*Discount*	*Gross cost*
	$	$	$	$		$
Current buying cost	350,000	600,000	60,000	1,010,000	5%	1,063,158
Saved cost	(17,500)	(30,000)	(60,000)			
New buying cost	332,500	570,000	0	902,500	5%	950,000
				921,500	3%	950,000
Lost discount				19,000		

Supervisor

There will be no saving or cost here as the supervisor will continue to be fully employed.

Short-term lease contract

The space currently issued for the TD will generate sublet income of $12,000.

Summary of relevant costs and benefits

Cash flow	$
Saved contribution – TD	12,000
Lost contribution – other products	(71,000)
Labour	(3,700)
Lost discount	(19,000)
Sublet income	12,000
Net cash flow	69,700

It is **not worthwhile** to cease production of the TD now rather than waiting 12 months.

(b) **Pricing strategies**

Complementary pricing

Since the washing machine and the tumble dryer are products that tend to be used together, Stay Clean could **link their sales** with a complementary price. For example they could offer customers a discount on the second product bought, so if they buy a TD for $80 then they can get a WM for at a discounted price.

Product line pricing

All the products tend to be **related** to each other and used in the utility room or kitchen. If customers are upgrading their utility room or kitchen, a sale may involve all three products. A package price could be offered and as long as Stay Clean make a **contribution** on the overall deal then they will be better off.

41 Bits and Pieces

Text references. Incremental costs and revenues are covered in Chapters 5 and 6.

Top tips. In part (a), use a clear layout, read the information carefully and make sure you state which costs should be excluded rather than not mentioning them at all.

Easy marks. There are plenty of easy marks available for the calculations in part (a).

Examiner's comments. Marks gained for part (a) were reasonable but the incremental heating cost was often incorrectly calculated for the whole year, rather than just the winter months as stated in the question.

This question required some common business sense which was lacking in many candidates with a lack of understanding or experience demonstrated in part (b).

Marking scheme

			Marks
(a)	Existing total sales	1	
	Existing total gross profit	1	
	New sales	1	
	New gross profit	1	
	Incremental gross profit	1	
	Existing purchasing	1	
	Discount allowed for	1	
	Incremental Sunday purchasing costs	1	
	Staff cost	1	
	Lighting cost and heating cost	1	
	Manager's bonus	1	
			11
(b)	Customer buying pattern	2	
	Customer dissatisfaction	2	
	Reputation of B&P	2	
			max 4
			15

(a) **Incremental revenue**

	Sales	*Gross profit*	*Gross profit*
	$	%	$
Average	10,000	70	
Sunday (60% more than average)	16,000	50	8,000
Annual Sunday sales (50 weeks)	800,000	50	400,000

Purchasing costs

Current annual spending = 50 weeks × 6 days × 10,000 × 30%
= $900,000

New annual spending with discount = (900,000 + 400,000) × 95%
= $1,235,000

Incremental purchasing cost = $(1,235,000 – 900,000)
= $335,000

Staff costs

Additional staff costs on a Sunday = 5 sales assistants × 6 hours × 50 weeks × 1.5 × $20
= $45,000

Manager's costs

The salary of the manager is a sunk cost and there will be no additional costs for his time.
He will be entitled to an extra bonus of 1% × $800,000 = $8,000

Lighting costs

50 weeks × 6 hours × $30 = $9,000

Heating costs

25 weeks × 8 hours × $45 = $9,000

Rent

The rent of the store is a sunk cost so is not relevant to this decision.

Net incremental revenue

Net incremental revenue = 800,000 – (335,000 + 45,000 + 9,000 + 9,000 + 8,000)
= **$394,000**

Conclusion

Incremental revenue exceeds incremental costs by $394,000 so Sunday opening is **financially justifiable**.

(b) **Price discounts and promotions**

B & P plans to offer substantial discounts and promotions on a Sunday to attract customers. This may indeed be a good **marketing strategy** to attract people to shop on a Sunday, but it is not necessarily good for the business.

Customer buying pattern

B & P wants to attract **new** customers on a Sunday but customers may simply **change the day** they do their shopping in order to take advantage of the discounts and promotions. The effect of this would be to **reduce the margin** earned from customer purchases and not increase revenue.

Customer dissatisfaction

Customers who buy goods at full price and then see their purchases for sale at lower prices on a Sunday may be disgruntled. They could then complain or switch their custom to another shop.

The **reputation** of B & P could be damaged by this marketing policy, especially if customers associate lower prices with **lower quality**.

42 BDU Co

Text reference. Risk and uncertainty techniques are covered in Chapter 7.

Top tips. The trickiest part of part (a) is dealing with the minimax regret decision rule. You do need to have a good understanding not only of how to do the calculations but also what they mean.

Part (b) is straightforward application of knowledge but do make sure you apply it to this specific company.

Marking scheme

			Marks
(a)	Discussion and application of maximax rule	2	
	Discussion and application of maximin rule	3	
	Discussion and application of minimax regret rule	5	
			10
(b)	Use of EV	1	
	Use of sensitivity analysis	2	
	Discussion of how BDU could use the techniques	2	
			5
			15

(a) **Maximax**

The **maximax criterion** looks at the **best possible results**. Maximax means 'maximise the maximum profit'. In this case, we need to **maximise the maximum contribution.**

Demand/price	*Maximum contribution*
1,000/$425	$255,000
730/$500	$240,900
420/$600	$180,600

BDU would therefore set a price of **$425**.

Maximin

The **maximin** decision rule involves choosing the outcome that offers the **least unattractive worst outcome**, in this instance choosing the outcome which **maximises the minimum contribution.**

Demand/price	*Minimum contribution*
1,000/$425	$165,000
730/$500	$175,200
420/$600	$142,800

BDU would therefore set a price of **$500**.

Minimax regret

The **minimax regret** decision rule involves choosing the **outcome that minimises the maximum regret** from making the wrong decision, in this instance choosing the outcome which **minimises the opportunity loss** from making the wrong decision.

We can use the calculations performed in (a) to draw up an **opportunity loss table.**

Variable cost		*Price*	
	$425	*$500*	*$600*
$170	–	$14,100	$74,400 (W1)
$210	–	$3,300	$51,200 (W2)
$260	$10,200	–	$32,400 (W3)
Minimax regret	$10,200	$14,100	$74,400

Minimax regret strategy (price of $425) is that which minimises the maximum regret ($10,200).

Workings

1 At a variable cost of $170 per day, the best strategy would be a price of $425. The opportunity loss from setting a price of $600 would be $(255,000 – 180,600) = $74,400.

2 At a variable cost of $210 per day, the best strategy would be a price of $425. The opportunity loss from setting a price of $600 would be $(215,000 – 163,800) = $51,200.

3 At a variable cost of $260 per day, the best strategy would be a price of $500. The opportunity loss from setting a price of $600 would be $(175,200 – 142,800) = $32,400.

(b) **Expected values**

Where probabilities are assigned to different outcomes we can evaluate the worth of a decision as the **expected value**, or weighted average, of these outcomes. The principle is that when there are a number of alternative decisions, each with a range of possible outcomes, the optimum decision will be the one which gives the highest expected value. The expected value will **never actually occur.**

Expected values are more valuable as a guide to decision making where they refer to outcomes which will occur **many times over**. Examples would include the probability that so many customers per day will buy a can of baked beans, the probability that a customer services assistant will receive so many phone calls per hour, and so on.

We have not been given information on probabilities of each demand occurring for BDU's pushchairs and it is unlikely that demand will be sufficiently predictable to use this technique successfully.

Sensitivity analysis

Sensitivity analysis can be used in any situation so long as the relationships between the key variables can be established. Typically this involves changing the value of a variable and seeing how the results are affected.

For example, BDU could use sensitivity analysis to estimate by **how much costs and revenues would need to differ** from their estimated values before the decision would change, or to estimate whether it would change if estimated costs were **x% higher** than estimated, or estimated revenues **y% lower** than estimated.

Sensitivity analysis can help to **concentrate management attention** on the most important factors and can be particularly useful when launching a new product.

43 Gym Bunnies

Text reference. Decision trees and calculating the value of perfect information are covered in Chapter 7 of the BPP Study Text.

Top tips. Always draw decision trees with a pencil initially, and use a ruler to make the tree as neat as possible. Clearly label all branches of the decision tree as well as any decision/outcome points. Ensure that you include all probabilities and cash flows on the tree diagram to assist in your calculations of expected values and to maximise your score.

To calculate the EV of perfect information, remember that perfect information only has value if it would lead to a change in the decision by producing a better result (in this case higher net income). Calculate what this difference would be and multiply it by the probability that this outcome will occur.

Easy marks. There are easy marks available for producing a well-structured decision tree. Sketch an answer in rough if you are not sure. When you think you know what the structure of the decision tree should be, draw it neatly.

Examiner's comments. Despite some labelling issues, a good number of candidates scored nearly full marks on part (a), maybe just losing half a mark for failing to multiply their values up by three to reflect the three-year period, or for failing to deduct the expansion cost of $360,000.

Part (b) was a very different story. This asked candidates to calculate the maximum price that the company should pay for perfect information about the expansion's exact effect on membership numbers. Very few candidates answered part (b) correctly. Candidates must revise this area well.

Marking scheme

			Marks
(a)	Decision tree diagram:		
	Start with decision point	0.5	
	Option 1 format	0.5	
	Option 2 format	4.0	
	Expected value and decision:		
	EV at A	1.0	
	EV at B	1.0	
	EV at C	2.0	
	Compare EVs at D	1.0	
	Recommendation that follows	1.0	
			11
(b)	Price of perfect information:		
	EV with 6,000 members, option 2	1.0	
	Compare with EV of option 1	1.0	
	Price of perfect information	2.0	
			4
			15

(a) See decision tree on next page.

Workings

Net income per member, per annum

Option 1: \$720 – \$80 = \$640 per annum

Option 2:

If costs \$120 per annum: \$720 – \$120 = \$600 per annum

If costs \$180 per annum: \$720 – \$180 = \$540 per annum

Expected values

EV at A = (0.5 × \$600 × 6,000) + (0.5 × \$540 × 6,000) = \$3.42m per annum

EV at B = (0.5 × \$600 × 6,500) + (0.5 × \$540 × 6,500) = \$3.705m per annum

EV at C = (0.4 × \$3.42m) + (0.6 × \$3.705m) = \$3.591m per annum

Decision

At D, compare EV of:

Option 1 = \$10.08m (3 years × \$3.36m per annum)

Option 2 = \$10.413m (3 years × \$3.591m – \$0.360m)

The expected value is higher with option 2; therefore expand the exercise studio.

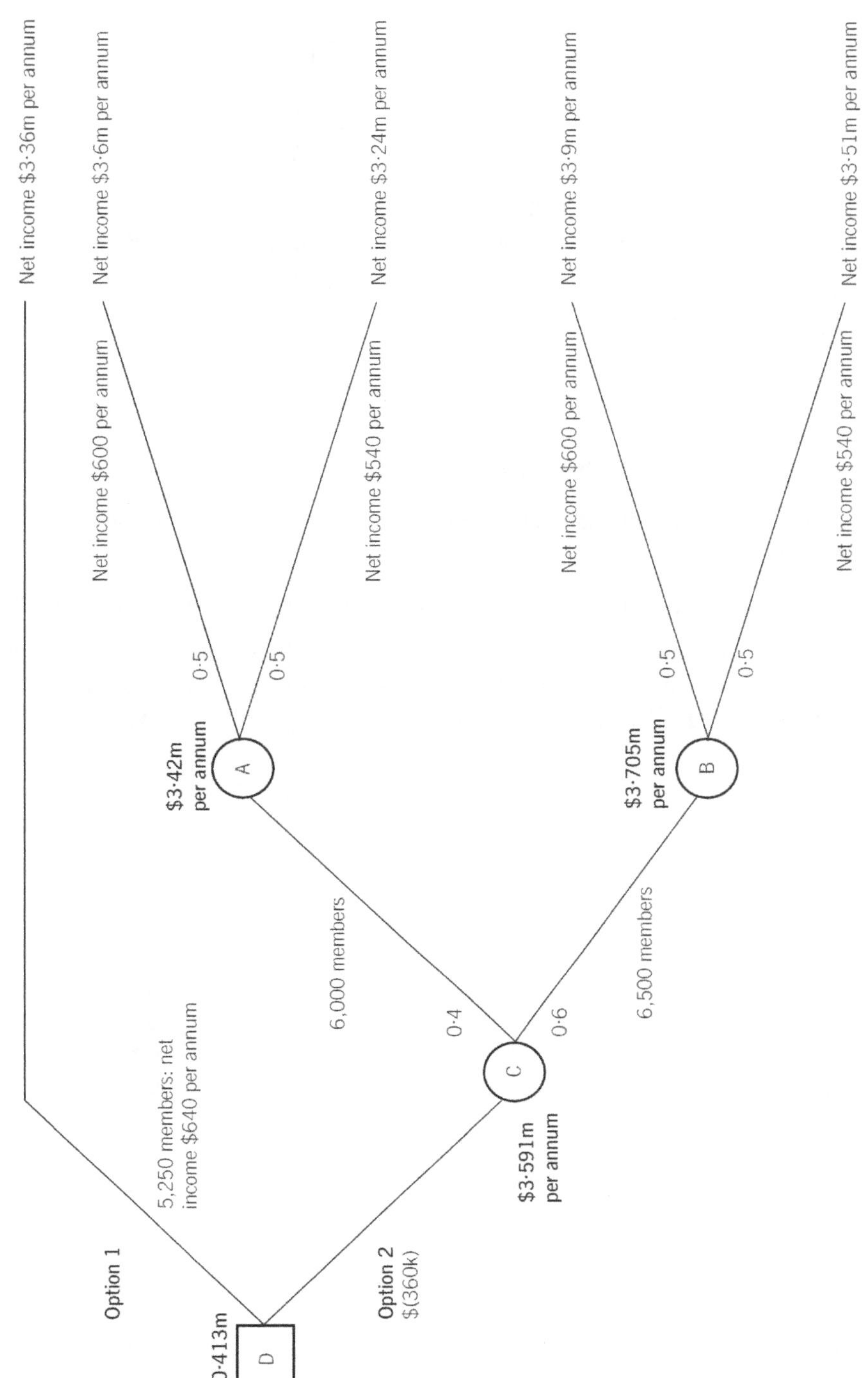

(b) **Maximum price that GB should pay for perfect information**

Perfect information has value only if it changes the decision from what it would otherwise have been. In the case of membership numbers, perfect information may result in a decision to choose option 1 rather than option 2, but only if membership numbers remain at 6,000.

(**Tutorial note**: Since option 2 has a higher EV of net income, it must be preferable to option 1 if membership numbers increase to 6,500.)

Option 1 will produce total net income over three years of $3.36m × 3 = $10.08 million

With option 2, if membership numbers are **6,000**:

	$m
EV = $3.42m per annum × 3 years	10.26
Less capital cost of exercise studio	(0.360)
	9.900

Therefore, with membership numbers of only 6,000 by choosing option 2, GB would choose option 1 instead, because the EV of net income over three years would be $0.18 million ($180,000) higher.

There is a 40% probability that membership numbers will be 6,000 with option 2; therefore the EV of perfect information is 0.40 × $180,000 = $72,000.

44 SH

Text reference. Risk and uncertainty is covered in Chapter 7.

Top tips. Part (a) is straightforward provided you read the information carefully and use a clear layout and workings. Make sure you relate you answer in part (b) to the specific circumstances of SH.

Easy marks. There are plenty of easy marks available for explanations even if you struggle with the calculations.

Examiner's comments. Part (a) was reasonably done by many but problems included a lack of understanding of information in the scenario, failing to include the goodwill adjustment and trying to calculate expected sales first then work out some sort of answer accordingly. Candidates often struggled to apply their knowledge to the question in part (b).

Marking scheme

			Marks
(a)	Profit calculations:		
	Small van sales	0.5	
	Small van VC	0.5	
	Small van goodwill or VC adjustment	0.5	
	Small van depreciation	0.5	
	Medium van – as above for small van	3.0	
	Large van – as above for small van	3.0	
	Presentation of profits table	1.0	
			9
(b)	Risk attitude issue	1.0	
	Optimist view	1.0	
	Pessimist view	1.0	
	Expected value calculation	1.0	
	Expected value discussion	1.0	
	Conclusion	1.0	
			6
			15

(a) **Profits table**

	Small van	*Medium van*	*Large van*
Capacity	100	150	200
Low demand (120 crates)	300 (W1)	468 (W3)	368 (W5)
High demand (190 crates)	300 (W2)	500 (W4)	816 (W6)

Working	*1*	*2*	*3*	*4*	*5*	*6*
Sales	1,000	1,000	1,200	1,500	1,200	1,900
Variable costs	(400)	(400)	(480)	(600)	(480)	(760)
Goodwill	(100)	(100)		(100)		
Variable cost adjustment at 10%			48		48	76
Depreciation	(200)	(200)	(300)	(300)	(400)	(400)
Profit	300	300	468	500	368	816

(b) The decision as to which van to buy depends on the managers' attitudes to risk.

Risk averse

If the managers are pessimistic and becoming **more cautious**, they will choose the van with the least unattractive worst outcome (the maximin criterion). This is the medium van with a profit of $468.

Risk taker

If the managers are **optimistic** about the future, they would choose the van with the best possible outcome (the maximax criteria). This is the large van as this has the highest profit of $816.

Expected values

Expected values support a **risk neutral attitude** and are used when a decision is being made more than once.

The expected values for this situation are:

Small van: $300
Medium van: ($468 × 0.4) + ($500 × 0.6) = $487
Large van: ($368 × 0.4) + (816 × 0.6) = $637

The large van therefore has the highest expected value.

Conclusion

The managers have become more cautious as the business has become more competitive so the medium van is probably the most likely to be chosen.

45 Gam Co

Text reference. Risk and uncertainty is covered in Chapter 7.

Top tips. Part (a) is straightforward provided you read the information carefully and use a clear layout and workings. Make sure you make a recommendation in your answer in part (b). Know the difference between maximin, minimax and maximax for part (c).

Examiner's comments. This was a very well answered question. Where mistakes were made it was through inaccurate reading of the question, incorrectly applying probabilities to profit figures (part (b)), or failure to recommend which option Gam Co would choose (part (b)). In part c, some candidates mixed up maximin with minimax regret or maximax and consequently gave the wrong explanation and recommendation.

Marking scheme

			Marks
(a)	Profit calculations:		
	Unit contribution up to 100,000 units	1	
	Unit contribution above 100,000 units	1	
	Each line of table for price of $30 (3 in total)	3	
	Each line of table for price of $35 (3 in total)	3	
			8

			Marks
(b)	Expected values		
	Expected value for $30	1.5	
	Expected value for $35	1.5	
	Recommendation	1	
			4
(c)	Maximin		
	Explanation	2	
	Decision	1	
			3
			15

(a) **Profit outcomes**

	$30	*$35*
Price per unit		
Contribution to 100,000 units ($30/$35 - $12)	$18	$23
Contribution above 100,000 units ($30/$35 - $11)	$19	$24

	1	*2*	*3*	*4*	*5*	*6*
	$	$	$	$	$	$
Sales price	30	30	30	35	35	35
Sales volume (units)	120,000	110,000	140,000	108,000	100,000	94,000
Unit contribution	19	19	19	24	23	23
Total contribution	2,280,000	2,090,000	2,660,000	2,592,000	2,300,000	2,162,000
Fixed costs	(450,000)	(450,000)	(450,000)	(450,000)	(450,000)	(450,000)
Advertising costs	(900,000)	(900,000)	(900,000)	(970,000)	(970,000)	(970,000)
Profit	930,000	740,000	1,310,000	1,172,000	880,000	742,000

(b) **Expected values**

	1	*2*	*3*	*4*	*5*	*6*
Sales price	**$30**	**$30**	**$30**	**$35**	**$35**	**$35**
Sales volume (units)	120,000	110,000	140,000	108,000	100,000	94,000
Profit	$930,000	$740,000	$1,310,000	$1,172,000	$880,000	$742,000
Probability	0.4	0.5	0.1	0.3	0.3	0.4
Ev OF Profit ($)	$372,000	$370,000	$131,000	$351,600	$264,000	$296,800
Totals			$873,000			$912,400

Using the expected value of profit as the basis for decision, a sales price of $35 should be chosen as it gives the highest expected value.

(c) **Maximin decision rule**

The maximin decision rule involves choosing the outcome that offers the least unattractive worst outcome, in this instance choosing the outcome which maximises the minimum profit. Management would therefore choose a selling price of $35, which has a lowest possible profit of $742,000. This is better than the worst possible outcome from a selling price of $30, which would provide a profit $740,000.

Question 46

46.1 C (Syllabus area C2(b))

There is likely to be a demotivating effect where an ideal standard of performance is set, because adverse efficiency variances will always be reported. It is important that adverse variances are not used to lay blame if targets have been set with the aim of motivation.

A low standard of efficiency is also demotivating, because there is no sense of achievement in attaining the required standards. Managers and employees will often outperform the standard or target when in fact they could have performed even better if they had been sufficiently motivated.

46.2 B (Syllabus area C4(a))

The mix variance is adverse because there is a higher proportion than expected of the more expensive Ingredient A in the actual production mix, and so a smaller than expected proportion of the cheaper Ingredient B.

To calculate a materials yield variance, we need information about actual and standard quantities of the ingredients used to make the actual production quantities. This data has not been provided.

46.3 B (Syllabus area C6(a))

Cumulative output	*Learning rate*	*Average time per batch*
Batches		Hours
1		45.00
2	75%	33.75
4	75%	25.3125
8	90%	22.78125

46.4 D (Syllabus area C5(a))

Administration costs are 100% fixed costs

	Production costs	*Selling costs*
	$'000	$'000
Cost of 7,000 units	231	19
Cost of 5,000 units	195	15
Variable cost of 2,000 units	36	4
Variable cost per unit	$18	$2
	$'000	$'000
Total cost of 5,000 units	195	15
Variable cost of 5,000 units	90	10
Fixed costs	105	5

	$'000
Variable cost of making 6,000 units (× $18)	108
Variable cost of selling 5,500 units (× $2)	11
Fixed costs (105 + 35 + 5)	145
Total budgeted cost allowance	264

46.5 B (Syllabus area C1(c))

An example of feedforward control is using the information from a forecast, rather than a historical result, to decide on appropriate control measures.

46.6 B (Syllabus area C2(b))

The zero base budgeting process seeks to identify short-term benefits and improvements, and there is a risk that these may be implemented at the expense of longer-term objectives. ZBB calls for management skills that managers often lack.

46.7 A (Syllabus area C3(e))

There may be a tendency to accept the figures produced by a spreadsheet without challenging the assumptions on which the figures have been prepared. Spreadsheets have greater practical application to budgeting for smaller business operations or restricted areas of operations, where the number of variables in the model is fairly limited. For more complex business operations, larger and more complex budgeting models are likely to be required.

46.8 C (Syllabus area C5(a))

This answer calculates the yield variance in terms of litres input.

	Litres of input
4,000 litres of output should require (× 10/9)	4,444.44
They did require	5,100.00
Yield variance in litres of input material	655.56 (A)
Standard weighted average price per litre of input	$2
Yield variance in $	$1,311 (A)

46.9 D (Syllabus area C7(c))

Planning variances may be the responsibility of 'senior management', but in practice this often means that no one takes responsibility for something that was 'unavoidable'. A severe criticism of planning and operational variances is the lack of objectivity that may be involved in deciding in retrospect what the standard cost should have been.

46.10 D (Syllabus area C7(c))

The planning variance for the labour rate is $2.50 per hour. It is an adverse variance, because the revised labour rate is more expensive than the original standard hourly rate. Applied to the actual hours worked, this gives a labour rate planning variance of 3,500 hours × $2.50 (A) = $8,750 (A).

Question 47

47.1 B (Syllabus area C2(b))

In ABB, the amount of resources allocated to each activity should be decided by the amount or level of the activity in the budget. An organisation should provide sufficient resources to ensure that the activity can be performed at the budgeted level of volume.

In ABB, a basic assumption is that by managing cost drivers, it should be possible to control costs more effectively than simply focusing on levels of expenditure.

47.2 B (Syllabus area C4(a))

Standard costing is not well suited to production where items are made to customer specifications. This is because items are not produced to standard specifications on which a standard cost can be based.

Similarly, standard costing is not consistent with a philosophy of continuous improvement and TQM, because if improvements are continually achieved, the standard costs will have to be continually reviewed and revised.

47.3 B (Syllabus area C6(a))

There are no standard profit figures, so the sales quantity variance should be calculated as a standard contribution figure.

Weighted average standard contribution per unit = [(5,000 × $8) + (3,000 × $14) + (2,000 × $16)]/(5,000 + 3,000 + 2,000) = $11.40 per unit.

Actual total sales = 10,300 units. Budgeted total sales = 10,000 units.

Sales quantity variance = 300 units (F) × $11.40 = $3,420 (F).

47.4 A (Syllabus area C5(a))

	Actual mix	Standard mix	Mix variance	Std price	Mix variance
	Litres	Litres	Litres	$	$
W	523	500	23 (A)	3	69 (A)
X	238	200	38 (A)	6	228 (A)
Y	239	300	61 (F)	4	244 (F)
	1,000	1,000	0		53 (A)

47.5 D (Syllabus area C2(b))

There are usually performance targets in a budget, but with incremental budgeting these are often not challenging. There is no incentive with incremental budgeting for managers to reduce costs; on the contrary, there is an incentive for managers to make sure that they spend up to their budget limit in order to retain the spending in next year's budget.

47.6 B (Syllabus area C2(b))

These reasons were given by the F5 examiner in an article on incremental and zero based budgeting. In private sector companies, objectives and outputs are fairly easy to identify, at least in the short term, as sales and profits. In the public sector, there are multiple non-financial objectives and many different ways of measuring output which creates complexity in the process. Budgeting within a spending limit should not necessarily make budgeting a difficult task.

47.7 A (Syllabus area C8(e))

An attainable standard provides a challenge to improve performance, for which bonuses should be paid. Ideal standards are too challenging and could be de-motivating. Current standards provide no incentive to improve. With basic standards, employees would be rewarded for efficiency improvements already achieved in the past.

47.8 A (Syllabus area C3(c))

b = log 0.85/log 2 = –0.0705811/0.30103 = –0.2344653

Average time to produce first 8 units = 800 × 0.85 × 0.85 × 0.85 = 491.30 hours

Average time to produce first 9 units = 800 × $9^{-0.2344653}$ = 800 × 5.3765756 = 477.917827 hours

	Hours
Total time for first 8 units (8 × 491.30)	3,930.40
Total time for first 9 units (9 × 477.917287)	4,301.26
Time for the 9th unit	370.86

47.9 C (Syllabus area C8(c))

Managers usually give budgeting too much of their time. Budgets protect rather than reduce costs because managers have a 'use it or lose it' mentality to spending their full budget expenditure allowance. Budgets discourage innovation and initiative because managers are discouraged from taking actions that are 'not in the budget'.

47.10 D (Syllabus area C3(a))

The high-low method takes the highest and lowest available activity/output levels.

	$
Total cost of 48,000 units	274,800
Total cost of 32,000 units	225,200
Variable cost of 16,000 units	49,600

Variable cost per unit = $49,600/16,000 = $3.1

	$
Total cost of 48,000 units	274,800
Variable cost of 48,000 units (× $3.1)	148,800
Fixed costs	126,000

Question 48

48.1 C (Syllabus area C8(e))

If targets are not communicated, they cannot provide an incentive, but they cannot be a disincentive either.

If targets are set at high levels that cannot realistically be achieved, this can be demotivating. Demotivation can also occur if targets are imposed by senior management; or if control reports are provided late so that the manager responsible is unable to take prompt action to deal with problems that may arise.

48.2 A (Syllabus area C7(d))

Operational variances compare actual performance with a realistic standard cost or budget, and so should provide a realistic reflection of what the causes of the variances have cost the organisation (in terms of cash flow or profit).

Planning variances are not the responsibility of operational managers, but their causes should be investigated, since lessons may be learned for the future.

48.3 D (Syllabus area C6(b))

In a competitive market, sales management are in a position to influence market share, for example through advertising, sales promotions and pricing initiatives. However it is difficult to influence total market size, because in a competitive market this is usually outside operational managers' control.

48.4 A (Syllabus area C3(a))

	$
Total cost of 38,000 units	282,000
Total cost of 24,000 units	247,000
Variable cost of 14,000 units	35,000

Variable cost per unit = $35,000/14,000 = $2.50

	$
Total cost of 38,000 units	282,000
Variable cost of 38,000 units (× $2.50)	95,000
Fixed costs	187,000

48.5 B (Syllabus area C3(c))

Average labour cost for first 39 batches = $\$50 \times 39^{-0.3219281}$ = $15.3731052
Average labour cost for first 40 batches = $\$50 \times 40^{-0.3219281}$ = $15.2483157

	$
Total labour cost for first 40 batches (× $15.2483157)	609.93
Total labour cost for first 39 batches (× $15.3731052)	599.55
Labour cost for the 40th batch	10.38

Standard variable cost per batch, including materials at $10, = $20.38. (Materials costs are not affected by the learning curve.)

48.6 D (Syllabus area C2(b))

By producing new plans at regular intervals, such as every three months, there may be a tendency for management to focus in changes to the plan rather than aspects of performance that should be controlled. They are time-consuming, and are only worthwhile when there is continual and substantial uncertainty about the future. (A simpler alternative if needed is to amend the annual budget when the budget is clearly unrealistic or out-of-date, by preparing an updated annual budget.)

48.7 D (Syllabus area C2(c))

The ranking process is used in ZBB to allocate resources to management budgets and activities within management budgets. However, ZBB is time-consuming and costly, and is likely to be a worthwhile undertaking every few years rather than every year (with incremental budgeting in the intervening years).

48.8 D (Syllabus area C5(a))

This answer calculates the yield variance in terms of litres output.

	Litres of output
5,750 litres of input should produce (× 100/120)	4,791.67
They did produce	5,000.00
Yield variance in litres of output	208.33 (F)
Standard material cost per litre of output	$2.70
Yield variance in $	$562.50 (F)

48.9 B (Syllabus area C5(d))

Rate of wastage = 500/8,000 = 6.25%
Average cost of input = $31,000/8,000 kg = $3.88 per kg produced
Output: input conversion ratio = 7,500:8,000 = 93.75%
Materials yield variance cannot be calculated without a figure for standard loss in input.

48.10 C (Syllabus area C7(c))

Training may help employees to improve their efficiency in a job. Overtime working should increase output, but there is no reason why it should improve efficiency (output per hour worked). Extra inspection and testing may reduce efficiency by taking up more time: they will not improve efficiency, because they do not test efficiency, only quality. Output capacity relates to potential output volume, not efficiency of working: for example output capacity may be increased by hiring extra workers, but this does not affect productivity.

Question 49

49.1 C (Syllabus area C2(b))

If it is difficult to forecast or plan costs and revenues accurately for more than three months ahead, it would be appropriate to prepare new annual budgets every three months, giving most emphasis to the budget for the next three-month period. The disadvantage is that this would require four annual budgets in every 12-month period.

49.2 A (Syllabus area C1(c))

The use of variances and key performance indicators are examples of feedback, but are not a general term for control information.

49.3 C (Syllabus area C2(b))

When senior managers impose budgets on managers below them in the organisation hierarchy, there is a risk that the imposed budgets will be unrealistic because senior managers may not have a full understanding of operational realities.

49.4 B (Syllabus area C3(c))

Standard costs are applicable in industries where learning curve applies, provided that enough units are made of each new product so that the labour time per additional unit eventually becomes close to a standard amount. Companies may sell early units of a new product at a loss in order to boost sales demand, so that labour costs (and unit costs) will fall to the point where a profit is made at that sales price.

49.5 A (Syllabus area C3(b))

When $Y = ax^b$, b = log 0.90/log 2 = -0.0457575/0.30103 = –0.1520031

Average labour time for first 49 batches = 2,000 × $49^{-0.1520031}$ = 2,000 × 0.5534584 = 1,106.916731 hours

Average labour time for first 50 batches = 2,000 × $50^{-0.1520031}$ = 2,000 × 0.5517614 = 1,103.522743

	Hours
Total labour time for first 50 units (× 1,103.522743)	55,176.14
Total labour time for first 49 units (× 1,106.916731)	54,238.92
Labour cost for the 50th batch	937.22

Standard time = 937 hours. Actual time = 980 hours. Labour efficiency variance for this unit = 43 hours (A) × $15 = $645 (A).

49.6 C (Syllabus area C7(b))

With road haulage and distribution, drivers' times on the road are measured automatically. Variable costs can be high (labour and fuel, for example). Standard costing is more common in manufacturing but in principle can be applied to service industries. The problem is to identify a standard item for which a cost can be measured and variances subsequently calculated. In road haulage for example a standard measure may be cost per tonne/kilometre delivered: this does not lend itself easily to variance analysis.

49.7 C (Syllabus area C7(c))

Excessive usage of materials is reported as a usage variance, not a price variance. The production manager should be responsible for price variances when he/she has responsibility for materials purchasing, or when the production department asks for an urgent materials order, resulting in higher purchasing prices than normal.

49.8 D (Syllabus area C5(a))

	Actual mix	*Standard mix*	*Mix variance*	*Std price*	*Mix variance*
	kg	kg	kg	$	$
P	820	750	70 (A)	3.0	210 (A)
Q	1,740	1,500	240 (A)	2.5	600 (A)
R	2,300	2,250	50 (A)	4.0	200 (A)
S	2,640	3,000	360 (F)	5.25	1,890 (F)
	7,500	7,500	0		880 (F)

49.9 D (Syllabus area C7(c))

Material usage is within the control of a production manager, whereas material price variances are usually the responsibility of the purchasing manager. Line managers are responsible for operational variances, but planning variances are commonly assumed to be the responsibility of someone in senior management.

49.10 B (Syllabus area C5(b))

Mix variances should only be calculated when a product contains two or more materials that can be mixed together in different proportions. For example, calculating a mix variance for the production of a bicycle out of its component parts would be meaningless. It is important to be aware of the interdependence between variances: a favourable mix variance – meaning a cheaper mix of materials in a product – may result in adverse total output of the product (adverse yield).

Question 50

50.1 D (Syllabus area C4(c))

Flexible budgets enable actual results to be compared with expected results for the same volume of activity, such as production and sales. To reconcile an original budgeted profit to actual profit with variances there must be a sales volume variance (measured in terms of either budgeted/standard contribution or profit, depending on the type of costing system used).

50.2 A (Syllabus area C6(a))

The loss of the advertising campaign means that sales of Product Y will be less than budgeted, which should lead us to expect adverse sales volume variance for Y and an adverse sales quantity variance for both products together. The price discounting for Product Y should lead us to expect an adverse sales price variance. The increase in the proportion of Product X units sold in the total sales mix should lead us to expect a favourable sales mix variance, because Product X has a bigger standard contribution, both per unit and per $1 of standard sales price, than Product Y.

50.3 B (Syllabus area C4(d))

This should be a fundamental principle of management control, but it is not always applied in practice.

50.4 C (Syllabus area C6(a))

Mix and yield variances measure costs and output quantities, not quality. A potential problem is that persistent **favourable** mix variances may have an adverse effect on sales volume variances and direct labour efficiency variances, because the cheaper materials mix may affect the quality of the product sold to customers and also make the product more difficult to handle. These consequences could lead to adverse sales volume and labour efficiency variances.

50.5 B (Syllabus area C8(g))

Standard costing systems are not compatible with a Total Quality Management approach to operations. With standard costing, the aim is to achieve standard cost or perhaps obtain some favourable variances. With TQM, guiding principles are 'continuous improvement' and 'zero defects'. Existing standards and methods of operating are always unsatisfactory and improvements should always be sought. This is not compatible with a standard costing 'philosophy'.

Standard costing tends to be of little value in a rapidly changing environment because products are not standardised for a sufficient length of time to make the preparation of standard costs worthwhile.

50.6 C (Syllabus area C3(c))

Learning curves are more difficult to apply in teams with a high labour turnover, as it can affect efficiency and knowledge significantly. Learning rates are affected by time gaps between the production of additional units of a product, because acquired learning may be forgotten with the passage of time unless the work continues regularly.

50.7 A (Syllabus area C3(d))

If an EV is used as a value in a budget, it represents a weighted average value that may not be expected to occur. If so, comparing actual results against the budget for control purposes would have limited value. The use of expected values and probabilities in budgeting is most useful when there is some, but a limited, amount of uncertainty about the future. When uncertainty is very high, the use of probabilities becomes little more than guesswork.

50.8 A (Syllabus area C5(a))

Product	*Actual sales*	*Actual sales in std mix*	*Sales mix variance*	*Std profit*	*Sales mix variance*
	Units	Units	Units	$	$
X	700	750.0	50.0 (A)	10	500 (A)
Y	1,200	937.5	262.5 (F)	6	1,575 (F)
Z	350	562.5	212.5 (A)	12	2,550 (A)
	2,250	2,250.0	0		1,475 (A)

50.9 D (Syllabus area C8(h))

Formal arrangements for monitoring performance are very widely used. Budgetary control reporting (if not standard costing variance reports) is an effective way of providing control information and performance information.

50.10 D (Syllabus area C2(b))

In an article in *Student Accountant* on incremental budgeting and zero based budgeting, the examiner described two reasons why ZBB is often considered more suitable for public sector service organisations than for private sector companies. One is that ZBB is more suited to costs where there is a lot of discretionary spending, as in the public sector services. The second reason is that activities of public sector organisations are more easily definable and so can usually be put into decision packages. (For example the activities of a local authority can be grouped into packages for local housing local education, local refuse collection and waste disposal, and so on.)

Question 51

51.1 D (Syllabus area C3(e))

The advantages of spreadsheets in budgeting include time-saving in preparing figures and the ability to carry out sensitivity analysis by analysing the effect of alterations to the value of key variables. It is also relatively easy to prepare alternative draft budgets or new draft budgets, simply by altering the value of variables in the spreadsheet budget model.

51.2 B (Syllabus area C4(b))

A basic standard is left unchanged, so that changes in variances over time indicate a trend in prices and efficiency over time.

51.3 D (Syllabus area C6(b))

If the sales mix is not a controllable item, and managers do not have control over it, sales mix variances do not provide meaningful control information. Sales volume variances for individual products would be more appropriate. If a company is trying to encourage customers to shift from one product to another, sales mix variance could provide useful control information – although other measures of performance might be just as good and possibly more suitable.

51.4 C (Syllabus area C7(c))

	Kg
120 units of product should use (× 3.50)	420
They did use	410
Operational usage variance in kg	10 (F)

Operational usage variance in \$ (× Standard price per kg \$4) = \$40 (F)

51.5 A (Syllabus area C2(b))

Rolling budgets are most likely to be used when the business environment changes rapidly or unpredictably. Preparing budgets more regularly helps to keep them more realistic, reflecting changes that occur. A disadvantage of rolling budgets is that, because budgets are prepared more frequently, the costs of budget administration are likely to be higher.

51.6 C (Syllabus area C8(c))

Management accountants should take measures where necessary to improve the quality of budgetary control reports. They do not have responsibility for management, however; senior management may be responsible for using control reports as a pressure device.

51.7 D (Syllabus area C1(a))

Budgets are sometimes described as being at a 'middle level' in the planning hierarchy, between strategic planning and short-term operational planning. Budgets are used both as plans and as a system for monitoring performance (budgetary control).

51.8 A (Syllabus area C2(b))

With bottom-up budgeting, the budgets of managers at a lower level in the organisation are prepared separately and then combined into a total operating budget. This is easier in practice in a fairly small and simple organisation than in a large and complex one.

51.9 C (Syllabus area C2(b))

Incremental budgets discourage managers from questioning the continuing need for certain activities. Incremental budgeting is not well suited to budgets for discretionary items of spending, because when there is choice about the level of spending (for example on advertising and sales promotion), the basis for decision making should not be 'last year's budget plus an amount for inflation'.

51.10 B (Syllabus area C6(a))

	Budgeted sales	*Std profit*	*Budgeted profit*
	Units	$ per unit	$
X	800	10	8,000
Y	1,000	6	6,000
Z	600	12	7,200
	2,400		21,200

Weighted average standard profit per unit = $21,200/2,400 = $8.8333

Quantity variance in units = 2,400 – 2,250 = 150 units (A)

Quantity variance in $ (standard profit) = 150 (A) × $8.8333 = $1,325 (A)

52 GH Consultancy

Text references. Costing methods are covered in Chapter 2. The objectives of budgetary control are covered in Chapter 8.

Top tips. The amount of information provided in the question can be confusing at first. Once you get going, however, and adopt a systematic approach to analysing the data, you should be able to sort it out to arrive at the required rates. These common-sense questions do not often require much technical knowledge but you do need to spend some time thinking them through before diving in.

Question (b) uses the word 'monitor', so you need to think about how they could control their income and costs. This required a focus on budgets and variances, which require efficient methods for recording and analysing time and costs.

Marking scheme

			Marks
(a)	Calculation of:		
	Available hours		
	Chargeable time	0.5	
	Travelling time	1.0	
	Productive time	0.5	
	Weighted chargeable time	0.5	
	Hourly rate: productive client work	0.5	
	Hourly rate for travelling	1.0	
	Rate per mile travelled	1.0	
		1.0	
			6
(b)	Budget preparation	1	
	Cost collection	1	
	Time recording	1	
	Comparisons with budgets	1	
	Variances	1	
			max 4
			10

(a) **Analysis of available time**

		Hours
Total hours per annum: (8 × 5 × 45) × 2 people: available hours		3,600
Less administration time	25.0%	(900)
idle time	22.5%	(810)
Chargeable time		1,890
Travelling time (25% of chargeable time)		472.5
Productive time (75% of chargeable time)		1,417.5

Travelling time is to be charged at one third of the normal hourly rate.

'Weighted' chargeable time	=	1,417.5 + (472.5/3)
	=	1,575 hours
∴ Rate per productive hours	=	$62,100/1,575
Hourly rate for productive client work	=	$39.43 per hour
Hourly rate for travelling (÷ 3)	=	$13.14 per hour
Rate per mile travelled	=	$10,080/18,000
	=	$0.56 per mile

(b) (i) **Preparation of budgets**

Costs and income should be budgeted on a monthly basis, allowing for any seasonal fluctuations. Cost behaviour patterns should be taken into account, so that fixed and variable costs can be analysed separately in each month's budget.

(ii) **Cost collection system**

An efficient cost collection system must be established. All costs should be analysed between professional services and vehicle costs so that the hourly rate can be carefully monitored.

(iii) **Time recording system**

An efficient time recording system will also be required. G and H must record how they use all of their time, analysing it between the categories of idle time, travelling time, productive time and so on. Efficient time recording will obviously be necessary so that clients can be charged quickly and correctly.

(iv) **Comparison with budgets**

Actual costs and income can then be compared with the budget for the month. If variable costs are significant and there are wide variations in activity levels, the budget allowance can be flexed to give a realistic control target for the actual activity level achieved.

(v) **Use of variances**

Any variances can be highlighted and remedial action can be taken to ensure that G and H achieve their objectives.

53 Sauce Co

Text reference. Budgeting styles are covered in Chapters 8 and 9.

Top tips. Aim to make five well-explained points.

Easy marks. There should be plenty of easy marks available. Remember to relate your answer to the scenario.

Examiner's comments. The question asked for a discussion of the impact of the top-down budgeting style being used. Many candidates scored full marks and some really good points were made.

Marking scheme

	Marks
Likely impact – 2 marks per point discussed	10

Business

Production volumes are currently based on **anticipated sales** rather than actual orders. As the managing director has overestimated sales, it is likely that Sauce Co has a large inventory of **perishable products**. Both inventory holding costs and the cost of disposing waste are likely to be high.

Sauce Co is likely to have too many staff, assuming **staffing levels** are based on forecast production volumes. Production is likely to slow down when it becomes apparent that sales of the sauces are lower than expected, resulting in **idle time** within the workforce. As well as being costly to the company, workers are likely to become de-motivated.

If inventory is held for some time (due to sales being lower than forecast), customers may receive goods that are close to the **expiry date** (the sauces must be used within three months). This could result in **poor customer feedback** and be damaging for the company's reputation.

Staff

Budgets at Sauce Co are **imposed by the managing director**. As such, operational managers are unlikely to voice their ideas and will not feel **valued**.

The absence of a participative style of budgeting is likely to adversely impact **staff morale** as they have not been involved in the budgeting process and have not had a chance to express their views.

Staff have not received a bonus for three years due to **unachievable sales targets**. This is likely to create a feeling amongst employees that 'all targets are unachievable' and that the bonus scheme is pointless. Team spirit is likely to be low and staff will not be motivated to work at an optimum level – many will do the bare minimum.

54 Wargrin

Text reference. Lifecycle costing is covered in Chapter 2c and budgeting in Chapter 9.

Top tips. Make sure you apply your answers to the specific circumstances of Wargrin. You need to use the high-low method to calculate the variable and fixed costs in part (a). Read the question carefully to make sure you answer the specific requirements.

Easy marks. The calculations in part (a) should provide plenty of easy marks provided you are happy with the high-low technique.

Examiner's comments. The calculations in part (a) were quite well done by most but a depressing number of candidates could not handle the stepped fixed cost aspect. A large number of candidates simply ignored the given targets in the assessment of performance. Far too many simply provided a description of figures without a qualitative comment.

Marking scheme

			Marks
(a)	Sales	1	
	Variable cost	1	
	Fixed cost	1	
	Marketing cost	1	
	Comments on profit performance	1	
	Consideration of all lifecycle costs	1	
			6
(b)	Why incremental budgeting is common – 1 mark per idea	max 2	
	Problems of incremental budgets – 1 mark per idea	max 2	
			4
			10

(a) **Budgeted results**

	Year 1	*Year 2*	*Year 3*	*Total*
	$	$	$	$
Sales revenue	240,000	480,000	120,000	840,000
Variable cost (W)	(40,000)	(80,000)	(20,000)	(140,000)
Fixed cost (W)	(80,000)	(120,000)	(80,000)	(280,000)
Marketing cost	(60,000)	(40,000)		(100,000)
Profit	60,000	240,000	20,000	320,000

Working

	Units	*Cost*
		$
Highest activity level	14,000	150,000
Lowest activity level	10,000	130,000
	4,000	20,000

Variable cost per unit = $20,000/4,000 units = $5

Fixed cost = Total cost – Variable cost

= 150,000 – (14,000 × 5)

= $80,000

If volumes exceed 15,000 units, fixed costs = $80,000 × 1.5 = $120,000

Assessment

The Stealth will make a **profit** in each of the three years with the highest profit in Year 2. In total, the **net profit margin** is 38% (320,000/840,000 × 100%) which is above the target 35%.

The **contribution rate** is 83% (30 – 5/30 × 100%) which is also above the expected 75%. This indicates that the production process is expected to be under control and reliable.

Wargrin may therefore be satisfied that using **traditional** performance measures, the Stealth will be successful. However, this fails to take into account the **design and development costs** of $300,000. If this is incorporated into the profit forecast, the profit is then only $20,000. This may still be acceptable but it does illustrate the importance of looking at costs throughout the **entire lifecycle**.

(b) **Incremental budgeting**

This is a traditional approach to budgeting which bases the budget on the current year's results plus an extra amount for estimated growth or inflation next year.

Why is it commonly used?

It is a **quick** and **relatively simple** process to prepare an incremental budget and people are usually comfortable and familiar with the technique.

The necessary information is usually **easily available** which again keeps the time needed and costs down.

Incremental budgeting is a reasonable procedure if current operations are as effective, efficient and economical as they can be. It is also appropriate for budgeting for costs such as staff salaries, which may be estimated on the basis of current salaries plus an increment for inflation and are hence administratively fairly easy to prepare.

Problems

In general, however, it is an **inefficient form of budgeting** as it **encourages slack** and **wasteful spending** to creep into budgets. Past inefficiencies are perpetuated because cost levels are rarely subjected to close scrutiny.

In a **rapidly changing** business environment, it is inappropriate as the past is not a reliable indicator of what will happen in the future. It can also be difficult to determine the level of the necessary increment.

55 Learning

Text reference. The learning curve is covered in Chapter 9.

Top tips. This is a straightforward computation problem that requires you to demonstrate your knowledge of the learning curve.

The main challenge is to calculate the cost of the 100th unit produced, because the learning effect ends after 100 units. It is important that you should be able to do this, because examination questions on the learning curve are likely to state that the learning effect ends after a given number of units have been produced.

Easy marks. Marks can be earned by calculating the labour time required for the first 100 units. More marks can be earned provided that you recognise how to calculate the labour time (and cost) for the 100th unit produced.

Examiner's comments. The question was tricky because it required candidates to calculate a revised life cycle cost per unit, taking into account the effect of the learning curve. Many candidates were easily able to score five marks for getting to the correct time per hour, after the first 100 units, of 0.33. It was after this that mistakes tended to be made because some people didn't really know how to progress from here.

Marking scheme

	Marks
Revised life cycle cost:	
Cost per unit and total cost of first 100	3
Cost per unit and total cost of first 99	3
Cost of 100th unit	1
Total cost in Year 1	1
Total cost in Year 2	1
Average cost over 2 years	1
	10

Revised life cycle cost for labour per unit

$Y = ax^b$

Where Y = cumulative average time per unit to produce x units

a = the time taken for the first unit of output

x = the cumulative number of units produced

b = the index of learning (log LR / log 2)

LR = the learning rate as a decimal

b = log 0.95/log 2

= -0.0740005 (given in the question)

A learning curve of 95% is expected to occur until the 100th unit has been completed.

Total labour time for first 100 units (x = 100)

The first unit is expected to take 0.5 hours (a = 0.5)

$Y = 0.5 \times 100^{-0.0740005}$

$= 0.5 \times 1/1.4060508$

= 0.3556 labour hours per unit

Therefore, labour time for 100 units = 0.3556 × 100 = 35.56 hours

Total labour time for 99 units

$Y = 0.5 \times 99^{-0.0740005}$

$= 0.5 \times 1/1.4050054$

= 0.3559 labour hours per unit

Therefore, labour time for 99 units = 0.3559 × 99 = 35.23 hours

Therefore, time for 100th unit = 35.56 hours – 35.23 hours = 0.33 hours

Total labour cost over life of product

First year

	Hours
100 units × 0.3556 hours per unit	36
99,900 units × 0.33 hours per unit	32,967
	33,003
at $24 per hour	$792,072

Second year

	Hours
200,000 units × 0.33 hours per unit	66,000
at $26 per hour	$1,716,000

Total revised life cycle cost for labour = $(792,072 + 1,716,000) = $2,508,072

Average labour cost per unit over the product life cycle = $2,508,072/300,000 = $8.36

56 HC

Text reference. Learning curves are covered in Chapter 9.

Top tips and easy marks. The calculations in this question require a logical approach and should be straightforward, provided you have practised this technique.

Examiner's comments. This was well done by many candidates despite it being a fairly demanding aspect of learning curves. A scientific calculator is essential and y should not be rounded.

Marking scheme

	Marks
Average time for 199th kitchen	1
Total time for 199 kitchens	1
Average time for 200th kitchen	1
Total time for 200 kitchens	1
200th kitchen time	1
Cost for first 200	1
Cost for next 400	1
Variable cost per hour	1
Fixed cost per month and hour	1
Cost summary	2
Maximum	10

Calculation of total cost

Cost	*Hours*	*Rate per hour*	*Total*
		$	$
Labour	9,247 (W1)	15	138,705
Variable overhead	9,247	8 (W2)	73,976
Fixed overhead	9,247	4 (W2)	36,988
Total cost			249,669

Workings

1 *Labour hours*

For 199 kitchens $y = ax^b$

$= 24 \times 199^{-0.074}$

$= 16.22169061$

Total time for 199 kitchens = 199×16.22169061

= 3,228.12 hours

For 200 kitchens $y = ax^b$

$= 24 \times 200^{-0.074}$

$= 16.21567465$

Total time for 200 kitchens = 200×16.21567465

= 3,243.13 hours

Time for the 200th kitchen = 3,243.13 – 3,228.12 = 15.01 hours

	Hours
1st 200 kitchens	3,243.13
Next 400 kitchens (15.01 × 400)	6,004.00
Total time	9,247.13

2 *Overheads*

	Hours	*Cost*
		$
Highest activity level	9,600	116,800
Lowest activity level	9,200	113,600
	400	3,200

Variable cost per hour = \$3,200/400 hours = \$8

Fixed cost = Total cost – Variable cost

= 116,800 – (9,600 × 8)

= \$40,000 per month

Annual fixed cost = \$40,000 × 12 = \$480,000

Fixed overhead absorption rate = \$480,000/120,000 hours = \$4 per hour

57 Mic Co

Text reference. The learning curve is covered in Chapter 9 of the BPP Study Text.

Top tips. There are quite a few calculations in this question, so you need to organise your presentation clearly and in a way that helps you to prepare your answer. Remember that every time output doubles, the cumulative average time per unit falls to the learning curve percentage figure of what the cumulative average time per unit was previously. You don't need the learning curve factor of -0.1844245 for most of your calculations.

The potential trick in the question is that the learning curve no longer applies in November, when the average time per batch is the same as the time required to produce the eighth batch in October. To calculate this time per batch, you need to calculate the average and total times for the seventh and eighth batches. The time for the 8th batch is the difference between the total times for the first seven and the first eight batches.

Easy marks. There are some easy marks to be won if you remember that every time output doubles the cumulative average time per unit is x% of what it was previously, where x is the learning curve percentage. If you can write your points reasonably quickly, there should be easy marks in the answer to part (b) too.

Marking scheme

			Marks
(a)	Cost each month: July and August (1 mark per month)	2	
	Cost each month: September and October (1.5 marks per month)	3	
	Cost in November	3	
			8
(b)	Maximum		2
			10

(a) Every time output doubles, the average time per batch is 88% of what it was previously. The learning curve effect ends in October and does not apply in November, when the average time per unit is the same as the time required to make the eighth batch in October.

Month	*Cumulative batches*	*Average time per batch*	*Total time*	*Incremental time in the month*	*Labour cost per month at \$12 per hour*
		Hours	Hours	Hours	\$
July	1	200.00	200.00	200.00	2,400
August	2	176.00	352.00	152.00	1,824
September	4	154.88	619.52	267.52	3,210
October	8	136.294	1,090.35	470.83	5,650

Average time to produce first 7 batches = 200 × 7 –0.1844245 = 200 × 1/1.4317157 = 139.6925 hours

Total time for first 7 batches = 7 × 139.6925 = 977.85 hours

Average time to produce first 7 batches = 200 × 8 –0.1844245 = 200 × 1/1.4674115 = 136.2944 hours

Total time for first 7 batches = 8 × 136.2944 = 1,090.35 hours

Time to make the 8th batch = 1,090.35 – 977.85 = 112.50 hours

Total labour cost in November = 8 batches × 112.50 per batch × $12 per hour = $10,800.

(b) The company sets selling prices on a cost plus basis, but in the first few months the cost per unit falls due to the 88% learning curve effect. The average time per batch was 200 hours for the first batch in July, but falls to 112.5 hours per batch from November onwards.

If cost plus pricing is used, and if the company wants to charge a stable price for its product, it should consider a cost plus price based on the longer-term unit cost from November onwards.

The company appears to have used actual cost plus to set the selling price on its initial batches, with the result that the price was high. This probably explains the disappointing initial sales.

Budgeting for labour time and labour costs should also take the learning curve into effect, because of the reduction in incremental labour time per batch in the months July – October.

58 Lock Co

Text references. Sales mix and quantity variances are covered in Chapter 11.

Top tips. As with all numerical requirements, show all of your workings in part (a). It is important to remember, however, that almost half the marks in the question are for the analysis of the variances in part (b).

Easy marks. There should be easy marks in part (a), but you need to be familiar with the method for calculating mix and yield variances. The question here asks for sales mix and yield variances, but the method is similar to calculating materials mix and yield variances.

Marking scheme

			Marks
(a)	Variance calculations:		
	Sales volume variance	2	
	Sales mix variance	2	
	Sales quantity variance	2	
			6
(b)	Likely reasons for variances:		
	1 mark per valid point		max 4
			10

(a) **Volume profit variance**

	Power Lock		Devil Lock
Budgeted sales	800 units		600 units
Actual sales	560 units		1,260 units
Sales volume variance in units	240 units (A)		660 units (F)
× standard margin per unit	× $5		× $3
Sales volume variance in $	$1,200 (A)		$1,980 (F)
Total sales volume variance		$780 (F)	

Sales mix variance

Top tips. The method for calculating the variance is as follows.

(i) Take the actual total of sales and convert this total into a standard or budgeted mix, on the assumption that sales should have been in the budgeted proportions or mix.

(ii) The difference between actual sales and 'standard mix' sales for each product is then converted into a variance by multiplying by the standard margin.

			Units
Total quantity sold (560 + 1,260)			1,820
Budgeted mix for actual sales:	4/7 Power Lock		1,040
	3/7 Devil Lock		780
			1,820

	'Should' mix Actual quantity Standard mix	*'Did' mix Actual quantity Actual mix*	*Difference*	*× Standard margin*	*Variance*
Power	1,040 units	560 units	480 (A)	× $5	$2,400 (A)
Devil	780 units	1,260 units	480 (F)	× $3	$1,440 (F)
	1,820 units	1,820 units	–		$960 (A)

Sales quantity variance

The sales quantity variance is calculated as follows.

	Actual sales Standard mix	*Standard sales Standard mix*	*Difference in units*	*× Standard profit*	*Variance*
Power	1,040 units	800 units	240 units (F)	× $5	$1,200 (F)
Devil	780 units	600 units	180 units (F)	× $3	$540 (F)
	1,820 units	1,400 units	420 units		$1,740 (F)

Alternative method of calculation, sales quantity variance

Weighted average budgeted profit per unit = $5,800/(800 + 600) units = $4.1428571

Quantity variance in units = Total budgeted sales – Total actual sales = 1,400 – 1,820 = 420 units (F)

Sales quantity variance = 420 units (F) × $4.1428571 = $1,740 (F)

Summary

	$
Sales mix variance	960 (A)
Sales quantity variance	1,740 (F)
Sales volume variance	780 (F)

Note. If an organisation uses standard marginal costing instead of standard absorption costing then standard contribution rather than standard profit margin is used in the calculations.

(b) The favourable **sales volume variance** indicates that a potential increase in profit was achieved as a result of the change in sales volume compared with the budgeted volume.

The **sales mix variance** is adverse due to the fact that a larger proportion of the less profitable Devil Lock was sold than budgeted.

Profit would have been $960 higher if the 1,820 units had been sold in the budgeted mix of Power Lock 4: Devil Lock 3.

The favourable **sales quantity variance** of $1,740 is the difference in profit because sales volumes of both products were higher than budgeted, possibly due to effective marketing campaigns.

Management are able to control the relative sales of each product through the **allocation of sales effort, advertising and sales promotion expenses**. However, if this is the case, the emphasis on marketing may have been on the less profitable Power Lock, resulting in the adverse mix variance.

On the other hand, total sales quantities were 420 units in excess of the budget, indicating that the marketing effort was successful.

Taking the mix and quantity variances together, the overall sales volume variance was favourable.

We do not know whether this favourable volume variance justifies any extra spending that may have been incurred on advertising and sales promotion.

59 Standard costing and TQM

Text references. Standard costing is covered in Chapter 13.

Top tips. The question asks you to discuss whether standard costing would still be appropriate if TQM was introduced. Make sure you answer the question – do not just put down everything you know about standard costing and TQM!

Examiner's comments. The question asked for a discussion of whether standard costing would still be appropriate if TQM was introduced. Most candidates failed to realise the changes that TQM will bring and how it will affect standard costing.

Marking scheme

	Marks
TQM and standard costing – up to 2 marks per valid point	max 10

TQM and standard costing

Standard costing concentrates on **quantity** and ignores other factors contributing to effectiveness. In a TQM environment, however, quantity is not an issue; **quality** is. Effectiveness in such an environment therefore centres on **high quality output** (produced as a result of high quality input and the **elimination of non-value adding activities**) and the cost of failing to achieve the required level of effectiveness is measured not in variances, but in terms of **internal and external failure costs**, neither of which would be identified by a traditional standard costing analysis.

For example, standard costing systems might measure **labour efficiency** in terms of individual tasks and **level of output**. In a total quality environment, labour is more likely to be viewed as a number of multi-task teams who are responsible for the completion of a part of the production process. The effectiveness of such a team is more appropriately measured in terms of **re-working required**, **returns from customers**, **defects** identified in subsequent stages of production and so on.

Similarly, traditional feedback control would seek to eliminate an **adverse material price variance** by requiring managers to source **cheaper**, possibly **lower quality supplies**. This may run counter to the aim of maximising **quality of output** (TQM).

It would seem there is **little point** in Lock Co running both a total quality management programme and a standard costing system simultaneously.

(a) **Predetermined standards** are at odds with the philosophy of continual improvement inherent in a total quality management programme.

(b) **Continual improvements** are likely to alter methods of working, prices, quantities of inputs and so on, whereas standard costing is most appropriate in a stable, standardised and repetitive environment.

(c) Material standard costs often incorporate a planned level of **scrap**. This is at odds with the TQM aim of **zero defects** and there is no motivation to 'get it right first time'.

(d) Attainable standards, which make some allowance for **wastage and inefficiencies** are commonly set. The use of such standards conflicts with the **elimination of waste** which is such a vital ingredient of a TQM programme.

(e) Standard costing control systems make **individual managers** responsible for the variances relating to their part of the organisation's activities. A TQM programme, on the other hand, aims to make **all personnel** aware of, and responsible for, the importance of supplying the customer with a quality product.

60 Choc Co

Text reference. Variance analysis is covered in Chapter 11.

Top tips. A number of calculations are required. Clearly label each variance and include all workings.

Remember, the mix variance compares actual quantities (standard mix v actual mix) whereas the yield variance compares the standard quantity with the actual quantity (standard mix).

Easy marks. There are easy marks available, providing you know the variance proformas.

Examiner's comments. This was probably the best answered question on the paper. A significant number of candidates scored full marks for the materials usage, mix and quantity variance. However, some candidates seemed to think it was acceptable merely to calculate the variances in kg and not convert them into a monetary value using the standard costs for each ingredient. Variances need to be given a value in order to be used properly within a business. It's not sufficient to simply stop at a quantity.

Marking scheme

	Marks
Material variances:	
(a) Usage variance	2
(b) Mix variance	4
(c) Yield variance	4
	10

(a) **Usage variance**

	Std usage for actual output (W1)	*Actual usage*	*Variance*	*Standard cost per kg (W2)*	*Variance*
	kg	kg	kg	$	$
Honey	2,020	2,200	180 (A)	20	3,600 (A)
Sugar	1,515	1,400	115 (F)	30	3,450 (F)
Syrup	1,010	1,050	40 (A)	25	1,000 (A)
	4,545	4,650			1,150 (A)

Workings

1 *Std usage for actual output*

There are 1,000 grams in a kilogram (kg).

Honey	20 grams per unit / 1,000	= 0.02 kg	× 101,000 units	= 2,020 kg
Sugar	15 grams per unit / 1,000	= 0.015 kg	× 101,000 units	= 1,515 kg
Syrup	10 grams per unit / 1,000	= 0.010 kg	× 101,000 units	= 1,010 kg

2 *Std cost per kg*

Honey	$0.02 per gram × 1,000	= $20 per kg
Sugar	$0.03 per gram × 1,000	= $30 per kg
Syrup	$0.025 per gram × 1,000	= $25 per kg

(b) **Mix variance**

	Actual quantity standard mix (W3)	*Actual quantity actual mix*	*Variance*	*Standard cost per kg (W2)*	*Variance*
	kg	kg	kg	$	$
Honey	2,066.67	2,200	133.33 (A)	20	2,666.60 (A)
Sugar	1,550.00	1,400	150.00 (F)	30	4,500.00 (F)
Syrup	1,033.33	1,050	16.67 (A)	25	416.75 (A)
	4,650.00	4,650	0		1,416.65 (F)

Workings

3 *Actual quantity standard mix*

	kg
Total quantity used:	
Honey	2,200
Sugar	1,400
Syrup	1,050
	4,650
Standard mix:	
Honey (20 grams / 45 grams per unit) × 4,650	2,066.67
Sugar (15 grams / 45 grams per unit) × 4,650	1,550.00
Syrup (10 grams / 45 grams per unit) × 4,650	1,033.33
	4,650.00

(c) **Yield variance**

	Std quantity standard mix (W1)	*Actual quantity standard mix (W3)*	*Variance*	*Standard cost per kg (W2)*	*Variance*
	kg	kg	kg	$	$
Honey	2,020.00	2,066.67	46.67 (A)	20	933.40 (A)
Sugar	1,515.00	1,550.00	35.00 (A)	30	1,050.00 (A)
Syrup	1,010.00	1,033.33	23.33 (A)	25	583.25 (A)
	4,545.00	4,650.00	105.00		2,566.65 (A)

Yield variance, alternative calculation

Weighted average standard cost per gram of material = $1.10/(20 + 15 + 10) grams = $0.024444

Weighted average standard cost per kg of material = $24.4444

101,000 units of Ooze should use in total (× 45 grams)	4,545 kg
They did use (2,200 + 1,400 +1,050)	4,650 kg
Yield variance in kg	105 kg (A)
× standard average cost per kg of material	× $24.4444
Yield variance	$2,566.66 (A)

61 DIY

Text references. Material price, mix and yield variances are covered in Chapter 11.

Top tips. Material price variances and reconciliation statements are assumed knowledge from Paper F2. You need to organise your workings separately from the reconciliation statement.

Easy marks. The easier marks in this question are for the variance calculations.

Marking scheme

	Marks
Standard materials cost	2
Price variances	2
Mix variance	2
Yield variance	3
Reconciliation of standard and actual cost	1
	10

Reconciliation statement

	$	$	$	
	F	A		
Standard material cost (7,800/100 × $210)			16,380	
Material price variance				
Material A (W1)		280		
Material B (W2)		270		
Material C (W3)		350		
Material D (W4)	190			
Material mix variance (W5)	1,050			
Material yield variance (W6)	–	420		
	1,240	1,320	80	(A)
Actual material cost			16,460	

Workings

1 *Material A price variance*

	$
2,800 litres should have cost (× $1.40)	3,920
But did cost (× $1.50)	4,200
	280 (A)

2 *Material B price variance*

	$
2,700 litres should have cost (× $1.20)	3,240
But did cost (× $1.30)	3,510
	270 (A)

3 *Material C price variance*

	$
1,000 litres should have cost (× $3.65)	3,650
But did cost (× $4.00)	4,000
	350 (A)

4 *Material D price variance*

	$
1,900 litres should have cost (× $2.60)	4,940
But did cost (× $2.50)	4,750
	190 (F)

5 *Material mix variance*

	Should mix Actual qty Std mix	*Did mix Actual qty Actual mix*	*Difference*	*Std price*	*Variance*
				$	$
A	2,240*	2,800	560 (A)	1.40	784 (A)
B	2,160	2,700	540 (A)	1.20	648 (A)
C	640	1,000	360 (A)	3.65	1,314 (A)
D	3,360	1,900	1,460 (F)	2.60	3,796 (F)
	8,400	8,400	0		1,050 (F)

Actual input = 8,400 litres

*Standard mix of actual input

A	28/105	× 8,400	=	2,240 litres
B	27/105	× 8,400	=	2,160 litres
C	8/105	× 8,400	=	640 litres
D	42/105	× 8,400	=	3,360 litres

6 *Material yield variance*

8,400 litres input should have yielded (÷ 105 = 80 × 100 litres)	8,000	litres
but did yield	7,800	litres
Variance in units	200	litres (A)
× standard cost ($210 ÷ 100 litres = $2.10)	× $2.10	
Variance	$420 (A)	

62 Valet Co

Text references. Mix and yield variances are covered in Chapter 11.

Examiner's comments. This is a very popular F5 topic. Students either knew how to calculate the variances and scored full marks, or did not and scored zero. Part (b) was not answered well even though it only asked for a brief description of the variances calculated in part (a). It really is a case of revising this area, learning the method and performing the calculations.

Marking scheme

	Marks
(a) Calculations	
Sales mix contribution variance	4
Sales quantity contribution variance	4
(b) Description	
One mark per description	2
	10

(a) Variances

(i) *Sales mix contribution variance*

	Should mix Actual qty Std mix	*Did mix Actual qty Actual mix*	*Difference*	*Std Contribution*	*Variance*
				$	$
Full	5,130 (W1)	4,000	1,130 (A)	22.30 (W2)	25,199 (A)
Mini	2,850 (W1)	3,980	1,130 (F)	16.50 (W2)	18,645 (F)
	7,980	7,980	0		6,554 (A)

Workings

1 *Actual sales quantity in standard mix*

Full	7,980	× (3,600/5,600)	=	5,130
Mini	7,980	× (2,000/5,600)	=	2,850

2 *Standard contributions per valet*

Full	$50	× 44.6%	=	$22.30 per valet
Mini	$30	× 55%	=	$16.50 per valet

(ii) *Sales quantity contribution variance*

	Should mix Actual qty Std mix	*Budgeted Std qty Std mix*	*Difference*	*Std Contribution*	*Variance*
				$	$
Full	5,130 (W1)	3,600	1,530 (F)	22.30 (W2)	34,119 (F)
Mini	2,850 (W1)	2,000	850 (F)	16.50 (W2)	14,025 (F)
	7,980	5,600	2,380		48,144 (F)

(b) Description

The sales mix variance occurs when the proportions of the various products sold are different from those in the budget.

The sales quantity variance shows the difference in contribution/profit because of a change in sales volume from the budgeted volume of sales.

63 PC Co

Text reference. Objectives of budgetary control and budgetary systems are covered in Chapter 8.

Top tips. Use the objectives identified in part (a) to structure your answer to part (b). Address each objective under a separate heading.

Easy marks. There are plenty of easy marks available in part (a), but keep an eye on the time. Do not overrun the allocated time for your answer.

Examiner's comments. Part (a) was where the bulk of the easy marks were on this paper and a good number of answers scored full marks.

Part (b) was a little more challenging: a requirement to discuss the concept of participative budgeting in terms of the objectives identified in part (a). Answers to this were mixed, with some good attempts but some poor ones too. A small number of candidates didn't know what participative budgeting was (the clue is in the title) so they scored nothing. Others managed to score marks by making some valid observations about it, even if they didn't necessarily tackle it in the best way, which was by using the objectives in part (a) as headings in order to give the answer some structure.

Marking scheme

			Marks
(a)	Objectives: For each objective: 1 – 1.5 marks		max 6
(b)	Participative style of budgeting:		
	Explanation of participative budgeting	1.5	
	Each objective discussed in relation to it: 1.5 marks per objective	7.5	
			9
			15

(a) **Objectives of a budgetary control system**

To compel planning

Budgeting forces management to look ahead and to set out detailed plans for **achieving targets** for each department, operation and (ideally) each manager within the organisation. It thus prevents management from relying on ad hoc or uncoordinated planning which may be detrimental to the performance of the organisation.

To communicate ideas and plans

A formal budgeting system is necessary to ensure that each person affected by management plans is aware of what he or she is supposed to be doing. Communication might be **one-way** with managers giving orders to subordinates, or there may be a **two-way dialogue** and exchange of ideas (participative budgeting).

To co-ordinate activities

Budgetary control systems help to coordinate the activities of different departments or sub-units of the organisation, ensuring **maximum integration** of effort towards common goals. The concept of coordination implies, for example, that the purchasing department should base its budget on production requirements and that the production budget should in turn be based on sales expectations. Co-ordination is difficult to achieve and there is often **conflict** between departmental plans in the budget so that the efforts of each department are not fully integrated into a combined plan to achieve the company's **best targets**.

To establish a system of control

A budget is a **benchmark** against which actual performance is **measured** and **assessed**. Control over actual performance is provided by the comparisons of actual results against the budget plan. Departures from budget can then be **investigated** and the reasons for the departures can be divided into controllable and uncontrollable factors.

To motivate employees to improve their performance

Employees can be motivated via a system of **feedback** of actual results, which lets them know how well or badly they are performing. The identification of controllable reasons for departures from budget with managers responsible provides an incentive for **improving future performance**.

Top tips. The question asks you to identify and explain **five** objectives of a budgetary control system. Other possible objectives include the following.

To provide a framework for responsibility accounting

Budgetary planning and control systems require that managers of **budget centres** are made responsible for the achievement of **budget targets** for the operations under their personal control.

To ensure the achievement of the organisation's objectives

Objectives can be set for individual departments and operations as well as the organisation as a whole. Quantified expressions of these objectives are then drawn up as **targets** to be achieved within the timescale of the **budget plan**.

To evaluate performance

Performance can be evaluated by **comparing actual results against the budget**. Employees are often rewarded with bonuses if performance **exceeds budget**. This makes more sense than simply comparing actual results against the previous year as economic conditions can change and events happen that may not be expected to re-occur.

(b) **Participative budgeting**

Under a participative style of budgeting budgets are developed by **lower-level managers** who then submit the budgets to their superiors. The budgets are based on the lower-level managers' perceptions of what is achievable and the associated necessary resources.

Each of the objectives from part (a) is addressed below, considering the extent to which participate budgeting hopes to achieve this.

To compel planning

Participative budgeting (bottom-up budgeting) will compel planning. Under this style of budgeting, participation starts at the **lowest level of management** and goes all the way up to the top. In this way, planning takes place at **all levels** within the organisation. As a result, plans should be **more accurate** as they will be based on information from employees who are most familiar with day-to-day operations.

To communicate ideas and plans

Communication of **ideas and plans** will be particularly effective with participative budgeting. If all levels of management actively participate in the budgeting process then they will all know what the plan is. However, budgets may be updated during the **review process** to conform with the expectations of top level management. If this happens, lower-level management will have to work towards budgets that differ from those that were originally submitted.

To coordinate activities

Co-ordination of activities is likely to take **significantly longer** under a style of participative budgeting. For everyone to know what the plan is, not only does there need to be co-ordination between departments but there also has to be co-ordination between the **different levels of management** within each department.

To establish a system of control

As stated above, budgets are likely to be more accurate if a participative style of budgeting is used, thus providing a solid **benchmark** against which to monitor actual results. However, the type of budgeting style used is largely irrelevant in establishing an effective **system of control**. Actual results should be compared against budget on a regular basis and any significant differences should be investigated, regardless of the budgetary system in place.

To motivate employees to improve their performance

Managers are more likely to think that a budget is **realistic** if they have been involved in the budget-setting process. They will therefore work harder to achieve the targets set. However, lower-level management may become disillusioned if top management make **significant changes** to the budget. They may be deliberately unproductive so that the final budget is not achieved and to prove that the budget they initially submitted was **more realistic/accurate**.

64 ZBB

Text reference. Budgetary systems are covered in Chapter 8.

Top tips. There are a number of marks available for explanations in this question. Include examples in your answers to maximise your score. Remember to refer back to the view given in your answer to part (d). Aim to include at least three well-explained limitations of zero-based budgeting.

Easy marks. There are easy marks available in parts (b) and (c) for simply explaining incremental budgeting and zero-based budgeting and the stages involved in ZBB.

Examiner's comments. There were some reasonable attempts to part (a), although too many candidates simply compared the two types of organisation without relating it to budgeting. Similarly, a significant number of candidates were clearly confused about the difference between public sector organisations as opposed to publicly listed companies, and answered the question entirely incorrectly!

The majority of candidates picked up the easy marks available in parts (b) and (c).

There were some reasonable attempts at part (d), although, as with part (a), some answers focused purely on the benefits and drawbacks of both methods without relating it back to the statement.

Marking scheme

			Marks
(a)	Explanation:		
	Difficulty setting objectives quantifiably	2	
	Difficulty in saying how to achieve them	1	
	Outputs difficult to measure	2	
	No relationship between inputs and outputs	2	
	Value for money issue	1	
			max 4
(b)	Incremental and zero-based budgeting:		
	Explaining 'incremental budgeting'	1	
	Explaining 'zero-based budgeting'	1	
			2
(c)	Stages involved in zero-based budgeting:		
	1 mark per stage		3
(d)	Any disadvantage of incremental budgeting that supports the statement	1	
	Incremental budgeting is quick and easy	1	
	Any disadvantage of ZBB that refutes the statement	1	
	Easier to define decision packages in public sector	2	
	More appropriate for discretionary costs	2	
	Conclusion	1	
			max 6
			15

(a) **Difficulties when budgeting in the public sector**

The main objective for most companies is to **maximise profit**. Effective budgeting can assist in meeting this objective by focussing efforts on reducing certain costs and increasing revenues by a certain amount or percentage. The **objectives of public sector organisations** are more **difficult to define in a quantifiable way**.

The **objectives of public sector organisations** such as hospitals are likely to **be largely qualitative**. For example, ensuring that ambulances reach patients within 20 minutes from an emergency call being received. Such objectives are difficult to define in a quantifiable way, whilst identifying how the objective is actually achieved can also be problematic.

Another problem why budgeting is so difficult in public sector organisations is that outputs in the public sector can seldom be measured in a way that is generally agreed to be meaningful. Whilst outputs for private companies can be measured in terms of sales revenue, outputs in the public sector are harder to pin down. For example in the education sector, are good exam results alone an adequate measure of the quality of teaching? In the public sector, **comparisons are often made between the funds available and the funds actually required**. Therefore, public sector budgeting naturally focuses on inputs, rather than the relationship between inputs and outputs.

Public sector organisations are under constant pressure to prove that they are economical, efficient and effective (offering value for money). **Resources are always kept to a minimum and each item of expenditure must be justified**. This makes the budgeting process more difficult.

(b) **Incremental budgeting**

Incremental budgeting **bases the budget on the current year's results plus an extra amount for estimated growth or inflation next year**. This form of budgeting is a reasonable procedure if current operations are as effective, efficient and economical as they can be.

Zero-based budgeting (ZBB)

ZBB rejects the assumption that underpins the concept of incremental budgeting; that next year's budget can be based on this year's costs plus an extra amount for estimated growth or inflation. ZBB involves **preparing a budget for each cost centre from a zero base**. Every item of **expenditure must be justified** in its entirety in order to be included in next year's budget.

(c) **Stages in zero-based budgeting**

ZBB involves three main stages.

Define activities (decision packages)

At the first stage, management identify the **key activities** within the organisation. These activities are described within a decision package. The decision package is originally **prepared at a base level** which shows the minimum level of resource required to meet the organisations objectives. **Incremental packages** may be prepared to show any **additional work** that could be done, at what cost and for what benefit.

Evaluate and rank each activity

Management will then rank each activity (decision package) on the basis of its benefit to the organisation. Minimum work requirements (those that are essential to get the job done) will be given high priority and so too will work which meets legal obligations. This process will **help management to decide what to spend and where to spend it**.

Allocate resources

At the final stage, management allocate resources in the budget **according to the funds available and the evaluation and ranking of the competing packages**.

(d) **The limitations of ZBB**

The major limitation of ZBB is the volume of **extra paperwork** created. Assumptions about costs and benefits in each package must be continually updated and new packages must be developed as new activities occur within the organisation.

ZBB is likely to require **management skills both in constructing decision packages and in the ranking process**. If management do not possess such skills they will require training in ZBB techniques which takes time and money.

The ranking process can also prove problematic. It can be difficult **to rank packages which appear to be equally vital**, for legal or operational reasons. Furthermore, it is difficult to rank activities which have **qualitative rather than quantitative benefits**.

ZBB can **give the impression that all decisions have to be made in the budget**. As a result, management may feel unable to carry out new ideas because they were not approved by a decision package and did not pass through the ranking process.

ZBB in practice

ZBB could be considered more **appropriate for public sector organisations**. The majority of costs in such organisations are **discretionary** and emphasis is placed on obtaining **value for money**. This objective is directly linked to the decision package ranking process within a ZBB system. Furthermore, it is easier to put activities into decision packages in organisations which undertake a number of set definable activities. Hospitals for example have set activities including outpatient wards, children's wards and A&E departments.

65 Northland

Text references. Budgeting is covered in Chapters 9 and 10.

Top tips. The expected value calculations in part (b) will need to carefully thought through. There are a number of ways of doing these calculations which are equally acceptable, but do make sure you show your workings clearly.

You must answer the specific requirements of the question in part (c) and apply your answer to the circumstances of a local government organisation.

Easy marks. There are easy marks available for the calculations and some straightforward textbook knowledge.

Examiner's comments. Part (a) was very well done as expected. Part (b) was a little more mixed with candidates getting into a tangle with the expected value calculations. Part (c) was less well done. Candidates can do the calculations but seem to have little idea as to why! The question did not ask for advantages and disadvantages of expected values.

Marking scheme

			Marks
(a)	Property cost	1	
	Central wages	1	
	Stationery	1	
			3
(b)	Basic budget	2	
	Contingency included	2	
	Expected value adjustment	2	
			6
(c)	Probability estimates difficult	1	
	Monetary values uncertain	1	
	EV not an actual value	1	
	Easy fall back for managers	1	
	Uncertainty issue	1	
	Weather	1	
	Other outside influences	1	
	Type of repairs variable	1	
			max 6
			15

(a) **Overheads budget for 20X2**

Property cost = \$120,000 + 5%
= \$120,000 × 1.05
= \$126,000

Central wages = (\$150,000 + 3%) + \$12,000
= (\$150,000 × 1.03) + \$12,000
= \$166,500

Stationery = $25,000 – 40%
= $25,000 × 0.6
= $15,000

(b) **Budget for road repairs**

Expected amount of road repairs = 2,000 metres + 10% contingency
= 2,000 × 1.1
= 2,200 metres

Expected value of weather related repair cost increase = (0.7 × 0%) + (0.1 × 10%) + (0.2 × 25%)
= 6%

After inflation road repair cost = $15,000 + 5% per metre
= $15,000 × 1.05
= $15,750

Budget for road repairs = 1.06 × $15,750 × 2,200 metres
= $36,729,000

(c) **Problems with using expected values in budgeting**

Probabilities

The probability of different types of weather conditions has been estimated and this is potentially **unreliable**. It is very difficult to accurately forecast long range weather conditions and this could have a major impact on potential budget errors.

Cost estimates

It is also difficult to accurately predict the **effect** of weather conditions on roads. 'Bad' weather could involve a number of different weather conditions such as extreme cold or heavy rain which would affect roads in different ways. Some repairs can be quick and cheap whilst other repairs will involve extensive and expensive work. The resulting **increase in repair costs** could therefore **vary** considerably and unpredictably.

Responsibility

The unpredictability of the weather gives managers responsible for road repair budgets a **good excuse** when actual costs are higher than budgeted. This limits the effectiveness of such budgets as a means of **control**.

Need for a contingency

The unpredictability of both weather conditions and the costs of repairs mean that there is a high degree of **uncertainty** associated with a road repair budget. A contingency therefore needs to be added to the budget in order to allow for unexpected increases in costs.

66 Big Cheese Chairs

Text reference. Target costing is covered in Chapter 2b and learning curves in Chapter 9.

Top tips. The question gives you the value of b and it is important to keep the accuracy by using all of the decimal places given. Show all your workings clearly and make sure you identify in both parts (a) and (b) what the final figures mean. In part (b), you need to apply your answer to the specific circumstances of Big Cheese Chairs and not just write a general description of how to close a cost gap.

Easy marks. There are easy marks available throughout this question.

Examiner's comments. Attempts at part (a) were reasonable. Whilst many candidates correctly identified ways of closing the gap in part (b), a number of answers included a suggestion to increase the selling price! This suggestion goes totally against the whole ideology of target costing and needless to say was not a mark earner!

There were some good attempts to part (c). Some candidates clearly did not understand the difference between a cumulative cost and an incremental cost and simply repeated their calculations from part (a).

Marking scheme

			Marks
(a)	Leather cost	1	
	Labour average time for 128 units	1	
	Labour total time for 128 units	1	
	Average cost per chair	1	
	Target cost and cost gap	1	
			5
(b)	Per suggestion: 1 mark		max 4
(c)	Frame	0.5	
	Leather	0.5	
	Average time per unit	2.0	
	Total time	1.0	
	Time for 128th chair	1.0	
	Conclusion	1.0	
			6
			15

(a) **Expected cost per unit**

		$ per chair
Frame and massage mechanism		51.00
Leather	2 metres × $10/m × 100/80	25.00
Labour (W)		20.95
Total cost		96.95
Target cost	$120 × 80%	(96.00)
Cost gap		0.95

Working

$y = ax^b$

$y = 2 \times 128^{-0.074000581}$

$y = 1.396674595$ hours

Average labour cost of a chair = 1.396674595 × $15

= $20.95

(b) **Closing the cost gap**

The chair's **design** could be looked at again to remove any **unnecessary features** which do not **add value** for the customer. This would reduce costs.

The **raw materials** are leather and the frame and it may be possible to **negotiate with the suppliers** for a better cost, perhaps as a bulk buying discount as volumes increase. However, reduced costs must not be at the expense of **quality**.

Reducing the level of **leather wasted** would save on cost. This could be achieved by better training of workers or improved processes.

Labour costs could be reduced by improving the **rate of learning** with better training and supervision. Alternatively, cheaper labour could be employed perhaps by reducing the skill level expected. This may however have the detrimental effect of quality reduction or increased wastage.

(c) Using the formula, we need to calculate the time taken for the first 127 chairs and deduct that from the time taken for the first 128 chairs.

$y = ax^b$
$y = 2 \times 127^{-0.074000581}$
$y = 1.39748546$ hours

Total time for 127 chairs = 127 × 1.39748546 = 177.48 hours
Total time for 128 chairs = 128 × 1.396674592 = 178.77 hours
Time for 128th chair = 178.77 – 177.48 = 1.29 hours

Cost of 128th chair

		$ per chair
Frame and massage mechanism		51.00
Leather	2 metres × $10/m × 100/80	25.00
Labour (W)	1.29 hours × $15	19.35
Total cost		95.35

The target cost is $96 so the target cost is now being achieved.

67 Designit

Text reference. Budgetary systems are covered in Chapter 8.

Top tips. There are easy marks available throughout this question so ensure you allocate enough time to each requirement. Refer to the scenario throughout your answer and, as a guide, aim for 1 mark per well-explained point.

Easy marks. You should be able to score well in part (a) by briefly explaining what a rolling budget is and how it would operate in Designit.

Examiner's comments. Answers to this question were weak in parts. Part (a) asked candidates to explain what a monthly rolling budget was and how it would operate at Designit. The question was looking for a few key points – the budget covers a twelve month period; it is updated monthly; one month is added whilst another is removed; the first month is prepared in a lot of detail compared to the other months. The most common problem with answers was that they talked about quarterly budgets and how they would operate, rather than monthly budgets.

Part (c) asked for a discussion of the problems with the current bonus scheme and a suggestion of an alternative more effective one. Many candidates identified the fact that, in the current scheme, the first target was too easy and the second target was too hard, meaning that the managers were not motivated to work hard. However, only a minority of candidates were able to discuss a feasible alternative scheme. The question wasn't looking for suggestions, just common sense answers suggesting perhaps a scheme with a number of different bonus rates over narrower bands of sales.

Marking scheme

			Marks
(a)	Explanation:		
	Updated after one month elapsed	1	
	Always 12 months	1	
	Example given	1	
	First month in detail	1	
	Later month less detail	1	
	Need to revisit earlier months	1	
			max 4

			Marks
(b)	Problems:		
	More time	1	
	Lack of experience	1	
	Too regular	2	
	Managers' resistance	2	
	Work harder	1	
	Holding back work	2	
			max 5
(c)	Simpler incentive scheme:		
	Current target too easy	1	
	Second target too hard	1	
	Other valid point re current scheme	1	
	New scheme outlined	3	
			6
			15

(a) **Rolling budget**

A **monthly rolling** budget is a budget which is **continuously updated** by adding a further month when the earliest month has passed.

For example, Designit would begin by preparing a 12-month budget covering the period 1 December 20X2 to 30 November 20X3. At the end of December 20X2, a budget for December 20X3 would be prepared, so that the **unexpired period covered by the budget is always 12 months.**

When the budget is initially prepared for the year ending 30 November 20X3, the budget for December 20X2 (the first month in the budget) should be prepared in detail. The later months will contain a lot **less detail** as there will be greater uncertainty regarding **internal resources** and **market conditions**.

When the budget for December 20X2 has elapsed and the budget for December 20X3 is prepared, the budget for January 20X3 should be **revised in greater detail**.

(b) **Problems**

Monthly rolling budgets **take time to prepare** and can be **complex**. The company's accounts department consists of a single part-qualified accountant who already has a **heavy workload**. As such it is unlikely that he has the **time or experience** required to successfully implement a system of monthly rolling budgets.

Rolling budgets are best suited to organisations that operate in **rapidly changing environments**. Designit is a **mature business and trading is fairly stable** year on year. A rolling budget updated on a **quarterly basis** (as opposed to a monthly basis) would probably be sufficient.

A monthly rolling budget will require **input from many staff**, reducing the time they have to dedicate to other tasks.

Sales managers are unlikely to embrace the new budgeting and incentive system. They will have become accustomed to **knowing their target for the whole year in advance** and will **be used to working to targets that are easily achievable**.

Under the proposed system sales managers may hold back work once they have achieved their monthly target and let it run into the following month to increase their chances of meeting next month's target. This is **not in the best interests of the business**.

(c) **Problems with the current bonus scheme**

The current bonus scheme consists of **two targets**. The first target ($1.5m of fee income) is **too easily reached** whilst the second target (a further $1.5m of fee income) appears **unrealistic** and has not been achieved by any of the sales managers.

Due to the above, sales managers are **not motivated to earn additional fees** once they have reached the first target of $1.5m.

Alternative bonus scheme

The company is currently paying each sales manager a bonus of $30,000 each year (20% of $150,000). This is 2% of $1.5m. Changing the bonus to **2% commission on all sales** as opposed to a percentage of salary would motivate the sales managers to bring in fees throughout the year.

Alternatively, the company may consider **revising the current bonus scheme** to include smaller bonuses paid out at more regular intervals; for example a bonus equivalent to 5% of salary for every $500,000 of fee income.

68 Newtown School

Text reference. Budgetary systems are covered in Chapter 8 of the BPP Study Text.

Top tips. This is a relatively straightforward question with a number of easy marks available, provided that you can work reasonably quickly.

Remember to clearly show all workings to part (a) and relate each point back to the scenario in part (c).

Easy marks. There are easy marks available for straightforward knowledge in parts (b) and (c).

Examiner's comments. In part (a) the calculations were quite straightforward and most candidates scored decent marks on this part of the question. The main error that arose was in relation to the salaries' cost. Many candidates were unable to split the year into two halves, deduct one staff member's cost and then apply the pay rise to only half of the year.

But, even if they had managed to do that, many candidates then went on to erroneously inflate the resultant cost of $599,940 by the rate given in the question, even though the pay rise was the relevant increment, not the rate of inflation.

Marking scheme

			Marks
(a)	Budgeted costs:		
	Budgeted income	1.5	
	Repairs and maintenance	1.0	
	Teachers' salaries	1.0	
	Capital expenditure	1.0	
	Deficit	0.5	
			5
(b)	Advantages and disadvantages:		
	Two advantages	2.0	
	Two disadvantages	2.0	
			4
(c)	Zero-based budgeting:		
	Explanation of ZBB process	max 4.0	
	Relevance to the school: 1 mark for each point made	max 4.0	
	Total for part (c)		max 6
			15

(a)

Budgeted income	$
Income from pupils registered on 1 June Year 1 (given in question)	724,500
Expected income from new joiners (W1)	26,100
Total expected income	750,600
Budgeted expenditure	
Repairs and maintenance ($30,000 × 1.03)	30,900
Salaries (W2)	595,900
Expected capital expenditure [(0.7 × $145,000) + (0.3 × $80,000)]	125,500
Total expected expenditure	752,300
Budget deficit	**1,700**

Workings

1 *Expected income from new joiners*

Expected number of new joiners = (0.2 × 50) + (0.3 × 20) + (0.5 × 26) = 29

$900 income from each new joiner × 29 = $26,100

2 *Salaries*

($590,000/2 + ($590,000 × 1.02)/2 = $595,900

(b) Incremental budgeting bases the budget on the results for the current period plus an amount for estimated growth or inflation in the next period. It is therefore suitable for organisations that operate in a **stable environment** where historical figures are a reliable guide to the future.

Advantages

Incremental budgeting is very **quick** compared to other methods of budgeting such as zero based budgeting. The information required to prepare a budget under this approach is also **readily available**.

For the above reasons, incremental budgeting is very **easy to perform**. This makes it possible for an employee with little accounting training to prepare a budget.

Disadvantages

Incremental budgeting is a reasonable procedure if current operations are as **effective, efficient and economical** as they can be. In general however, it is an inefficient form of budgeting as it encourages **slack** and **wasteful spending** to creep into budgets. Past inefficiencies are perpetuated because cost levels are rarely subjected to close scrutiny.

There is also a risk that **errors** from one year are carried to the next, since the previous year's figures are not questioned.

(c) The principle behind **zero based budgeting** is that the budget for each cost centre should be prepared from 'scratch' or zero. Every item of expenditure must be justified to be included in the budget for the forthcoming period.

The ZBB process involves identifying decision packages, which are activities or items of expenditure about which a decision should be made about cost. There are two types of decision package.

Mutually exclusive packages are alternative ways of getting the same job done. The best option among the packages must be selected by comparing costs and benefits and the other packages are then discarded.

Incremental packages analyse an activity into different levels of effort. The 'base' package will describe the minimum amount of work that must be done to carry out the activity and the other incremental packages describe what additional work could be done, at what cost and for what benefits.

Packages are ranked in order of priority, and given a limited budget (limited cash and other resources), the preferred mutually exclusive and incremental packages are selected for the budget.

Use of ZBB at Newtown School

Implementing ZBB would enable the school to distinguish between **necessary** and **discretionary expenditure**, and allocate resources accordingly.

For example, although some level of sports education is needed, the extent of the different activities offered is discretionary. As a bare minimum, it is essential that children have somewhere safe and secure to exercise. ZBB could be used to put together **decision packages** which reflect the **different levels of sports facilities** available to the children. For example, the most basic level could be to continue to hold all sports classes inside in the existing gym. The next level would be to offer a combination of indoor and outdoor sports classes which would require the sports field to be maintained. Finally, the highest level would be a state of the art gym and sports pitches. At Newtown School the sports staff could **prepare the decision packages** and they would be decided upon by the head teacher, who would **rank them accordingly**.

ZBB can a take long time to implement however and would **not be appropriate for all categories of expenditure** at the school. Incremental budgeting could still be **used as a basis for essential expenditure** such as repairs and maintenance, since the costs of the checks and repairs needed to comply with health and safety standards seem to stay largely the same year on year, with an inflationary increase.

69 Spike Limited

Text reference. Revised budgets and planning and operational sales variances are covered in Chapter 12.

Top tips. Part (a) does not require detailed technical knowledge but should be based on your knowledge of how budgets and control systems can operate effectively. Argue your points clearly and try not to waffle!

The variance calculations in part (b) are very straightforward but you may need to think a little more about the variances in part (c). The key is to consider what is controllable and what is not.

Easy marks. The variance calculations should provide some easy marks.

Examiner's comments. Part (a) was often very poorly done. Candidates seemed to have avoided any understanding of the practical problems involved in planning and operational variances.

Part (a) needed arguments in favour and against with points separated and a consistent conclusion.

In part (c) candidates often provided a discussion rather than the required analysis.

Marking scheme

			Marks
(a)	Materials discussion	3	
	Conclusion	1	
	Labour discussion	2	
	Conclusion	1	
			7
(b)	Sales price variance	2	
	Sales volume variance	2	
			4
(c)	Market size variance	2	
	Market share variance	2	
			4
			15

(a) **Materials**

Arguments for a revision

The problem arose due to a liquidation of a supplier which is **outside the control** of the buyer who is unlikely to have been aware it was going to happen.

The buyer will expect this revision to be allowed as it is outside his control and is likely to be demoralised and demotivated if it is refused.

Arguments against a revision

The buyer accepted the deal with the new supplier **without attempting to negotiate**. This may have been a panicked reaction to the immediate problem which has increased Spike Limited's costs.

The buyer is responsible for sourcing the cheapest materials and this could have been achieved with an alternative local supplier. A more **considered, careful approach** would have achieved a better deal.

A buyer should also have a good knowledge of his supplier's circumstances and it could be argued that some advance knowledge of liquidity problems could have been expected.

Conclusion

The budget revision should not be allowed. Although the liquidation was outside the control of the buyer, he could have achieved a better price.

Labour

Arguments for a revision

The Board made the decision to change the recruitment policy and this decision was outside the control of the departmental manager. The departmental manager is therefore not responsible for the extra cost.

Arguments against a revision

The **organisation as a whole** is in control of this decision so the cost is controllable.

The departmental manager **requested** a change in recruitment so is responsible for the extra cost involved.

The **productivity increases** have benefited the department involved so it should also be charged with the costs involved.

Conclusion

This was an **operational decision** that the departmental manager requested and agreed to. It has had the desired effects so no budget revision should be allowed.

(b) **Total sales price variance**

	$
Sales revenue for 176,000 units should have been (× $17.00)	2,992,000
but was	2,886,400
Variance	105,600 (A)

Total sales volume variance

Budgeted sales volume	180,000 units
Actual sales volume	176,000 units
Variance in units	4,000 units (A)
× Standard contribution per unit	× $7.00
Variance	$28,000 (A)

(c) **Market size variance**

Revised sales volume (1.6/1.8 × 180,000)	160,000 units
Budgeted sales volume	180,000 units
Variance in units	20,000 units (A)
× Standard contribution per unit	× $7.00
Market size variance in $	$140,000 (A)

Market share variance

Revised sales volume	160,000 units
Actual sales volume	176,000 units
Variance in units	16,000 units (F)
× Standard contribution per unit	$7
Market share variance in $	$112,000 (F)

Check:	$
Market size variance	140,000 (A)
Market share variance	112,000 (F)
Total sales volume variance	28,000 (A)

70 Carat

Text references. Variance analysis is covered in Chapters 11 and 12. Standard costing is covered in Chapter 13.

Top tips. This type of question requires practice of the different types of variance so be prepared before you go to the exam and make sure you know how to do these.

Easy marks. In part (a) calculating each variance.

Marking scheme

			Marks
(a)	Sales volume contribution variance	1	
	Sales volume planning variance	2	
	Sales volume operational variance	2	
	Material price variances	1	
	Material mix variances	2	
	Material yield variances	2	
			max 9
(b)	Sales volume, planning and operational variances	3	
	Material price, mix and yield variances	3	
			6
			15

(a)

		$
Standard sales price		12.00
Material A	$1.70 × 2.5	4.25
Material B	$1.20 × 1.5	1.80
Labour	$6.00 × 0.45	2.70
Standard contribution		3.25

(i) **Sales volume contribution variance**

Budgeted sales volume	50,000 units
Actual sales volume	48,000 units
Sales volume variance in units	2,000 units (A)
× standard contribution per unit ($3.25)	× $3.25
Sales volume variance	$6,500 (A)

(ii) **Sales volume planning variance**

Original budgeted sales	50,000 units
Revised budget sales (– 5%)	47,500 units
	2,500 units (A)
× standard contribution per unit ($3.25)	× $3.25
Sales volume planning variance	$8,125 (A)

Sales volume operational variance

Revised budget sales (– 5%)	47,500 units
Actual sales	48,000 units
	500 units (F)
× standard contribution per unit ($3.25)	× $3.25
Sales volume planning variance	$1,625 (F)

(iii) **Direct material price variances**

	$
121,951 kgs of A should have cost (× $1.70)	207,317
but did cost	200,000
Material A price variance	7,317 (F)

	$
67,200 kgs of B should have cost (× $1.20)	80,640
but did cost	84,000
Material B price variance	3,360 (A)

Material mix variances

	kg
Total quantity used (121,951 + 67,200) kgs	189,151
Standard mix for actual use 2.5/4 A	118,219
1.5/4 B	70,932

Material	*Actual quantity standard mix*	*Actual quantity actual mix*	*Variance*	*Standard cost per kg*	*Variance*
	kg	kg	kg	$	$
A	118,219	121,951	3,732 (A)	1.70	6,344 (A)
B	70,932	67,200	3,732 (F)	1.20	4,478 (F)
	189,151	189,151	0		1,866 (A)

Material yield variance

		$
Each unit of product ZP requires	2.5 kg of A, costing	4.25
	1.5 kg of B, costing	1.80
	4.0 kg	6.05

Standard average price per kg = $6.05/4 kg = $1.5125 per kg

189,151 kg should have yielded (÷ 4 kg)	47,288 units
But did yield	48,000 units
Yield variance in units	712 units (F)
× standard cost per unit of output	× $6.05
Yield variance	$4,308 (F)

Alternative calculation, yield variance

48,000 units of ZP should use in total (× 4)	192,000 kg
They did use (121,951 + 67,200)	189,151 kg
Yield variance in kg	2,849 kg (F)
× standard average cost per kg of material	× $1.5125
Yield variance	$4,309 (F)

(b) The **sales volume variance** of $6,500 (A) can be split into planning and operational variances. The **adverse planning variance** of $8,125 is a result of the fall in market size during 20X3 which is uncontrollable by the management of Carat.

Given the decrease in market size, the company should have expected to sell 47,500 units. The company actually sold 48,000 units, giving rise to a **favourable operational variance** of $1,625. The operational variance is controllable and management are likely to have **preserved market share** through effective advertising and marketing.

The **favourable Material A price variance** shows that it cost less than standard. This could have been because of an out of date standard, price changes by the supplier or perhaps a discount. In contrast the **adverse Material B price variance** shows that it cost more than standard, possibly due to careless purchasing or a change in the standard of material.

The **adverse Material A mix variance** shows that the actual mix included a bigger proportion than standard of the more expensive Material A and a smaller proportion of Material B, which has a favourable mix variance.

The favourable yield variances indicate that more output was produced than expected. This could be due to better operating processes or a superior workforce.

71 Crumbly Cakes

Text references. Variance analysis is covered in Chapters 11 and 12.

Top tips. You may find part (a) quite tricky. You need to plan a structured answer using the headings suggested by the question. Make some sensible, common sense suggestions and if you run out of ideas, move on to part (b) where easier marks are available. Read the information very carefully and layout your workings clearly.

Easy marks. There are some easy variance calculations in part (b) as well as some trickier mix and yield variances.

Examiner's comments. Many candidates completely missed the point in part (a). If a business fundamentally changes its business process without altering the standard costs of the process, it renders the variances that are produced meaningless. Some candidates tried to discuss each variance in turn rather than carry out a performance assessment of each manager. This is not as effective a method. Motivation is a complex topic and credit was given for any sensible comments.

Part (b) was well done with many candidates scoring good marks.

Marking scheme

			Marks
(a)	Production manager assessment	2	
	Sales manager assessment	2	
	Bonus scheme comment	3	
			7
(b)	Price variance	2	
	Mix variance	3	
	Yield variance	3	
			8
			15

(a) **Production manager**

The production manager instigated the new organic cake production approach and this has **fundamentally changed** the nature of the business. Before the new system started, there were **favourable material variances** for price and yield and the production manager would have received a bonus as a result.

Organic ingredients are **more expensive** and this results in **adverse** material price and mix variances in March. The **material yield** variance is favourable but not by enough to compensate for the adverse variances. This means that the production manager would not receive a bonus under the current scheme.

Sales of the cakes have improved significantly so customers presumably appreciate the new flavour and mix of ingredients. The production manager does not receive any credit for the favourable sales variances and that does not seem fair.

Sales manager

In contrast, the **sales variances** that the sales manager is responsible for have moved from adverse in February to favourable in March. The new organic approach has therefore been a **success** with customers. The sales manager will have had to sell the new organic cakes to customers and is therefore **partly responsible** for the improvement, but the original impetus came from the production manager.

Bonus scheme

The bonus scheme does not seem to be fair as it will **not reward** the two managers fairly for their efforts. They are both responsible for the improved sales but it is very difficult to **fairly allocate responsibility** in this situation. Some form of **sharing** of responsibility and reward is required.

The **standards** that the variances are based on need to be changed to reflect the new approach that the business is taking. For example, the standard price of the materials needs to be increased.

(b) **Material price variances**

	$
5,700 kg of flour should have cost (× $0.12)	684
but did cost	741
Material price variance	57 (A)

	$
6,600 kg of eggs should have cost (× $0.70)	4,620
but did cost	5,610
Material price variance	990 (A)

	$
6,600 kg of butter should have cost (× $1.70)	11,220
but did cost	11,880
Material price variance	660 (A)

	$
4,578 kg of sugar should have cost (× $0.50)	2,289
but did cost	2,747
Material price variance	458 (A)

	$
Total material price variance	2,165 (A)

Material mix variances

Total quantity used = 5,700 + 6,600 + 6,600 + 4,578 = 23,478 kg
Standard mix of actual use of each ingredient is in equal proportions = 23,478/4 = 5,869.5 kg

	Actual quantity Actual mix	*Actual quantity Standard mix*	*Variance*	*Standard cost per kg*	*Variance*
	kg	kg	kg	$	$
Flour	5,700	5869.5	169.5 (F)	0.12	20.34 (F)
Eggs	6,600	5869.5	730.5 (A)	0.70	511.35 (A)
Butter	6,600	5869.5	730.5 (A)	1.70	1,241.85 (A)
Sugar	4,578	5869.5	1,291.5 (F)	0.50	645.75 (F)
	23,478	23,478.0			1,087.11 (A)

Material yield variance

Standard cost of a cake

		$
Flour	0.1 kg × $0.12	0.012
Eggs	0.1 kg × $0.70	0.070
Butter	0.1 kg × $1.70	0.170
Sugar	0.1 kg × $0.50	0.050
		0.302

	Cakes
The actual quantity of inputs are expected to yield (23,478/0.4)	58,695
Actual output	60,000
Yield variance in cakes	1,305 (F)
× standard cost per cake ($0.302)	$394.11 (F)

Alternative method

	Kg of output
23,478 kg of inputs are expected to yield (0.36/0.4)	21,130.2
Actual output in kg	21,600.0
Yield variance in kg of output	469.8 (F)
× standard cost per kg of output ($0.302/0.36)	$394.11 (F)

72 Secure Net

Text reference. Planning and operational variances are covered in Chapter 12.

Top tips. For part (a) the examiner stated that any methods applied consistently would score full marks. This answer shows the BPP approach and the approach used in the article previously written by the examiner. If you get stuck on the details of which numbers to use where, make an attempt at something sensible and move on.

Part (b) is a straightforward discussion of the production manager's performance. Even if you struggled with the calculations in part (a), you should be able to pick up on the clues given in the scenario for factors that would have been controllable and uncontrollable.

Easy marks. There are easy marks available in part (b) just from describing factors in the scenario.

Examiner's comments. Answers for part (a) could have been better. As we know from articles that have been written on operational and planning variances in the past, there are often different approaches to calculating some of them. Candidates should remain assured that, whichever approach they adopted, full credit would be given if they were consistent.

Part (b) produced some mixed answers. Candidates need to be reminded to state the obvious points: operational variances are deemed to be within the control of the production manager, planning variances are not; the net effect of usage and price variances must be considered when assessing the production manager's performance.

Marking scheme

			Marks
(a)	Planning price variance	2	
	Planning usage variance	2	
	Operational price variance	2	
	Operational usage variance	2	
			8
(b)	Explanation of external problems beyond control of manager	4	
	Assessment of factors within the control of the manager	4	
			max 7
			15

(a) **Planning price variance**

	$
Original standard price per kg	4.00
Revised standard price per kg	4.80
Planning price variance per kg	0.80 (A)
Quantity used = 100,000 × 0.035	3,500 kg
Planning price variance in $	$2,800 (A)

Planning usage variance

	kg
Original standard: 100,000 units should use (× 0.04)	4,000
Revised standard: 100,000 units should use (× 0.042)	4,200
Planning usage variance in kg	200 (A)
Original standard price per kg	$4
Planning usage variance in $	$800 (A)

Operational price variance

	$
Actual price of actual materials (3,500 kg)	18,375
Revised standard price of actual materials ($4.80 × 3,500 kg)	16,800
Operational price variance	1,575 (A)

Operational usage variance

Actual quantity should have been	4,200 kg
but was	3,500 kg
Operational usage variance in kg	700 kg (F)
× original standard cost per kg	× $4
Operational usage variance in $	$2,800 (F)

Check:	$	$
Actual cost of materials: 3,500kg × $5.25		18,375
Original standard cost: 100,000 units × 40g × $4 per kg		16,000
Total materials cost variance		2,375 (A)
Variances:		
Price planning	2,800 (A)	
Usage planning	800 (A)	
Price operational	1,575 (A)	
Usage operational	2,800 (F)	
		2,375 (A)

(b) **Worldwide standard size**

The size of the security card has to fit the reader of that card and if the **industry specification changes** there is nothing that the production manager can do about it. This is **beyond his control** and therefore a planning error and should not be used to assess his performance.

Oil prices

World-wide oil prices have increased which have **increased plastic prices** and again the production manager **cannot control** that. This is another planning error and should be ignored in an assessment of his performance.

New supplier

The decision to use a new supplier cost an extra $1,575 which is the **operational price variance** and could be regarded as **poor performance** by the production manager. However, the manager seems to have agreed to the higher price on the promise of **better quality** and **reliability**.

The **operational usage variance** is $3,360 favourable and this could be as a result of improved quality.

Increase in production and sales

Production levels increased significantly from 60,000 to 100,000 which could potentially have caused problems for the production manager. However, the ability to increase production suggests that the new supplier's reliability was good.

The total materials operational variance shows a favourable variance of $1,785 which reflects well on the performance of the production manager. The ability to react and be flexible can often form a part of a performance assessment.

In **conclusion** the manager could be said to have performed well.

73 Carad Co

Text reference. Sales variances are covered in Chapter 11. Planning and operational variances are covered in Chapter 13.

Top tips. In part (a) the examiner has stated that any methods applied consistently would score full marks. This answer shows the BPP approach. If you get stuck on the details of which numbers to use where, make an attempt at something sensible and move on.

Part (b) is a straightforward discussion of planning and operational variances. Even if you struggled with the calculations in part (a), you should be able to explain a few reasons why Carad would be interested in planning and operational variances.

Easy marks. Part (a)(ii) should be an easy 2 marks and there are easy marks available in part (b) just for explaining planning and operational variances and relating your answer to the scenario.

Examiner's comments. There were plenty of easy marks in this question, but if anyone didn't understand variances properly, they would have struggled.

The most common error in part (b) was that candidates didn't read the requirement properly. They expected it to be asking them how the manager had performed and this was what they wrote about. Every exam sitting, this proves a problem – candidates pre-empting the question and not reading it properly. It should not be assumed that every single variance question will give you some variances, maybe ask you to calculate some more, and then ask for a discussion of management's performance. Exam papers cannot be allowed to become that predictable as examinees would then start to only partly prepare for them, on the basis that they know what will be examined, more or less. Candidates that did read the question, however, tended to make a reasonable attempt at this part.

Marking scheme

				Marks
(a)	(i)	Sales volume contribution variance	1.0	
		Sales mix variance	3.0	
		Sales quantity variance	3.0	
				7
	(ii)	Purchasing planning variance	1.5	
		Purchasing efficiency variance	1.5	
				3
(b)	1 mark per valid reason			5
				15

(a) (i) **Sales volume contribution variance**

	Actual sales volume (units)	*Budgeted sales volume (units)*	*Difference (units)*	*× Standard contribution*	*Sales volume variance*
				$	$
Plasma TVs	750	590	160 (F)	190	30,400 (F)
LCD TVs	650	590	60 (F)	180	10,800 (F)
	1,400	1,180	220		41,200 (F)

Sales mix variance

	'Should' mix: Actual quantity Standard mix (units)	*'Did' mix: Actual quantity Actual mix (units)*	*Difference (units)*	*× Standard contribution*	*Sales mix variance*
				$	$
Plasma TVs	700	750	50 (F)	190	9,500 (F)
LCD TVs	700	650	50 (A)	180	9,000 (A)
	1,400	1,400	0		500 (F)

Sales quantity variance

	Actual sales Standard mix (units)	*Standard sales Standard mix (units)*	*Difference (units)*	*× Standard contribution*	*Sales quantity variance*
				$	$
Plasma TVs	700	590	110 (F)	190	20,900 (F)
LCD TVs	700	590	110 (F)	180	19,800 (F)
	1,400	1,180	220 (F)		40,700 (F)

Sales quantity variance, alternative method

	Units
Budgeted total sales	1,180
Actual total sales	1,400
Sales quantity variance in units	220 (F)
Average standard contribution per unit $(190 + 180)/2	$185
Sales quantity variance in $	$40,700 (F)

(ii) **Material price planning variance**

	$
Original standard price of component X	60
Revised standard price of component X	85
Material price planning variance	25 (A)
Actual units used/purchased (1,400 units in total)	1,400
Material price planning variance in $	$35,000 (A)

Material price operational variance

	$
Cost of X for 1,400 units should have been (× $85)	119,000
Actual price paid ($80.00)	112,000
Material price operational variance	7,000 (F)

(b) **Material price variance**

The adverse material price variance could arise due to a number of **controllable** and **uncontrollable factors.** For this reason, it is important to analyse the variance in further detail to provide a true and fair assessment of the efficiency of the purchasing department.

Splitting the total variance into planning and operational components will enable Carad to distinguish between variances that have arisen due **to inaccurate planning and faulty standards** (planning variances) and those which have been caused by **adverse or favourable operational performance** (operational variances).

Material price planning variance

Planning variances arise because the **original standard and revised standards are different**. It is unlikely that the purchasing department could do anything to alter the planning variance as it is not controlled by operational functions, but by senior management. The material price planning variance shows how skilled management are in estimating future prices.

Material price operational variance

Operational variances **compare actual results with a realistic standard or budget**. The material price operational variance measures the purchasing department's efficiency given the market price at the time that materials were purchased.

The operational variance ignores factors that the purchasing department cannot control and is likely to gain greater acceptance as a performance measure as staff know that **they will not be held responsible for poor planning and faulty standard setting**. The favourable operational variance for material price indicates **good purchasing performance** by the manager responsible for buying component X.

74 Noble

Text references. Flexed budgets are covered in Chapter 10. Sales mix and quantity variances are covered in Chapter 11.

Top tips. When you prepare a flexed budget, remember its format should replicate the original budget to which it relates. For example, if the original budget totals up variable costs, so should the flexed budget. This makes it easier to compare like with like.

Easy marks. There are 11 marks available for preparing a flexed budget in part (a). The steps involved in preparing a flexed budget should be familiar to you from your earlier studies.

Examiner's comments. Many candidates answered part (a) well and easily scored (most of) the marks available, tripping up only on staff wages and energy costs calculations.

Many candidates confused the sales mix variance with the materials mix variance and talked about the latter in part (b). Also many candidates could not describe the quantity variance or identify why it had arisen. There is clearly a lack of understanding about variances, with candidates perhaps learning formulae in order to churn out calculations but not really understanding what variances mean to a business. This area needs more work by the majority of students.

Marking scheme

			Marks
(a)	Flexed budget:		
	Food sales	1.0	
	Drink sales	1.0	
	Total revenue	1.0	
	Staff wages	1.0	
	Food costs	1.0	
	Drink costs	1.0	
	Energy costs	1.0	
	Variable costs total	1.0	
	Contribution	1.0	
	Manager's and chef's pay	0.5	
	Rent & rates	0.5	
	Operating profit	1.0	
			11
(b)	Explanation of variances	2.0	
	Suggestions of reason for variances	2.0	
			4
			15

(a) **Flexed budget**

Number of meals	1,560	
	$	$
Revenue:		
Food sales (W1)	62,400	
Drink sales (W1)	15,600	
		78,000
Variable costs:		
Staff wages (W2)	(12,672)	
Food costs (W3)	(7,800)	
Drink costs (W4)	(3,120)	
Energy costs (W5)	(4,234)	
		(27,826)
Contribution		50,174
Fixed costs:		
Manager's and chef's pay	(8,600)	
Rent, rates and depreciations	(4,500)	
		(13,100)
Operating profit		37,074

Workings

1 *Revenue*

Food revenue = 1,560 × (($45 + $35)/2) = $62,400

Drinks revenue = 1,560 × ($2.50 × 4) = $15,600

2 *Staff wages*

Average number of orders per day = 1,560/(6 days × 4 weeks) = 65 orders per day

Therefore extra orders = 15 per day (65 – 50). 15/5 = 3 therefore, 3 × 0.5 hours (1.5 hours) of overtime must be paid.

8 staff × 1.5 hours × 6 days × 4 weeks = 288 extra hours

Extra wages = 288 extra hours × $12 = $3,456 extra wages

Total flexed wages = $9,216 + $3,456 = $12,672

3 *Food costs*
Food costs = 12.5% × \$62,400 = \$7,800

4 *Drink costs*
Drink costs = 20% × \$15,600 = \$3,120

5 *Energy costs*
Standard total hours worked = (8 staff × 6 hours) × 6 days × 4 weeks = 1,152 hours
Extra hours worked = 288 (W2)
Total hours = 1,152 + 288 = 1,440
Total energy costs = 1,440 hours × \$2.94 per hour = \$4,234

(b) **Sales mix contribution variance**

The sales mix contribution variance measures the effect on profit when the proportions of products sold are different from those in the standard mix.

The sales mix variance is adverse. Meal B generates a higher contribution than meal A. This means that more of meal A must have been sold, relative to meal B, than budgeted.

Sales quantity contribution variance

The sales quantity contribution variance shows the difference in contribution/profit because of a change in sales volume from the budgeted number of sales.

The sales quantity variance is favourable. This means that the total number of meals sold (in the standard mix) was higher than expected. Indeed, 1,560 meals were sold (budget was 1,200 meals).

75 Block Company

Text reference. Sales mix and quantity variances are covered in Chapter 11 of the BPP Study Text. Sales planning and operational variances are covered in Chapter 12.

Top tips. You may have been surprised that this question focussed on sales variances rather than cost variances, but the principles are very similar. In part (a), the planning and operational variances for Commodity 1 have already been calculated and the information is available to calculate the variances for both commodities, so you can check your logic as you calculate the variances for Commodity 2.

The use of a proforma layout in part (b) is essential for clarity of presentation.

Easy marks. There are easy marks available in part (c) providing you understand what the variances you have calculated in parts (a) and (b) mean for the business and refer to the scenario throughout your answer.

Examiner's comments. Part (a) was really well answered with the majority of candidates scoring the full marks. Part (b) tested the sales mix and sales quantity variances. This was well answered by some candidates, but the main error that did arise was the failure to realise that the company was using absorption costing, which meant that the variances should have been based on the profit margins of each product rather than the contribution margins. Quite a few candidates had calculated their variances using selling prices rather than profit margins.

Finally, another common error was to calculate the sales volume variance rather than the sales quantity variance. This is an error in understanding, since the sales volume variance is the total variance which breaks down into its two component parts of sales mix and sales quantity.

Marking scheme

			Marks
(a)	Planning and operational variances:		
	Operational variance	2	
	Planning variance	2	
			4
(b)	Mix and quantity variances:		
	Standard profit per unit	1	
	Mix variance	3	
	Quantity variance	3	
			7
(c)	Discussion:		
	1 mark per valid comment		max 4
			15

(a) **Sales price operational variance for Commodity 2**

	$
Actual sales (25,600 units × $40.40)	1,034,240
Revised budget at market price (25,600 units × $39.10)	1,000,960
Sales price operational variance	33,280 (F)

Sales price planning variance for Commodity 2

	$
Revised 'standard' sales price budget	39.10
Original standard sales price	41.60
Sales price planning variance per unit	2.50 (A)
Units sold	25,600
Sales price planning variance in total	$64,000 (A)

(b) **Total sales mix variance**

	Actual total sales in standard mix (W1)	*Actual total sales in actual mix*	*Sales mix variance in units*	*× Standard profit margin (W2)*	*Variance*
					$
Commodity 1	29,700 units	29,840 units	140 (F)	× $9.20	1,288 (F)
Commodity 2	25,740 units	25,600 units	140 (A)	× $12.00	1,680 (A)
	55,440 units	55,440 units			392 (A)

Total sales quantity variance

Actual total sales units	55,440
Budgeted total sales units (30,000 + 26,000)	56,000
Total sales quantity variance in units	560 (A)
Average standard profit per unit (W3)	$10.50
Total sales quantity variance in units	$5,880 (A)

Workings

1 *Actual sales quantity in standard mix at standard profit margin*

Product	*Actual quantity in standard mix*
Commodity 1: 55,440 × 30/56 =	29,700
Commodity 2: 55,440 × 26/56 =	25,740
	55,440

2 *Standard profit margins per unit*

Product	*Commodity 1*	*Commodity 2*
	$	$
Standard selling price	30.00	41.60
Variable production costs	(18.00)	(26.40)
Fixed production overheads	(2.80)	(3.20)
Standard profit margin	9.20	12.00

3 *Average standard profit per unit*

	Budgeted sales units	*Standard profit per unit*	*Budgeted profit*
		$	$
Commodity 1	30,000	9.20	276,000
Commodity 2	26,000	12.0	312,000
	56,000		588,000

Budgeted average profit per unit = $588,000/56,000 = $10.50

(c) **Sales price**

The sales manager cannot be held responsible for any difference between the original standard sales price and the 'realistic' average market price for the period. The sales planning variances are due to inaccurate forecasts by the market specialist.

However, the sales manager should be accountable for the actual selling prices achieved compared with the realistic average market prices, as measured by the sales price operational variances. These were $35,808 adverse for Commodity 1 and $33,280 favourable for Commodity 2.

These are large amounts. The sales manager appears to have performed well in selling Commodity 2 as a price higher than the market average, but he has performed disappointingly in selling Commodity 1 at below the average market price.

Sales volumes

The total sales volume variance is $6,272 adverse ($392 adverse for mix and $5,880 adverse for total sales quantity). Total sales volumes were 1% lower than expected, which is another indication of disappointing performance by the sales manager. The sales mix variance, however, seems relatively small when compared with the other variances, and so does not seem significant.

Total sales variance

The total sales price operational variance is $2,528 adverse (35,808 – 33,280) and the total sales volume variance is $6,272 adverse, giving total sales variances of $8,800 adverse for the period. In the context of a budgeted profit of $588,000 this is probably fairly insignificant. However, the large differences in the sales price operational variances for the two products are large and should be investigated.

76 Bedco

Text reference. Planning and operational variances are covered in Chapter 12 of the BPP Study Text.

Top tips. To answer this question within the allocated time, you need to be familiar with planning and operational variances. You should identify that the planning variance for material usage applies to pillow cases only.

Remember that when calculating an operational variance for usage, the standard cost to apply is the standard cost per unit of material in the original standard cost.

If you have time, comment on the usage operational variances for bed sheets and pillow cases separately.

Part (b) of the question is worth seven marks, so make sure that you allocate the right amount of time to this part of your answer.

Easy marks. When answering a question on planning and operational variances, calculate the original standard cost and the revised standard cost. This should indicate what the planning variances are, per unit or price or usage. Having done this, the task is then to convert the planning variance as a price per unit of material or a quantity used of material into a total variance.

Marking scheme

			Marks
(a)	For each variance: 2 marks		8
(b)	Responsibility for operational variances but not planning variances	1	
	Comments on production volume, but not relevant to materials variances	1	
	Comments on price operational variance	1	
	Comments on total operational usage variance	2	
	Comments on usage variances for bed sheets and pillow cases individually	2	
			7
			15

(a)

Original standard cost		
Sheets	$2m^2 \times \$5$ per m^2	\$10 per unit
Pillow cases	$0.5m^2 \times \$5$ per m^2	\$2.50 per unit
Revised standard cost		
Sheets	$2m^2 \times \$6$ per m^2	\$12 per unit
Pillow cases	$0.55m^2 \times \$6$ per m^2	\$3.30 per unit

Material price planning variance

	\$
Original standard price of materials per m^2	5.0
Revised standard price	6.0
Material price planning variance per m^2	1.0 (A)
Actual quantity used/purchased (248,000 + 95,000)	343,000
Material price planning variance in \$	\$343,000 (A)

Material price operational variance

	\$
Revised standard price of materials per m^2	6.0
Actual price paid	5.8
Material price planning variance per m^2	0.2 (F)
Actual quantity used/purchased (248,000 + 95,000)	343,000
Material price planning variance in \$	\$68,600 (F)

Material usage planning variance

This applies to pillow cases only

	m^2
180,000 pillow cases should use: original standard (× 0.5)	90,000
180,000 pillow cases should use: revised standard (× 0.55)	99,000
Material usage planning variance in m^2	9,000 (A)
Original standard price per m^2	$5
Material usage planning variance in $	$45,000 (A)

Material usage operational variance

This applies to pillow cases only

	m^2
180,000 pillow cases should use: revised standard (× 0.55)	99,000
120,000 sheets should use (× 2)	240,000
Together they should use	339,000
They did use	343,000
Material usage operational variance in m^2	4,000 (A)
Original standard price per m^2	$5
Material usage planning variance in $	$20,000 (A)

Check:	$	$
Actual cost of materials: 343,000 m^2 × $5.80		1,989,400
Original standard cost: (120,000 sheets × $10) + (180 pillow cases × $2.50)		1,650,000
Total materials cost variance		339,400 (A)
Variances:		
Price planning	343,000 (A)	
Usage planning	45,000 (A)	
Price operational	68,600 (F)	
Usage operational	20,000 (A)	
		339,400 (A)

(b) The production manager is not responsible for setting the standard costs and is therefore not responsible for any planning variances. He is responsible however for the operational variances (including the price variance, since he has responsibility for materials purchasing).

The manager is also not responsible for the production shortfall of 10,000 pillow cases in the month, since this was caused by the change in customer requirements. However, this did not affect the materials variances. (It is much more likely to have affected labour efficiency or idle time variances in the month.)

Assessing performance on operational variances only, it would appear that the production manager has performed well. Although the expected material price rose to $6 per m^2, he was able to purchase materials at $5.80 per m^2, which 'saved' $68,600 in purchase costs.

The materials usage operational variance was adverse in total, by 4,000 m^2. The usage of materials on bed sheets (248,000m^2) was more than the expected 240,000 m^2 for 120,000 sheets produced (120,000 × 2). On the other hand, materials usage for pillow cases (95,000m^2) was 4,000 m^2 less than the expected usage of 99,000 m^2 for the 180,000 pillow cases produced (180,000 × 0.55). The production manager should therefore be asked to explain the adverse usage of materials in producing the bed sheets.

The large favourable variance for materials usage on pillow cases should also be explained, to make sure that the pillow cases are being made properly to the new standard requirement.

Question 77

77.1 D (Syllabus area D4(e))

The quality of products or services is an aspect of operational performance. Quality affects customer perceptions, but is under the control of management. It should therefore normally be used as a measure from the operational perspective rather than a customer perspective (where customer views, attitudes or behaviour is more significant).

77.2 D (Syllabus area D4(b))

Customers ceasing their subscription = 0.6 million

Average number of subscribers = (5.6 + 6.0)/2 = 5.8 million

Churn rate = 0.6/5.8 = 0.103 or 10.3%

77.3 A (Syllabus area D1(a))

Divisionalisation means creating divisions or business units, where responsibility for profit, and not just cost, is delegated to divisional managers. The use of transfer pricing, ROI as a performance measure and incentives for improving performance are often aspects of divisionalisation, but they do not describe or explain the term.

77.4 B (Syllabus area D1(a))

The term 'management control' refers to both planning and control at the 'tactical' level within an organisation, and is sometimes called 'tactical planning'. This is the middle layer of management planning and control, between strategic planning and operational planning and control.

77.5 C (Syllabus area D1(b))

Unlike traditional management accounting systems, strategic management accounting systems draw on data from external as well as internal sources, and include non-financial as well as financial information. Executive information systems also draw on data from internal and external sources, but are much less extensive that strategic management accounting systems.

77.6 C (Syllabus area D2(b))

Market research information is primary data, but it is obtained from external sources. As a general rule, external information is less reliable than internally produced information, because with external information there is often uncertainty about the source, accuracy and completeness of the information.

77.7 D (Syllabus area D4(b))

The cost of a bus route and the cost of a journey are not comparable measures of performance because they do not compare like with like. The cost per passenger kilometre provides a comparison based on both numbers of passengers and distance travelled, that can be used for comparisons between different routes and over time.

77.8 B (Syllabus area D4(e))

Fitzgerald and Moon identified six dimensions or aspects of performance in a service business: financial performance, competitiveness, quality, resource utilisation, flexibility and innovation.

77.9 A (Syllabus area D5(c))

A fair comparison is not possible if, for example, one division has non-current assets that are quite old (and so have a small net book value) and another division has non-current assets that are mostly new, so valued at close to their cost. To measure ROI, profit is calculated after deducting depreciation but without deducting any interest on capital employed.

77.10 B (Syllabus area D5(d))

In a system of performance reporting where managers are held responsible only for the costs that they are in a position to control, the divisional manager should be held responsible for the gross profit less operating costs that are attributable to divisional activities, and so which are presumable directly controllable or influenced by the divisional manager.

Question 78

78.1 D (Syllabus area D5(b))

Internal transfers should be preferred to external purchases because the company will have better control over output quality from Division A and the scheduling of production and deliveries. Transfer prices determine how total profit will be shared between the divisions.

78.2 C (Syllabus area D6(a))

Not-for-profit organisations do have financial objectives, which may sometimes be described as financial constraints. For example a charity organisation may want to maximise its funding and a government department may seek to carry out its activities within the spending budget for the department.

The outputs produced by commercial organisations can be measured simply by profit, which is a measure of the value created by the organisation in a period. Outputs of not-for-profit organisations cannot be measured as easily because they often have many different objectives, each measured in different ways.

78.3 B (Syllabus area D5(d))

Gross profit ignores other expenses other than cost of sales. Profit before tax and profit after tax are after deducting items that do not relate to divisional performance (costs of interest on company debt and tax charges). Profit before interest and tax is the most appropriate measure of the four, and it will often be the same as operating profit.

78.4 A (Syllabus area D5(a))

The minimum transfer price is the marginal cost of production in Division A, because any transfer price in excess of this amount will add to the division's contribution and profit. The maximum transfer price is the external market price of Component X, because any price in excess of this amount will lead to Division B sourcing Product X externally.

78.5 D (Syllabus area D6(b))

Adherence to appointment times means starting an appointment at the scheduled time. One suitable measure might be the percentage of appointments that begin late more than a certain amount of time, say 15 minutes. Of the performance measurements in the question, average waiting time on the appointment date would be the most appropriate.

78.6 C (Syllabus area D3(b))

Passwords are used to prevent access to files and programs within a system, rather than preventing access to the system at all.

78.7 C (Syllabus area D4(e))

R&D expenditure on its own is not a measure of performance, and costs in the previous year will not relate to all four products introduced to the market in the past two years.

The most appropriate of these measures as an indication of innovation within the organisation is revenue from new products as a percentage of total revenue. (This is more meaningful for comparison purposes than simply measuring average revenue per new product.)

78.8 A (Syllabus area D6(b))

Number of patients treated per $1 spent relates outputs to inputs, and is a measure of efficiency. Reducing a departmental budget is a measure of economy. A crime clear-up rate and an examination pass rate are measures of effectiveness for the police force and the state-owned college respectively.

78.9 A (Syllabus area D2(b))

For example systems for recording attendance times at work are more reliable when recorded automatically by a card reader system than if individuals sign in and sign out in a manual attendance record. However, time recording systems (such as time sheets for recording time spent on different jobs) must sometimes rely on human records. Secondary information is usually much cheaper to collect than primary data.

78.10 C (Syllabus area D5(a))

For example if the marginal cost of a transferred item is $5 and it has an external intermediate market of $7 but external selling costs of $0.50; and if the transferring-in division can use the transferred item to make an end product that earns a contribution of $10, the maximum transfer price should be the lower of $7 and $10. The minimum transfer price should be $5 + $(7 – 5 – 0.50) = $6.50.

Question 79

79.1 D (Syllabus area D4(e))

The target is to improve the efficiency of dealing with customer calls. This may affect customer satisfaction and profitability, but its prime objective is to reduce call times and improve efficiency in the call centre.

79.2 D (Syllabus area D1(b))

Management information, often of an operational nature, is often produced as summary data output from a transaction processing system. Management information systems are based mainly on internal data sources rather than sources that are external to the organisation.

79.3 B (Syllabus area D1(a))

Budgeting is commonly associated with decision making at the tactical planning level (management control level) within a management hierarchy.

79.4 A (Syllabus area D1(b))

EIS systems often present key information in a 'visually friendly' format.

79.5 B (Syllabus area D2(a))

Data from a government source is external data since it comes from a source outside the organisation. It is secondary data because it was not produced for the specific purpose for which management are using it.

79.6 A (Syllabus area D2(b))

Feedback is information captured within an organisation by measuring output from the system. Information from an external source cannot be feedback.

79.7 B (Syllabus area D4(e))

Making repeat orders is possibly a measure of customer satisfaction, and so might be used as a measure of performance from a customer perspective in a balanced scorecard. The growth in the product range is more relevant to innovation, and speed of order processing and orders per sales representative are measures of operational efficiency and effectiveness rather than customer attitudes to the organisation and its products.

79.8 C (Syllabus area D6(d))

Providing value for money (VFM) means providing a service that is economical, efficient and effective. 'Economical' means getting the best price, but this does not necessarily mean 'cheap'. Measuring the percentage of collected refuse that is recycled is a measure of effectiveness, if recycling refuse is an objective of the service. (Efficiency measures an amount of output or benefit per unit of resource input.)

79.9 D (Syllabus area D5(a))

The minimum transfer price is a price that should be sufficient to make the manager of Division A wiling to transfer units of Component X to Division B. This is the marginal cost of manufacture plus the opportunity cost of not being able to sell the component in the external market.

This is $8 + $(16 – 8 – 1) = $15.

79.10 B (Syllabus area D5(c))

When divisional performance is measured by residual income, a fair comparison of divisional performances is not possible, because the divisional residual incomes are not related to the size and asset value of each division. For example residual income of $50,000 when divisional assets are $10 million is not as impressive as residual income of $50,000 when divisional assets are only $100,000.

When a transfer price is based on cost, the size of the profit mark-up is a matter for negotiation, and one of the divisional managers (or even both of them) are likely to consider the agreed transfer price as 'unfair', favouring the other division.

Question 80

80.1 D (Syllabus area D4(b))

Time between order and despatch is a measure of speed, which is an aspect of efficiency.

80.2 A (Syllabus area D4(e))

In the Fitzgerald and Moon model there are six dimensions of performance. Two of these reflect past results and achievements: financial performance and competitiveness. The other four dimensions of performance are determinants of future performance: flexibility, innovation, quality and resource utilisation.

80.3 B (Syllabus area D4(d))

There is a risk of dysfunctional decision making and a lack of goal congruence with divisionalisation. Divisional managers may base investment decisions on whether they will improve ROI, which is inappropriate. Transfer pricing disputes too may lead to bad decisions by divisional managers. However, the risk can be avoided or minimised if divisional management and head office management are aware of the potential problem.

Authority is delegated to divisional managers; therefore there is some loss of head office control over operations, but decision making at 'local' operational level should be faster since the decision does not have to be referred to head office for a decision. There is likely to be some duplication of costs, since each division will have its own administration activities.

80.4 B (Syllabus area D5(c))

Capital employed at start of 20X2 = $2 million + $0.2 million + $0.8 million + $0.1 million = $3.1 million

Capital employed at the end of 20X2 is the capital employed at the beginning of the year minus depreciation of $0.4m on the 'old' assets and $0.2m on the 'new' asset.

Capital employed at end of 20X2 = $1.6 million + $0.2 million + $0.6 million + $0.1 million = $2.5 million

Mid-year capital employed = $(3.1 m + 2.5m)/2 = $2.8 million

Profit = $0.5 million + $0.35 million – depreciation $0.2 million = $0.65 million

ROI = 0.65/2.8 = 0.232 = 23.2%

80.5 B (Syllabus area D5(c))

ROI is measured as divisional operating profit: this is after deducting depreciation charges.

80.6 D (Syllabus area D3(a))

Controls are needed over internally-produced information to prevent excessive amounts of information being circulated - leading to waste of management time. Controls are also needed to ensure that unauthorised information is not circulated. Controls may extend to the use of e-mails containing 'off the record' comments which could potentially have legal implications for the organisation.

80.7 D (Syllabus area D2(b))

Feedback is information produced by a system as control information for management. Benchmarking means comparing performance of an organisation, or part of an organisation, with a 'benchmark'. The benchmark may be an external organisation, such as a competitor company, or another department or division within the same organisation.

80.8 D (Syllabus area D5(a))

When an organisation is structured into divisions, there will almost inevitably be some transfer of goods or services between divisions, for which transfer prices are required.

Statement 2 is one of the guiding rules for identifying the optimal transfer price.

80.9 B (Syllabus area D6(b))

The cost of resources (inputs) per member of the local community is a measure of the resources spent on the fire service, without providing any measure of outputs obtained from the resources. A measure of the cost of the service provides an indication of the resources committed to it, but does not measure the value or benefits obtained from them.

80.10 D (Syllabus area D4(e))

The growth perspective is concerned with: 'Can we continue to improve and create value?' The process efficiency perspective, also called the operational perspective, is concerned with operational efficiency and excellence.

Question 81

81.1 D (Syllabus area D4(d))

Holding on to outdated assets valued at a negligible carrying amount, provided they help to earn some profit, will provide a good ROI and a positive residual income. Managers may therefore be encouraged to hold on to out-of-date assets when it would better for the organisation to modernise and obtain new assets. Key Performance Indicators are a term used for measurements that are used to set targets and compare actual performance with target.

81.2 C (Syllabus area D7(d))

Good performance measurements may be either financial or non-financial measurements.

81.3 D (Syllabus area D2(e))

The main problem with information overload is that managers may be given so much information that they are unable to identify what is important and what is irrelevant or unimportant. The consequence could be wasted time searching for the important information, or poor decision making because the important information has not been recognised.

81.4 C (Syllabus area D4(a))

Liquidity and cash flow are improved by reducing the average time that customers take to pay and by extending the length of credit taken from suppliers.

81.5 D (Syllabus area D4(c))

Non-financial performance measures are often a useful guide to future financial performance. A problem with using multiple performance measures, however, is that they have different performance objectives. For example a measurement of output quality has an objective of improving quality, but this may be inconsistent or incompatible with a measure of cost of output. You can have better quality or lower cost, but it is not so easy to have both.

81.6 D (Syllabus area D5(a))

Transfers should not be at actual cost, because there is no incentive for the transferring division to control the costs of the transferred item. A transfer price based on actual cost plus would be even worse, since the transferring division (Division A) would make a profit on any overspending that it incurs. Standard cost plus is preferable to standard cost because the profit margin provides an incentive for Division A to make and transfer the item.

81.7 B (Syllabus area D5(c))

	$'000	$'000
Sales (7,000 units × $154)		1,078
Variable costs in Division B; (7,000 × $33)	231	
Costs of transfers (14,000 × $43)	602	
		833
		245
Fixed costs		160
Operating profit		85
Notional interest (16% × $500,000)		80
Residual income		5

81.8 A (Syllabus area D5(c))

	Profit	*Capital employed*
	$	$
Original forecast	65,000	210,000
Effect of machine sale	(2,500)	(6,000)
Effect of machine purchase	5,200	15,000
	67,700	219,000

Revised ROI = 67,700/219,000 = 30.9%

81.9 D (Syllabus area D6(c))

When an organisation has multiple objectives, outputs must be measured for each objective and these outputs cannot be easily compared with each other. Providing suitable comprehensive measures of performance may be impracticable.

Schools may be tempted to manipulate figures to improve their reported performance in examinations, for example by preventing poor students from taking the examinations. The temptation is to focus on the reported performance measures than the achievement of the objectives that the performance measures are intended to assess.

81.10 D (Syllabus areas D1 (b) and (c))

ERP systems should ensure that different departments or functions within an organisation, such as sales and marketing, production, HR management and accounts, all use the same data files and so the same data for information purposes. An open system is a system that interacts with its environment and is influenced by it. All systems involving people are open systems.

82 ERP

Text reference. Strategic information systems and ERP systems are covered in Chapter 14.

Top tips. You should think about the potential benefits of a company-wide IT system, in terms of the quality of information and how the information can be used to improve performance. Think particularly about the context in which Trendy operates, and how it can increase the value it provides for its customers.

Marking scheme

		Marks
Definition of ERP	max 2	
Continual updating	1	
Immediate access to system	1	
Integration of information systems for all functions	max 2	
Examples of uses	max 4	
Automated decisions	1	
Better quality/consistent quality of management information	max 2	
Maximum		10

An **ERP system** integrates the information required by all functions within an organisation into a single system, so that everyone uses the same data and information. A properly-designed system will also provide for **continual updating**, so that the information it contains is both current and accurate. It should also enable employees who are away from the company's premises to have **immediate access to the system**, both to input data and to obtain information. It appears that a large proportion of the company's employees are out of the office for much of the time, speaking with potential customers and visiting their premises, so it will be important for them to be able to easily access up-to-date information about Trendy's performance.

Trendy also needs to be **flexible** and **responsive** to its customer's demands. Its retail customers are not particularly loyal to their suppliers; instead they are looking for quick delivery and low prices, as well as items of clothing that will sell well. By integrating its manufacturing and inventory systems, the ERPS should help Trendy increase the flexibility and efficiency of its production, which are characteristics the retailers value.

An ERP system should enable Trendy to **respond to customer requests** promptly. The sales representative can access the **inventory files** to check whether inventory is available for immediate delivery. If there is insufficient inventory, the system should be able to provide an estimate of when the items can be produced and delivered. The system should also hold information about the current state of **work in progress**, so that information about **delivery dates** for these items can also be given to retailers. The customer can therefore be given **reliable information** about availability and delivery.

If a retailer asks for a special batch of an item, the Trendy representative should be able to quickly obtain a **price quotation** from the accounts data on the IT system.

Orders from retailers can be fed into the system prompting **automatic decisions** about producing new items. The system may also provide information for predicting future orders so that items can be produced in anticipation of orders – allowing the company to deliver orders more quickly when they are eventually obtained.

Data on **production and delivery costs** should be recorded immediately, so that up-to-date product costs can be measured and reported. Sales prices can be adjusted as appropriate in response to changing costs.

Trendy has some retail outlets of its own. The checkout function in each of these outlets can be linked to the ERP system, providing immediate information about **sales in each retail outlet**. The sales information can be used to predict future order quantities for each of the outlets, and the managers of each outlet should also be able to input orders to the central system. By linking checkout to order and delivery systems, the retail outlets should be kept better stocked to **meet customer demand**.

In summary, an ERP system should provide an **integrated IT system** that allows for input from different locations, including remote input from representatives, and for the provision of up-to-date information about inventory, work-in-progress, sales demand for different products, sales orders and costs. In a competitive environment, this should help Trendy to respond immediately to customer requests and queries, and so provide a **better service** to the customer and (hopefully) secure a **higher volume of sales**.

By integrating the IT system for the company as a whole, the ERP will provide access for many employees to data that was previously unattainable that they can use to perform their jobs more effectively.

83 ICE

Text reference. Sources of management information are covered in Chapter 15.

Top tips. We think the requirement of this question sounds more complex than the information you actually need to provide! You may have got bogged down in the intricacies of designing information systems, but all that you really needed to do was **comment** on the **issues that needed to be considered**.

- Aspects of the environment that need to be monitored
- Sources of information
- Who will collect the information
- The way in which it will be disseminated

It was important to note that you were supposed to be commenting on **formal** methods and procedures. Informal methods such as discussions between employees should not have been covered.

You could also have made mention of **security** of information systems and **controls** over distribution of information if you had time.

Marking scheme

		Marks
External information requirements	max 4	
Sources of information	max 4	
Responsibilities for obtaining the information	1	
System/methods for dissemination within the organisation	max 3	
Maximum		10

Some aspects of ICE's **external environment** will be more important for the company than others. Just what the most important aspects are vary from organisation to organisation. The first step that should therefore be taken is for an individual or a committee to be appointed to establish (and subsequently review) what aspects of the external environment should be monitored by formal methods and procedures.

The aspects of the environment that might be monitored include the following.

(a) **Competitors**. Information should be gathered about what competitors are doing, how successful they are and how much of a threat they are. New contracts awarded by food companies will be of interest to ICE.

(b) **Suppliers**. Information should be gathered about suppliers and potential suppliers, their prices, product or service quality and delivery dates.

(c) **Customers**. An organisation should always try to be aware of the needs of its customers, to identify changes in these needs, to recognise potential market segments, and to assess the size of a potential market. Customer awareness is vital for new product development and successful selling.

(d) **Legal changes**. Changes in the law might affect how an organisation operates, and any such changes should be monitored. For example, changes in data protection legislation.

(e) **Political changes**. Some organisations are affected by national or local politics. If politics can be important, the organisation should try to monitor political decisions at both national and local level.

(f) **Financial and economic conditions**. Most organisations have to monitor developments in financial and economic conditions. For example, the general rate of inflation is significant for decisions about wage increases for employees.

(g) **Environmental pressures.** The use of CFCs in packaging has been identified as contributing to the hole in the ozone layer. Companies such as ICE therefore need to find alternative materials to use in their products.

Once the main types of environmental information have been identified, ICE should then establish the following.

(a) The most **appropriate sources** for obtaining this information. This will vary according to the nature of the information.

(b) The individuals or departments **whose task** it should be to gather the information, and where appropriate, disseminate it through the organisation to other people who might need it.

(c) The **form** in which the information should be disseminated through the organisation.

Sources of information

(a) **Suppliers**' price lists and brochures.

(b) **Published reports and accounts** (of competitors, suppliers and business customers).

(c) **Government** reports (often, reports on specific topics. Economic and trade reports, for example, are frequently produced by central government).

(d) Government statistics.

(e) External databases, provided by specialist organisations and often available over the **Internet**. Treasury departments, for example, use external databases to obtain information about current interest rates and foreign exchange rates.

(f) Newspaper and other **media** reports.

Individuals or departments should be made **responsible** for obtaining information about certain aspects of the environment. In some cases, the individual department will collect information that it wishes to use itself. In other cases, there will be a need to distribute information throughout the rest of the organisation, and procedures should be established for doing this. Methods of distributing information would include the following.

(a) Routine reports or in-house circulars
(b) The company magazine
(c) A company database, to which access is via computer terminals
(d) An executive information system
(e) Email
(f) An intranet

84 Biscuits and Cakes Part 1

Text references. Return on investment and residual income are covered in Chapter 17.

Top tips. Parts (a) and (b) ask you to calculate the **annualised** return on investment and residual income. Remember to multiply the monthly net profit figure by 12, to reflect that there are 12 months in a year.

Part (c) asks you to conclude as to whether the two divisions have performed well, using additional calculations as necessary. In order to fairly assess performance, take time to recalculate ROI and/or RI using controllable profit.

Easy marks. There are four marks up for grabs in parts (a) and (b) for calculating the annualised ROI and RI.

Examiner's comments. This was a straightforward performance measurement question in a divisional context. Parts (a) and (b) were relatively straightforward.

In part (c), stronger candidates realised that, in order to discuss the performance of the divisions well, they needed to recalculate the ROI and/or RI using controllable profit. Where candidates did this, they generally accompanied it with some good discussion and scored full marks.

Weaker answers performed other calculations on the two divisions and gave some general commentary, even though the question asked for a discussion 'using both ROI and RI'.

Marking scheme

			Marks
(a)	ROI/RI calculations:		
	ROI for B	1	
	ROI for C	1	
			2
(b)	ROI/RI discussion:		
	RI for B	1	
	RI for C	1	
			2
(c)	Discussion:		
	ROI discussion	2	
	RI discussion	2	
	Extra ROI calculation under old method	1	
	Valid conclusion drawn	1	
			6
			10

(a) **Annualised return on investment (ROI)**

ROI = (Net profit / Net assets) × 100%

Division B

Net profit = $311,000 × 12 months = $3,732,000

ROI = ($3,732,000 / $23,200,000) × 100%

= 16.09%

Division C

Net profit = $292,000 × 12 months = $3,504,000

ROI = ($3,504,000 / $22,600,000) × 100%

= 15.5%

(b) **Annualised residual income (RI)**

	Division B	*Division C*
	$'000	$'000
Net profit (part (a))	3,732	3,504
Less imputed interest charge:		
$23.2m × 10%	(2,320)	nil
$22.6m × 10%	nil	(2,260)
	1,412	1,244

(c) **Performance based on ROI**

The ROIs calculated for each division in part (a) are both significantly below the company's **target ROI** (20%). This would suggest that both divisions are performing poorly.

However, both divisions are now required to deduct a share of **head office costs** in their respective operating statements before arriving at 'net profit' which is then used to calculate ROI. The company's target ROI has not been reduced to take account of these **uncontrollable costs**.

Using the old method (prior to head office costs being recharged to divisions), ROI for both divisions would have **exceeded the 20% target**, and increased ROIs for the last three months (Division B: 22% pa, Division C: 23% pa) showing that both divisions have actually **improved their performance**.

ROI using the old method

Division B net profit = ($311,000 + $155,000) × 12 = $5,592,000

Division B ROI = $5,592,000 / $23,200,000 × 100% = 24.1%

Division C net profit = ($292,000 + $180,000) × 12 = $5,664,000

Division C ROI = $5,664,000 / $22,600,000 × 100% = 25.06%

Performance based on RI

Division B and Division C both have healthy RI figures of $1.4m and $1.2m respectively. These figures are impressive when you consider that they are based on **net profits** as opposed to **controllable profits**.

However, the company's cost of capital of 10% is significantly lower than the target return on investment (20%). This makes the residual income figure show a more **positive position**.

85 Biscuits and Cakes Part 2

Text references. Return on investment and residual income are covered in Chapter 17.

Top tips. Parts (a) and (b) ask you to calculate the **annualised** return on investment and residual income. Remember to multiply the monthly net profit figure by 12, to reflect that there are 12 months in a year.

Easy marks. This question tests your knowledge and understanding of the influence of management behaviour or motivation of ROI and residual income as measures of divisional performance.

You should try to remember, however, that both ROI and RI are mostly used as measures of historical performance. They are unreliable measures when it comes to making investment decisions for the future, although in this respect ROI is more unreliable than RI.

Examiner's comments. In part (b) candidates were supposed to identify the fact that changing the basis for calculating ROI and using this for performance measurement without changing the target ROI would cause managers to be demotivated. Many candidates answered this well, although some simply discussed the general problems encountered when using ROI, which were relevant to a degree but shouldn't have been the sole answer.

Marking scheme

			Marks
(a)	ROI/RI after investment:		
	ROI calculation	2	
	RI calculation	2	
	Comments and conclusion	2	
			6
(b)	Behavioural issues:		
	ROI of investment – 1 mark per valid point		max 4
			10

(a) **Division B's revised annualised net profit and opening net assets after investment**

Depreciation = ($2,120,000 – $200,000) / 48 months = $40,000 per month

Net profit for July = $311,000 + ($600,000 × 8.5%) – $40,000 = $322,000

Annualised net profit = $322,000 × 12 = $3,864,000

Opening net assets after investment = $23,200,000 + $2,120,000 = $25,320,000

Division B ROI

ROI = (Net profit / Net assets) × 100%

= $3,864,000 / $25,320,000 × 100% = 15.26%

Division B will not proceed with the investment as it will cause a decrease in ROI.

Division B RI

	$'000
Net profit	3,864
Less imputed interest charge:	
$25.32m × 10%	(2,532)
Residual income	1,332

This calculation shows that, if the investment is undertaken, RI is actually lower than without the investment. So, if either ROI or RI is considered by Division B's manager when deciding whether to undertake the investment, the investment will not be undertaken. This decision will be in the best interests of the company as a whole, since the RI of the investment alone is actually negative ($132,000 – $212,000 = $(80,000)).

(b) **Behavioural problems**

Staff in both divisions are used to exceeding the target ROI of 20% and being rewarded for doing so. As a result of including head office costs in the calculation of net profit, staff will see that their respective divisions are no longer meeting the target ROI despite performance actually improving.

The target ROI should be revised to take account of the uncontrollable allocated costs.

Staff are likely to become demotivated by the fact that they are no longer meeting the target ROI despite continuing to operate at the same level as before. They may feel that management have deliberately altered how performance is measured in order to avoid paying staff bonuses for exceeding targets.

Staff may deliberately work slowly and refuse to work overtime to show their opposition to the new system. The company should resolve the situation as soon as possible to avoid a decrease in production output and product quality.

86 Brash Co

Text references. The balanced scorecard approach to performance measurement is covered in Chapter 16.

Top tips. Make your answer easy to mark. Start with a short introduction then write a little bit about each perspective under separate headings.

Easy marks. Although it is based in the context of a company, the requirement in the question is really generic. You should score highly providing your answer covers all four perspectives of the balanced scorecard.

Examiner's comments. There were some really good answers although the structure of answers could have been better. It is really hard to mark a question like this where candidates' answers include no headings and often not even any paragraphs.

Marking scheme

	Marks
Balanced scorecard approach:	
Stating what it is	2
Financial perspective	2
Customer perspective	2
Internal perspective	2
Learning and growth perspective	2
	10

Balanced scorecard

The **balanced scorecard** approach to performance measurement emphasises the need to provide management with a set of information which covers all relevant areas of performance in an objective and unbiased fashion.

The information provided may be both financial and non-financial and cover areas such as profitability, customer satisfaction, internal efficiency and innovation.

The balanced scorecard focuses on **four different perspectives**, as follows.

Customer perspective

The customer perspective considers how new and existing customers view the organisation. This perspective should identify targets that matter to customers such as cost, quality, delivery, inspection and so on.

The customer perspective is linked to revenue/profit objectives in the financial perspective. If customer objectives are achieved, it is likely that revenue/profit objectives will also be achieved.

Internal perspective

The internal perspective makes an organisation consider what processes it must excel at in order to achieve financial and customer objectives.

The perspective aims to improve internal processes and decision making.

Innovation and learning perspective

The innovation and learning perspective requires the organisation to consider how it can continue to improve and create value.

Organisations must seek to acquire new skills and develop new products in order to maintain a competitive position in their respective market(s) and provide a basis from which the other perspectives of the balanced scorecard can be accomplished.

Financial perspective

The financial perspective considers whether the organisation meets the expectations of its shareholders and how it creates value for them.

This perspective focuses on traditional measures such as growth, profitability and cost reduction.

87 Brace Co

Text references. Return on investment and residual income are covered in Chapter 17.

Top tips. This question should be a straightforward test of your ability to calculate ROI and residual income, and to comment on divisional performance on the basis of these ratios.

Easy marks. This question offers easy marks, but only if you know how to calculate ROI and residual income.

Examiner's comments. About 50% of candidates scored full marks on the calculations but some had no idea how to calculate ROI/RI. As for the commentary, most answers were poor, showing that there is little understanding of what these figures actually mean.

Marking scheme

		Marks
ROI/RI:		
ROI for A	1	
ROI for B	1	
RI for A	2	
RI for B	2	
Comments:		
A rejects, B accepts under ROI	1	
Both accept under RI	1	
ROI produces wrong decision for company	1	
RI produces right decision	1	
Manager right	1	
Other factors to consider	1	
		max 10

Division A

Return on investment (ROI):
Net profit = \$44.6m × 28% = \$12.488m
ROI = (profit / capital employed) × 100%
= \$12.488m / \$82.8m = 15.08%

Residual income (RI):
Net profit = \$12.488m
Capital employed = \$82.8m
Imputed interest charge = \$82.8m × 12% (cost of capital for both divisions) = \$9.936m
RI = net profit – imputed interest charge
= \$12.488m – \$9.936m = \$2.552m

Division B

Return on investment (ROI):
Net profit = \$21.8m × 33% = \$7.194m
ROI = \$7.194m / \$40.6m = 17.72%

Residual income (RI):
Net profit = \$7.194m
Capital employed = \$40.6m
Imputed interest charge = \$40.6m × 12% = \$4.872m
RI = \$7.194m – \$4.872m = \$2.322m

Comments

The current return on investment (ROI) of each division is 16%. It is likely that the manager of Division A will reject any proposal based solely on ROI as the Division A investment only has a ROI of 15.08%. The proposed investment would reduce Division A's ROI by 0.92 percentage points.

In contrast, the manager of Division B is likely to accept the proposal as the Division B investment has an ROI of 17.72%. The proposed investment would increase Division B's ROI by 1.72 percentage points.

Both divisions are likely to accept the proposal based on residual income as both have a healthy RI (\$2.552m and \$2.322m respectively).

The views of the new manager of Division A are correct. The use of ROI as the sole decision tool in the past has led to a lack of goal congruence between Division A and the company as a whole.

It is clear that the use of RI as an investment measure will help the divisions to make decisions that are in the best interests of the company.

88 Wash Co

Text reference. Transfer pricing is covered in Chapter 17. Activity based costing is covered in Chapter 2a.

Top tips. There are a number of calculations to make in parts (a) and (b). Label each calculation clearly and show all your workings.

You are told that company policy is to transfer the machines from the assembly division to the retail division at full cost plus 10%. Ensure that you calculate a 10% mark-up, not a 10% margin!

Easy marks. You should be able to score a number of quick and easy marks in part (a) using knowledge from your previous studies.

Examiner's comments. Part (a) asked for a recalculation of the transfer prices using activity based costing to allocate the overheads. Many candidates scored full marks, although when errors were made, the main ones were to use machine hours as the driver for machine set up costs and the number of set ups as the driver for machine maintenance costs. This error always seems to occur with these two categories of costs and I don't really understand why. I can only put it down to poor reading of the question.

Marking scheme

			Marks
(a)	Transfer price using ABC:		
	Cost driver rates	2.0	
	Total overheads allocated	2.0	
	Overhead cost per unit	0.5	
	Total cost per unit	0.5	
	Transfer price per unit	1.0	
	Comment on retail manager's target sales prices	2.0	
			8
(b)	ABC profit calculation: 1 mark per division		2
			10

(a) **Transfer prices using ABC**

	Product S	*Product R*
	$	$
Materials cost	117.00	95.00
Labour cost ($12 per hour)	6.00	9.00
Overhead cost (W1)	160.57	66.75
Total cost	283.57	170.75
10% mark-up	28.36	17.08
Transfer price using ABC	311.93	187.83

The transfer price for Product S would be much higher than it is currently and the transfer price for Product R would be much lower. At this lower cost, the manager of the retail division could sell Product R more cheaply at his target price of $230, but it would Product S would make very little profit if it is sold at $320 when its activity based cost is nearly $312.

Workings

1 *Overhead cost using ABC*

Machine set up costs

Driver = number of production runs
Total number of production runs = 30(S) + 12(R) = 42
Cost per set up = $306,435/42 = $7,296.07

Machine maintenance costs

Driver = machine hours
Total number of machine hours = 6,400(S) + 5,450(R) = 11,850
Cost per machine hour = $415,105 / 11,850 = $35.03

Ordering costs

Driver = number of purchase orders
Total number of purchase orders = 82(S) + 64(R) = 146
Cost per order = $11,680 / 146 = $80.00

Delivery costs

Driver = number of deliveries
Total number of deliveries = 64(S) + 80(R) = 144
Cost per delivery = $144,400 / 144 = $1,002.78

Allocation of overheads to each product

	Product S	*Product R*
	$	$
Materials set-up costs ($7,296.07 per set up)	218,882	87,553
Machine maintenance costs ($35.03 per machine hr)	224,192	190,913
Ordering costs ($80.00 per order)	6,560	5,120
Delivery costs ($1,002.78 per delivery)	64,178	80,222
Total overheads allocated	513,812	363,808
Number of units produced	3,200	5,450
Overhead cost per unit	$160.57	$66.75

(b) **ABC monthly profit**

Using the ABC transfer price from part (a):

Assembly division	*Product S*	*Product R*	*Total*
Production and sales	3,200	5,450	
	$	$	
10% mark up	28.36	17.08	
Profit	90,752	93,086	$183,838

Retail division	*Product S*	*Product R*	*Total*
Production and sales	3,200	5,450	
	$	$	
Selling price	320.00	260.00	
Cost	(311.93)	(187.83)	
Profit per unit	8.07	72.17	
Total profit	25,824	393,327	$419,151

89 PC

Text reference. Performance measurement is covered in Chapters 16 and 17.

Top tips. This is the style of performance measurement question that we should probably expect from this examiner, with a financial performance measure giving a misleading picture of a company's performance. Use a clear layout for your calculations and headings to give a structure to your discussions and explanations. Each part of the question can be answered separately so if you get stuck or are unsure what is required, move on.

Easy marks. The calculations are straightforward provided you are happy with calculating ROI and there are plenty of marks available for common sense explanations.

Examiner's comments. Many candidates scored reasonable marks in part (a) but in part (b) few candidates understood how performance can be manipulated with most only suggesting depreciation. Far too few suggested accruals and tampering with sales timing.

Marking scheme

			Marks
(a)	Sales calculation	0.5	
	Sales revenue assessment	1.0	
	Gross margin calculation	0.5	
	Gross margin assessment	1.0	
	Overhead control and flexibility	1.0	
	ROI calculation	1.0	
	ROI comment	1.0	
			6
(b)	Timing of decision problem	1.0	
	Revenue acceleration	1.0	
	Delay of cost (0.5 per example)	1.0	
	Manipulation of accounting policy	1.0	
			4
			10

(a) **Calculation of performance measures**

	20X5	*20X6*	*20X7*	*20X8*
ROI (net profit/net assets × 100%)	13.0%	17.5%	16.7%	20.0%
Gross profit margin (gross profit/sales × 100%)	40%	35%	35%	30%
Net profit margin (net profit/sales × 100%)	6.5%	7.0%	5.6%	4.7%
Change in sales	–	0%	–10%	–5.6%
Overheads (Gross – net profit)	$67,000	$56,000	$53,000	$43,000

ROI

The **target ROI** is 15% and this has been achieved every year apart from 20X5. This looks impressive but it is **not due** to increasing profits. **Net assets have fallen in value** each year due to depreciation. It is this fall which has compensated for the fall in net profits and enabled the target ROI to be achieved.

Change in sales

The market in which PC operates has been growing steadily but **sales revenues have been declining** in store W. This is a worrying sign and indicates that PC is either failing to compete effectively or is reducing selling prices.

Gross profit margin

PC's stores typically generate a 40% gross profit margin and this has only been achieved in 20X5. This could be due to reduced selling prices or an increase in the cost of sales, for example increased labour costs. As sales revenue has fallen, it looks like **sales prices have been reduced** in an effort to improve sales.

Overheads

Overheads have been **reducing** year on year and this is usually considered to be positive, especially as sales have fallen. However, the cost cutting could have damaged customers' experiences in the store and contributed to the decline in sales.

Net profit margin

Even though overheads have been reduced, net profit margin has still been **falling**. This is again primarily due to the fall in gross margin.

Conclusion

The positive ROI information **fails to reflect** the true performance of store W. Profitability and sales revenue have declined and it seems hard to justify awarding a bonus to the manager of store W based on an inappropriate performance measure.

(b) The manager's aim would be to **just hit** the target 15% each year rather than exceed the target in one year and fail to meet it in another.

The manager would not have been awarded a bonus in 20X5 because ROI was below the target. In order to gain the bonus in 20X5 he would have had to manipulate the results so that $2,000 less profit was made in 20X6 and more in 20X5.

Manipulation methods

Accelerate revenue by allocating sales made early in 20X6 to 20X5. This could be achieved by dating an invoice when an order is received in late 20X5 but not actually sending it to the customer until delivery is made in 20X6.

Delay costs by not recording suppliers' invoices until 20X6, even though goods were received in 20X5.

Manipulate provisions and accruals so that less costs are charged in 20X5.

Manipulate accounting policies such as inventory values or depreciation charges so that more profit is made in 20X5. For example, closing inventory could be overstated.

90 Rotech Group

Text reference. Performance measurement is covered in Chapters 16 and 17.

Top tips. Use a clear layout for your calculations and headings to give a structure to your discussions and explanations. Each part of the question can be answered separately so if you get stuck or are unsure what is required, move on.

Easy marks. The calculations are straightforward and there are plenty of marks available for common sense explanations.

Examiner's comments. The calculations in the first part of the question were done quite well, although a common mistake was to combine the two divisions of W Co an calculate the ratios for W Co as a whole. This was presumably caused by insufficient reading of the requirement. Students had difficulty dealing with the discussion that followed the calculations with candidates failing to identify the difficulty comparing a design business to a manufacturing business.

Marking scheme

		Marks
Ratios		
Calculating ROCE	1.5	
Calculating asset turnover	1.5	
Calculating operating profit margin	1.5	
Marks per valid comment (max 5.5)	5.5	
		10

Financial ratios

		W Co Design	*W Co Gearbox*	*C Co*
Return on capital employed	Profit before interest and tax / Capital employed %	\$6,000/\$23,540 = 25.49%	\$3,875/\$32,320 = 11.99%	\$7,010/82,975 = 8.45%
Asset turnover	Sales / Capital employed	\$14,300/\$23,540 = 0.61 times	\$25,535/\$32,320 = 0.79 times	\$15,560/\$82,975= 0.19 times
Operating profit margin	Profit before interest and tax / Sales %	\$6,000/\$14,300 = 41.96%	\$3,875/\$25,535 = 15.18%	\$7,010/\$15,560 = 45.05%

Return on capital employed:

ROCE shows how much profit has been made in relation to the amount of resources invested. C Co and both divisions of W Co are profitable. The Design division of W Co has the highest ROCE at over 25% while the Gearbox division and C Co are significantly lower at 11.99% and 8.45% respectively. This is primarily due to the nature of the design business which derives its profits from personnel rather than physical assets. Employees generate profits by designing products, rather than using expensive machinery. Therefore the Design divisions capital employed (asset) figure is significantly lower.

C Co has the largest asset base, and this is reflected in a relatively low ROCE. The Gearbox division is closer to this than to the design division but this is as a result of similarities in the nature of the business rather than division performance alone.

Asset turnover:

Asset turnover is a measure of how well the assets of a business are being used to generate sales. The Gearbox division has the highest level at 79%, while C Co has the lowest at 19%. This is probably due in part to the fact that the Gearbox division buys from C Co, therefore C Co must hold a large asset base to produce the relevant components. Both divisions of W Co do not have the same requirement and this is reflected in the higher asset turnover figures.

Operating profit margin:

C Co comes out on top in the final profitability measure, which is he operating profit margin at just over 45%, while the Gearbox division is the lowest at 15.18%. The Design division performs well at 41.96%, as it did in asset turnover. This was to be expected from the ROCE of 25%, which is a combination of the other two ratios. The Design division has both high unit profitability and generates sales at a high lever compared to its asset base.

There are limitations to these types of comparisons due to the differing nature of the businesses. It would be more useful to compare each business unit to an industry average for similar businesses, as well as comparing year on year figures to monitor the units on an ongoing basis.

91 Story

Text reference. Management information systems are discussed in Chapter 14.

Top tips. This is quite a long and complicated scenario. You'll improve your chances of writing a good answer by reading the scenario carefully and then planning your answer.

We suggest that you start by making brief notes as a rough sketch for your answer. Then elaborate your notes into your answer, using headings and paragraphs, and picking out the main points from the question. So, for example, head up a paragraph 'open systems' and write a paragraph on open systems. This makes it much clearer to mark and uses the key phrases the examiner is looking for in a good answer.

Part (b) of this question illustrates the importance of being able to apply theory to the scenario. You may not be able to give any examples of closed systems as these rarely occur. Just make sure you put down an explanation so that you get credit for knowing what a closed system is.

Marking scheme

			Marks
(a)	Discussion of advantages	2	
	Discussion of costs	2	
	Discussion of changes	4	
			8
(b)	Discussion of open systems	2	
	Discussion of closed systems	2	
	Application to the case study	3	
			7
			15

(a) **Issues in upgrading the existing information system**

The issues involved in an upgrade of the existing information system include achieving the potential advantages at minimum cost and anticipating and managing necessary changes.

(i) **Advantages of upgrade**

A networked system would allow the **transmission** of information both to and from the business units and head office at Story. As such it is likely that performance indicators, financial statistics and similar **information** could be **rapidly gathered, processed and disseminated**. **Improved communication** between units and head office should improve, leading to **rapid reaction** to changes both within the organisation and outside it. This should result in a responsive, evolving organisation capable of meeting the challenges of the market place. It would also get rid of the problems currently experienced where some countries do not have the most up-to-date information on products and prices.

(ii) **Costs**

The **costs** of providing a fully networked computer system, changeover costs and the costs of future maintenance and training must be evaluated and budgeted for. The development and implementation of **security measures** to prevent the misuse of corporate data, and to prevent fraud by unauthorised users (who may be employees or external to the organisation) have to be considered and costed. In addition, there may be a possible need to **recruit** specialised staff to implement the changes to the existing information system. All of these costs are foreseeable and can be planned.

(iii) **Changes**

Upgrading corporate information systems usually results in many unforeseen changes to the **culture** of the organisation and to the **working practices** of staff at all levels. For example, would greater efficiency be achieved by allowing staff to have more flexible hours of attendance? Can costs be reduced by allowing some staff to telecommute on a regular basis, thus allowing hot-desking to take place? Is it likely that morale will be adversely affected by staff who may be concerned about using new technology or staff who fear that they may lose their jobs through the changes?

The proposed changes are unlikely to change the **role and remit of management** in relation to the directing of staff, although it is likely that there will be some impact upon organising staff tasks as new needs arise. **Strategic and tactical planning** are likely to change in response to the improved, and more rapid, flow of information that the information system will provide.

Operational decisions can be taken at lower levels of the corporate hierarchy as information becomes available more rapidly and in an appropriate format. As well as providing a swift response to changes in the business environment, it is possible that the organisation will, in time, evolve into one with a **flatter hierarchy**. This would particularly suit the autonomous business unit structure in Story which already operates with devolved decision making. However, there is always the danger of '**information overload**' which can reduce efficiency and morale within the organisation.

(b) **Closed systems and open systems**

Closed system

A closed system is one that **does not react to external stimuli or allow communication from internal processes to interact with the outside environment**. They are seldom, if ever, found in naturally occurring situations. A typical example of a closed system would be a chemical reaction that takes place under controlled conditions within a laboratory. Closed systems can be created to eliminate external factors and then used to investigate the relationship between known variables in an experiment.

Open system

An open system is one that **interacts fully with its environment**. It accepts **inputs** from its surroundings, processes the inputs in some manner and then produces an **output**. The input parameters can be foreseen or be unpredictable. Similarly, outputs can either be predicted or unforeseen. For example, predictable inputs of a metal smelting works would include items like the raw materials and coal while the predictable outputs would be ash, smoke and the smelted metal. If the raw material to be smelted became contaminated in some way, it is likely that an undesirable product would be produced. These are examples of unforeseen inputs and outputs.

Examples in the question

Turning to the question, we can see that Story is clearly an **open system**. It reacts, albeit imperfectly, to inputs from its environment and produces outputs. Sales figures are collated and analysed and predictions are made based upon this information. Hence the organisation responds to external stimuli and reacts appropriately.

The question also provides instances of **sub-systems** within the organisation that are themselves open systems. For example, the information system, the corporate management team, the business units and retail outlets are examples of sub-systems within the business that are all open.

92 Viga

Text reference. Procedures to ensure the secrecy of highly confidential information are covered in Chapter 15.

Top tips. The examples in the question indicate some of the ways in which confidential information may become 'public knowledge'. You should consider the potential consequences in part (a) and then go on to consider ways in which confidentiality and secrecy can be protected in part (b). Unfortunately, control measures cannot be guaranteed to succeed, and the rigour of the controls that are put in place may depend to some extent on the potential consequences of public disclosure of the information.

Marking scheme

			Marks
(a)	Reasons for improper release of confidential information	4	
	Possible consequences	3	
			7
(b)	Measures to improve confidentiality of sensitive information (maximum 2 marks per point)		max 8
			15

(a) There are several reasons why confidential information may be improperly released. Most reasons can be described in terms of **weak or non-existent controls** to protect confidentiality.

(i) **Confidential information** may be released through carelessness. The example of Viga's company secretary leaving their computer on a train illustrates one way in which confidential information could find its way into the public domain; but information could also be released by employees making a careless comment within the hearing of an 'outsider', or failing to keep confidential reports in a secure place. When confidential information is discovered due to carelessness, there is a risk that it will be **read and passed on**.

(ii) There may be a **deliberate breach of security** to access confidential information. There may be a big risk to commercial organisations from external **'hackers'**. Employees may also deliberately find a way of gaining **unauthorised access** to confidential files.

(iii) There may be **loose controls** over the disposal of information. There have been occasional reports in the press of confidential reports being found by investigators in rubbish bins.

Reasons for breaches of confidentiality may also be analysed in terms of the motivation of the individuals who acquire it. Individuals who **sell confidential information** to a rival organisation do so for personal selfish motives. In the case of the member of the accounts department who had details of his private life disclosed, the breach of confidentiality was probably motivated by a desire to retaliate against the whistle blower. **Leaking information** (even though it was not fully correct) about the closure of the production centre may have been prompted by a desire to help the employees affected; to try to prevent them losing their jobs.

The consequences for an organisation of the release of confidential information depend on the **nature** of the 'leak'.

(i) Information may be returned **un-read and unused**, in which case there has been a breach of security controls but no adverse consequence, as appears to have been the case with the company secretary's laptop.

(ii) When **confidential information** is released to employee representatives, there may be an immediate threat of **strike action**, or a change in **negotiating position** (when a matter such as pay is currently under negotiation). A strike would have operational and financial consequences. In the longer term, there may be damage to the trust between management and employees, and uneasy **industrial relations** within the company.

(iii) The release of confidential information to the media, such as information about Viga's health and safety inspection, creates adverse publicity and can have **adverse consequences** for the company's **reputation**. The consequences of damage to reputation may be difficult to assess.

(iv) The release of confidential information about an employee, leading to the resignation of the employee, can have **legal and financial consequences**. Employees who are victimised in this way have a right to appeal for **constructive dismissal** and could potentially receive substantial compensation.

(v) The loss of confidential information to a **rival organisation** could have serious commercial consequences, because the information could help the rival to decide its **competitive strategy** in a way that enables it to gain an **advantage in the market**. In an extreme case, the unauthorised disclosure of the secret recipe for its drink product could have a long-term impact on Viga's business position. The recipe currently represents a source of **competitive advantage** for Viga, but if the recipe details were disclosed to a rival company, it could make use of the recipe information to improve its own product.

(b) The procedures that Viga is going to put in place should be set out clearly in a **policy document**.

(i) The company's policy should include an **element of deterrence**, to discourage employees from trying to access or use confidential information. This policy should include ensuring that any breach of confidentiality is investigated, perhaps by an external firm of investigators. There should be **disciplinary measures** for breaches of confidentiality, ranging from an official warning (for example, for leaving a laptop on a train) to dismissal or even referral to the police for a criminal matter. Although these measures are retrospective (because they occur after the security breach has occurred) their existence should help act as a deterrent against employees committing breaches of security in the future.

(ii) There should be physical protection for files or other documents containing confidential information. Paper files may be kept in a safe. Viga's secret recipe is presumably kept off site in a **secure deposit** with a reputable custodian such as a major bank.

Viga should also consider the use of **encryption software** for securing files on its computers, and/or email messages. This would prevent third parties from **recovering information** even if they gain access to a laptop or computer files.

(iii) All confidential papers distributed to a restricted list of recipients should be marked on every page to identify the recipient, and should be **signed for on receipt**. If a photocopy or photograph of the document is subsequently leaked, the **individual responsible can be identified**. This should encourage the individual to make sure that the documents are kept secure.

(iv) Access to computer files containing confidential information can be restricted to specific users and by means of **passwords**. Attempts at unauthorised access should be logged automatically as security violations and investigated.

(v) The company should have a **strict emails policy**, instructing managers to avoid any mention of confidential issues in the emails they send.

(vi) Viga should review its **whistle blowing procedures** and consider ways in which the identity of whistle blowers (and, initially, the information they provide) is kept secret until any subsequent investigation has been completed. The problem at Viga may be due to the fact that the person authorised to hear the whistle blower's allegation did not keep the matter sufficiently hidden and out of sight, or did not investigate the allegation in an appropriate way.

(vii) Confidential information may be accessed by individuals from **outside the organisation**, but the person responsible is often an employee. Confidential information should only be made available to individuals who can be trusted. An important control may therefore be the **careful selection of individuals** for appointment to jobs in the organisation, and impressions of honesty, integrity and trustworthiness may be factors to consider when making the appointment.

93 Lewisville

Text references. Performance measures are covered in Chapter 16 and not-for-profit organisations in Chapter 18.

Top tips. In part (a), the first three ratios are well-known financial performance measures. You might find average cost per passenger mile a bit difficult to work out at first. However, the information is in the question so you just need to read carefully.

Make sure you can make at least one point on each measure as it applies to the bus service.

In part (b) make sure that the measures you suggest are indeed non-financial. Probably the most common fault in answers to this section will be confusion between what is to be measured (for example customer satisfaction) and the performance measure (level of complaints).

Easy marks. The ratio calculations in part (a) should be mostly straightforward, and you should try to provide a comment on each ratio that you calculate.

Marking scheme

			Marks
(a)	One mark per ratio	4	
	One mark per ratio explained	4	
	One mark per comment on performance	4	
			12
(b)	1.5 marks per indicator and its importance		3
			15

(a) **Return on capital employed (ROCE)**

ROCE (also called return on investment (ROI)) is calculated as (profit/capital employed) × 100%. This shows how much profit has been made in relation to the amount of resources invested. In the case of the bus service, the measure is calculated by using the surplus figure as profit.

Profit = $20,000

Capital employed (or total assets less liabilities) = $2,210,000

Therefore ROCE = (20,000/2,210,000) × 100% = 0.9% = 1%

The bus service appears to have a very low return compared to private bus companies. However the bus service does not have investors nor does it have the same profit maximisation objectives as private operators. As a public service, it operates to provide a public good and has public service requirements such as availability to all, unlike private companies. It also has low fares and so could be unable to increase profitability. The Lewisville bus service is only generating an annual profit of 0.9 cents for every $1 invested. Private bus companies are showing a return of 10 cents or 10%.

Return on sales

This is a simple measure of performance, which calculates the profit margin and thus alerts managers to excessive costs when compared to industry averages. The profit margin (profit to sales ratio) is calculated as (profit ÷ sales) × 100%. For the bus service, taking the surplus figure as above and using income from passenger fares as sales:

Return on sales = (20,000/1,200,000) × 100% = 1.7%

The bus service has low margins compared to the private sector. Once again, this may be partly explained by its public service ethos and lack of discretion in charging fares. Of course it also means that costs will have to be looked at in case these are excessive.

The Lewisville bus service is making a return on sales of 1.7% or 1.7 cents per $1 of sales. Its private sector equivalents are making a return of 30 cents per $1 of sales.

Asset turnover

Asset turnover is a measure of how well the assets of a business are being used to generate sales. It is calculated as (sales ÷ capital employed). Sales are passenger fares and capital employed is as stated in ROCE above.

Asset turnover = 1,200,000/2,210,000 = 0.54 times.

The figure for the bus service is better than that for the private sector. However this may also mean that capital employed is lower and so less investment has been made which is not necessarily ideal.

The Lewisville bus service manages to generate sales of 54 cents for every $1 of capital employed compared to 33 cents for every $1 among the private bus companies.

Average cost per passenger mile

When service organisations are being measured, the cost unit needs to be relevant to the service and reflect what is being provided.

For the bus service, take the cost of providing the service as $1,180k and divide by the number of passenger miles travelled:

Average cost per revenue mile = $1,180,000/4,320,000 = 27.3c

This is a measure of the costs of transporting passengers per mile travelled. Based on this measure the public service is more economic than its comparators.

The Lewisville bus service is cheaper on this measure than the private bus companies. It has a cost of 27.3 cents per passenger mile compared to 37.4 cents per mile in these companies.

Conclusion

In conclusion, the bus service performs better than its comparators on some measures and worse on others. However as it does not have the same objectives, it would be more sensible to compare the bus service with operators who have similar objectives.

(b) (Note that only two indicators are required)

Non-financial performance indicator	*Importance*
% of buses on time	Punctuality is important to passengers and a well-understood target
% of buses cancelled	Reliability is important to passengers
Accidents per 1,000,000 passengers	Safety is vital in any form of travel
Customer rating of cleanliness of facilities	Passengers require good quality service
% utilisation of staff	Underused staff are a waste of resources
% of new customers	New customers are vital for sustained growth
Employee morale	Happy employees (particularly those who deal with customers), are vital for success in a service business

94 Heighway

Text references. Performance measurement is covered in Chapter 16.

Top tips. Make sure that you are confident with the definition of standard accounting ratios (such as return on capital employed and net profit margin) as required in part (a).

Part (b) requires a commentary on the company's financial performance. Suggest causes of changing performance which are appropriate to the circumstances of the railway company.

Part (c) requires you to suggest non-financial performance indicators appropriate to a railway company. Probably the most common fault in answers to this section will be confusion between what is to be measured (for example customer satisfaction) and the performance measure (level of complaints).

Marking scheme

		Marks
(a)	For each financial ratio: 0.5 marks	4
(b)	Comment on each ratio and possible causes of change	8
(c)	For each non-financial ratio, and justification: 1 mark each	3
		15

(a) **Financial ratios**

		20X3	*20X4*
Return on capital employed	$\frac{\text{Profit before interest and tax}}{\text{Capital employed}}\%$	$\frac{18}{105.6} = 17\%$	$\frac{16.5}{123.2} = 13.4\%$
Net profit margin	$\frac{\text{Profit before interest and tax}}{\text{Sales}}\%$	$\frac{18}{180} = 10\%$	$\frac{16.5}{185.0} = 8.9\%$
Asset turnover	$\frac{\text{Sales}}{\text{Capital employed}}$	$\frac{180}{105.6}$ = 1.7 times	$\frac{185}{123.2}$ = 1.5 times
Current ratio	$\frac{\text{Current assets}}{\text{Current liabilities}}$	$\frac{13.6}{8.4}$ = 1.6 : 1	$\frac{11.9}{9.2}$ = 1.3 : 1

(b) **Profitability**

Return on capital employed has fallen from 20X3 to 20X4, caused by a **decrease in operating profit** and an **increase in capital employed**. The fall in operating profit may have been caused by an **increase in costs**, whilst the **new investment programme** will have caused an increase in capital employed.

Asset turnover has fallen. Sales have only increased by 2.8% between 20X3 and 20X4 so the new investment programme may not yet have had a significant effect upon sales.

In the **short term**, the investment programme has increased assets and costs but has not yet influenced sales.

Liquidity

The **current ratio** has deteriorated so the firm's ability to meet its short-term obligations from its short-term resources has been reduced. The expenditure on the investment programme may have decreased the cash balance between 20X3 and 20X4, causing the deterioration in liquidity.

(c) (Note that only three indicators are required.)

Non-financial performance indicator	*Importance*
% of trains on time	Punctuality is important to passengers and a well-understood target

% of trains cancelled	Reliability is important to passengers
Accidents per 1,000,000 passengers	Safety is vital in any form of travel, and an important PR issue for railways in recent times
Customer rating of cleanliness of trains	Passengers require good quality service facilities
% utilisation of rolling stock profits	Underused assets do not earn maximum profits
% utilisation of staff	Underused staff do not help to grow profits
% of new customers	New customers are vital for sustained growth
Employee morale	Happy employees (particularly those who deal with customers), are vital for success in a service business

95 Web Co

Text reference. Performance measurement is covered in Chapter 16.

Top tips. This question may look daunting at first glance, given the 20 marks available for a single requirement. Use the information in the scenario as a framework when structuring your answer and address each performance indicator under a separate heading. Don't forget to highlight any instances where further information is required.

Examiner's comments. As usual, it was necessary to do some preliminary calculations in order to assess performance and candidates should be reminded that absolute figures are rarely useful and percentage changes are far more informative.

The most common weakness in answers was the classic commentary stating that, for example, 'Sales have gone up, which is good'. Comments such as these simply won't score marks. Candidates needed to consider the relationship between the data and calculations with the information given in the question, in this case relating to the changes and incentives introduced. If this link is not being made, rarely will comments score marks.

Good candidates identified that, although sales had increased by 25%, net profit had decreased by 33%, but this was due to the mass of expenses that had been incurred in bringing about the changes. Consequently, the benefits of these changes would be expected to continue for some time, and it would certainly be useful to see quarter 3's results when these were available.

Poorer candidates seemed to think that the decrease in net profit margin was a sign that things were going wrong and cost of sales must be increasing dramatically. Again, I would emphasize that, at this level, candidates are expected to link the information in the scenario with the data and their calculations in order to draw valid conclusions.

Marking scheme

	Marks
Calculations	4
Discussion and further analysis (2–3 marks per point)	10
Conclusion	1
	15

Total sales revenue

Web Co's total **sales revenue has increased 25%** (W1) on Quarter 1 (Q1), from $2.2m to $2.75m. This is impressive given the decision to give a $10 discount to all customers who spend over $100. It is not possible to attribute the increase to any particular change or incentive without analysing the **performance indicators** below.

Net profit margin

The net profit margin has fallen from 25% to 16.7%. Net profit was $550,000 in Q1 and $459,250 in Q2 (W2). If the profit margin had remained at 25%, net profit for Q2 would have been $687,500. Net profit for Q2 is therefore $228,250 **lower** due to the fall in margin.

This significant fall in net profit is largely due to the fee of $200,000 paid for an advert on **the webpage of a well-known fashion magazine**. A further $20,000 is attributable to the fee paid to the **website consultant**.

Number of orders from customers/customers spending over $100

The number of orders received from customers has increased by 22%, from 40,636 in Q1 to 49,600 in Q2 (W3). This 22% increase is roughly **in line with the 25% increase in sales revenue**.

The number of customers spending more than $100 per visit has increased by 37%, from 4,650 in Q1 to 6,390 in Q2. So although the discount reduces the net sales price, it appears to have resulted in higher sales volume. The overall effect of the discount cannot be estimated easily from the data available.

Number of visits to website

The number of visits to the website has also increased significantly, from 101,589 to 141,714 (39.5% (W4)). Of this increase, 28,201 (W5) can be attributed to visitors coming through the **fashion magazine's website**. The remainder of the increase is likely to be due to the work of the website consultant.

It is clear that both changes have been effective in increasing the number of visitors to Web Co's online store. At a cost of $20,000, the work of the web consultant represents excellent **value for money**. However Web Co's sales are not really high enough to justify an outlay of $200,000 for the web magazine advert, hence the **significant fall in net profit margin** (detailed above).

Conversion rate – visitor to purchaser

The conversion rate has decreased by 5 percentage points, from 40% to 35%. This is to be expected, given the substantial increase in visitors to the website as a result of the **web magazine advert** and **search engine optimisation**.

Readers of the fashion magazine may have clicked on the advert link out of curiosity and may return to the site and purchase products at a **later date**.

Website availability

Website availability has remained at 95%. This indicates that the changes made by the IT department **have not corrected the problem(s).**

Lack of availability **may have lost Web Co a significant number of sales.**

Conclusion

In summary, **Web Co performed well in Q2**. With the exception of the work performed by the IT department to make the website more available, all other changes have increased sales.

It appears that the business has **responded well to the changes and incentives introduced**.

The cost of the web advert ($200,000) was so high that **profits have decreased substantially despite the incentives** and changes detailed above.

Workings

1 *Increase in sales revenue*

$2.75m – $2.2m / $2.2m = 25% increase

2 *Net profit*

Quarter 1 = $2.2m × 25% = $550,000
Quarter 2 = $2.75m × 16.7% = $459,250

3 *Increase in orders*

49,600 – 40,636 / 40,636 = 22%

4 *Increase in number of visits to website*

141,714 – 101,589 / 101,589 = 39.5%

5 *Customers accessing website through magazine advert*

141,714 × 19.9% = 28,201

96 Bath Co

Text reference. Transfer pricing is covered in Chapter 17.

Top tips. You may find part (a) particularly time pressured. Ensure your profit statement is neatly presented and remember to split sales and costs figures into external sales and inter-divisional transfers.

Easy marks. There are some easy marks in part (a) of this question.

Examiner's comments. This question covered transfer pricing and really separated out the strong candidates from the weak ones. Part (a) contained the easy marks, with a simple requirement to prepare a profit statement under the current transfer pricing system.

Part (b) asked for a calculation of the maximum profit that could be earned if transfer pricing was optimised. 'Optimised' meant set at a level that would make the total company profit as high as possible. In order for this to be the case, the transfer price needed to be set somewhere between Division B's marginal cost of $20 and the current market price of the fittings of $65 per set. Any price between this range would make sure that Division A bought the fittings from Division B, provided that Division A was told that it could only buy the fittings from outside the group if the price was lower than the price being charged by Division B. If Division B was allowed to sell to the external market too, then the profit could be maximised at $11,060. This logic was totally lost on the majority of candidates. However, many of them managed to get to the maximum profit by having Division B selling 180,000 sets of fittings outside the group and then selling the remaining 20,000 sets of fittings to B at $75. This was a half decent attempt at the question but the reality would be, of course, that, in the real world, Division A would not want to pay $75 for the fittings if it could buy them from an external supplier for only $65. This is not, therefore, optimisation of transfer pricing, because this would require the company to have a policy of making Division A buy from B, **even** if fittings were cheaper elsewhere and this would cause behavioural issues, with Division A's manager becoming demotivated.

Marking scheme

			Marks
(a)	Profit statement:		
	Sales revenue:		
	External	1	
	Inter-divisional transfers	1	
	External material costs	1	
	Inter-divisional transfers	1	
	Labour costs	1	
	Fixed costs	1	
	Profit	1	
			7
(b)	Revised profit:		
	External sales	1	
	Inter-divisional transfers	1	
	Material costs	2	
	Internal transfers (materials)	1	
	Labour costs	1	
	Fixed costs	1	
	Profit	1	
			8
			15

(a) **Profit statement**

	Division A	Division B	Company
	$'000	$'000	$'000
Sales revenue:			
External (W1)	36,000	9,600	45,600
Inter-divisional transfers	0	6,000	–
	36,000	15,600	45,600
Variable costs:			
External material costs (W2)	(16,000)	(1,000)	(17,000)
Inter-divisional transfers (W3)	(6,000)	0	–
Labour costs (W4)	(3,600)	(3,000)	(6,600)
	(25,600)	(4,000)	(23,600)
Fixed costs	(7,440)	(4,400)	(11,840)
Profit	2,960	7,200	10,160

Workings ($'000)

1 *External sales*

Division A: 80,000 units × $450 = $36,000
Division B: 120,000 units × $80 = $9,600
Division B: 80,000 units × $75 = $6,000

2 *External material costs*

Division A: 80,000 units × $200 = $16,000
Division B: 200,000 units × $5 = $1,000

3 *Inter-divisional transfers*

Division A: 80,000 units × $75 = $6,000

4 *Labour costs*

Division A: 80,000 units × $45 = $3,600
Division B: 200,000 units × $15 = $3,000

(b) **Bath Co's profit is transfer pricing is optimised**

	Division A	Division B	Company
	$'000	$'000	$'000
Sales revenue:			
External sales (W1)	36,000	14,400	50,400
Internal sales (W2)	0	1,300	–
	36,000	15,700	50,400
Variable costs:			
External material costs (W3)	(19,900)	(1,000)	(20,900)
Inter-divisional transfers (W2)	(1,300)	0	–
Labour costs	(3,600)	(3,000)	(6,600)
	(24,800)	(4,000)	(27,500)
Fixed costs	(7,440)	(4,400)	(11,840)
Profit	3,760	7,300	11,060

Note. The above statement has been prepared on the assumption that Bath Co will introduce the policy discussed in part (b) of the question. Assuming that the transfer price is set between Division B's marginal cost ($20) and the cost to Division A of buying from outside the group ($65), the actual transfer price is irrelevant in this calculation. The overall profit of the company will be the same.

Workings ($'000)

1 *External sales*

Division A: 80,000 units × $450 = $36,000
Division B: 180,000 units × $80 = $14,400

2 *Internal sales*

20,000 units × $65 = $1,300

3 *External material costs*

Division A: 60,000 units × $265 + (20,000 units × $200) = $19,900
Division B: 200,000 units × $5 = $1,000

97 Process Co

Text reference. Further processing decisions covered in Chapter 6 and transfer pricing is covered in Chapter 17 of the BPP Study Text.

Top tips. Part (a) of this question is on whether to further process products or whether to sell them at the split-off point, without further processing. This question has an added complication that there is loss in the further process, which affects both sales revenue and also further processing variable costs.

There are various ways in which the figures could be presented, but the key to a good answer is to sort out the logic of the problem. If necessary, draw a sketch of the processes and the input/output quantities for each process, to get the problem clear in your mind. Then present the answer as clearly as you can, showing your workings.

The answer to part (b) calls for a discussion of transfer prices. You should be able to explain why transfers at marginal cost would be unsatisfactory for Division A, whilst allowing Division A to sell the products at the split off point instead of transferring them, is also undesirable. Internal transfers should in general be preferred to external sales and purchases.

Easy marks. An important first step in answering part (a) is to understand the problem. Because there is some loss in further processing, it may help to draw a sketch of the two processes, with input and output quantities. If you do this correctly, you should be able to identify the relevant revenues and variable costs for your analysis.

For part (b), you can earn marks by explaining the basic principles of transfer pricing, and why marginal cost is not a suitable transfer price.

Marking scheme

			Marks
(a)	Revenue at split-off point for products L, M and S	1.5	
	Normal losses in further processing	1.5	
	Incremental revenue less incremental costs from FP:		
	Product LX	2.0	
	Product MX	2.0	
	Product SX	2.0	
	Conclusion	1.0	
			10
(b)	Common on 'ideal' transfer price	1.0	
	Comment on reason why marginal cost is not a suitable TP	1.0	
	Comments on selling products at split-off point	1.0	
	Comments on other transfer price arrangements including the most appropriate in this situation	2.0	
			5
			15

(a)

	L/LX	M/MX	S/SX
Sell at split-off point			
Quantity (kg)	1,200	1,400	1,800
Sales price per kg	$5.60	$6.50	$6.10
Revenue if sold at split off point (A)	$6,720	$9,100	$10,980
Sell after further processing			
Quantity (kg): 5% normal loss	1,140	1,330	1,710
Sales price per kg	$6.70	$7.90	$6.80
Revenue if sold after further processing (B)	$7,638	$10,507	$11,628
	$	$	$
Incremental sales revenue from further processing (B) – (A)	918	1,407	648
Incremental variable costs of FP (Working)	570	931	(1,368)
Incremental gain/(loss) from further processing	348	476	(720)

Working

It is assumed that variable costs relate to output units, since loss occurs at the beginning of the further process.

LX: 1,140 × $0.50 = $570
MX: 1,330 × $0.70 = $931
SX: 1,710 × $0.80 = $1,368

Conclusion

Products L and M should be further processed, but product S should not.

(b) A transfer pricing system should seek to establish transfer prices that will provide an incentive for the managers of each profit centre to make and sell quantities of products that will maximise the company's total profit and in doing so also maximise their own divisional profit.

The proposal to set a transfer price at marginal cost is inadvisable. At this price, Division A will not make any profit at all on the units of L and M that it produces, and it will not even be able to cover its divisional fixed costs. It will therefore be transferring units at a net loss.

Even transferring units at full cost is undesirable because Division A would make zero net profit on the transfers.

The manager of Division A will want to sell the units of L and M externally, in order to earn a profit for the division. However as the solution to part (a) shows, the company would not benefit if this were to happen. Division B would have to buy the same quantity of units in the external market. Internal transfers should in general be preferred to external sales and purchases, because there is better management control and (often) lower administration and distribution costs.

An appropriate transfer price for units of L and M would be a price that represents opportunity costs. For Division A, this is the opportunity cost of not being able to sell the units externally at the external selling price. For Division B this is the opportunity cost of being able to purchase in the market at the market price for L and M instead of buying them internally at the transfer price.

The most appropriate transfer prices for L and M are therefore their market price at the split-off point – $5.60 and $6.50 per kg respectively.

98 Hammer

Text references. Transfer pricing is covered in Chapter 17.

Top tips. Do not forget to exclude fixed costs from your calculations in part (a). The question states that the current pricing policy is variable cost plus 30%.

Easy marks. Four marks are available in part (d) for discussing factors to consider when purchasing from outside suppliers.

Examiner's comments. The numerical parts to the question were quite well answered by most candidates. However, a disappointing number of answers included the fixed costs within part (a) and part (b) which defied the purpose of the whole question really. That having been said, most answers were good.

The quality of answers to part (c) was really poor. The question was looking for a couple of key points, for example, that including fixed costs guarantees a profit for the seller but invites manipulation of overheads and passes on inefficiencies from one part of the business to another. Also, that this strategy causes fixed costs of one division to be turned into a variable cost for another division.

Similarly, part (d) rarely produced answers scoring full marks. It asked whether retail stores should be allowed to buy in from outside suppliers. Key points in any answer should have been that the overall profitability of the company is key, as is goal congruence; these points were rarely made. Thankfully, many candidates did spot the more obvious points such as that the quality and reliability of any external supplier would need to be assessed.

Marking scheme

				Marks
(a)	Steel	1.0		
	Other material	1.0		
	Labour	0.5		
	Variable overhead	0.5		
	Delivery	0.5		
	Margin	0.5		
				4
(b)	Fixed cost	2.0		
	Margin	0.5		
	Increase in transfer price	0.5		
				3
(c)	Covers all cost	1		
	Risk	1		
	Fixed cost accounting	1		
	Converts a FC to VC	2		
			max	4
(d)	Market price may be temporary	1		
	Brand	1		
	Profitability	1		
	Flexibility	1		
	Control	1		
	Motivation	1		
	Performance assessment	1		
			max	4
				15

(a) **Price Nail would charge under existing policy (cost plus 30%)**

	$
Steel (0.4kg/0.95 (5% steel loss)) × $4.00	1.68
Other materials ($3.00 × 0.9 × 0.1)	0.27
Labour ($10 × 0.25)	2.50
Variable overhead ($15 × 0.25)	3.75
Delivery	0.50
Total variable cost	8.70
Mark-up (30%)	2.61
Transfer price	11.31

(b) **Price Nail would charged under total cost plus 10%**

	$
Total variable cost from part (a)	8.70
Extra fixed cost (0.25 × $15 × 0.8)	3.00
Total cost	11.70
Mark up (10%)	1.17
Transfer price	12.87

The increase in price if the pricing policy switches to total cost plus 10% is $1.56 per unit ($12.87 – $11.31).

(c) Fixed costs can be accounted for in a number of ways. As such, including the fixed cost within the transfer price could lead to **manipulation of overhead treatment**. For example employing absorption costing or activity based costing.

Including the fixed costs in the transfer price will benefit the manufacturer who can ensure that **all costs** incurred during the manufacturing process are **covered**. Assuming the fixed overhead absorption calculations are accurate, the manufacturing division should be **guaranteed a profit**.

The main **problem** with this pricing strategy is **fixed costs** are **effectively treated as variable costs** from the perspective of the stores, as they are included within the variable buy-in price. This could lead to **poor decision making** from a **group perspective**.

(d) Managers of the retail stores are likely to be more **motivated** if they are given **freedom** in which to **operate** and are able to purchase from outside suppliers if prices are cheaper.

In addition, the performance of **store managers will be easier to assess** in an environment in which managers are able to control greater elements of the business.

Price differences are perhaps to be expected given that products are rarely identical. There is a **risk** that store managers purchase cheaper shears of **inferior quality** to those produced internally (whilst claiming they are comparable) in order to achieve a greater margin. Such scenarios jeopardise the **reputation** of the brand for the benefit of individual stores.

Allowing store managers to purchase from cheaper suppliers could result in Hammer **losing control** of its business as retail stores could potentially stock different shears and other products from a range of different suppliers. On the other hand **flexibility is increased** and profits could increase as store managers find bargain prices.

In a competitive market, it is unlikely that suppliers will offer products significantly cheaper to Hammer for a sustained period of time. Any cheap prices accessed by store managers are likely to be the result of a sale or special promotion. If this is the case, it would not be advisable for Hammer to grant store managers the power to purchase from cheaper external suppliers in the long term.

Overall profitability of the company is key. The retail stores and Nail should be working in a way that is best for the company overall. This is known as **goal congruence**.

99 Woodside

Text reference. Operating statements are covered in Chapter 11 and not-for-profit organisations in Chapter 18.

Top tips. In part (a), fixed costs do not relate to any particular activity of the charity and so a marginal costing approach has to be used in analysing the budgeted and actual information provided.

Part (b) is a straightforward discussion using knowledge that you should be familiar with for this exam but again, you must specifically refer to the issues that Woodside faces.

Marking scheme

			Marks
(a)	Budgeted surplus	2.5	
	Actual deficit	2.0	
	Funding shortfall	0.5	
	Cost variances (0.5 each)	4.0	
	Reconciliation	1.0	
			10
(b)	Problems: 1 mark per valid point		max 5
			15

(a) **Operating statement**

	Favourable $	Adverse $	$
Budgeted surplus (W1)			98,750
Free meals (W4)			
Price variance		4,000	
Usage variance		8,750	
Overnight shelter (W5)			
Price variance		4,380	
Usage variance	31,000		
Advice centre (W6)			
Price variance		9,100	
Usage variance		7,500	
Campaigning and advertising (W7)			
Expenditure variance		15,000	
Fixed cost (W8)			
Expenditure variance		18,000	
	31,000	66,730	
Total spending variances		35,730	
Funding shortfall (W3)		80,000	
Overspend and funding shortfall			(115,730)
Actual shortfall (W2)			(16,980)

Workings

1 *Budgeted figures*

	$	
Free meals provision	91,250	(18,250 meals at $5 per meal)
Overnight shelter (variable)	250,000	(10,000 bed-nights at $30 – $5 per night)
Advice centre (variable)	45,000	(3,000 sessions at $20 – $5 per session)
Fixed costs	65,000	(10,000 × $5) + (3,000 × $5)
Campaigning and advertising	150,000	
	601,250	
Surplus for unexpected costs	98,750	
Fundraising target	700,000	

2 *Actual figures*

	$	
Free meals provision	104,000	(20,000 meals at $5.20 per meal)
Overnight shelter	223,380	(8,760 bed-nights $25.50 per night)
Advice centre	61,600	(3,500 sessions at $17.60 per session)
Fixed costs	83,000	
Campaigning and advertising	165,000	
	636,980	
Funds raised	620,000	
Shortfall	16,980	

3 Funding shortfall = 700,000 – 620,000 = $80,000 (A)

4 Free meals price variance = (5.00 – 5.20) × 20,000 = $4,000 (A)
Free meals usage variance = (18,250 – 20,000) × 5.00 = $8,750 (A)

5 Overnight shelter price variance = (25.00 – 25.50) × 8,760 = $4,380 (A)
Overnight shelter usage variance – (10,000 – 8,760) × 25 = $31,000 (F)

6 Advice centre price variance = (17.60 – 15.00) × 3,500 = $9,100 (A)
Advice centre usage variance = (3,000 – 3,500) × 15·00 = $7,500 (A)

7 Campaigning and advertising expenditure variance = 150,000 – 165,000 = $15,000 (A)

8 Fixed cost expenditure variance = 65,000 – 83,000 = $18,000 (A)

There was a **fundraising shortfall** of $80,000 compared to the target and **costs were over budget** in all areas except overnight shelter provision.

(b) Financial management and control in a not-for-profit organisation (NFPO) such as the Woodside charity needs to recognise that such organisations often have **multiple objectives** that can be **difficult to define** and are usually **non-financial**.

Performance of such organisations is judged in terms of inputs and outputs and hence the **value for money** criteria of economy, efficiency and effectiveness.

Economy means that inputs should be obtained at the lowest cost. **Efficiency** involves getting as much as possible for what goes in ie using the charity's resources as efficiently as possible to provide the services offered by the charity. **Effectiveness** means ensuring the outputs ie the services provided, have the desired impacts and achieve the charity's objectives.

Performance measures to determine whether objectives have been achieved can be difficult to formulate for an organisation such as Woodside.

Measures such as the number of free meals served, number of advice sessions given and number of bed-nights used, show that quantitative measures can be used to demonstrate that the charity is meeting a growing need.

Financial management and control in this organisation will primarily be concerned with preparing budgets and controlling costs.

Preparing budgets

Budgets rely on **forecasting** and accurate forecasts can be difficult to prepare for a charity such as Woodside. The level of activity is driven by the needs of the homeless and therefore **difficult to predict**. A high degree of **flexibility** is required to meet changing demand so provision needs to be built into budgets for this.

It is unlikely that Woodside has carried out a **detailed analysis of costs** and they have probably used an **incremental** approach to budgeting. This will limit the accuracy of their forecasts but staff may not have the necessary financial skills to use more advanced techniques.

Controlling costs

This is a key area of financial management due to the need for efficiency and economy. Inputs such as food, drink, bedding etc can be sourced as cheaply as possible and expenses such as electricity and telephone usage can be kept to an absolute minimum through careful use.

The responsibility for cost control would probably be the responsibility of the full-time members of staff but a culture of economy and efficiency can be encouraged amongst the volunteers.

Woodside will also need to provide **annual accounts** in order to retain charitable status and to show the providers of funds that their donations are being used as they intended.

100 PAF Co

Text reference. Performance measurement is covered in Chapter 16 of the BPP Study Text.

Top tips. This question allows you to analyse performance as much as you can within the available time. For every ratio or other performance measure that you calculate, be ready to comment on its significance answer. Even if a ratio does not seem significant, you can say so.

Some ratios for measuring performance might seem easy to identify, but remember to use the information given in the question. There are five items in particular you could use.

(1) The aim five years ago was to become the market leader in Sista.

(2) Division S left its prices for products and services unchanged in 20X3 rather than increasing them in line with its competitors so increases in sales volume are down to sales volume entirely.

(3) Skilled staff are in short supply – so it is worth looking at labour costs.

(4) In Sista fire safety regulations were introduced, and this could have an impact on the requirement for labour.

(5) In addition, the property tax has affected rental costs, so these should be looked at too.

And where possible, compare the relative performance of the two divisions.

There is a lot you could write about – but remember to keep your time discipline and do not exceed your allocated time for the question.

Easy marks. The question enables you to make as many ratio calculations as you can, and you should be able to calculate some quite easily – such as the increase in sales revenue and profit in each division, and the change in the ratio of operating profit to sales from one year to the next. However, there are twice as many marks available for discussion of performance as for calculation of ratios, so make sure that you comment on the measures you have calculated.

Marking scheme

	Marks
Sales revenue and volume growth	3
Market share	2
Profitability: gross profit	2
Profitability: net profit	2
Labour costs	3
Property costs	2
Summary	1
	15

Workings

	Division S 20X3	*Division S 20X2*	*Division C 20X3*	*Division C 20X2*
Increase in sales revenue	44%		9%	
Increase in gross profit	32%		6%	
Increase in operating profit	86%		5%	
Gross profit as % of revenue	56%	61%	65%	67%
Operating profit as % of revenue	11.1%	8.6%	21.5%	22.2%
Increase in labour costs	70%		14%	
Average salary per employee	$27,000	$25,021	$21,000	$20,000
Increase in employee numbers	58%		9%	
Increase in property costs	78%		5.6%	
Increase in administration costs	6.5%		0.3%	

Commentary

Sales revenue growth and volume growth

Division S achieved a huge increase of 44% in sales revenue in 20X3. The division did not increase its selling prices; therefore this revenue increase is attributable entirely to increase in sales volume.

Without further information it is not possible to assess whether the increase in sales volume can be attributed mainly to the price freeze, or whether the size of the market in Sista is expanding very rapidly.

In comparison, sales growth in Division C was only 9%. This indicates very different market conditions in the two countries.

Market share

Five years ago the company set itself a target of becoming the market leader in Sista. In 20X3 its market share was 30%. There are two major competitors, who presumably have about 70% of the market between them. This suggests that the company has not yet achieved market leadership, but with sales growth of 44% in 20X3 it may well be catching up with, or even overtaking, at least one of these two competitors.

In contrast, Division C is already the market leader, and succeeded in increasing its market share slightly in 20X3.

Profitability

Gross profit increased in Division S by 32% and operating profit increased by 86%. The gross profit as a percentage of revenue fell however from 61% to 56%, although the ratio of operating profit to revenue increased from 8.6% to 11.1%. Increases in some costs of sales (discussed later) meant that gross profit margins were reduced, and the increase in the operating profit margin is attributable to relatively small increases in administration costs (just 6.5% in spite of revenue and volume growth of 44%) and to a lesser extent distribution and marketing costs.

We do not know how administration costs have been kept under control to such an extent, in view of the very rapid growth in the business volume.

In contrast, Division C achieved just 6% growth in gross profit and 5% growth in operating profit, suggesting that Calana is a mature market. However although gross profit margins fell from 67% to 65%, they are higher than in Sista. Similarly, operating profit as a percentage of revenue although it fell in 20X2, was 21.5%, much higher than in Division S.

Labour costs

With its rapid expansion, Division S has taken on a large number of new employees, and employee numbers increased by 58% in 20X3 – more than the increase in sales volume. In addition, possibly because skilled labour is in short supply, the average salary cost per employee rose by about 8% to $27,000. The increase in average salary costs was only 5% and labour costs rose by 9%, in line with the increase in revenue.

Division S may find that if it continues to grow rapidly in 20X4, labour costs will become an even greater problem.

Property costs

The fall in gross profit as a percentage of revenue in Division S is attributable largely to rising labour costs and rising property costs. Property costs rose by 78% in Division S in 20X3, much more than in Division C. This may be largely attributable to the increase in property tax and property rental costs. If so, it might be expected that there will be no further substantial increases in property costs in 20X4 and that the effects of the higher tax and rental costs have now been fully incorporated into costs.

Summary

In summary, the company appears to have had a successful year in 20X3, although the fall in gross profit margin may be a matter of some concern. Opportunities for growth seem much greater for Division S, but there is some volatility in costs as well as huge growth in customer numbers.

Division C may be achieving some further growth in market share and profits, but further growth will probably be relatively modest in amount – as it was in 20X3. Even so, Division C performed well during the year.

101 Ties Only Limited

Text reference. Performance analysis is covered in Chapter 16.

Top tips. In both parts (a) and (b) you need to analyse and comment on each part of the given results. Make sure your percentages calculation technique can cope with this!

Easy marks. Using your common sense will gain you easy marks throughout this question. Use headings to make your answer easy for the marker to identify where to award marks.

Examiner's comments. Calculating a ratio without real comment did not gain full marks. An opinion such as 'impressive growth' was required. Candidates should offer an opinion as to why the ratio has occurred.

Marking scheme

			Marks
(a)	Sales	1	
	Gross profit	1	
	Website development	2	
	Administration	1	
	Distribution	1	
	Launch marketing	1	
	Comment on recent and future profit	3	
			max 9

			Marks
(b)	Number of tie sales	1	
	Tie price calculation	1	
	On time delivery	2	
	Returns	2	
	System down time	1	
	Summary comment	1	
			max 6
			15

(a) **Financial performance**

Sales growth

Ties Only Limited appear to have made an excellent start with initial sales of $420,000 growing by 62% ((680,000 – 420,000)/420,000 × 100%) to Quarter 2. This is particularly impressive given the acknowledged competitiveness of this business sector.

Gross profit

The gross profit margin in Quarter 1 was 52% (218,400/420,000 × 100%) and 50% (339,320/680,000 × 100%) in Quarter 2. The level of margin may be as expected for this business sector but we would need industry average data for comparison.

However, a **fall in margin** needs to be investigated. It could be that Ties Only was initially able to source cheaper ties but the rapid growth meant that alternative, more expensive suppliers had to be found. Alternatively, competitors quickly responded to this new entrant and lowered their prices in response. This pressure could have forced Ties Only to lower their prices.

Website development

All website development costs are being **written off as incurred** so we would expect costs to be higher in the initial quarters. The website costs are over a third of total expenses, so the initial loss is mostly explained by this write-off and does not therefore give any major cause for concern.

Administration costs

Although administration costs have risen in absolute terms, as a **percentage of sales** they have **fallen** from 23.9% (100,500/420,000 × 100%) to 22.2% (150,640/680,000 × 100%). Administration costs are the second biggest expense so very important to control.

This could indicate that administration costs are being **effectively controlled** which is good news. It could also be because fixed overheads are being **spread over a larger volume** and this will continue to improve as the business grows.

Distribution costs

These costs form the **smallest proportion** of total expenses (about 6%) and the proportion of distribution costs to sales has **remained constant** at 4.9% (20,763/420,000 × 100%). These costs will be subject to external influences such as a general rise in postage costs.

Launch marketing

This is similar to the website costs as it is expected to fall once the business is established. Ties Only will need to **continue to market** their website but this is likely to be cheaper than the initial big launch marketing campaign. The negative impact on profitability will therefore reduce over time.

Other variable expenses

These have again increased in line with the sales volume and are 11.9% of sales (50,000/420,000 × 100%).

Much of the loss in the first two quarters is due to the website development costs which will not be incurred again. Websites do need to be maintained and continually improved but this cost will be much lower. Launch marketing is another initial cost which will fall rapidly. If we deduct these expenses, the business made an **underlying profit** of $47,137 in Quarter 1 and $75,360 in Quarter 2, an encouraging **upward trend**.

These figures illustrate that a short-term view of a new business is not necessarily a good indicator of future performance.

(b) **Non-financial performance indicators**

Average price of ties

Quarter 1: $420,000/27,631 = $15.20
Quarter 2: $680,000/38,857 = $17.50

In part (a) it was suggested that **the fall in gross profit margin** might be due to a price reduction. This data provides evidence that this is **not** the case. There must therefore be an alternative explanation.

On time delivery

This has dropped significantly from 95% to 89% and this is worrying. The service provided to customers is a **key differentiator**, especially if the company is competing on quality not price. Customers will go elsewhere if their expectations are not met. Action will need to be taken to remedy this problem.

Sales returns

This is again a key indicator of **quality** and whether **customers' expectations** are being met. Returns have risen from 12% to 18% and are now above the industry average of 13%. Returns are to be expected on Internet sales where the product may look different in reality, but a higher than average rate means that the internet is **not adequately describing and illustrating** the products. Again, quality may be less than customers expect.

Alternatively, the **pressure to dispatch orders** may be resulting in **errors** or packaging problems. Either of these reasons does not bode well for the business and action must be taken to remedy the problem.

System downtime

Customers who use shopping websites are usually **time pressured** individuals who will not react well to delays in loading pages. It is all too easy to immediately switch to a competitor's website so it is essential that system downtime is kept to an absolute minimum to **avoid lost sales**.

It would be useful to compare the figures with an **industry average** but the important point is that system downtime has **doubled**. This could be due to **pressure on the website** as a result of the volume of demand. As the website development has been such a costly and important part of the business set-up, the owners of Ties Only should have an urgent discussion with the website developers to come up with a solution.

Conclusion

Ties Only are doing well in terms of sales growth and potential profitability for a brand new business. However the owners need to focus their attention on the accuracy of order delivery, website reliability and the quality of the product. Further investigation needs to be made of the fall in gross profit margin.

102 Squarize

Text reference. The balanced scorecard is covered in Chapter 16 of the BPP Study Text.

Top tips. It is important to read and understand the facts and details in this question. It is easy to get carried away in part (a) and simply write all you know the balanced scorecard – the question asks you to identify **just one** objective for each balanced scorecard perspective **and** a corresponding performance measure for each objective. Present your answer in a table to ensure you answer all of the requirements and make your answer easy to mark.

Some sensible suggestions will score well in part (b).

Easy marks. There are easy marks available throughout this question provided you have a sound knowledge of the balanced scorecard.

Examiner's comments. In part (a) of the requirements, candidates were asked to identify goals and performance measures for each perspective of the balanced scorecard that would help the company assess whether the changes had been successful. The requirement also read 'justify the use of each performance measure that you choose.' The reason that this last bit of the requirement was put in was so that candidates would not simply write generic performance measures such as 'compare net profit margin' without actually thinking about what was relevant for this company.

There were three main problems with answers. Firstly, by far the biggest issue was that candidates didn't write any objectives or performance measures at all, they simply wrote pages and pages of words about the company, discussing how it was performing and the issues it faced. This was really disappointing.

Many candidates who had made a proper attempt at answering the actual requirement simply did not read the requirement carefully enough and therefore did not bother to give their reasons for selecting their performance measure.

The third issue was that a number of candidates simply wrote everything that they knew about the balanced scorecard. Since this was an application not a knowledge requirement, such candidates scored very low marks.

Marking scheme

			Marks
(a)	Balanced scorecard: Identifying a goal (1 mark) and a performance measure (2 marks) for each of the four perspectives in the balanced scorecard.	max	11
(b)	Each point discussed – 2 marks	max	4
			15

(a) **Objectives and performance measures**

Objective	Performance measures	Comment
Customer perspective		
Increase number of new customers	Volume of sales to new customers for each product/service	This measure will help to assess whether the decision to withdraw the packaged product has been successful.
Internal business perspective		
Reduce number of contracts cancelled due to broadband service not working	Number of contracts cancelled within 14 day cancellation period	This measure is to assess whether resolving the problems with customers' broadband service has reduced the number of contract cancellations.
Innovation and learning perspective		
Increase employees' satisfaction	Percentage decrease in staff turnover	This performance measure will help to monitor the effect the changes on staff morale.
Financial perspective		
Increase operating profit margin	Percentage increase in operating profit	The changes have been implemented partly to increase revenues and reduce costs. This profit measure will enable Squarize to measure the extent to which operating profit has increased.

Note. Other reasonable suggestions would have scored marks.

(b) **Minimum contract term**

Currently, Squarize offers a **minimum contract term of three months**. It is likely that considerable resource is required to set up new customer accounts, and if customers then choose to leave after only three months then the company has **little time to recover costs relating to these customers and earn a profit**. The company may consider increasing the minimum contract term to 12 months, or alternatively offering customers a **loyalty reward** at certain milestones. For example, 25% off their next invoice for all customers who receive their sixth invoice.

Pay-TV boxes

Currently, pay-TV boxes are **sold to customers** upon setting up a new contract. Due to the economic climate, a number of customers appear to be cancelling their contract after the minimum term (3 months) and keeping the pay-TV box so that they can continue to watch a number of pre-set free channels on the box, free of charge. Squarize may wish to consider **loaning the boxes** to customers rather than selling them at the beginning of the contract.

103 Jump

Text references. Performance measurement is covered in Chapter 16.

Top tips. Ensure that your answer to part (b) supports both arguments. Use headings in your answer, one for each target.

Easy marks. There should be easy marks to gain from performance measurement, but remember to comment on the measures that you calculate.

Examiner's comments. Answers to part (a) were good on the whole. For a narrative requirement, part (b) was fairly well answered overall.

Marking scheme

			Marks
(a)	Per target, 2 marks	2	
			6
(b)	For each target – supporting controllability	1.5	
	For each target – denying controllability	1.5	
			9
			15

(a) **Bonus calculation**

	Qtr to 30 June 20X1	*Qtr to 30 September 20X1*	*Qtr to 31 December 20X1*	*Qtr to 31 March 20X2*	*Bonus hits*
Staff on time?					
On-time %	95.5%	94.2%	94.0%	95.8%	
	(430/450)	(452/480)	(442/470)	(460/480)	
Bonus earned?	Yes	No	No	Yes	2
Member visits					
Target visits	21,600	23,040	23,760	24,480	
	(60% × 3,000 × 12)	(60% × 3,200 ×12)	(60% × 3,300 × 12)	(60% × 3,400 × 12)	
Actual visits	20,000	24,000	26,000	24,000	
Bonus earned?	No	Yes	Yes	No	2

	Qtr to 30 June 20X1	*Qtr to 30 September 20X1*	*Qtr to 31 December 20X1*	*Qtr to 31 March 20X2*	*Bonus hits*
Personal training					
Target visits	300	320	330	340	
	(10% × 3,000)	(10% × 3,200)	(10% × 3,300)	(10% × 3,400)	
Actual visits	310	325	310	339	
Bonus earned?	Yes	Yes	No	No	2

Total number of bonus hits from table above = 6

The earned by the manager is 6 x $400 = $2,400. This represents 50% of the total bonus available.

(b) It is essential that the targets set are based on elements of the job that the local managers are able to control. Targets that are based on elements that local managers are unable to influence will be seen as pointless and unrealistic and could **demotivate staff** at the local manager level.

Staff on time

Individual members of staff may be late for work as a result of external factors including home pressures or delayed public transport. Such factors cannot be controlled by the local manager. However if such problems occur on a regular basis to certain members of staff, the local manager does have the power **to amend their contract of employment**.

The way in which the local manager manages staff will impact upon how **motivated** they are to work and to arrive on time. The **local manager** has the power to **devise shift patterns** that best their team and can **reward** them accordingly through their ability to amend employment contracts.

In summary, **lateness** to work **can be controlled** by the local manager.

Personal training sessions

The local manager has control over prices charged to customers. If demand for personal training sessions falls he/she can reduce prices or make special offers in a bid to increase customer numbers.

A number of potential customers may view personal training sessions as a luxury, particularly in the current economic climate. Also, the personal training market is particularly competitive which may make it difficult for the local managers to increase sales. Local managers can take steps to improve the service offered by the sports club but any significant expenditure requires approval at Board level.

In summary, the local manager can only **partly control** the number of **personal training sessions** that are booked.

Member use of facilities

The local manager controls the staff and hence the level of customer service. It is likely that a **high level of customer service** could encourage some **members to use** the facilities **more often**. The local manager also has the ability to influence member numbers by **adjusting membership prices**.

However, external factors such as **work pressures** and level of **health** may prevent some members from visiting the club as often as they would like.

In summary, the local manager can only **partly control** the **number of member visits**.

104 The Accountancy Teaching Co

Text reference. Performance measurement is covered in Chapter 16.

Top tips. At first glance, you may not know where to begin with this question! Take care to structure your answer around the headings given in the requirement and set out your workings clearly to maximise your score in each area.

Be sure to explain what your calculations mean for AT Co, to add depth to your answer. Finally, do not forget to comment on each of the non-financial performance indicators.

Easy marks. There are easy marks available throughout this question (providing you spend enough time on each heading provided in the question requirement!).

Examiner's comments. This was a typical performance measurement question. There was quite a lot of information to absorb but I strongly believe that, unless you are given plenty of information to work with, it is only possible to make very generalised, insipid comments. This is not what F5 is all about. I want candidates to be able to handle information and make some quality analysis about it. It requires common sense and ability to link information. Needless to say, answers were poor. Anyone who had read my article on this area, or indeed my predecessor's article on this area, would know that insipid comments such as 'turnover decreased by 8.3%, which is poor' will score only a calculation mark, for working out the 8.3%. Is this decrease in turnover poor? Well, it depends on the market in which the company is operating. You have to read the scenario. When you take into account the fact that there has been a 20% decline in the demand for accountancy training, AT Co's 8.3% looks relatively good. You must link information; this is an essential skill for any accountant. Nothing is ever what it seems...ask any auditor!

Let me also take the opportunity to distinguish between an acceptable comment, which might earn one mark, compared to a good point, which might earn two marks. Cost of sales fell by $10.014m in the year. Part of this reduction was down to a fall in freelance lecture costs. A good candidate would have commented that, whilst the company requested that freelance lecturers reduce their fees by 10%, the actual fee reduction gained was 15%, a strong performance. A comment such as this would have earned two marks. A less observant comment, earning one mark, would have been that the reduction in cost of sales was partly due to the fact that the company requested freelance lecturers to reduce their fees by 10%.

I hope that this question will serve as a good revision question to future examinees of F5. The information given is there to help you make worthwhile comments. When planning the question, you should annotate it carefully, cross-referencing different parts of the question, linking financial and non-financial information etc.

Marking scheme

		Marks
Turnover:		
8.3% decrease	0.5	
Actual turnover 14.6% higher	0.5	
Performed well CF market conditions	1.0	
Transfer of students	1.0	
		max 2
Cost of sales:		
19.2% decrease	0.5	
63.7% of turnover	0.5	
15% fee reduction from freelance staff	1.0	
Other costs of sale fell by $3.555m	1.0	
Online marking did not save as much as planned	1.0	
		4
Gross profit – numbers and comment	1.0	
Indirect expenses:		
Marketing costs:		
42.1% increase	0.5	
Increase necessary to reap benefits of developments	1.0	

		Marks
Staff training:		
163.9% increase	0.5	
Necessary for staff retention	1.0	
Necessary to train staff on new website etc	1.0	
Less student complaints	1.0	
Interactive website and student helpline:		
Attracted new students	1.0	
Increase in pass rate	1.0	
Enrolment costs:		
Fall of 80.9%	0.5	
Result of electronic system being introduced	1.0	
Reduced number of late enrolments	1.0	
		max 7
Net operating profit:		
Fallen to $2.106	0.5	
Difficult market	1.0	
Staff training costs should decrease in the future	1.0	
Future increase in market share	1.0	
Lower advertising cost in future	1.0	
Charge for website	1.0	
		max 2
		15

Turnover

Turnover has decreased by 8.3% from $72.025 million in 20X1 to $66.028 million in 20X2. Given the 20% **decline in demand for accountancy training**, AT Co's turnover would have been expected to fall to $57.62m in line with market conditions. As such, it would appear that **AT has performed well in a tough market as its actual turnover is 14.6% higher than expected**.

Non-financial performance indicators show that the number of students who transferred to AT from an alternative training provider in has increased to 20% in 20X2 (from 8% in 20X1). This **increase in market share** is likely to be directly linked to **the improved service provided to students** as a result of the new student helpline and interactive website as well as other developments.

Cost of sales

Cost of sales has decreased by 19.2% from $52.078m in 20X1 to $42.056m in 20X2. In 20X1, cost of sales represented 72.3% of turnover and in 20X2 this figure was 63.7%. The reasons for this substantial decrease are considered below.

Freelance costs in 20X1 were $14.582m. Given that a minimum 10% reduction in fees had been requested to freelance lecturers and the number of courses run by them was the same year on year, the expected cost for freelance lecturers in 20X2 was $13.124m. The **reduction in costs was successful** as actual costs were $12.394m (a reduction of 15%).

Prior to any cost cuts and **assuming a consistent cost of sales to turnover ratio**, costs of sales for 20X2 were expected to be $47.738m. The actual cost of sales was $5.682m lower at $42.056m. Freelance lecturer costs fell by $2.188m, meaning that the remaining $3.494m is made up of decreases in other costs of sales.

Employees were told they would not receive a pay rise for at least one year and the average number of employees hardly changed year on year. As such, **the decreased costs are unlikely to be related to staff costs**.

The introduction of the **electronic marking system was expected to save the company $4m**. It is possible that the system did not save as much as predicted, hence the $3.494m fall. Alternatively, the saved marking costs may have been partially counteracted by an increase in another cost included in cost of sales.

Gross profit

As a result of the increased market share and cost savings discussed above, the **gross profit margin has increased** in 20X2 from 27.7% to 36.3%.

Indirect expenses

Marketing costs

AT Co has increased spend on marketing campaigns to make students aware of the improved service and the range of facilities that the company offer. As such, marketing costs have increased by 42.1% in 20X2. It would appear that the marketing campaigns have been a success, with higher student numbers relative to the competition in 20X2. It is important to recognise the time lag between the cost outlay and the benefit received from such campaigns. It is likely that many of the benefits will not be felt until 20X3.

Property costs

Property costs have remained in line with 20X1, indicating no significant investment in company premises.

Staff training

Training costs have increased dramatically from $1.287m in 20X1 to $3.396m in 20X2, an increase of 163.9%. In 20X1 and before, AT Co had experienced problems with staff retention which resulted in a lower quality service being provided to students.

Considerable time and money is likely to have been spent on training staff to use the new interactive website as well as the electronic enrolment and marking systems. If the company had not spent this money on essential training, the quality of service would have deteriorated further and more staff would have left as they became increasingly dissatisfied with their jobs.

The number of student complaints has fallen dramatically in 20X2 to 84 from 315, indicating that the staff training appears to have improved the quality of service being provided to students.

Interactive website and the student helpline

Interactive website and student helpline costs have not been incurred in previous years and have arisen from the drive towards providing students with an improved service and to increase pass rates. The percentage of students passing exams first time increased from 48% in 20X1 to 66% in 20X2 which would suggest that the developments have improved the student learning environment.

Enrolment costs

Enrolment costs have fallen by $4.072m (80.9%), largely due to the new electronic enrolment system that was launched in 20X2. It is likely that the new system has contributed to the reduction in late enrolments from 297 in 20X1 to 106 in 20X2.

Net operating profit

Net operating profit has fallen from $3.635m to $2.106m (42%). Whilst this is a significant decrease, AT Co has been operating in tough market conditions in 20X2. The company may have considered charging students a fee to use the interactive website in order to recoup some of the funds invested. This would have increased net operating profit.

Going forward, staff training costs are likely to decrease as staff become familiar with the new developments and staff retention improves. Higher pass rates are likely to attract more students in the coming years which will further increase market share.

As the AT brand becomes established in the market, it is likely that fewer advertising campaigns will take place, resulting in lower marketing costs.

Workings (**Note.** All workings are in $'000.)

1 *Turnover*

Decrease in turnover = $72,025 – $66,028/$72,025 = 8.3%

Expected 20X2 turnover given 20% decline in market = $72,025 × 80% = $57,620

Actual 20X2 turnover CF expected = $66,028 – $57,620/$57,620 = 14.6% higher

2 *Cost of sales*

Decrease in cost of sales = \$42,056 – \$52,078/\$52,078 = 19.2%

Cost of sales as percentage of turnover: 20X1 = \$52,078/\$72,025 = 72.3%

20X2 = \$42,056/\$66,028 = 63.7%

3 *Freelance staff costs*

In 20X1 = \$41,663 × 35% = \$14,582

Expected cost for 20X2 = \$14,582 × 90% = \$13,124

Actual 20X2 cost = \$12,394

\$12,394 – \$14,582 = \$2,188 decrease

\$2,188/\$14,582 = 15% decrease in freelancer costs

4 *Expected cost of sales for 20X2*

Before costs cuts, = \$66,028 × 72.3% = \$47,738

Actual cost of sales = \$42,056

Difference = \$5,682, of which \$2,188 relates to freelancer savings and \$3,494 relates to other savings.

5 *Gross profit margin*

20X1: \$19,947/\$72,025 = 27.7%

20X2: \$23,972/\$66,028 = 36.3%

6 *Increase in marketing costs*

\$4,678 – \$3,291/\$3,291 = 42.1%

7 *Increase in staff training costs*

\$3,396 – \$1,287/\$1,287 = 163.9%

8 *Decrease in enrolment costs*

\$960 – 5,032/5,032 = 80.9%

9 *Net operating profit*

Decreased from \$3,635 to \$2,106. This is fall of 1,529/3,635 = 42.1%

105 Bridgewater Co

Text references. Performance measurement is covered in Chapter 16.

Top tips. The key to success in this type of question is reading the information in the question very carefully and making full use of it. When the examiner asks for 'comment', he requires an opinion not simply a re-statement of the proposals.

Easy marks. For half marks in part (a) all that was expected was a statement (with simple supporting calculations) of whether or not the manager would meet each of the targets.

Examiner's comments. Candidates must be able to assess performance which means interpret financial and other data and make sensible comments on it. Few candidates realised that the division's improving performance in Quarters 3 and 4 came too late for the promotion at the end of Quarter 2. Many only commented on the profits of the division and ignored all the other targets. Many also assessed the performance more generally, calculating amongst other things % margins and ignored the targets altogether. This was very disappointing.

Part (b) was also poorly performed and misreading the question was common. Candidates must learn to read performance management questions more carefully.

For Part (c) candidates answers primarily consisted of a re-statement of the different steps being proposed with little or no comment at all. A comment requires opinion and anything sensible scored marks.

Candidates should prepare themselves to assess the performance of a business, both financially and non-financially if they want to pass.

Marking scheme

			Marks
(a)	Per target discussed, maximum 2.0 marks	2.0	
			max 7
(b)	Revised forecasts		
	New software sales effect	1.0	
	Extra trainer cost from extra courses	1.0	
	Extra room hire cost of extra courses	1.0	
	Staff training increase	0.5	
	Software cost	0.5	
	Overall revised profit calculation	1.0	
			max 5
(c)	Per idea commented on	1.5	
			max 3
			15

(a) **Each quarter, sales should grow and annual sales should exceed budget**

In the Northwest division, sales are forecasted to fall by 10% (4/40 × 100%) from Quarter 1 to Quarter 2 but then start to grow. Average growth per quarter over the year is 14.5% ($\sqrt[3]{(60/40)} - 1$). Annual sales are forecast to exceed the sales budget by $6,000 (186 – 180).

It would therefore appear that the annual **target will be met**. However, the promotion decision is to be taken in Quarter 3 and the **slow start** to the year may not reflect well on the manager of the Northwest division.

Trainer costs should not exceed $180 per teaching day

The manager is paying $200 (8,000/40) per teaching day in trainer costs which **exceeds the target**. He believes in quality and therefore appears to be paying more to attract better teaching staff. This may well improve sales in the long-term as the reputation for quality delivery becomes known, but it is at the expense of increased costs in the short-term.

Room hire costs should not exceed $90 per teaching day

The manager of this division is also **spending more** on room hire costs than the target. He is spending $100 per teaching day rather than $90. This could be again part of his quality improvement policy as he is hiring better facilities, but it could also be due to poor negotiation and buying strategy.

Each division should meet its budget for profit per quarter and annually

The achievement of this target suffers from the same problem as the sales target. The manager will meet the target for the year by $2,500, but is **below target** in the first two quarters.

This again will impact on his promotion prospects which overall are not looking good. He is failing to meet any of the targets in the first two quarters and will have to hope that the senior managers agree with his **long-term** rather than **short-termist** approach.

(b) **Revised forecasts**

	Q1	*Q2*	*Q3*	*Q4*	*Total*
	$'000	$'000	$'000	$'000	$'000
Existing sales	40.0	36.0	50.0	60.0	186.0
Software training			10.0	12.0	22.0
	40.0	36.0	60.0	72.0	208.0
Less:					
Existing trainer costs	8.0	7.2	10.0	12.0	37.2
Additional training costs ($200 × teaching days)			2.0	2.4	4.4
Room hire	4.0	3.6	5.0	6.0	18.6
Additional room hire ($100 × teaching days)			1.0	1.2	2.2
Staff training	1.0	1.0	1.0	1.0	4.0
Additional staff training	0.5	0.5			1.0
Other costs	3.0	1.7	6.0	7.0	17.7
Software	1.8				1.8
Total costs	18.3	14.0	25.0	29.6	86.9
Forecast net profit	21.7	22.0	35.0	42.4	121.1
Original budget profit	25.0	26.0	27.0	28.0	106.0

(c) **Software upgrade**

It is essential that a software training company uses the **latest software technology** on its courses. The investment in software and staff training is therefore a **necessity** and cannot be avoided.

The courses will generate **extra revenue** but not until Quarters 3 and 4. This software upgrade will therefore further damage the achievement of targets in Quarters 1 and 2, as costs will rise but the extra revenue will be too late for the promotion assessment.

It is to be hoped that the senior managers will recognise the essential long-term planning being undertaken.

Delaying payments to trainers

This is not a good idea. None of the performance targets will be affected, as the plan will not affect costs or profits. The only positive impact will be on **cash flow**. The worrying aspect is the negative impact it may have on **relationships with trainers**. Software training is a competitive market and good trainers will be in demand by a number of training providers. If the company is to offer quality training, it must have the best trainers and this is not the way to retain them.

In conclusion, if all the proposals were taken together, they will **not improve** the manager's chance of promotion as any benefits will accrue after Quarter 2.

106 Oliver's Salon

Text references. Performance measurement is covered in Chapter 16.

Top tips. This is quite a long scenario with lots of information to deal with. Part (a) relates only to financial performance so a range of ratios need to be calculated and explained. The approach to use is to calculate a ratio, make a qualitative statement and suggest a cause or some other comment.

Part (b) gives you the headings to give a structure to your answer. Quality and resource utilisation are two of the dimensions in the Building Block Model. The question does not ask for recommendations for Oliver so make sure you stick to the requirements of the question.

Easy marks. The ratio analysis in part (a) has plenty of easy marks available but make sure you do more than just calculate the ratios.

Examiner's comments. In part (a) there was some improvement in candidate's ability to assess performance. There were problems however. Mathematical descriptions are not performance assessments; simply stating the % increases in numbers is not enough; indicating the absolute change in a cost is rarely that useful; too narrow a range of figures considered, virtually all the numbers in the question carry marks.

In part (b) answers on quality dealt with the complaints issue well, but very few talked about the new members of staff and how their performance might be suspect. The lack of a pay rise can be de-motivating and so quality might suffer, this too was rarely picked up.

On resource utilisation candidates had a mixed result. The male throughput per specialist was very high but this was perhaps due to the fact that male hair tends to be easier (quicker) to cut. The female situation was different, with fewer clients for more staff. Many candidates recognised this. Very few talked about the property utilisation at all.

Marking scheme

			Marks
(a)	Sales growth	3	
	Gross margin	3	
	Rent	1	
	Advertising spend	1	
	Staff costs	1	
	Electricity	1	
			10
(b)	Quality – single gender	1	
	Quality – wage levels	1	
	Quality – other	1	
	Resource utilisation – property	1	
	Resource utilisation – staff	1	
	Resource utilisation – other	1	
			max 5
			15

(a) **Financial performance**

Sales growth

Sales have grown by 19.25% ((238,500 – 200,000)/200,000 × 100%) from 20X8 to 20X9. This is particularly impressive as Oliver's Salon experiences high levels of competition.

This growth has come from the new **male hairdressing** part of the business as female sales have fallen by 15% ((200,000 – 170,000)/200,000 × 100%). There was **no price increase** during this time so this fall is due to less female client visits.

Gross profit

The gross profit margin in 20X8 was 53% (106,000/200,000 × 100%) and in 20X9 had **fallen** to 47.2% (112,500/238,500 × 100%). This is predominantly due to a 40% ((91,000 – 65,000)/65,000 × 100%) in **staff costs** as a result of the recruitment of two new staff.

The new specialist hairdresser for male clients is on a salary of $17,000 (91,000 – 65,000 – 9,000) whereas the female hairdressers were paid an average of $16,250 (65,000/4) in 20X8.

However it is the **female client** business which has been responsible for the drop in gross profit margin.

	20X8 Female	20X9 Female	20X9 Male
	$	$	$
Sales	200,000	170,000	68,500
Less cost of sales:			
Hairdressing staff	(65,000)	(74,000)	(17,000)
Hair products – female	(29,000)	(27,000)	
Hair products – male			(8,000)
Gross profit	106,000	69,000	43,500
Gross profit margin	106/200 × 100% = 53%	69/170 × 100% = 40.6%	43.5/68.5 × 100% = 63.5%

The gross profit margin from male clients is higher than for female clients.

Rent

This has not changed so is a **fixed cost** at the moment.

Administration salaries

These have increased by only 5.6% ((9,500 – 9,000)/9,000 × 100%) which is impressive given the expansion in the business.

Electricity

This has increased by 14.3% ((8,000 – 7,000)/7,000 × 100%. More clients would involve more electricity so it is a **semi-variable cost**. There may also have been a **general increase** in electricity prices which would be beyond the control of Oliver.

Advertising

This has increased by 150% ((5,000 – 2,000)/2,000 × 100%) which could be expected at the **launch of a new service**. Provided the advertising has generated new clients, it should not be a cause for concern.

Net profit

Net profit has only increased by 2.6% ((80,000 – 78,000/78,000 × 100%) which is disappointing compared to a 19.25% increase in sales.

(b) **Non-financial performance**

Quality

The number of complaints has increased significantly by 283% ((46 – 12)/12 × 100%). This is not just due to the increase in client numbers.

Complaints per customer visit have increased from 0.15% (12/8,000 × 100%) to 0.44%. This is a cause for concern in a service business, especially as many customers will not actually complain but will just not come back.

The complaints could be from the new male clients who are not happy with the new hairdresser, or they could be from female clients who do not like having men in the salon. More information is needed and action to be taken to reduce the complaints.

Resource utilisation

The resources in Oliver's Salon are the **salon** itself and the **staff**. The salon is being utilised more as a result of the increase in clients from 8,000 in 20X8 to 10,225 (6,800 + 3,425) in 20X9. This is a 27.8% ((10,225 – 8,000)/8,000 × 100%) increase. This increase in utilisation has not however resulted in a proportionate increase in profit.

The **female specialist hairdressers** served 2,000 (8,000/4) clients per specialist in 20X8 and this fell to 1,360 (6,800/50) in 20X9, following the recruitment of two new staff. Oliver may be prepared to accept this reduction in resource utilisation in order to boost service levels and reduce complaints.

This contrasts with the higher figure of 3,425 clients per **male specialist** in 20X9. The time taken per male client is much less so.

Mock exams

ACCA

Paper F5

Performance Management

Mock Examination 1

Question paper	
Reading and planning	15 minutes
Writing	3 hours
This paper is divided into two sections:	
Section A – ALL TWENTY questions are compulsory and MUST be answered	
Section B – ALL FIVE questions are compulsory and MUST be answered	

DO NOT OPEN THIS PAPER UNTIL YOU ARE READY TO START UNDER EXAMINATION CONDITIONS

Section A – ALL TWENTY questions are compulsory and MUST be attempted

Each question is worth 2 marks.

1 The following statements have been made when making comparisons between traditional absorption costing and activity-based costing.

(1) ABC has evolved as a response to the increase in support activities in modern organisations.

(2) Absorption costing uses volume as a basis for cost allocation, and so tends to allocate too great a proportion of overheads to low volume products.

Which of the above statements is/are true?

A 1 only
B 2 only
C Neither 1 nor 2
D Both 1 and 2

2 Highfly Co manufactures two products, X and Y, and any quantities produced can be sold for $60 per unit and $25 per unit respectively.

Variable costs per unit of the two products are as follows:

	Product X	*Product Y*
	$	$
Materials (at $5 per kg)	15	5
Labour (at $6 per hour)	24	3
Other variable costs	6	5
Total	45	13

Next month, only 4,200 kg of material and 3,000 labour hours will be available. The company aims to maximise its profits each month.

The company wants to use the linear programming model to establish an optimum production plan. The model considers 'x' to be number of units of product X and 'y' to be the number of units of product Y.

Which of the following objective functions and constraint statements (relating to material and labour respectively) is correct?

	Objective function	*Material constraint*	*Labour constraint*
A	60x + 25y	3x + y ≤ 4,200	4x + 0.5y ≤ 3,000
B	15x + 12y	3x + y ≥ 4,200	4x + 0.5y ≥ 3,000
C	15x + 12y	3x + y ≤ 4,200	4x + 0.5y ≤ 3,000
D	60x + 25y	3x + y ≥ 4,200	4x + 0.5y ≥ 3,000

3 The following statements have been made about the balanced scorecard.

(1) It focuses solely on non-financial performance measures.
(2) It looks at both internal and external matters concerning the organisation.

Which of the above statements is/are true?

A 1 only
B 2 only
C Neither 1 nor 2
D Both 1 and 2

4 The following statements have been made about changing budgetary systems.

(1) The costs of implementation may outweigh the benefits.

(2) Employees will always welcome any new system which improves planning and control within the organisation.

Which of the above statements is/are true?

A 1 only
B 2 only
C Neither 1 nor 2
D Both 1 and 2

5 A manufacturing company uses throughput accounting. It manufactures two products, X and Y, using the same types of machine (Machine M and Machine T) for both products. Machine time on Machine Type M is a production bottleneck. The following information is available.

	Product X	*Product Y*
Throughput accounting ratio	2.4	3.0
Machine M time per unit produced	15 minutes	30 minutes
Machine T time per unit produced	30 minutes	20 minutes

There is unlimited sales demand for both products.

If extra production capacity is made available, amounting to 10 extra machine M hours and 10 extra machine T hours, how many additional units of output would be produced in order to maximise profit?

A 10 units of Product Y and 20 units of Product X
B 20 units of Product Y and 40 units of Product X
C 20 units of Product Y
D 40 units of Product X

6 A company has entered two different new markets.

In market A, it is initially charging low prices so as to gain rapid market share while demand is relatively elastic.

In market B, it is initially charging high prices so as to earn maximum profits while demand is relatively inelastic.

Which price strategy is the company using in each market?

A Penetration pricing in market A and price skimming in market B
B Price discrimination in market A and penetration pricing in market B
C Price skimming in market A and penetration pricing in market B
D Price skimming in market A and price discrimination in market B

7 The following are all types of control within an organisation.

(i) Logical access controls
(ii) Database controls
(iii) Hierarchical passwords
(iv) Range checks

Which of the above controls help to ensure the security of highly confidential information?

i and ii only
i and iii only
i, ii and iii only
All of the above

8 Total production costs for 900 units of output are $58,200 and total production costs for 1,200 units are $66,600.

The variable cost per unit is constant up to a production level of 2,000 units per month but a step up of $6,000 in the monthly total fixed cost occurs when production reaches 1,100 units per month.

What is the total cost for a month when 1,000 units are produced?

A $54,200
B $55,000
C $59,000
D $60,200

9 S Company is a manufacturer of multiple products and uses target costing. It has been noted that Product P currently has a target cost gap and the company wishes to close this gap.

Which of the following may be used to close the target cost gap for product P?

A Use overtime to complete work ahead of schedule
B Substitute current raw materials with cheaper versions
C Raise the selling price of P
D Negotiate cheaper rent for S Company's premises

10 The following statements have been made about management information systems.

(1) They are designed to report on existing operations.
(2) They have an external focus.

Which of the above statements is/are true?

A 1 only
B 2 only
C Neither 1 nor 2
D Both 1 and 2

11 The following are some of the areas which require control within a division.

(i) Generation of revenues
(ii) Investment in non-current assets
(iii) Investment in working capital
(iv) Apportioned head office costs

Which of the above does the manager have control over in an investment centre?

A i, ii and iii only
B ii, iii and iv only
C i, ii and iv only
D All of the above

12 An investment centre in a manufacturing group produced the following results in the previous financial year:

	£'000
Operating profit	360
Capital employed: non-current assets	1,500
current assets	100

For the purpose of performance measurement, non-current assets are valued at cost. The investment centre is considering a new investment that will increase annual operating profit by £25,000, and will require an investment of £100,000 in a non-current asset and an additional £30,000 in working capital.

Will the performance measurement criteria of (1) Return on Investment (ROI) and (2) residual income (RI) motivate the centre manager to undertake the investment? Assume a notional capital charge of 18% on divisional capital.

	ROI	*RI*
A	Yes	Yes
B	Yes	No
C	No	Yes
D	No	No

13 For a charitable organisation providing relief services to underdeveloped economies, which one of the following performance measurements would be the most suitable measurement of the effectiveness in the use of the charity's aid funds?

A Percentage of funds spent on frontline activities
B Ratio of volunteer helpers to full-time employees in the organisation
C Size of operating surplus (fund income less expenditure)
D Total spending by the charity on its operations

14 A company introduced Product C to the market 12 months ago and is now about to enter the maturity stage of its life cycle. The maturity stage is expected to last for three months. The Director of Sales and Marketing has suggested four possible prices that the company could charge during the next three months. The following table shows the results of some market research into the level of weekly demand at alternative prices:

Selling price per unit	$300	$255	$240	$225
Weekly demand (units)	1,800	2,400	3,600	4,200

Each unit of product C has a variable cost of $114 and takes one standard hour to produce.

Which selling price will maximise the weekly profit during this stage of the product life cycle?

A $225
B $240
C $255
D $300

15 A company has received a special order for which it is considering the use of material B which it has held in its inventory for some time. This inventory of 945 kg was bought at $4.50 per kg. The special order requires 1,500 kg of material B. If the inventory is not used for this order, it would be sold for $2.75 per kg. The current price of material B is $4.25 per kg.

What is the total relevant cost of material B for the special order?

A $4,957.50
B $6,375
C $4,125
D $6,611.25

16 Which one of the following approaches to budgeting is most likely to reduce budgetary slack in administration budgets?

A Rolling budget
B Activity based budget
C Incremental budget
D Zero based budget

17 The following cost information relates to product XY, which is produced in a continuous process from several different materials.

	$
Actual quantity of materials at standard price	19,960
Actual quantity of materials at actual price	23,120
Actual yield at standard materials cost	20,800
Standard yield from actual input of materials at standard cost	19,552

What is the materials yield variance for the period?

A $1,248 (F)
B $2,320 (A)
C $840 (F)
D $3,568 (F)

18 Which one of the following reduces uncertainty in decision making?

A Expected value analysis
B Market research
C Sensitivity analysis
D Relevant costing

19 Budgeted set-up costs in a manufacturing department are $120,000. The following budgeted information is also available.

Number of batches produced	40 batches
Number of orders handled	200 orders
Number of machine hours	8,000 machine hours
Quantities of products produced	30,000 units (four different products)

In an activity based costing system, what is likely to be the overhead recovery rate for set-up costs?

A $3,000 per batch
B $600 per order
C $15 per machine hour
D $4 per unit produced

20 A manufacturing company wants to measure the learning rate that it has achieved with the manufacture of a new product item. The first item produced took 6 hours to make and the average time for the first 16 units was 3.3 hours.

What has been the learning rate for this product, to the nearest 1%?

A 69%
B 70%
C 80%
D 86%

(40 marks)

Section B – ALL FIVE questions are compulsory and MUST be attempted

1 Brunti is a manufacturing company which manufactures and assembles car components. The following budgeted information relates to Brunti for the forthcoming period.

	Products		
	XYI	*YZT*	*ABW*
	'000	'000	'000
Sales and production (units)	50	40	30
	$	$	$
Selling price (per unit)	45	95	73
Prime cost (per unit)	32	84	65
	Hours	*Hours*	*Hours*
Machine department (machine hours per unit)	2	5	4
Assembly department (direct labour hours per unit)	7	3	2

Overheads can be re-analysed into 'cost pools' as follows.

Cost pool	$'000	*Cost driver*	*Quantity for the period*
Machining services	357	Machine hours	420,000
Assembly services	318	Direct labour hours	530,000
Set up costs	26	Set ups	520
Order processing	156	Customer orders	32,000
Purchasing	84	Suppliers' orders	11,200
	941		

You have also been provided with the following estimates for the period.

	Products		
	XYI	*YZT*	*ABW*
Number of set-ups	120	200	200
Customer orders	8,000	8,000	16,000
Suppliers' orders	3,000	4,000	4,200

Required

Prepare and present a profit statement for each product using activity based costing.

(A total profit statement is not required.) **(10 marks)**

2 Cement Co is a company specialising in the manufacture of cement, a product used in the building industry. The company has found that when weather conditions are good, the demand for cement increases since more building work is able to take place. Cement Co is now trying to work out the level of cement production for the coming year in order to maximise profits. The company has received the following estimates about the probable weather conditions and corresponding demand levels for the coming year:

Weather	*Probability*	*Demand*
Good	25%	350,000 bags
Average	45%	280,000 bags
Poor	30%	200,000 bags

Each bag of cement sells for $9 and costs $4 to make. If cement is unsold at the end of the year, it has to be disposed of at a cost of $0.50 per bag. Cement Co has decided to produce at one of the three levels of production to match forecast demand. It now has to decide which level of cement production to select.

Required

(a) Construct a pay-off table to show all the possible profit outcomes. **(8 marks)**

(b) Determine the level of cement production the company should choose, based on the decision rule of maximin. Show your calculations clearly and justify your decision. **(2 marks)**

(Total = 10 marks)

3 The following figures for the years ending 31 December 20X4 and 20X3 relate to the Boats and Cladding divisions of Cordeline.

The return on capital employed (ROCE) figure is the basis for awarding a 20% bonus to the manager of the Boats division (actual ROCE/target ROCE). The below target ROCE for the Cladding division has resulted in a zero bonus award to its manager.

	Division			
	Boats		*Cladding*	
	20X4	*20X4*	*20X4*	*20X3*
	$'000	$'000	$'000	$'000
Sales	9,850	7,243	4,543	2,065
Profit before interest and taxes (PBIT)	1,336	1,674	924	363
Included in profit calculation:				
Depreciation for year	960	919	1,300	251
Net book value (NBV) of non-current assets*	5,540	6,000	7,700	2,600
Original cost of non-current assets	12,600	12,100	9,500	3,100
Replacement cost of non-current assets	25,000	24,500	9,750	3,350
New investment in non-current assets	500	750	6,400	2,400
Cost of capital	8%	8%	8%	8%
Return on capital employed**	24%	28%	12%	14%
Target return on capital	20%	20%	20%	20%

* Net book value is original cost less accumulated depreciation to date.

** Cordeline consider ROCE for bonus purposes to be PBIT as a % of NBV.

Required

(a) Explain what type of possible counter-productive behaviour could result from using the current ROCE calculation for performance appraisal. **(6 marks)**

(b) Suggest a revised ROCE measure and justify your suggestion. **(4 marks)**

(Total = 10 marks)

4 Thatcher International Park (TIP) is a theme park and has for many years been a successful business, which has traded profitably. About three years ago, the directors decided to capitalise on their success and as a result they reduced the expenditure made on new thrill rides, reduced routine maintenance where possible (deciding instead to repair equipment when it broke down) and made a commitment to regularly increase admission prices. Once an admission price is paid, customers can use any of the facilities and rides for free. These steps increased profits considerably, enabling good dividends to be paid to the owners and bonuses to the directors.

The last two years of financial results are as follows:

	Year 1	*Year 2 (most recent)*
	$'000	$'000
Sales	5,250	5,320
Less expenses:		
Wages	2,500	2,200
Maintenance – routine	80	70
Repairs	260	320
Directors' salaries	150	160
Directors' bonuses	15	18
Other costs (including depreciation)	1,200	1,180
Net profit	1,045	1,372

Other information	Year 1	Year 2 (most recent)
Book value of assets at start of year ($'000)	13,000	12,000
Dividend paid ($'000)	500	650
Number of visitors	150,000	140,000

TIP operates in a country where the average rate of inflation is around 1% per annum.

Required

Assess the financial performance of TIP using the information given above. **(15 marks)**

Note. There are 5 marks available for calculations and 10 marks available for discussion.

5 Truffle Co makes high quality, hand-made chocolate truffles which it sells to a local retailer. All chocolates are made in batches of 16, to fit the standard boxes supplied by the retailer. The standard cost of labour for each batch is $6.00 and the standard labour time for each batch is half an hour. In November, Truffle Co had budgeted production of 24,000 batches; actual production was only 20,500 batches. 12,000 labour hours were used to complete the work and there was no idle time. All workers were paid for their actual hours worked. The actual total labour cost for November was $136,800. The production manager at Truffle Co has no input into the budgeting process.

At the end of October, the managing director decided to hold a meeting and offer staff the choice of either accepting a 5% pay cut or facing a certain number of redundancies. All staff subsequently agreed to accept the 5% pay cut with immediate effect. At the same time, the retailer requested that the truffles be made slightly softer. This change was implemented immediately and made the chocolates more difficult to shape. When recipe changes such as these are made, it takes time before the workers become used to working with the new ingredient mix, making the process 20% slower for at least the first month of the new operation.

The standard costing system is only updated once a year in June and no changes are ever made to the system outside of this.

Required

(a) Calculate the following variances for Truffle Co:

(i) Labour rate planning variance
(ii) Labour rate operational variance
(iii) Labour efficiency planning variance
(iv) Labour efficiency operational variance **(8 marks)**

(b) Assess the performance of the production manager for the month of November. **(7 marks)**

(Total = 15 marks)

Formulae Sheet

Learning curve

$Y = ax^b$

Where Y	=	cumulative average time per unit to produce x units
a	=	the time taken for the first unit of output
x	=	the cumulative number of units produced
b	=	the index of learning (log LR/log2)
LR	=	the learning rate as a decimal

Demand curve

P	=	$a - bQ$
b	=	$\dfrac{\text{Change in price}}{\text{Change in quantity}}$
a	=	price when $Q = 0$
MR	=	$a - 2bQ$

End of Question Paper

Answers

DO NOT TURN THIS PAGE UNTIL YOU HAVE COMPLETED THE MOCK EXAM

A PLAN OF ATTACK

If this were the real Performance Management exam and you had been told to turn over and begin, what would be going through your mind?

An important thing to say (while there is still time) is that it is vital to have a good breadth of knowledge of the syllabus because the requirements for each question will relate to different areas of the F5 syllabus. With 20 multiple choice questions and five longer questions, you can expect most areas of the syllabus to be covered. However, don't panic. Below we provide guidance on how to approach the exam.

Which order to do the questions

Use the 15 minutes' reading time to **look through** the **paper in detail** and establish the **order** in which to attempt the questions. You may have a preference for attempting the multiple choice questions first and the Section B questions after that; or you may prefer to attempt Section B first. Whichever approach you take, you need to be disciplined about time: in the three hours of writing time, don't spend more than 72 minutes (40% of the three hours) on Section A and don't spend more than 108 minutes on Section B. If you begin with the multiple choice questions and are running out of the allocated time, don't use precious minutes struggling with questions that you are not sure about. Move on.

It is vital to attempt all the questions in the paper to increase your chances of passing. The best way to do this is to make sure you stick to the time allocation for each question – both in total and for each of the question parts. The worst thing you can do is run over time in one question and then find that you don't have enough time for the remaining questions. If you end up rushing the final Section B question, or even find that you don't have time to start your answer, you will have thrown away any chance of earning what could be important marks.

Section A multiple choice questions

If you decide to attempt the multiple choice questions first, remember that you don't have to answer them in their numerical order. You ought to find some MCQs easier than others, so look for the marks first that you think are easy.

If any question seems difficult, or would take too much time to answer, move on to the next question. If you still have time allocated time left after working through all the MCQs, you can go back to the questions you haven't answered.

Section B 10-mark and 15-mark questions

If you are challenged by the Section B questions in this paper, do the **questions in the order of how well you think you can answer them.**

- **Question 1** requires you to perform some activity based costing calculations. If you have practised with ABC questions, you should find this quite straightforward. However, present your calculations clearly and keep your eye on the time.
- **Question 2** is mainly about throughput accounting. Unlike Question 1, most of the marks in this question are for interpretation and discussion, so you need to do the calculations quickly. Poor exam technique would be to spend most of the time on the calculations, leaving you with just enough time to make some sketchy and hastily-explained comments for the rest of your answer.
- **Question 3** is about the use of return on capital employed (return on investment) and how measuring performance with this measure could lead to dysfunctional decision making. There are quite a few numbers in the question, but the answer is more about discussion and explanation rather than calculations.

  In the 15-minute reading time at the start of the exam, you may have identified this as a potentially tricky question for 10 marks, and you may therefore choose to leave this until last.
- **Question 4** is about linear programming, including calculating a shadow price. The problem can be solved using a graph, but you are unlikely to have graph paper handy and your answer may therefore be a bit untidy. However the question does not ask you to use the graphical method to reach a solution. You may prefer to go straight to simultaneous equations to identify the combination of the two variables that will maximise contribution. Working through simultaneous equations may be faster for you than drawing a graph. It's down to your preference.

- **Question 5** asks for calculations of variances and an interpretation of what they may signify. You should have practised these calculations many times in your studies. The task is to calculate the variances quickly in the time available, and leave yourself enough time to provide useful comment for 6 marks. The danger is to spend too much time on the calculations. Even if your calculations are perfect, that's only 9 marks of the 15 available.

Keep your discipline

So you **must allocate your time** according to the marks for the question in total, and for the parts of the questions. And you must also **follow the requirements of each question exactly.** If you are required to comment on some calculations or figures, make sure that you are answering the actual question, instead of writing around the subject without actually dealing with the specific question that is asked.

And try not to panic. There is a good chance that at least one Section B question and one or two Section A questions will confuse you. Don't worry. For Section A questions, just move on to the next question. And for Section B questions, do as much as you can, that you think is correct. Focus on the marks you find easier to earn.

Finished with fifteen minutes to spare?

If this happens, it looks like you slipped up on the time allocation. However if you have finished early, make sure you don't waste the last few minutes; go back to **any questions or parts of questions that you didn't finish** because you ran out of your allocated time.

Then forget about it!

Forget about what? Excellent, you already have.

Section A

1 A ABC involves the identification of factors known as cost drivers, which drive the costs of an organisation's major activities. Support Overhead costs of support services are then charged to products on the basis of their usage of an activity.

Absorption costing uses volume as a basis for cost allocation, and so tends to allocate too great a proportion of overheads to high volume products and too low a proportion of overheads to low volume products.

2 C Contribution for X = $15 ($60 – $45)

Contribution for Y = $12 ($25 – $13)

Objective function is to maximise: 15x + 12y

Constraints:

Material = $3x + y \leq 4{,}200$ (as X uses 3 kg of material (15/5), Y uses 1 kg (5/5))

Labour = $4x + 0.5y \leq 3{,}000$ (as X uses 4 labour hrs (24/6), Y uses 0.5 hrs (3/6))

3 B The balanced scorecard includes a financial perspective. It also has a customer perspective, which means that it is concerned with external as well as internal matters.

4 A The costs of introducing a new system may exceed the benefits. Employees are often inclined to resist change, even though the planned changes may improve planning and control within the organisation.

5 C Priority for production, in order to maximise profit, should be given to the product with the higher throughput accounting ratio. This is Product Y. With Machine M as a bottleneck, extra Machine T hours could not be utilised. With the additional 10 machine M hours, it would be possible to make and sell 20 units of Product Y (10 hours at 30 minutes per unit).

6 A Charging low prices initially to gain a large market share is market penetration pricing. Charging high prices in order to maximise unit profits is market skimming. Market penetration pricing is most effective when demand for the product is elastic (sensitive to price) and market skimming can maximise profitability when demand is inelastic (fairly insensitive to price).

Price elasticity of demand can be reduced by trying to persuade customers to buy products for reasons other than price, such as quality or design features. Advertising and sales promotion can also have the effect of reducing price elasticity.

7 C A range check is a control within specific IT applications to check that an input item of data has a value within an acceptable range, and any input items with a value outside the range are reported as errors.

8 C

	$
Total cost at 1,200 units	66,600
Deduct step increase in fixed costs	(6,000)
Total cost at 1,200 units excluding step cost increase	60,600
Total cost of 900 units	58,200
Therefore variable cost of 300 units	2,400

Variable cost per unit = $8

	$
Total cost of 900 units	58,200
Variable cost of 900 units (at 8 each)	7,200
Therefore fixed costs at this level of output	51,000

Total costs of 1,000 units = $51,000 + $(8 × 1,000) = $59,000

9 B Reducing the target cost gap should focus on ways of reducing the direct or variable costs of the product. This can be achieved by using a substitute cheaper raw material, but without affecting product quality. Reducing fixed overhead costs is not a way of reducing the gap. Using overtime is likely to increase costs and the target cost gap. Raising the selling price does not affect the cost gap directly, although it may lead to a reassessment of the target cost.

10 A Management information systems provide information to management about existing operations, and have an internal focus.

11 A The manager of an investment centre should have control over costs, revenues, and non-current assets and working capital of the centre, but does not have control over general head office costs.

12 C Current ROI 360/1,600 = 22.5% Residual income (in £'000) = 360 – (18% × 1,600) = £72,000
The new project: ROI = 25,000/130,000 = 19.2%. This is less than 22.5%; therefore ROI will fall.

New project RI = 25,000 – (18% × 130,000) = + £1,600. RI would increase.

13 A Effectiveness is a measure of the way in which resources (inputs) are used to create desired outputs, which in the case of the charity is the provision of relief services. Of the four measures, the percentage of funds spent on front-line activities, rather than on the organisation's administration, is the most appropriate measure of resource inputs to outputs.

14 A

Selling price/unit ($)	300	255	240	225
Contribution/unit ($)	186	141	126	111
Demand (units)	1,800	2,400	3,600	4,200
	$334,800	$338,400	$453,600	$466,200

15 A Incremental purchases = (1,500 – 945)kg × $4.25 per kg = $2,358.75

Opportunity cost of materials already purchased = 945 kg × $2.75 = $2,598.75

Total relevant cost = $2,358.75 + $2,358.75 = $4,957.50

16 D Zero based budgeting encourages the elimination of wasteful spending or budgetary slack because budgets are built from a zero base. This contrasts with incremental budgeting, where budgets for next year are based on the current year, with increments for growth or inflation.

17 A Standard yield from actual input of materials at standard cost: $19,552

Actual yield at standard materials cost: $20,800

Mix variance (19,552 – 20,800): $1,248 (F)

18 B Market research is used to obtain data about customer/consumer attitudes and preferences to products or markets, and the quantitative or qualitative information obtained from market research can help to reduce uncertainty for some elements of decision making, such as pricing and product design decisions.

19 A Set-up costs are most likely to be driven by the number of set-ups. The likelihood is that there will be a new set-up for each batch production run. So set-up costs are commonly driven by the number of production runs or number of batches produced.

20 D The cumulative average time falls to r% of what it was previously every time that output doubles. Between the first unit and the 16th unit, output has doubled four times.

Therefore $3.3/6 = r^4$

$r^4 = 0.55$

r = 0.861 or 86.1%

Section B

1 Brunti

Text references. Activity based costing is covered in Chapter 2a.

Top tips. This question calls for a straightforward ABC calculation which should not cause any problems. However you should be able to complete the calculations and present them neatly within the allocated time for the question.

Marking scheme

	Marks
Rate per cost driver	2
Overhead costs for each activity for each product	5
Overhead cost statement for each product	3
	10

(a) **Activity based costing**

Step 1 **Calculate the rate per cost driver for each of the cost pools**

Cost pool	*Cost*	*Quantity of cost drivers*	*Rate per cost driver*	
	$'000		$	
Machining services	357	420,000	0.850	per machine hour
Assembly services	318	530,000	0.600	per direct labour hour
Set up costs	26	520	50.000	per set up
Order processing	156	32,000	4.875	per customer order
Purchasing	84	11,200	7.500	per supplier's order

Step 2 **Allocate costs to the different products.**

	XYI	*YZT*	*ABW*
Units produced/sold	50,000	40,000	30,000
Machining services			
Machine hrs/unit	2	5	4
Total machine hours	100,000	200,000	120,000
Cost at $0.85/hr	$85,000	$170,000	$102,000
Assembly services			
Assembly hrs/unit	7	3	2
Total assembly hours	350,000	120,000	60,000
Cost at $0.60/hr	$210,000	$72,000	$36,000
No of set-ups	120	200	200
Cost at $50/set-up	$6,000	$10,000	$10,000
No of customer orders	8,000	8,000	16,000
Cost at $4.875/order	$39,000	$39,000	$78,000
No of suppliers' orders	3,000	4,000	4,200
Cost at $7.50/order	$22,500	$30,000	$31,500

Activity based costing profit statement

	XYI	YZT	ABW	Total
Units produced/sold	50,000	40,000	30,000	120,000
	$'000	$'000	$'000	$'000
Sales	2,250.00	3,800.00	2,190.00	8,240.00
Less:				
Prime cost	1,600.00	3,360.00	1,950.00	6,910.00
Overheads:				
Machining services	85.00	170.00	102.00	357.00
Assembly services	210.00	72.00	36.00	318.00
Set up costs	6.00	10.00	10.00	26.00
Order processing	39.00	39.00	78.00	156.00
Purchasing	22.50	30.00	31.50	84.00
	1,962.50	3,681.00	2,207.50	7,851.00
Profit/(loss)	287.50	119.00	(17.50)	389.00

Alternative approach

The overheads can also be allocated using ratios, without calculating rates per cost driver.

	XYI	YZT	ABW	Total
	$'000	$'000	$'000	$'000
Machining services (by machine hours) 10:20:12 (= 42)	85.0	170.0	102.0	357
Assembly services (by direct labour hours) 35:12:6 (= 53)	210.0	72.0	36.0	318
Set up costs (by number of set ups) 12:20:20 (= 52)	6.0	10.0	10.0	26
Order processing (by number of customer orders) 8:8:16 (= 32)	39.0	39.0	78.0	156
Purchasing (by number of supplier orders) 3:4:4.2 (= 11.2)	22.5	30.0	31.5	84
	362.5	321	257.5	941

Profit/loss for each product can then be calculated as sales revenue less prime cost and overheads.

2 Cement Co

Text reference. Pay-off tables and the maximin decision rule are covered in Chapter 7.

Top tips. You need to identify that since the question asks you to use the maximin decision rule, probabilities and expected values are not relevant. The probabilities are included in the question as a trick, to confuse you.

When you start to put the profit figures in the table for each combination of production quantity and demand, it may help to begin with the figures for produce and sell 200,000; produce and sell 280,000; and produce and sell 350,000. The profit is $5 per bag made and sold.

You can work out the other profit figures from this base. Another potential error to watch out for is to remember that if a bag of cement is produced but not sold, the resulting loss is not $0.50 per bag – the disposal cost. The loss is the cost of production as well as the disposal cost.

In answering part (b), let the examiner/marker know that you understand the maximin decision rule – state briefly what it is, before showing how it applies in this particular problem.

Easy marks. There are easy marks available in part (a) for constructing the framework of the pay-off table. One side of the table is for the decision choices – how many bags of cement to produce. The other side of the table is for the different possible outcomes – in this case different possible weather conditions and so different possible demand volumes.

Marking scheme

			Marks
(a)	Pay-off table		
	Calculation of profit	1.0	
	Calculation of loss	1.0	
	'Demand' label	0.5	
	'Supply' label	0.5	
	Weather column	0.5	
	Supply column – 350,000	1.5	
	Supply column – 280,000	1.5	
	Supply column – 200,000	1.5	
			8
(b)	Decision criterion		
	Maximin		
	Calculation	1.0	
	Justification	1.0	
	Labour efficiency planning variance		2
			10

(a) **Pay-off table**

The figures in $000 are profits for each given combination of production quantity and demand.

		Produce ('000 bags)		
		200	280	350
Weather	*Demand ('000 bags)*	$'000	$'000	$'000
Poor	200	1,000	640	325
Average	280	1,000	1,400	1,085
Good	350	1,000	1,400	1,750

Workings

Profit per bag sold = $9 – $4 = $5
Loss per bag produced but not sold = $4 + $0.50 = $4.50

1: (200 × 5) – (80 × 4.50) = 640
2: (200 × 5) – (150 × 4.50) = 325
3: (280 × 5) – (70 × 4.50) = 1,085

(b) **Decision based on maximin criterion**

The maximin criterion is that when given a choice between mutually exclusive courses of action, the preferred choice should be the one that has the best 'worst outcome'.

Make 200,000 bags: The profit will be $1,000,000 regardless of the weather.

Make 280,000 bags: The worst outcome would be a profit of $640,000, if the weather is poor.

Make 350,000 bags: The worst outcome would be a profit of $325,000, if the weather is poor.

The best 'worst possible' outcome is a profit of $1,000,000, which will be obtained by making 200,000 bags. The decision should therefore be to make 200,000 bags.

3 Boats and Cladding

Text references. Performance measures are covered in Chapters 16, 17 and 18.

Top tips. Use information provided in the question to illustrate your answer as necessary.

To justify your selection in part (b), it would be useful to present illustrative calculations. Without doing this, you may be struggling for something to write in part (b) to justify 4 marks.

Marking scheme

			Marks
(a)	Sub-optimality of ROI	3	
	Further disadvantages of ROI using net book values	3	
			6
(b)	Alternative ROI measure	1	
	Justification	3	
			4
			10

(a) **Possible counter-productive behaviour resulting from using the current ROCE calculation for performance appraisal**

Under the current method of performance appraisal, managers are judged on the basis of the **ROCE** that their divisions earn, the ROCE being calculated using the net book value of non-current assets. The use of ROCE as a method of appraising performance has disadvantages, whilst there are additional disadvantages of using ROCE based on the net book value of non-current assets.

(i) As managers are judged on the basis of the ROCE that their divisions earn each year, they are likely to be **motivated** into taking decisions which increase the division's short-term ROCE and rejecting projects which reduce the short-term ROCE even if the project is in excess of the company's target ROCE and hence is desirable from the company's point of view.

Suppose that the manager of the Boats division was faced with a proposed project which had a projected return of 21%. He would be likely to reject the project because it would reduce his division's overall ROCE to below 24%. The investment would be desirable from Cordeline Co's point of view, however, because its ROCE would be in excess of the company's target ROCE of 20%. This is an example of **sub-optimality** and a **lack of goal congruence** in decision making.

(ii) A similar misguided decision would occur if the manager of the Cladding division, say, was worried about the low ROCE of his division and decided to reduce his investment by scrapping some assets not currently being used. The reduction in both depreciation charge and assets would immediately improve the ROCE. When the assets were eventually required, however, the manager would then be obliged to buy new equipment.

(iii) The current method bases the calculation of ROCE on the **net book value of assets**. If a division maintains the same annual profits and keeps the same asset without a policy of regular asset replacement, its ROCE will increase year by year as the assets get older. Simply by allowing its non-current assets to depreciate a divisional manager is able to give a false impression of improving performance over time.

The level of new investment in non-current assets by the Cladding division was over three times that of the Boats division in 19X3 and nearly 13 times that of the Boats division in 19X4. The Boats division is using old assets that have been depreciated to a much greater extent than those of the Cladding division and hence the basis of the ROCE calculation is much lower. Consequently it is able to report a much higher ROCE.

(iv) The method used to calculate ROCE therefore also provides a **disincentive** to divisional mangers to **reinvest** in new or replacement assets because the division's ROCE would probably fall. From the figures provided it is obvious that the Cladding division has replaced assets on a regular basis, the difference between original and replacement costs of its assets being small. The manager of the Boats division, on the other hand, has not replaced assets, there being a marked difference between original and replacement cost of the division's assets.

(v) A further disadvantage of measuring ROCE as profit divided by the net book value of assets is that it is not easy to **compare fairly** the performance of one division with another. Two divisions might have the same amount of working capital, the same value of non-current assets at cost and the same profit. But if one division's assets have been depreciated by a much bigger amount, perhaps because they are older, that division's ROCE will be bigger.

In some respects this is the case with the Boats and Cladding divisions. Both the profit and the original asset cost of the Cladding division are about the same proportion of the Boats division's profit and original asset cost but the ROCE of the Boats division is twice that of the Cladding division.

(b) **A revised ROCE measure**

Instead of using the net book value of non-current assets to calculate ROCE, it could be calculated using the gross book value of non-current assets. This would remove the problem of ROCE increasing over time as non-current assets get older and will enable comparisons to be made more fairly.

Using the alternative method, the ROCE for the two divisions in the two years would be as follows.

Boats	20X3	13.8%
	20X4	10.6%
Cladding	20X3	11.7%
	20X4	9.7%

Although the Boats division still has a greater ROCE, the difference between the ROCE of the two divisions is much less.

4 Thatcher International Park

Text reference. Performance measurement is covered in Chapter 16.

Top tips. The challenge with questions on performance measurement is often to provide a convincing interpretation of the performance figures. You should have relatively little difficulty in identifying aspects of performance for comment and ratios to calculate.

Better answers will offer a meaningful discussion of the reasons for the different performance in Year 1 and Year 2, and a big hint is given in the question. The directors began to cut costs and raise admission prices three years ago, and switched from routine maintenance to repairs when equipment breaks down. We only have the performance figures for two years, but higher prices, lower costs (especially wages costs) and higher repair costs may all be attributable to this change in policy. You may also remember that measures to improve performance in the short term may have negative consequences over the longer term.

Easy marks. The question does not say how many aspects of performance you are required to discuss in your answer, so you could begin by selecting aspects of performance that you are familiar with, such as sales growth, profit margin and return on capital employed. Keep looking for more aspects of performance until you run out of time your allocated for the question. But remember to make some comment on each of the aspects of performance that you select.

Marking scheme

	Marks
Sales growth	3
Maintenance	3
Directors' pay	2
Wages	2
Net profit	2
Return on assets	3
	15

TIP's financial performance can be assessed in a number of ways:

Revenue growth and revenue per visitor

Sales increased by about 1.3% in Year 2 compared with Year (W1). Revenue consist entirely of admission charges, and the revenue per customer (admission prices) increased by about 8.6% (W2).

The increase in admission prices, is probably a major reason for the fall in visitor numbers by 10,000 or 6.7%.

The directors will need to consider whether further large price increases will reduce visitor numbers to the point where total sales revenue also falls.

Maintenance and repairs

The directors decided to reduce routine maintenance and repair equipment when it breaks down. The figures indicate that maintenance costs fell by $10,000 but repair costs rose by $60,000. This might suggest that the reduction in routine maintenance has been a costly mistake. However we do not know whether costs of maintenance engineers were included in the wages cost, so that the reduction in wages costs by $300,000 (12%) is due to partly to cuts in the number of engineering staff.

The large reduction in wages by 12% may be a consequence of the falling visitor numbers. However it may also raise concerns about the quality of service in the theme park – whether the reliability of the equipment or the standards of service to customers. Reductions in routine maintenance and an increase in equipment breakdowns may also increase health and safety risks – for both customers and staff.

Directors' pay

Directors' salaries increased by 6.7% and bonuses rose by $3,000 or 20%. Total pay including bonuses amounted to about 3.1% of revenue and 15.8% of net profit in Year 1, and to about 3.3% of revenue and 13.0% of net profit in Year 2. The directors are presumably being rewarded to the increase in profits, and this is likely to motivate them to pursue further price increases and cost reductions in the future.

The short-term rewards and incentives for the directors may, however, have negative implications for the longer-term prospects of TIP for revenue and profits.

Net profit

Net profit increased by 31.3% (W3) in Year 2 compared with Year 1. Net profit as a percentage of sales revenue was 19.9% in Year 1 and 25.8% in Year 2.

It would seem that the main reason for this big improvement in profits and profit margin is the fall in wages costs. If total wages had remained the same as in Year 1, profits in Year 2 would have been just $1,072,000, or 20.2% of sales.

This again raises questions about future profitability. It may not be possible to cut the wages costs by as much in future years. The improvement in results in Year 2 may be short-term in nature, and future growth may be much less certain.

Return on assets and investment in the theme park

The return on capital employed (or ROI) rose from 8.0% in Year 1 to 11.4% in Year 2 (W4). This was due to a combination of the large increase in net profit and also the fall in the book value of assets by $1,000,000 or 7.7%.

These figures suggest that the depreciation charge on equipment was at least $1,000,000 in Year 2, and the fall in book value suggests that the equipment is getting older. At some time in the future, the ageing equipment may become unreliable and will need replacing. As TIP has been paying good dividends out of profits, it may not have the money to purchase new equipment.

Again, this suggests that TIP is achieving short-term financial benefits, but the long-term consequences for the business could be adverse.

Workings

1 Sales growth is $5,320,000/$5,250,000 = (1.013 – 1) or 1.3%

2 Average admission prices were:

Year 1: $5,250,000/150,000 = $35 per person

Year 2: $5,320,000/140,000 = $38 per person

Increase = $(38 – 35)/$35 = 0.0857 or 8.57%

3 Net profit increase = up by (1,372 – 1,045)000/1,045 = 0.313 or 31.3%

4 Return on assets:

Year 1: $1,045,000/$13,000,000 = 0.08 or 8.0%

Year 2: $1,372,000/$12,000,000 = 0.114 or 11.4%

5 Truffle Co

Text reference. Planning and operational variances are covered in Chapter 12.

Top tips. When dealing with a question on planning and operational variances, you need to begin by establishing the original standard cost and the revised standard cost. Planning variances are calculated from the difference between the original and revised standards, and in principle operational variances are calculated using the revised standard.

There is a problem, however, in that planning and operational variances can be calculated in two different ways, and this can be confusing. The approach we recommend, and use in our answers is that:

- The rate planning variance is applied to actual hours worked (just as a material price planning variance would be applied to the actual quantities of material bought and used, and
- The efficiency operational variance is priced at the original standard rate per hour of $12 (just as a material usage operational variance would be measured using the original standard price per unit of materials).

In this way, the total of planning and operational variances add up to the correct amount.

Easy marks. To obtain easy marks for this question, you need to establish the original standard labour cost and the revised standard cost. The planning variance can be calculated from the difference between the original and the revised standards for labour rate per hour and labour time per unit.

Operational variances are calculated in much the same way as for 'normal' variances, although you may then have a problem in deciding the rate per hour to use for the operational efficiency variance.

Marking scheme

			Marks
(a)	Calculation of planning and operational variances:		
	Labour rate planning variance	2	
	Labour rate operational variance	2	
	Labour efficiency planning variance	2	
	Labour efficiency operational variance	2	
			8
(b)	Discussion:		
	Only operational variances controllable	1	
	No labour rate operating variance	1	
	Planning variance down to company, not manager	2	
	Labour efficiency total variance looks bad	2	
	Manager has performed well as regards efficiency	2	
	Standard for labour time was to blame	2	
	Conclusion	2	
			max 7
			15

(a) **Planning and operational variances**

The original standard labour cost = 0.5 hours × \$12 per hour = \$6 per unit
The revised standard cost = (0.5 hours × 1.20) × \$(12 × 0.95) per hour
= 0.6 hours × \$11.40 = \$6.84 per unit

Labour rate planning variance

	\$	
Original standard rate per hour	12.00	
Revised standard rate per hour	11.40	
Rate planning variance per hour	0.60	(F)

Actual hours paid = 12,000

Rate planning variance = 12,000 × \$0.60 (F) = \$7,200 (F)

(**Tutorial note**. The planning variance is favourable because the revised standard is a lower cost than the original standard.)

Labour rate operational variance

	\$
12,000 hours paid for should cost (revised standard) × \$11.40 per hour	136,800
They did cost	136,800
Labour rate operational variance	0

Labour efficiency planning variance

	Hours	
Original standard time per batch	0.5	
Revised standard time per batch	0.6	
Efficiency planning variance per batch	0.1	(A)

Batches produced = 20,500
Efficiency planning variance in hours
= 20,500 × 0.1(A) = 2,050 hours (A)
Original standard rate per hour = $12
Efficiency planning variance in $ = 2,050 × $12
$24,600 (A)

(**Tutorial note**. The planning variance is adverse because the revised standard is a longer time and so higher cost than the original standard.)

Labour efficiency operational variance

	Hours	
20,500 batches should take (revised standard) × 0.6 hours	12,300	
They did take	12,000	
Labour efficiency operational variance in hours	300	(F)

Original standard rate per hour $12
Labour efficiency operational variance in $ = $3,600 (F)

Tutorial note. Check

		$	
20,500 batches at original standard cost	(× $6)	123,000	
Rate planning variance		7,200	(F)
Rate operational variance		0	
Efficiency planning variance		24,600	(A)
Efficiency operational variance		3,600	(F)
Actual labour cost		136,800	

(b) **Performance of production manager**

The performance of the production manager should be assessed by the operational variances, and not the planning variances over which he has no control.

The operational labour rate variance was $0, which means that the labour force were paid exactly the reduced rate of $11.40 per hour that was agreed at the end of October. The manager presumably did not have to pay anyone for overtime, which would have produced an adverse rate variance (for overtime premium payments).

The reduction in the rate per hour to $11.40 was negotiated by the managing director, and was not within the control of the production manager. This planning variance is measured as a favourable variance, although it was agreed in order to avoid redundancies. To the extent that this can be regarded as favourable performance, the managing director should be given the credit.

The planning variance for labour efficiency is $24,600 adverse. This is because of the change in the standard labour time per batch as a result of the change in the ingredient mix. This is measured as a planning variance because, in the short term at least, extra time must be expected to complete batches until the work force gets used to the change. The production manager cannot be held responsible for this disruption to labour efficiency.

On the assumption that the revised standard time of 0.6 hours per batch is a reliable measurement, the production manager does have control over the operational variance for labour efficiency. This was $3,600 favourable. This suggests that the production manager may have succeeded in getting the work force to adapt to the new ingredient mix more quickly, and this reflects good performance for which he should be given credit.

In conclusion, the manager has performed well, given the change in the ingredient mix for batches. Due to better-than-expected labour efficiency.

ACCA

Paper F5

Performance Management

Mock Examination 2

Question paper	
Reading and planning Writing	15 minutes 3 hours
This paper is divided into two sections: Section A – ALL TWENTY questions are compulsory and MUST be answered Section B – ALL FIVE questions are compulsory and MUST be answered	

DO NOT OPEN THIS PAPER UNTIL YOU ARE READY TO START UNDER EXAMINATION CONDITIONS

Section A – ALL TWENTY questions are compulsory and MUST be attempted

Each question is worth 2 marks.

1 A company manufactures a product which requires four hours per unit of machine time. Machine time is a bottleneck resource as there are only ten machines which are available for 12 hours per day, five days per week. The product has a selling price of $130 per unit, direct material costs of $50 per unit, labour costs of $40 per unit and factory overhead costs of $20 per unit. These costs are based on weekly production and sales of 150 units.

What is the throughput accounting ratio (to 2 decimal places)?

A 1.33
B 2.00
C 0.75
D 0.31

2 A company makes a single product which it sells for $2 per unit.

Fixed costs are $13,000 per month.

The contribution/sales ratio is 40%.

Sales revenue is $62,500.

What is the margin of safety (in units)?

A 15,000
B 16,250
C 30,000
D 31,250

3 The following statements have been made about different types of standards in standard costing systems.

(1) Basic standards provide the best basis for budgeting because they represent an achievable level of productivity.

(2) Ideal standards are short-term targets and useful for day-to-day control purposes.

Which of the above statements is/are true?

A 1 only
B 2 only
C Neither 1 nor 2
D Both 1 and 2

4 A budget that is continuously updated by adding a further accounting period (a month or quarter) when the earlier accounting period has expired is known as a:

A Zero base budget
B Rolling budget
C Periodic budget
D Flexible budget

5 Division X and Division Y are profit centres in the same company. Division X makes a single component product. It has a fixed contract to supply an external customer with 5,000 units each month at a price of $35 per unit. All other sales are to Division Y at $30 per unit. Budgeted monthly profits for Division X are as follows:

	$
Sales: External	350,000
Sales to Division Y	150,000
	500,000
Variable costs	(270,000)
Fixed costs	(170,000
Profit	60,000

An external supplier offers to sell 4,000 units of the component to Division Y at a price of $25 per unit, for one month only. Division X would not be able to sell additional components externally.

If Division Y chooses to buy the components from the external supplier, how will profits for the month be affected?

A Division X profit will be $0. The company's profit will be $20,000 lower
B Division X profit will be $0. The company's profit will be $28,000 lower
C Division X profit will be $12,000. The company's profit will be $20,000 lower
D Division X profit will be $12,000. The company's profit will be $28,000 lower

6 The following are types of management accounting techniques.

(i) Flow cost accounting
(ii) Input/output analysis
(iii) Life cycle costing
(iv) Activity based costing

Which of the above techniques could be used by a company to account for its environmental costs?

A i only
B i and ii only
C i, ii and iii only
D All of the above

7 A business makes two components which it uses to produce one of its products. Details are:

	Component A	*Component B*
Per unit information:	$	$
Buy in price	14	17
Material	2	5
Labour	4	6
Variable overheads	6	7
General fixed overheads	4	3
Total absorption cost	16	21

The business wishes to maximise contribution and is considering whether to continue making the components internally or buy in from outside.

Which components should the company buy in from outside in order to maximise its contribution?

A A only
B B only
C Both A and B
D Neither A nor B

8 The following are all types of costs associated with management information.

(i) Use of bar coding and scanners
(ii) Payroll department's processing of personnel costs
(iii) Completion of timesheets by employees

Which of the above are examples of direct data capture costs?

A i only
B i and ii only
C i and iii only
D All of the above

9 To produce 19 litres of product X, a standard input mix of 8 litres of chemical A and 12 litres of chemical B is required.

Chemical A has a standard cost of $20 per litre and chemical B has a standard cost of $25 per litre.

During September, the actual results showed that 1,850 litres of product X were produced, using a total input of 900 litres of chemical A and 1,100 litres of chemical B (2,000 litres in total).

The actual costs of chemicals A and B were at the standard cost of $20 and $25 per litre respectively.

It was expected that an actual input of 2,000 litres would yield an output of 1,900 litres (95%). The actual yield for September was only 1,850 litres, which was 50 litres less than expected.

For the total materials mix variance and total materials yield variance, was there a favourable or adverse result in September?

A The total mix variance was adverse and the total yield variance was favourable
B The total mix variance was favourable and the total yield variance was adverse
C Both variances were adverse
D Both variances were favourable

10 Which one of the following may be used to study possible future outcomes when there are many different variables in the situation and the relationships between variables are not predictable?

A Sensitivity analysis
B Stress testing
C Pay-off table
D Simulation model

11 The following costs arise in relation to production of a new product.

(i) Research and development costs
(ii) Design costs
(iii) Testing costs
(iv) Advertising costs
(v) Production costs

In calculating the lifetime costs of the product, which of the above items would be **excluded**?

A i, ii, and iii only
B ii and iii only
C iv and v only
D None of the above

12 The following statements have been made about zero based budgeting.

(1) Employees will focus on eliminating wasteful expenditure.
(2) Short-term benefits could be emphasised over long-term benefits.

Which of the above statements is/are true?

A 1 only
B 2 only
C Neither 1 nor 2
D Both 1 and 2

13 Which of the following is the best definition of a traceable divisional cost?

A A variable cost incurred in a division

B A cost incurred in a division over which the divisional manager has control

C A cost attributable directly to a division over which the manager may or may not have control

D Costs charged to a division, including both directly attributable costs and a share of general overheads

14 A company makes and sells Product P. At the current selling price of $6 per unit, weekly demand is 4,000 units. It is estimated that for every $0.50 increase in price, sales demand will fall by 200 units, and for every $0.50 reduction in price, sales demand will increase by 200 units.

What is the formula for the sales demand curve for this product, where P is the sales price and Q is the quantity demanded?

A $P = 6 - 0.0025Q$
B $P = 16 - 0.0025Q$
C $P = 6 - 0.005Q$
D $P = 16 - 0.005Q$

15 The following statements have been made about activity based costing.

(1) There may be more than one cost driver for an activity.
(2) ABC involves some arbitrary allocation or apportionment of overhead costs.

Which of the above statements is/are true?

A 1 only
B 2 only
C Neither 1 nor 2
D Both 1 and 2

16 Tech World is a company which manufactures mobile phone handsets. From its past experiences, Tech World has realised that whenever a new design engineer is employed, there is a learning curve with a 75% learning rate which exists for the first 15 jobs.

A new design engineer has just completed his first job in five hours.

Note. At the learning rate of 75%, the learning factor (b) is equal to -0·415.
How long would it take the design engineer to complete the sixth job?

A 2.377 hours
B 1.442 hours
C 2.564 hours
D 5 hours

17 The following statements have been made about performance measures.

(1) Non-financial measures are often termed 'indicators of future performance'. Good results in these measures can lead to a good financial performance. For example if a business delivers good quality to its customers then this could lead to more custom at higher prices in the future.

(2) Financial performance indicators will generally only give a measure of the past success of a business, but not the future.

Which of the above statements is/are true?

A 1 only
B 2 only
C Neither 1 nor 2
D Both 1 and 2

18 The selling price of Product X is set at $550 for each unit and sales for the coming year are expected to be 800 units.

A return of 30% on the investment of $500,000 in Product X will be required in the coming year.

What is the target cost for each unit of Product X?

A $385
B $165
C $187.50
D $362.50

19 A company makes two products, X and Y. Each product earns a contribution of $6 per unit. Direct labour hours and machine hours are both effective limiting factors on production and sales. Relevant information is as follows.

	Product X per unit	*Product Y per unit*	*Total available per period*
Direct labour hours	0.4	0.8	36,000 hours
Machine hours	0.2	0.1	12,000 hours

The maximum contribution achievable is $420,000, by making and selling 50,000 units of X and 20,000 units of Y.

What is the shadow price of a direct labour hour?

A $3.75
B $5.00
C $7.50
D $15.00

20 What are the three building blocks in Fitzgerald and Moon's performance model for a service business?

A Objectives, standards and rewards
B Dimensions, standards and rewards
C Objectives, standards and measures
D Dimensions, rewards and measures

(40 marks)

Section B – ALL FIVE questions are compulsory and MUST be attempted

1 Brick by Brick (BBB) is a business which provides a range of building services to the public. Recently they have been asked to quote for garage conversions (GC) and extensions to properties (EX) and have found that they are winning fewer GC contracts than expected.

BBB has a policy to price all jobs at budgeted total cost plus 50%. Overheads are currently absorbed on a labour hour basis, resulting in a budgeted total cost of $11,000 for each GC and $20,500 for each EX. Consequently, the products are priced at $16,500 and $30,750 respectively.

The company is considering moving to an activity based cost approach. You are provided with the following data:

Overhead category	*Annual overheads* $	*Activity driver*	*Total number of activities per year*
Supervisors	90,000	Site visits	500
Planners	70,000	Planning documents	250
Property related	240,000	Labour hours	40,000
Total	400,000		

A typical GC costs $3,500 in materials and takes 300 labour hours to complete. A GC requires only one site visit by a supervisor and needs only one planning document to be raised. The typical EX costs $8,000 in materials and takes 500 hours to complete. An EX requires six site visits and five planning documents. In all cases, labour is paid $15 per hour.

Required

(a) Calculate the cost and the quoted price of a GC and an EX using activity based costing (ABC). **(5 marks)**

Assume that the cost of a GC falls by approximately 7% and the cost of an EX rises by approximately 2% as a result of a change to ABC.

Required

(b) Suggest possible pricing strategies for the two products which BBB sells and suggest one reason other than high prices for the current poor sales of the GC. **(5 marks)**

(Total = 10 marks)

2 The Q Organisation is a large, worldwide respected manufacturer of consumer electrical and electronic goods. Q constantly develops new products that are in high demand.

Market research has discovered that the price-demand relationship for a new DVD recorder product during the initial launch phase will be as follows.

Price $	*Demand* Units
100	10,000
80	20,000
69	30,000
62	40,000

Production of the DVD recorder would occur in batches of 10,000 units and the production director believes that 50% of the variable manufacturing cost would be affected by a learning curve. This would apply to each batch produced and continue at a constant rate of learning up to a production volume of 40,000 units when the learning would be complete. The production director estimates that the unit variable manufacturing cost of the first batch would be $60 ($30 of which is subject to the effect of the learning curve, and $30 of which is unaffected), whereas the average unit variable manufacturing cost of all four batches would be $52.71.

There are no non-manufacturing variable costs associated with the DVD recorder.

Required

(a) Calculate the rate of learning that is expected by the production director. **(2 marks)**

(b) Calculate the optimum price at which Q should sell the DVD recorder in order to maximise its profits during the initial launch phase of the product. **(8 marks)**

(Total = 10 marks)

3 Brace Co is split into two divisions, A and B, each with their own cost and revenue streams. Each of them is managed by a divisional manager who has the power to make all investment decisions within the division. The cost of capital for both divisions is 12%. Historically, investment decisions have been made by calculating the return on investment (ROI) of any opportunities and at present, the return on investment of each division is 16%.

A new manager who has recently been appointed in division A has argued that using residual income to make investment decisions would result in 'better goal congruence' throughout the company.

Each division is currently considering the following separate investments:

	Division A	*Division B*
Capital required for investment	$82.8 million	$40.6 million
Sales generated by investment	$44.6 million	$21.8 million
Net profit margin	28%	33%

Required

(a) Calculate the return on investment for each of the two divisions. **(2 marks)**

(b) Calculate the residual income for each of the two divisions. **(4 marks)**

(c) Comment on the results, taking into consideration the manager's views about residual income. **(4 marks)**

(Total = 10 marks)

4 (a) A paint manufacturer uses skilled staff to operate the machinery that converts the raw materials for the paint into the finished product. The standard direct labour hours for each 100 litres of white paint produced are as follows: 8 direct labour hours at $24 per hour.

During February, 640 direct labour hours were worked to produce 7,800 litres of paint, at a total cost of $16,500. It has now been realised that a new wage rate of $26 per hour had been agreed with the workers.

Required

(i) Calculate the labour rate planning variance for February. **(2 marks)**

(ii) Calculate the operational labour rate variance and the operational labour efficiency variance for February. **(4 marks)**

(b) Explain the importance of separating variances into their planning and operational components. You should use the figures calculated in part (b) to illustrate your answer. **(4 marks)**

(c) Discuss the problems that can arise from using standard costs in a rapidly changing environment. **(5 marks)**

(Total = 15 marks)

5 Colour Co is a paint manufacturer with a number of divisions. Brief details of the Green and Blue divisions are set out below for the year ended 30 September 20X8.

	Green	*Blue*
	$m	$m
Net profit for year ended 30 September 20X8	4.2	5.6
Net book value of non-current assets at 1 October 20X7	20.0	32.0
Additions to non-current assets on 2 October 20X7	4.5	
Depreciation for year ended 30 September 20X8	(4.0)	(6.2)
Net book value of non-current assets at 30 September 20X8	20.5	25.8
Net current assets	11.5	10.2
Total net assets at 30 September 20X8	32.0	36.0

There were no sales of non-current assets during the year. Depreciation has been charged on the basis of assets in use. The cost of capital used by Colour plc is 12%.

The budgeted assets and profits for Green and Blue for the year ended 30 September 20X9 are identical to those in use at the end of the previous year. A new investment in computerised mixing equipment is available to either Green or Blue at the beginning of the year 20X9. This investment would increase total net assets by $25m and produce annual net profits of $3.5m for many years.

Required

(a) Calculate for Green and Blue, using 'net assets in use' as a basis:

(i) Return on investment (ROI) for year ended 30 September 20X8;

(ii) Residual income (RI) for year ended 30 September 20X8. **(4 marks)**

(b) Comment briefly on the performance of Blue and Green in 20X8. **(2 marks)**

(c) Discuss whether Blue or Green would want to take the new investment opportunity in the year 20X9 described above. Provide calculations to support your comments.

(9 marks)

(Total = 15 marks)

Formulae Sheet

Learning curve

$Y = ax^b$

Where			
	Y	=	cumulative average time per unit to produce x units
	a	=	the time taken for the first unit of output
	x	=	the cumulative number of units produced
	b	=	the index of learning (log LR/log2)
	LR	=	the learning rate as a decimal

Demand curve

$$P = a - bQ$$

$$b = \frac{\text{Change in price}}{\text{Change in quantity}}$$

a = price when Q = 0

$$MR = a - 2bQ$$

End of Question Paper

Answers

DO NOT TURN THIS PAGE UNTIL YOU HAVE COMPLETED THE MOCK EXAM

A PLAN OF ATTACK

If this were the real Performance Management exam and you had been told to turn over and begin, what would be going through your mind?

An important thing to say (while there is still time) is that it is vital to have a good breadth of knowledge of the syllabus because the requirements for each question will relate to different areas of the F5 syllabus. With 20 multiple choice questions and five longer questions in Section B, you can expect most of the syllabus to be covered somehow. However, don't panic. Below we provide guidance on how to approach the exam.

Which order to do the questions

Use the 15 minutes' reading time to **look through** the **paper in detail** and establish the **order** in which to attempt the questions. You may have a preference for attempting the multiple choice questions first and the Section B questions after that; or you may prefer to attempt Section B first. Whichever approach you take, you need to be disciplined about time: in the three hours of writing time, don't spend more than 72 minutes (40% of the three hours) on Section A and don't spend more than 108 minutes on Section B. If you begin with the multiple choice questions and are running out of the allocated time, don't use precious minutes struggling with questions that you are not sure about. Move on.

It is vital to attempt all the questions in Section B of the paper to increase your chances of passing. The best way to do this is to make sure you stick to the time allocation for each question – both in total and for each of the question parts. The worst thing you can do is run over time in one question and then find that you don't have enough time for the remaining questions. If you end up rushing the final Section B question, or even find that you don't have time to start your answer, you will have thrown away any chance of earning what could be important marks.

With Section A it is less essential to answer all the questions. If you don't answer a question, you have lost only two marks, and this may not be disastrous. On the other hand, as you do not get negative marks for a wrong answer, there is nothing to lose by giving an answer and choosing between A, B, C and D. Not ideal, of course, but it's not against the rules.

Section A multiple choice questions

If you decide to attempt the multiple choice questions first, remember that you don't have to answer them in their numerical order. If any question seems difficult, or would take too much time to answer, move on to the next question. If you have time after working through all the MCQs, you can go back to the questions you haven't answered.

You ought to find some MCQs easier than others, so look for the marks first that you think are easy.

Section B 10-mark and 15-mark questions

If you are challenged by the Section B questions in this paper, do the **questions in the order of how well you think you can answer them.**

- **Question 1** is about target costing. The challenge here is the amount of calculation required to complete your answer in time. You have to calculate the expected cost and the target cost gap, but there is no requirement for discussion or comment. It's all down to speed and efficiency of calculations.
- **Question 2** is about the learning curve. Having to begin your answer by calculating the learning rate. This may create some difficulty if you haven't seen this type of problem before. So if you can't see a way into the solution, you may choose to come back to the question after you have attempted the rest of the questions in Section B. If you can't see how to calculate the learning rate, and so can't answer this question, study our suggested answer very carefully!
- **Question 3** is about a make-or-buy decision, but there is a lot of information to take in, and only seven marks are available for the calculations. The main challenge here may be to complete your answer in the available time. Remember that neat and clear workings can be an enormous help to you when you are working under time pressure.
- **Question 4** is mainly about planning and operational variances, but only six marks are available for the calculations. Four marks – almost as many as for the calculations – are available for an explanation or analysis of your figures. Then there are five marks for part (c): this has some link to planning variances, and the need to

keep amending standards in a changing business environment. However, it may be asked whether the benefits of standard costing are worth the cost for any business that operates in a continually changing environment.

- **Question 5** is about divisional performance measurements and the use of ROI and residual income. The calculations should be straightforward, but you need to do them quickly and competently. Nine marks are available for discussion, so you should spend most of the time writing down points and ideas rather than calculating numbers.

Keep your discipline

So you **must allocate your time** according to the marks for the question in total, and for the parts of the questions. And you must also **follow the requirements of each question exactly.** If you are required to comment on some calculations or figures, make sure that you are answering the actual question, instead of writing around the subject without actually dealing with the specific question that is asked.

And try not to panic. There is a good chance that at least one Section B question and one or two Section A questions will confuse you. Don't worry. For Section A questions, just move on to the next question. And for Section B questions, do as much as you can, that you think is correct. Focus on the marks you find easier to earn.

Finished with fifteen minutes to spare?

Looks like you slipped up on the time allocation. However if you have finished early, make sure you don't waste the last few minutes; go back to **any questions or parts of questions that you didn't finish** because you ran out of your allocated time.

Then forget about it!

Forget about what? Excellent, you already have.

Section A

1 A Return per factory hour = ($130 – $50)/4 hours = $20

Factory costs per hour = $20 + $40/4 = $15

Throughput accounting ratio = $20/$15 = 1.33

2 A Sales = $62,500

Break even sales = $13,000/0.40 = $32,500

Margin of safety (sales revenue) = $62,500 – $32,500 = $30,000
Margin of safety (units) $30,000/$2 =15,000 units

3 C A basic standard is a historical standard, and will often no longer represent current levels of productivity. Ideal standards are not achievable in the short term, but may be longer-term targets.

4 B A rolling budget is also known as a continuous budget.

5 D External sales are 10,000 units and internal transfers are 5,000 units. The marginal cost per unit produced in Division X is $270,000/(10,000 + 5,000) = $18.

The marginal cost of making the units is $18 and the cost of external purchase would be $25. By purchasing externally, the company as a whole would incur additional costs of $(25 – 18) × 4,000 units = $28,000.

Division profit	$
Sales: External	350,000
Sales to Division Y (1,000 units)	30,000
	380,000
Variable costs (11,000 × $18)	(198,000)
Fixed costs	(170,000)
Profit	12,000

Division Y profits would increase by $20,000, Division X profits would fall be $48,000 and the company as a whole would suffer a fall in profit of $28,000.

6 D Material flow cost accounting (MFCA) and input-output analysis are environmental management accounting techniques. Life cycle costing is concerned with analysing costs of a product over its entire life cycle from initial development to eventual withdrawal from the market. However, as long as you are aware that activity based costing is a management accounting technique, the answer to this question is straightforward. Only Option D includes ABC.

7 B For a make-or-buy decision, we compare the marginal cost (relevant cost) of in-house production with the cost of buying in the item. Profit is maximised by selecting the lower cost.

Component A: Relevant cost = $(2 + 6 + 4) = $12. Buy in cost = $14. Therefore produce in-house.

Component B: Relevant cost = $(5 + 6 + 7) = $18. Buy in cost = $17. Therefore buy in from an external supplier.

8 C Bar codes and scanners capture sales and inventory data, for example in retail stores. Timesheets capture data about labour hours worked. Processing personnel costs is an example of processing data that has been captured, and (often also) producing output data.

Operational gearing is a measure of how much operating profit will change, given a change in sales revenue. Operational gearing is high when the contribution/sales ratio is high, and variable costs are a small proportion of total operating costs (and most costs are fixed costs).

9 B The actual yield was less than the expected (standard) yield; therefore the yield variance must be adverse. There is no requirement to calculate the amount of the variance.

Mix variance:

	2,000 litres input			*Standard*	
Material	*Standard mix*	*Actual mix*	*Mix variance*	*price per litre*	*Mix variance*
	Litres	Litres	Litres	£	£
A	(40%) 800	900	100 (A)	20	2,000 (A)
B	(60%) 1,200	1,100	100 (F)	25	2,500 (F)
	2,000	2,000			500 (F)

The other checks are all methods of restricting access to systems, data files or programs.

10 D Sensitivity analysis is a term used to describe any technique whereby decision options are tested for their vulnerability to changes in any 'variable' such as expected sales volume, sales price per unit, material costs, or labour costs. It can be used in any situation so long as the relationships between the key variables can be established. Stress tests are used to test for extreme possible circumstances and what the outcome might then be.

Simulation models can be used to deal with decision problems involving a large number of uncertain variables, when the relationship between the variables is uncertain or unpredictable. In practice, simulation modelling is carried out using a computer model.

11 D All the costs are included in the lifetime costs of a product.

12 D Zero based budgeting begins by looking at the minimum budgeted expenditure, and building a budget from this zero base. This encourages employees to focus on wasteful and unnecessary spending.

However the focus is on short-term savings and may give insufficient consideration to longer-term benefits of current spending.

13 C A distinction can be made between controllable fixed costs of a division, which are fixed costs over which the divisional manager has some control or influence, and traceable fixed costs which are costs attributable to a division but over which the manager has no control. For example, if a division is located in separate premises, the rental cost or depreciation cost of the premises is a traceable cost to the division, but the divisional manager may have no control over the amount of the expense.

14 B If $P = a - bQ$, a is the price when $Q = 0$

$Q = 0$ when $P = 6 + [(4{,}000/200) \times 0.50] = 16$

Demand falls by 200 for every $0.5 change in the price, so the demand curve formula is:

$P = 16 - (0.5/200) \times Q$

$P = 16 - 0.0025Q$

15 D There may be more than one cost driver for an activity, but in order to simplify the ABC system, it is usual to use just one cost driver per activity. ABC does involve some arbitrary apportionment of overhead costs to activities, such as factory rental and heating costs. Alternatively, general overheads are absorbed into costs on a direct labour hour or machine hour basis: this too is an arbitrary method of charging overheads.

16 B $Y = ax^b$

$b = \log 0.75/\log 2 = -0.1249/0.3010 = -0.415$

When $x = 6$, $x^{-0.415} = 1/6^{-0.415} = 0.4754$

Average time for six jobs:

$Y = 5 \times 0.4754 = 2.377$ hours

Total time required for six jobs = 6×2.377 hours = 14.262 hours

Average time for five jobs: $5 \times 5^{-0.415} = 2.564$ hours

Total time required for five jobs = 5×2.564 hours = 12.820 hours

Time required to perform the 6th job = Total time required for six jobs – Total time required for five jobs.

Therefore, time required to perform the 6th job = 14.262 hours – 12.820 hours = 1.442 hours

17 D Good results in non-financial measures can lead to a good financial performance in the future. For example if a business delivers good quality to its customers then this could lead to more custom at higher prices in the future.

There is no guarantee that a good past financial performance will lead to a good **future** financial performance.

18 D Required return: $500,000 × 30% = $150,000

Total sales revenue: $550 × 800 units = $440,000

Therefore total cost = $440,000 – $150,000 = $290,000

Unit cost = $290,000/800 = $362.50

19 B If one more labour hour is available, contribution will be maximised where:

(1)	0.4x + 0.8y	=	36,001
(2)	0.2x + 0.1y	=	12,000

Multiply (2) by 2

(3)	0.4x + 0.2y	=	24,000
Subtract (3) from (1)	0.6y	=	12,001
	y	=	20,001.667

Substitute in (2) 0.2x + 2,000.1667 = 12,000

x	=	49,999.166

Total contribution = (20,001.667 + 49,999.166) × $6 = $420,005. This is an increase of $5; therefore the shadow price of labour hours is $5 per hour.

20 B In the Fitzgerald and Moon model, there are three building blocks. Dimensions are the bases for measuring performance, such as financial performance and quality. For each dimension of performance there must be standards or targets for achievement. And there should be a reward system to provide incentives to managers and other employees to achieve the targets or standards.

Section B

1 Brick by Brick

Text reference. Activity based costing is covered in Chapter 2a.

Top tips. This question may call for relatively straightforward calculations of cost, but you need to work quickly and accurately. With ABC, overhead costs are the main challenge, and you need to identify the different overhead activities and calculate a cost per unit of the driver for each activity.

For part (b), you may need to note carefully the wording of the question which asks about possible pricing strategies. You will earn more marks by recognising that although BBB currently sets sales prices at cost plus 50% – and may continue to do so – other pricing strategies are also possible.

Easy marks. The cost per unit of GC and EX is the sum of the cost of materials, labour and three elements of overheads. The price is cost plus 50%. You can set out a table for unit costs, and quickly enter the materials and labour costs.

For part (b), you can earn marks by stating that a change in costs may result in a reduction or increase in the selling price. A higher price should result in lower sales and a lower price should result in higher sales.

Marking scheme

			Marks
(a)	**Price under ABC**		
	Materials	0.5	
	Labour	0.5	
	Supervisor overheads	1.0	
	Planner overheads	1.0	
	Property overheads	1.0	
	Price	1.0	
			5
(b)	**Pricing discussion**		
	GC – reduce price by 7%	1.0	
	GC – produce price by less than 7%	1.0	
	Quality, reputation, reliability, sales documentation	2.0	
	EX – increase price by 2%	1.0	
	EX – hold price unchanged	1.0	
		max	5
			10

(a) **Costs and quoted prices for the GC and the EX using ABC to absorb overheads**

		GC per unit $		*EX* per unit $
Materials		3,500		8,000
Labour	(300 × $15)	4,500	(500 × $15)	7,500
Overheads				
– Supervisor	(1 × $180)	180	(6 × $180)	1,080
– Planners	(1 × $280)	280	(5 × $280)	1,400
– Property	(300 × $6)	1,800	(500 × $6)	3,000
Total cost		10,260		20,980
Quoted price				
At cost + 50%		15,390		31,470

Workings

	Cost $	*Number of drivers*	*Cost per driver unit* $
Supervisor	90,000	500	180
Planners	70,000	250	280
Property	240,000	40,000	6

(b) BBB can choose its pricing strategy and is not committed to charging a price that is equal to cost plus 50%.

GC

However, if BBB continues its policy of charging cost plus 50%, a fall in the cost of GC by 7% would result in a fall in the selling price by 7%. At this lower price, BBB might expect to sell a larger quantity of GC.

BBB is currently not selling as many units of GC as it expected, and this may be due to the price that it is charging (in comparison with the prices of competitors).

BBB could reduce the price from its current level, but by less than 7% – say by 5%. There should still be some increase in sales demand, and the unit profit (and profit as a percentage of cost) would be higher than if the price is reduced by 7%.

The selling price may not be the only reason, or even the main reason, why sales of GC are less than expected. Poor selling and marketing of GC would have a negative impact on demand from customers. Another possibility is that although BBB may have a good reputation for the quality of its EX, its GC are poor quality; and BBB may have earned a reputation among potential customers for poor product quality. Poor service to customers may also affect the reputation of BBB for its GC: for example BBB may not be reliable in meeting its promised dates for starting or completing jobs.

However, price is usually significant factor affecting sales demand, and if BBB wants to increase demand for GC, it may wish to consider a large reduction in price – perhaps larger than the reduction of 7% considered above.

EX

If BBB continues its policy of charging cost plus 50%, a rise in the cost of GC by 2% would result in an increase in the selling price by 2%. At this lower price, BBB might expect to sell a smaller quantity of GC; however we do not know what effect a fairly small increase would have on sales volume.

BBB may choose instead to keep the price of EX unchanged. The unit profit (and profit as a percentage of cost would fall, but the budgeted sales volume should remain unchanged.

2 Q Organisation

Text references. Pricing is covered in Chapter 5 and the learning curve in Chapter 9.

Top tips. Part (a) is difficult and requires you to know how to calculate a rate of learning and a learning curve.

Part (b) should just follow on: once you have total variable costs for each level of demand you can calculate the optimal contribution.

Marking scheme

			Marks
(a)	Calculation of r		2
(b)	Calculation of average cost of first 30,000 units	2	
	Table to calculate profit for each price/quantity level prices	5	
	Identify optimum price	1	
			8
			10

(a)

Cumulative number of units	*Total variable cost/unit*	*Affected by learning*	*Not affected by learning*
	$	$	$
10,000	60.00	30.00	30.00
20,000	56.10 (W2)	26.10	30.00
30,000	54.06 (W3)	24.06	30.00
40,000	52.71	22.71	30.00

Workings

1 *Calculation of rate of learning*

Every time output doubles, the cumulative average time per unit is r% of what it was previously, where r is the rate of learning.

At 10,000 units, variable cost affected by learning = $30

At 40,000 units, variable cost affected by learning = $22.71

Let the rate of learning be r.

$22.71/30 = r^2$

$r^2 = 0.757$

$r = 0.87$

(**Note.** Also, using the average costs per unit for 10,000 and 20,000 units: 26.10/30 = r; therefore r = 0.87.)

(b) We can now derive the variable cost affected by learning for 20,000 units,

$= 30r = 30 \times 0.87 = \$26.10$

To calculate the variable cost affected by learning for 30,000 units requires the use of a formula for the learning curve.

a = $30

= 3

b = log 0.87/log 2

= −0.201

Thus Y= aX^b

= $30 \times 3^{-0.201}$

= 24.06

Optimum price at which the DVD recorder should be sold.

Demand in units	*Price/unit* $	*Variable cost /unit* $	*Contribution/ unit* $	*Total contribution* $
10,000	100	60.00	40.00	400,000
20,000	80	56.10	23.90	478,000
30,000	69	54.06	14.94	448,200
40,000	62	52.71	9.29	371,600

The price which gives the optimum contribution is $80/unit.

3 Brace Co

Text reference. Return on Investment and residual income are covered in Chapter 17.

Top tips. Show your workings for ROI and RI clearly. Then don't forget to state the 'obvious' – using ROI as a basis for making an investment decision, what would each divisional manager decide? And using RI as a basis for making an investment decision, what would each divisional manager decide? Unless you make these points specifically in your answer, you will fail to get all the marks available.

Easy marks. There are easy marks available for calculating ROI and residual income for each division, but you need to make the calculations fairly quickly, to leave yourself enough time for the comments or conclusions.

Marking scheme

			Marks
(a)	Return on investment		
	ROI of A	1	
	ROI of B	1	
			2
(b)	Residual income		
	RI of A	2	
	RI of B	2	
			4
(c)	Comments		
	A rejects, B accepts under ROI	1	
	Both accept under RI	1	
	ROI produces wrong decision for company and RI produces right decision	1	
	Manager right	1	
			4
			10

(a) **Return on investment (ROI)**

Division A

Net profit = $44.6m × 28% = $12.488m

ROI = $12.488m/$82.8m = 15·08%

Division B

Net profit = $21.8m × 33% = $7.194m

ROI = $7.194m/$40·6m = $17.72%

(b) **Residual income**

Division A

Profit (see (a)) = $12.488m

Capital employed = $82.8m

Imputed interest charge = $82.8m × 12% = $9.936m

Residual income = $(12.488m – 9.936)m = $2.552m

Division B

Profit = $7.194m

Capital employed = $40.6m

Imputed interest charge = $40.6m × 12% = $4.872m

Residual income = $(7.194 – 4·872)m = $2.322m

(c) **Comments**

If a decision about whether to proceed with the investments is based on ROI, the manager of division A is likely to reject the proposed investment. This is because the ROI of the investment would be 15.08% but the ROI of the division is currently 16%. Making the investment would reduce the division's ROI.

The manager of division B will accept the proposal. This is because the ROI of the investment would be 17.72%, which is higher than the current ROI for the division. As a result of the investment, the division's ROI would increase.

Both investments would achieve a return in excess of the cost of capital of 12%. Although it is incorrect to compare accounting ROI with cost of capital, there is nevertheless good reason to suppose that both investments may be worthwhile.

Residual income is calculated by charging each division with notional interest on capital invested at a rate equal to the cost of capital. In both cases, RI would be positive, indicating that profit would exceed an estimated cost of the capital invested. If a decision about whether to proceed with the investments is based on RI, both managers would want to accept their proposed investment.

It is inappropriate to base an investment decision on whether it would increase or educe the existing ROI. Investment decisions add value and are worthwhile if they achieve returns in excess of the cost of capital. For this reason RI is a better basis for decision-making than ROI. In this case, using ROI would produce the 'wrong' answer for division A but using RI would produce the 'right' answer for both divisions.

4 Paint manufacturer

Text references. Planning and operational variances are covered in Chapter 12.

Top tips. Part (a) tests your knowledge and understanding of planning and operational variances, and you should try to make the calculations quickly, using your preferred approach to the calculations and their presentation.

Part (c) is more of a challenge, but it deals with the important issue of whether standard costing has any validity in a fast-changing industrial environment.

Easy marks. The easier marks in this question are for the variance calculations.

Marking scheme

				Marks
(a)	(i)	Labour rate planning variance		2
	(ii)	Operational rate variance	2	
		Operational efficiency variance	2	
				4
(b)	Controllability		2	
	Motivation		1	
	Improved standard setting		1	
				4
(c)	For each point: 1 mark			max 5
				15

(a) (i) **Labour rate planning variance**

	$
Original standard rate per hour	24
Revised standard rate per hour	26
Labour rate planning variance per hour	2 (A)
Hours worked	640
Labour rate planning variance in $	1,280 (A)

(ii) **Operational labour efficiency variance**

7,800 litres should have taken (7,800/100 × 8 hrs)	624 hrs
But did take	640 hrs
Operational efficiency variance in hours	16 hrs (A)
× Original standard rate per hour	× $24
Operational labour efficiency variance	$384 (A)

Operational labour rate variance

	$
640 hours should have cost ($26 × 640)	16,640
Actual cost	16,500
Operational labour rate variance	140 (F)

(b) **Controllable versus uncontrollable**

The analysis highlights those variances which are **controllable** and those which are **non-controllable**. By analysing the total labour rate variance between planning and operational, management can focus on the underlying operational causes of the total variances and thus identify the controllable increase in costs which could have been avoided. In part (b) the labour rate variance was $1,280 (A) + $140 (F) = $1,140 (A) but it is clear that the reason for this adverse variance is because of a planning error ($1,280 (A)). Planning errors are not within the control of operational management.

Motivation

Managers' acceptance of the use of variances for performance measurement, and their motivation, is likely to increase if they know that they will **not be held responsible for poor planning** and faulty standard setting.

Improved standard setting

The planning and standard setting process should improve. Standards should be more **accurate**, **relevant** and **appropriate**.

(c) **Standard costs in a rapidly changing environment**

Standard costing is most appropriate in a **stable, standardised and repetitive** environment. One of the main objectives of standard costing is to ensure that processes conform to standards, that they do not vary, and that variances are eliminated. This could be **restrictive** and **inhibiting** in a fast-changing business environment.

Variance analysis concentrates on only a **narrow range of costs** and does not give sufficient attention to issues such as quality and customer satisfaction.

Standard costing places **too much emphasis on direct labour costs**. Direct labour is only a small proportion of costs in the modern manufacturing environment and so this emphasis is not appropriate.

Many of the variances in a standard costing system focus on the control of **short-term variable costs**. In most modern manufacturing environments, the majority of costs, including direct labour costs, tend to be fixed in the short run.

The use of standard costing relies on the existence of **repetitive operations** and relatively **homogeneous** output. Nowadays many organisations are forced continually to respond to customers' changing requirements, with the result that output and operations are not so repetitive.

Standard costing systems were **developed** when the **business environment** was more **stable** and **less prone to change**. The current business environment is more dynamic and it is not possible to assume stable conditions.

Standard costing systems **assume** that **performance to standard is acceptable**. Today's business environment is more focused on continuous improvement.

Most standard costing systems produce **control statements weekly or monthly**. The modern manager needs much more prompt control information in order to function efficiently in a dynamic business environment.

5 Colour Co

Text reference. Performance measures are covered in Chapters 16 and 17.

Top tips. Parts (a) to (c) are fairly standard calculations on ROI and RI, involving a comparison between different divisions and calculating the effect of a changed situation. The superiority of residual income as a measure will always need to be discussed in answers.

Easy marks. The calculations in part (a) should be straightforward if you can remember the methods involved.

Marking scheme

			Marks
(a)	1 mark for each correct calculation		4
(b)	1 mark for each relevant comment		2
(c)	1 mark for each correct calculation	4	
	1 mark for each relevant comment about the results shown by ROI and RI max	3	
	Comment on superiority of RI	2	
			9
			15

(a) In the case of Blue division, the **value of net assets** should exclude the non-current assets purchased on 29 September 20X8, because these were bought at the end of the year and so have not yet been able to make any contribution to the division's profitability.

(i) **ROI**

	Green	Blue
Net profit	$4.2 m	$5.6 m
Net assets	$32.0 m	$36.0 m
Return on investment (ROI)	13.1%	15.6%

(ii) **RI**

	Green	Blue
	$m	$m
Net profit	4.20	5.60
Notional interest (12% of net assets)	3.84	4.32
	0.36	1.28

(b) **ROI and RI values**

Both Green and Blue have achieved a return on investment that is higher than the company's cost of capital, and so both have a positive residual income.

Comparison of divisions

Blue division has achieved a higher ROI and a higher residual income than Green division, suggesting that it has achieved the better performance. In the case of Green division, a fall in profitability by more than $360,000 would mean that its ROI would be less than the cost of capital, and the residual income would be negative.

(c) **Assumptions**

The ROI and residual income of Green and Blue can be calculated, on the assumption that the new investment is undertaken and other results in 20X9 will be the same as in 20X8.

		Green		Blue
Net profit	(4.2 + 3.5)	$7.7 m	(5.6 + 3.5)	$9.1 m
Net assets	(32 + 25)	$57.0 m	(36 + 25)	$61.0 m
ROI		13.5%		14.9%

	Green	Blue
	$m	$m
Net profit	7.70	9.10
Notional interest (12% of net assets)	6.84	7.32
RI	0.86	1.78

Green division

The manager of Green division would want to undertake the investment, because it would result in an **increase in both the ROI** and the **residual income** of the division. This is because the ROI of the investment is (3.5/25) = 14%, higher than the ROI currently achieved by the division, and there is an addition to residual income because the extra net profit of $3.5 million exceeds the extra notional interest charge of (12% of $25 million) = $3 million.

Blue division

If the performance of Blue division is judged by **ROI**, the manager would be reluctant to undertake the investment. The ROI of the investment is 14%, which is higher than the company's cost of capital, but lower than the ROI currently being achieved by Blue. As a result, the division's ROI would fall, and reported performance would be worse. If on the other hand the performance of Blue is judged by **residual income**, the manager would want to undertake the investment. The return from the investment would exceed the company's cost of capital, and so residual income would rise (by $500,000).

Conclusion

This situation illustrates the **advantage** of **residual income** over ROI as a measure of divisional performance. Unlike ROI, residual income as a measure of performance will 'reward' divisional managers who invest in projects that earn an annual return in excess of the company's cost of capital.

ACCA

Paper F5

Performance Management

Mock Examination 3

December 2014 exam paper

Question paper	
Reading and planning Writing	15 minutes 3 hours
This paper is divided into two sections: Section A – ALL TWENTY questions are compulsory and MUST be answered Section B – ALL FIVE questions are compulsory and MUST be answered	

DO NOT OPEN THIS PAPER UNTIL YOU ARE READY TO START UNDER EXAMINATION CONDITIONS

Section A – ALL TWENTY questions are compulsory and MUST be attempted

Each question is worth 2 marks.

1 Dust Co has two divisions, A and B. Each division is currently considering the following separate projects:

	Division A	*Division B*
Capital required for the project	\$32·6 million	\$22·2 million
Sales generated by project	\$14·4 million	\$8·8 million
Operating profit margin	30%	24%
Cost of capital	10%	10%
Current return on investment of division	15%	9%

If residual income is used as the basis for the investment decision, which Division(s) would choose to invest in the project?

A Division A only
B Division B only
C Both Division A and Division B
D Neither Division A nor Division B

2 The following costs have arisen in relation to the production of a product:

(i) Planning and concept design costs
(ii) Testing costs
(iii) Production costs
(iv) Distribution and customer service costs

In calculating the life cycle costs of a product, which of the above items would be included?

A (iii) only
B (i), (ii) and (iii) only
C (i), (ii) and (iv) only
D All of the above

3 Which of the following describes a 'basic standard' within the context of budgeting?

A A standard which is kept unchanged over a period of time

B A standard which is based on current price levels

C A standard set at an ideal level, which makes no allowance for normal losses, waste and machine downtime

D A standard which assumes an efficient level of operation, but which includes allowances for factors such as normal loss, waste and machine downtime

4 The following statements have been made about planning and control as described in the three tiers of Robert Anthony's decision-making hierarchy:

(1) Strategic planning is concerned with making decisions about the efficient and effective use of existing resources

(2) Operational control is about ensuring that specific tasks are carried out efficiently and effectively

Which of the above statements is/are true?

A 1 only
B 2 only
C Neither 1 nor 2
D Both 1 and 2

5 P Co makes two products – P1 and P2 – budgeted details of which are as follows:

	P1	*P2*
	$	$
Selling price	10.00	8.00
Cost per unit:		
Direct materials	3.50	4.00
Direct labour	1.50	1.00
Variable overhead	0.60	0.40
Fixed overhead	1.20	1.00
Profit per unit	3.20	1.60

Budgeted production and sales for the year ended 30 November 2015 are:

Product P1	10,000 units
Product P2	12,500 units

The fixed overhead costs included in P1 relate to apportionment of general overhead costs only. However, P2 also includes specific fixed overheads totalling $2,500.

If only product P1 were to be made, how many units (to the nearest unit) would need to be sold in order to achieve a profit of $60,000 each year?

A 25,625 units
B 19,205 units
C 18,636 units
D 26,406 units

6 A company has the following production planned for the next four weeks. The figures reflect the full capacity level of operations. Planned output is equal to the maximum demand per product.

Product	*A*	*B*	*C*	*D*
	$ per unit	$ per unit	$ per unit	$ per unit
Selling price	160	214	100	140
Raw material cost	24	56	22	40
Direct labour cost	66	88	33	22
Variable overhead cost	24	18	24	18
Fixed overhead cost	16	10	8	12
Profit	30	42	13	48
Planned output	300	125	240	400
Direct labour hours per unit	6	8	3	2

The direct labour force is threatening to go on strike for two weeks out of the coming four. This means that only 2,160 hours will be available for production rather than the usual 4,320 hours.

If the strike goes ahead, which product or products should be produced if profits are to be maximised?

A D and A
B B and D
C D only
D B and C

7 The following table shows the number of clients who attended a particular accountancy practice over the last four weeks and the total costs incurred during each of the weeks:

Week	*Number of clients*	*Total cost*
		$
1	400	36,880
2	440	39,840
3	420	36,800
4	460	40,000

Applying the high low method to the above information, which of the following could be used to forecast total cost ($) from the number of clients expected to attend (where x = the expected number of clients)?

A 7,280 + 74x
B 16,080 + 52x
C 3,200 + 80x
D 40,000/x

8 Oxco has two divisions, A and B. Division A makes a component for air conditioning units which it can only sell to Division B. It has no other outlet for sales.

Current information relating to Division A is as follows:

Marginal cost per unit	$100
Transfer price of the component	$165
Total production and sales of the component each year	2,200 units
Specific fixed costs of Division A per year	$10,000

Cold Co has offered to sell the component to Division B for $140 per unit. If Division B accepts this offer, Division A will be shut.

If Division B accepts Cold Co's offer, what will be the impact on profits per year for the group as a whole?

A Increase of $65,000
B Decrease of $78,000
C Decrease of $88,000
D Increase of $55,000

9 The following statements have been made in relation to activity-based costing:

(1) A cost driver is a factor which causes a change in the cost of an activity
(2) Traditional absorption costing tends to underestimate overhead costs for high volume products

Which of the above statements is/are true?

A 1 only
B 2 only
C Neither 1 nor 2
D Both 1 and 2

10 A linear programming model has been formulated for two products, X and Y. The objective function is depicted by the formula C = 5X + 6Y, where C = contribution, X = the number of product X to be produced and Y = the number of product Y to be produced.

Each unit of X uses 2 kg of material Z and each unit of Y uses 3 kg of material Z. The standard cost of material Z is $2 per kg.

The shadow price for material Z has been worked out and found to be $2·80 per kg.

If an extra 20 kg of material Z becomes available at $2 per kg, what will the maximum increase in contribution be?

A Increase of $96
B Increase of $56
C Increase of $16
D No change

11 The following statements have been made about both standard costing and total quality management (TQM):

(1) They focus on assigning responsibility solely to senior managers
(2) They work well in rapidly changing environments

Which of the above statements is/are true?

A 1 only
B 2 only
C Neither 1 nor 2
D Both 1 and 2

12 The following statements have been made about environmental cost accounting:

(1) The majority of environmental costs are already captured within a typical organisation's accounting system. The difficulty lies in identifying them

(2) Input/output analysis divides material flows within an organisation into three categories: material flows; system flows; and delivery and disposal flows

Which of the above statements is/are true?

A 1 only
B 2 only
C Neither 1 nor 2
D Both 1 and 2

13 Def Co provides accounting services to government departments. On average, each staff member works six chargeable hours per day, with the rest of their working day being spent on non-chargeable administrative work. One of the company's main objectives is to produce a high level of quality and customer satisfaction.

Def Co has set its targets for the next year as follows:

(1) Cutting departmental expenditure by 5%
(2) Increasing the number of chargeable hours handled by advisers to 6·2 per day
(3) Obtaining a score of 4·7 or above on customer satisfaction surveys

Which of the above targets assesses economy, efficiency and effectiveness at Def Co?

	Economy	*Efficiency*	*Effectiveness*
A	1	3	2
B	2	1	3
C	3	2	1
D	1	2	3

14 Which of the following is an advantage of non-participative budgeting as compared to participative budgeting?

A It increases motivation
B It is less time consuming
C It increases acceptance
D The budgets produced are more attainable

15 The following are all steps in the implementation of the target costing process for a product:

(1) Calculate the target cost
(2) Calculate the estimated current cost based on the existing product specification
(3) Set the required profit
(4) Set the selling price
(5) Calculate the target cost gap

Which of the following represents the correct sequence if target costing were to be used?

A (1), (2), (3), (4), (5)
B (2), (3), (4), (1), (5)
C (4), (3), (1), (2), (5)
D (4), (5), (3), (1), (2)

16 What is the name given to a budget which has been prepared by building on a previous period's budgeted or actual figures?

A Incremental budget
B Flexible budget
C Zero based budget
D Functional budget

17 Tree Co is considering employing a sales manager. Market research has shown that a good sales manager can increase profit by 30%, an average one by 20% and a poor one by 10%. Experience has shown that the company has attracted a good sales manager 35% of the time, an average one 45% of the time and a poor one 20% of the time. The company's normal profits are $180,000 per annum and the sales manager's salary would be $40,000 per annum.

Based on the expected value criterion, which of the following represents the correct advice which Tree Co should be given?

A Do not employ a sales manager as profits would be expected to fall by $1,300
B Employ a sales manager as profits will increase by $38,700
C Employ a sales manager as profits are expected to increase by $100
D Do not employ a sales manager as profits are expected to fall by $39,900

18 A company manufactures two products, C and D, for which the following information is available:

	Product C	*Product D*	*Total*
Budgeted production (units)	1,000	4,000	5,000
Labour hours per unit/in total	8	10	48,000
Number of production runs required	13	15	28
Number of inspections during production	5	3	8
Total production set up costs			$140,000
Total inspection costs			$80,000
Other overhead costs			$96,000

Other overhead costs are absorbed on the basis of labour hours per unit.

Using activity-based costing, what is the budgeted overhead cost per unit of product D?

A $43·84
B $46·25
C $131·00
D $140·64

19 X Co uses rolling budgeting, updating its budgets on a quarterly basis. After carrying out the last quarter's update to the cash budget, it projected a forecast cash deficit of $400,000 at the end of the year. Consequently, the planned purchase of new capital equipment has been postponed.

Which of the following types of control is the sales manager's actions an example of?

A Feedforward control
B Negative feedback control
C Positive feedback control
D Double loop feedback control

20 The following circumstances may arise in relation to the launch of a new product:

(i) Demand is relatively inelastic
(ii) There are significant economies of scale
(iii) The firm wishes to discourage new entrants to the market
(iv) The product life cycle is particularly short

Which of the above circumstances favour a penetration pricing policy?

A (ii) and (iii) only
B (ii) and (iv)
C (i), (ii) and (iii)
D (ii), (iii) and (iv) only

(40 marks)

Section B – ALL FIVE questions are compulsory and MUST be attempted

1 Chair Co has developed a new type of luxury car seat. The estimated labour time for the first unit is 12 hours but a learning curve of 75% is expected to apply for the first eight units produced. The cost of labour is $15 per hour. The cost of materials and other variable overheads is expected to total $230 per unit.

Chair Co plans on pricing the seat by adding a 50% mark-up to the total variable cost per seat, with the labour cost being based on the incremental time taken to produce the 8th unit.

Required

(a) Calculate the price which Chair Co expects to charge for the new seat.

Note: The learning index for a 75% learning curve is –0·415. **(5 marks)**

(b) The first phase of production has now been completed for the new car seat. The first unit actually took 12·5 hours to make and the total time for the first eight units was 34·3 hours, at which point the learning effect came to an end. Chair Co are planning on adjusting the price to reflect the actual time it took to complete the 8th unit.

Required

(i) Calculate the actual rate of learning and state whether this means that the labour force actually learnt more quickly or less quickly than expected. **(3 marks)**

(ii) Briefly explain whether the adjusted price charged by Chair Co will be higher or lower than the price you calculated in part (a) above. You are **not** required to calculate the adjusted price. **(2 marks)**

(Total = 10 marks)

2 Glam Co is a hairdressing salon which provides both 'cuts' and 'treatments' to clients. All cuts and treatments at the salon are carried out by one of the salon's three senior stylists.

The salon also has two salon assistants and two junior stylists. Every customer attending the salon is first seen by a salon assistant, who washes their hair; next, by a senior stylist, who cuts or treats the hair depending on which service the customer wants; then finally, a junior stylist who dries their hair. The average length of time spent with each member of staff is as follows:

	Cut	*Treatment*
	Hours	Hours
Assistant	0.1	0.3
Senior stylist	1	1.5
Junior stylist	0.5	0.5

The salon is open for eight hours each day for six days per week. It is only closed for two weeks each year. Staff salaries are $40,000 each year for senior stylists, $28,000 each year for junior stylists and $12,000 each year for the assistants. The cost of cleaning products applied when washing the hair is $0·60 per client. The cost of all additional products applied during a 'treatment' is $7·40 per client. Other salon costs (excluding labour and raw materials) amount to $106,400 each year.

Glam Co charges $60 for each cut and $110 for each treatment.

The senior stylists' time has been correctly identified as the bottleneck activity.

Required

(a) Briefly explain why the senior stylists' time has been described as the 'bottleneck activity', supporting your answer with calculations. **(4 marks)**

(b) Calculate the throughput accounting ratio (TPAR) for 'cuts' and the TPAR for 'treatments' assuming the bottleneck activity is fully utilised. **(6 marks)**

(Total = 10 marks)

3 The Hi Life Co (HL Co) makes sofas. It has recently received a request from a customer to provide a one-off order of sofas, in excess of normal budgeted production. The order would need to be completed within two weeks. The following cost estimate has already been prepared:

Direct materials:		*Note*	$
Fabric	200 m^2 at \$17 per m^2	1	3,400
Wood	50 m^2 at \$8·20 per m^2	2	410
Direct labour:			
Skilled	200 hours at \$16 per hour	3	3,200
Semi-skilled	300 hours at \$12 per hour	4	3,600
Factory overheads	500 hours at \$3 per hour	5	1,500
Total production cost			12,110
Administration overheads at 10% of total production cost		6	1,211
Total cost			13,321

Notes

1 The fabric is regularly used by HL Co. There are currently 300 m^2 in inventory, which cost \$17 per m^2. The current purchase price of the fabric is \$17·50 per m^2.

2 This type of wood is regularly used by HL Co and usually costs \$8·20 per m^2. However, the company's current supplier's earliest delivery time for the wood is in three weeks' time. An alternative supplier could deliver immediately but they would charge \$8·50 per m^2. HL Co already has 500 m^2 in inventory but 480 m^2 of this is needed to complete other existing orders in the next two weeks. The remaining 20 m^2 is not going to be needed until four weeks' time.

3 The skilled labour force is employed under permanent contracts of employment under which they must be paid for 40 hours' per week's labour, even if their time is idle due to absence of orders. Their rate of pay is \$16 per hour, although any overtime is paid at time and a half. In the next two weeks, there is spare capacity of 150 labour hours.

4 There is no spare capacity for semi-skilled workers. They are currently paid \$12 per hour or time and a half for overtime. However, a local agency can provide additional semi-skilled workers for \$14 per hour.

5 The \$3 absorption rate is HL Co's standard factory overhead absorption rate; \$1·50 per hour reflects the cost of the factory supervisor's salary and the other \$1·50 per hour reflects general factory costs. The supervisor is paid an annual salary and is also paid \$15 per hour for any overtime he works. He will need to work 20 hours' overtime if this order is accepted.

6 This is an apportionment of the general administration overheads incurred by HL Co.

Required

Prepare, on a relevant cost basis, the lowest cost estimate which could be used as the basis for the quotation.

Explain briefly your reasons for including or excluding each of the costs in your estimate.

(10 marks)

4 Jamair was founded in September 2007 and is one of a growing number of low-cost airlines in the country of Shania.

Jamair's strategy is to operate as a low-cost, high efficiency airline, and it does this by:

– Operating mostly in secondary cities to reduce landing costs.
– Using only one type of aircraft in order to reduce maintenance and operational costs. These planes are leased rather than bought outright.
– Having only one category of seat class.
– Having no pre-allocated seats or in-flight entertainment.
– Focusing on e-commerce with customers both booking tickets and checking in for flights online.

The airline was given an 'on time arrival' ranking of seventh best by the country's aviation authority, who rank all 50 of the country's airlines based on the number of flights which arrive on time at their destinations. 48 Jamair flights were cancelled in 2013 compared to 35 in 2012. This increase was due to an increase in the staff absentee rate at Jamair from 3 days per staff member per year to 4·5 days.

The average 'ground turnaround time' for airlines in Shania is 50 minutes, meaning that, on average, planes are onthe ground for cleaning, refuelling, etc for 50 minutes before departing again. Customer satisfaction surveys have shown that 85% of customers are happy with the standard of cleanliness on Jamair's planes.

The number of passengers carried by the airline has grown from 300,000 passengers on a total of 3,428 flights in 2007 to 920,000 passengers on 7,650 flights in 2013. The overall growth of the airline has been helped by the limited route licensing policy of the Shanian government, which has given Jamair almost monopoly status on some of its routes. However, the government is now set to change this policy with almost immediate effect, and it has become more important than ever to monitor performance effectively.

Required

(a) Describe each of the four perspectives of the balanced scorecard. **(6 marks)**

(b) For each perspective of the balanced scorecard, identify one goal together with a corresponding performance measure which could be used by Jamair to measure the company's performance. The goals and measures should be specifically relevant to Jamair. For each pair of goals and measures, explain why you have chosen them. **(9 marks)**

(Total = 15 marks)

5 The Safe Soap Co makes environmentally-friendly soap using three basic ingredients. The standard cost card for one batch of soap for the month of September was as follows:

Material	*Kilograms*	*Price per kilogram ($)*
Lye	0.25	10
Coconut oil	0.6	4
Shea butter	0.5	3

The budget for production and sales in September was 120,000 batches. Actual production and sales were 136,000 batches. The actual ingredients used were as follows:

Material	*Kilograms*
Lye	34,080
Coconut oil	83,232
Shea butter	64,200

Required

(a) Calculate the total material mix variance and the total material yield variance for September. **(8 marks)**

(b) In October the materials mix and yield variances were as follows:

Mix: $6,000 adverse
Yield: $10,000 favourable

The production manager is pleased with the results overall, stating:

'At the beginning of September I made some changes to the mix of ingredients used for the soaps. As I expected, the mix variance is adverse in both months because we haven't yet updated our standard cost card but, in both months, the favourable yield variance more than makes up for this. Overall, I think we can be satisfied that the changes made to the product mix are producing good results and now we are able to produce more batches and meet the growing demand for our product.'

The sales manager, however, holds a different view and says:

'I'm not happy with this change in the ingredients mix. I've had to explain to the board why the sales volume variance for October was $22,000 adverse. I've tried to explain that the quality of the soap has declined slightly and some of my customers have realised this and simply aren't happy but no-one seems to be listening. Some customers are even demanding that the price of the soap be reduced and threatening to go elsewhere if the problem isn't sorted out.'

Required

(i) Briefly explain what the adverse materials mix and favourable materials yield variances indicate about production at Safe Soap Co in October.

Note: You are NOT required to discuss revision of standards or operational and planning variances. **(4 marks)**

(ii) Discuss whether the sales manager could be justified in claiming that the change in the materials mix has caused an adverse sales volume variance in October. **(3 marks)**

(Total = 15 marks)

Formulae Sheet

Learning curve

$Y = ax^b$

Where			
	Y	=	cumulative average time per unit to produce x units
	a	=	the time taken for the first unit of output
	x	=	the cumulative number of units produced
	b	=	the index of learning (log LR/log2)
	LR	=	the learning rate as a decimal

Demand curve

$$P = a - bQ$$

$$b = \frac{\text{Change in price}}{\text{Change in quantity}}$$

a = price when $Q = 0$

$MR = a - 2bQ$

End of Question Paper

Answers

DO NOT TURN THIS PAGE UNTIL YOU HAVE COMPLETED THE MOCK EXAM

A PLAN OF ATTACK

If this were the real Performance Management exam and you had been told to turn over and begin, what would be going through your mind?

An important thing to say (while there is still time) is that it is vital to have a good breadth of knowledge of the syllabus because the question requirements for each question will relate to different areas of the F5 syllabus. However, don't panic. Below we provide guidance on how to approach the exam.

Which order to do the questions

Use the 15 minutes' reading time to **look through** the **paper in detail** and establish the **order** in which to attempt the questions. You may have a preference for attempting the multiple choice questions first and the Section B questions after that, or you may prefer to attempt Section B first. Whichever approach you take, you need to be disciplined about time. In the three hours of writing time, don't spend more than 72 minutes (40% of the three hours) on Section A and don't spend more than 108 minutes on Section B. If you begin with the multiple choice questions and are running out of the allocated time, don't use precious minutes struggling with questions that you are not sure about. Move on.

It is vital to attempt all of the questions in the paper to increase your chances of passing. The best way to do this is to make sure you stick to the time allocation for each question – both in total and for each of the question parts. The worst thing you can do is run over time in one question and then find that you don't have enough time for the remaining questions. If you end up rushing the final Section B question, or even find that you don't have time to start your answer, you will have thrown away any chance of earning what could be important marks.

Section A multiple choice questions

If you decide to attempt the multiple choice questions first, remember that you don't have to answer them in their numerical order. If any question seems difficult, or would take too much time to answer, move on to the next question. If you have time after working through all of the MCQs, you can go back to the questions you haven't answered.

You ought to find some MCQs easier than others, so look for the marks first that you think are easy.

Section B 10-mark and 15-mark questions

If you are challenged by the Section B questions in this paper, do the **questions in the order of how well you think you can answer them.**

- **Question 1** is a learning curve question. It tells you that the learning index for 75% is -0.415 so don't waste time calculating this. Read the question carefully. You need to calculate the cumulative average time per unit for 8 units and multiply it by 8. Then you need to work out the cumulative average time per unit for 7 units and multiply it by 7. Deducting one from the other will give you the incremental time for the 8th unit. The 50% mark-up applies to the total variable cost per seat.
- **Question 2** is about bottlenecks and the throughput accounting ratio. You need to explain the term bottleneck and use calculations to support your answer. You need to have learnt the formula for the TPAR.
- **Question 3** is a full question on relevant costing. You absolutely must explain why you have included or excluded each figure.
- **Question 4** is probably the most difficult question on the paper, particularly if you cannot remember the four perspectives of the balanced scorecard. Read part (b) very carefully. You must set out a goal, a measure and an explanation of why the goals are relevant to Jamair. Use the information in the question.
- **Question 5** asks for calculations of mix and yield variances and an explanation of what they mean. This should be fairly straightforward. Part (b)(ii) is trickier because you must discuss whether the mix variance has caused the adverse sales volume variance. Remember that there could be other reasons for the sales volume variance.

Keep your discipline

You **must allocate your time** according to the marks for the question in total, and for the parts of the questions. And you must also **follow the requirements of each question exactly.** If you are required to comment on some calculations or figures, make sure that you are answering the actual question, instead of writing around the subject without actually dealing with the specific question that is asked.

And try not to panic. There is a good chance that at least one Section B question and one or two Section A questions will confuse you. Don't worry. For Section A questions, just move on to the next question. And for Section B questions, do as much as you can, that you think is correct. Focus on the marks you find easier to earn.

Finished with fifteen minutes to spare?

Looks like you slipped up on the time allocation. However if you have finished early, make sure you don't waste the last few minutes; go back to **any questions or parts of questions that you didn't finish** because you ran out of your allocated time.

Then forget about it!

Forget about what? Excellent, you already have.

Section A

1 A

	Division A	*Division B*
Profit generated by project (sales × operating profit margin)		
(\$14.4m × 30%)	\$4.32m	
(\$8.8m × 24%)		\$2.11m
Less: Imputed interest (capital required × cost of capital)		
(\$32.6m × 10%)	(\$3.26m)	
(\$22.2m × 10%)		(\$2.22m)
Residual income	\$1.06m	\$(0.11m)

2 D A product's life cycle costs are incurred from its design stage through development to market launch, production and sales, and finally to its eventual decline and withdrawal from the market.

3 A A basic standard is a long-term standard which remains unchanged over the years and is used to show trends. The descriptions given in B, C, and D describe a current standard, an ideal standard, and an attainable standard respectively.

4 B Statement 1 is a definition of management control. Strategic planning is the process of deciding on objectives for the organisation, on changes in these objectives, on the resources to attain these objectives, and on the policies that are to govern the acquisition, use and disposition of these resources.

5 C Sales volume to achieve a target profit = $\frac{\text{fixed cost + target profit}}{\text{contibution per unit}}$

Fixed costs = (\$1.2 × 10,000) + (\$1 × 12,500) – \$2,500 = \$22,000
Contribution per unit of P = \$3.20 + \$1.20 = \$4.40
(\$22,000 + \$60,000)/\$4.40 = 18,636 units

6 A

Product	*A*	*B*	*C*	*D*
Selling price per unit	\$160	\$214	\$100	\$140
Contribution per unit	\$46	\$52	\$21	\$60
Labour hours per unit	6	8	3	2
Contribution per unit of limiting factor	\$7.67	\$6.5	\$7	\$30
Priority for manufacture	2	4	3	1

7 B

	Week	*No. of clients*	*Total cost*
High	1	400	\$36,880
Low	4	460	\$40,000
		60	\$3,120

Variable cost per client:	\$3,120/60 = \$52
Fixed costs:	\$36,880 – (\$52 × 400) = \$16,080
Total costs (where X = expected number of clients):	\$16,080 + \$52x

8 B Profits of Division A: [2,200 × (\$165 – \$100)] – \$10,000 = \$133,000

Potential savings of purchasing the component from Cold Co for Division B:

(\$165 – \$140) × 2,200 = \$55,000

Impact of purchasing the component from Cold Co on the group as a whole:

\$55,000 – \$133,000 = \$78,000

9 A Traditional absorption tends to overestimate overhead costs for high volume products.

10 B \$2.80 × 20 kg = \$56. The shadow price is the extra contribution that may be earned if one more unit of limiting factor becomes available.

11 C Standard costing control systems make individual managers responsible for the variances relating to their part of the organisation's activities. A TQM programme, on the other hand, aims to make all personnel aware of, and responsible for, the importance of supplying the customer with a quality product. Therefore, statement 1 is false. Statement 2 is also false as it can be argued that standard costs have limited relevance and value in the modern business world, where the environment is continually changing, and the life cycle of products can be very short.

12 A Statement 2 refers to flow cost accounting rather than input/output analysis. Under the flow cost accounting technique, material flows within an organisation are divided into three categories: material flows; system flows; and delivery and disposal flows.

13 D Economy is attaining the appropriate quantity and quality of inputs at lowest cost.
Efficiency is the relationship between inputs and outputs.
Effectiveness is the relationship between an organisation's outputs and its objectives.

14 B The following are advantages of participative budgeting. Morale and motivation are improved. Employees feel more involved and that their opinions matter to senior management. Although they consume more time, in general they are more realistic.

15 C Step 1 Calculate the target cost.
Step 2 Set the required profit.
Step 3 Calculate the target cost.
Step 4 Calculate the estimated current cost based on the existing product specification.
Step 5 Calculate the target cost gap.

16 A Incremental budgeting is a method of budgeting in which next year's budget is prepared by using the current's year's actual results as a starting point, and making adjustments for expected inflation, sales growth or decline and other known changes.

A flexible budget is a budget which, by recognising different cost behaviour patterns, is changed as the volume of output and sales changes.

Zero based budgeting involves preparing a budget for each cost centre or activity from a zero base and justify every item of expenditure to be included in the next year's budget.

Functional budgets are budgets for the different departments or functions within the organisation.

17 A Expected value of increase in profit of hiring a sales manager:

Good manager:	$180,000 × 30% × 35% =	$18,900
Average manager:	$180,000 × 20% × 45% =	$16,200
Poor manager:	$180,000 × 10% × 20% =	$3,600
Expected value		$38,700
Less the sales manager's salary		($40,000)
Effect on profit of hiring sales manager		($1,300)

18 B ABC approach

	Labour hours
Product C = 1,000 units × 8 hours	8,000
Product D = 4,000 units × 10 hours	40,000
	48,000

Using ABC the overhead costs are absorbed according to the cost drivers. The absorption rate for each cost pool is as follows.

	$		*Absorption rate, ABC*
Production run driven costs	140,000 ÷ 28 production runs	=	$5,000 per production run
Inspection driven costs	80,000 ÷ 8 inspections	=	$10,000 per inspection
Labour hour driven costs	96,000 ÷ 48,000 labour hours	=	$2 per labour hour

Overhead costs are therefore as follows.

	Product D
	$
Production run driven costs (15 runs × $5,000)	75,000
Inspection driven costs (3 inspections × $10,000)	30,000
Labour hour driven costs (40,000 hrs × $2)	80,000
	185,000
Production units budgeted	4,000
Overhead cost per unit	$46.25

19 A Feedforward control is control based on forecast results. In other words if the forecast is bad, control action is taken well in advance of actual results.

Negative feedback indicates that results or activities must be brought back on course, as they are deviating from the plan.

Positive feedback results in control action continuing the current course.

Double loop feedback is information used to change the plan itself. For example, if sales targets are not reached, the company may need to change the plan.

20 A (i) is incorrect because a penetration policy is favourable in circumstances where demand is relatively **elastic**. The circumstance in (iv) favours a market skimming policy.

Section B

1 Chair Co

Text reference. Learning curve theory is covered in Chapter 10.

Top tips. Show your workings clearly to gain as many marks as possible. The calculations in this question require a logical approach and should be straightforward, provided you have practised this technique. A scientific calculator is essential for both (a) and (b). If you are in any doubt of the answer to part (b) (ii) you should substitute the different learning rates into your calculations to prove your answer correct.

Easy marks. There are easy marks available in part (a). Read the question carefully to ensure that you finish the question (and don't just stop after calculating the time taken to produce the 8th unit) so that you pick up the easy marks for calculating the labour cost, total cost and selling price.

Marking scheme

					Marks
1	(a)	Price			
		Cumulative average time per unit for 8 units		1	
		Total time for 8 units		0.5	
		Cumulative average time per unit for 7 units		1	
		Total time for 7 units		0.5	
		Incremental time for 8th unit		0.5	
		Cost for 8th unit		0.5	
		Total cost		0.5	
		Price		0.5	
					5
	(b)	(i)	Learning rate		
			Calculating learning rate	2.5	
			Saying whether better or worse	0.5	
					3
		(ii)	Effect on price		2
			Total marks		10

(a) **Time to produce the first 8 units**

$Y = ax^b$

$b = -0.415$

$Y = 12 \times (8^{-0.415}) = 12 \times 0.421907898 = 5.062894777$ hours

Total time for first 8 units = 8 × 5.062894777 hours = 40.50 hours

Time to produce the first 7 units

$Y = 12 \times (7^{-0.415}) = 12 \times 0.445948095 = 5.351377144$ hours

Total time for first 7 units = 7 × 5.351377144 hours = 37.46 hours

Time to produce the 8th unit = (40.50 – 37.46) = 3.04 hours

Budgeted labour cost = 3.04 hours × \$15 per hour = \$45.60

Budgeted material and overhead cost = \$230

Total cost = \$275.60

Proposed selling price = \$275.60 × 150% = \$413.40 per seat

(b) **(i) Actual learning rate:**

Let the rate of learning be r.

Cumulative production	*Cumulative average time*	*Cumulative total time*
1	12.5	12.5×1
2	$12.5 \times r$	$12.5 \times r \times 2$
4	$12.5 \times r^2$	$12.5 \times r^2 \times 4$
8	$12.5 \times r^3$	$12.5 \times r^3 \times 8$

Cumulative total time for the first 8 units was 34.3 hours

$\therefore \quad 12.5 \times r^3 \times 8 = 34.3$ hours

$100\ r^3 = 34.3$

$r^3 = 0.345$

$r = 0.70$

$\therefore$ The rate of learning is 70%.

The rate of learning forecast was 75%, which means that the labour force actually learned more quickly than expected.

Note. You can test this by substituting the budgeted learning rate of 75% into the equation $12.5 \times r^3 \times 8$ (the cumulative total time for producing the first 8 units). The result is 42.1875 hours, which is longer than the actual total time given in the question (34.3 hours).

(ii) Adjusted price

The adjusted price charged by Chair Co will be lower than the price calculated in part (a). The actual total time taken to produce the 8th unit is 34.3 hours, which is lower than the budgeted total time of 40.5 hours (calculated in part (a)). We can deduce therefore, that the actual incremental time taken to produce the 8th unit is lower than the budgeted figure. The budgeted labour cost is based on the incremental time taken to produce the 8th unit, and the price is based on this cost. Therefore it is logical to conclude that the adjusted price will be lower than the price calculated in part (a).

2 Glam Co

Text reference. Throughput accounting is covered in Chapter 2d.

Top tips. In this question, throughput accounting is tested in a service industry context rather than the usual traditional manufacturing context. Don't let this confuse you. In part (a) there are a number of different time frames you could use to illustrate that the senior stylist's time is the bottleneck factor, such as daily hours available, or annual hours available. Think logically about the processes and you should be able to illustrate the bottleneck clearly.

Easy marks. The calculations in part (b) should provide easy marks, provided you have learnt how to calculate a throughput accounting ratio.

Marking scheme

				Marks
2	(a)	Calculation and justification of bottleneck	3	
		Explanation of bottleneck	1	
				4
	(b)	TPAR		
		Throughput	1	
		Throughput per bottleneck	1	
		Total salon costs	1	
		Cost per hour	1	
		TPAR	2	
				6
		Total marks		10

(a) **Bottleneck activity**

The salon is open for 8 hours per day. There are no figures given for the projected ratio of cuts to treatment, therefore we must calculate on the basis that in one day 100% of the services requested are cuts, and on another day 100% of the services required are treatments. The maximum number of clients that could receive a treatment or a cut can be calculated as follows:

	Cut
Assistant (8 hrs ÷ 0.1 hrs per client × 2 assistants)	160
Senior stylist (8 hrs ÷ 1 hrs per client × 3 senior)	24
Junior stylist (8 hrs ÷ 0.5 hrs per client × 2 junior)	32

	Treatment
Assistant (8 hrs ÷ 0.3 hrs per client × 2 assistants)	53
Senior stylist (8 hrs ÷ 1.5 hrs per client × 3 senior)	16
Junior stylist (8 hrs ÷ 0.5 hrs per client × 2 junior)	32

It is clear from the above that the bottleneck activity is the work performed by the senior stylists whether the service required is a cut or a treatment. Despite the extra senior stylist (3 senior stylists but only 2 assistants and 2 junior stylists), the assistants and the junior stylists can attend to a greater number of clients than the senior stylist can. The salon throughput can not be increased by increasing the number or efficiency of the assistants or junior stylists.

(b) **Throughput accounting ratio (TPAR)**

	Cut	*Treatment*
	$	$
Selling price	60	110
Direct material	0.60	8
Throughput	59.40	102
Bottleneck hour	1	1.5
Throughput per bottleneck hour	59.40	68

Total salon costs: [$106,400 + (3 × $40,000) + (2 × $28,000) + (2 × $12,000)] = $306,400

Total units of bottleneck resource (senior stylist hours): (3 × 8 hours × 6 days × 50 weeks) = 7,200 hours

Factory cost per bottleneck resource $306,400 ÷ 7,200 = $42.56

		Cut		*Treatment*
TPAR	(59.40 / 42.56)	1.4	(68 / 42.56)	1.6

3 Hi Life Co

Text reference. Relevant cost analysis is covered in Chapter 6.

Top tips. Show all your workings and make sure that you explain why each cost is included or excluded from the cost statement. It is important to set out adequate narrative analysis for each item on the pricing schedule. Remember to look only at the incremental costs, and ensure that you read each note carefully so that you choose and apply the correct rates.

Easy marks. For easy marks in relevant costing questions, you must state the obvious. For example, you must say that the agency workers are cheaper than the semi-skilled workers. There are also easy marks for stating that you have excluded items because they are not incremental costs.

Marking scheme

		Marks
3	Fabric calculation	0.5
	Fabric reason	0.5
	Wood calculation	1
	Wood reason	1
	Skilled labour calculation	1
	Skilled labour reason	1
	Semi-skilled labour calculation	0.5
	Semi-skilled labour reason	1
	Factory overheads calculation	0.5
	Factory overheads reason	1.5
	Administration overheads reason	1
	Total relevant cost (lowest cost estimate)	0.5
	Total marks	10

		Note	$
Direct materials:			
Fabric	200 m^2 at $17.50 per m^2	1	3,500
Wood	20 m^2 at $8.20 per m^2		
	30 m^2 at $8.50 per m^2	2	419
Direct labour:			
Skilled	50 hours at $24 per hour	3	1,200
Semi skilled	300 hours at $14 per hour	4	4,200
Factory overheads	20 hours at $15 per hour	5	300
Total production cost			
Administrative overheads at 10% of total production cost		6	
Total cost			9,619

Notes

1 The relevant cost is the replacement cost as the material is in regular use by HL Co.

2 30 m^2 must be bought immediately from the alternative supplier, the remaining 20 m^2 can be obtained from inventory and replaced in future from the current supplier.

3 The skilled workers have spare capacity of 150 hours, therefore the relevant cost is the additional 50 hours work required, at a rate of time and a half.

4 The relevant cost is the cheaper option, which is the use of agency workers at a rate of $14 per hour.

5 The only relevant cost is the overtime paid to the supervisor. The other overheads are non incremental overheads.

6 The administrative overheads are non incremental and therefore should not be included.

4 Jamair

Text reference. The balanced scorecard is covered in Chapter 16

Top tips. It is extremely important in part (b) that the measures chosen are specific to the case study. No marks will be awarded for generic measures, therefore read the case study carefully and choose logical goals that you can back up with appropriate performance measures.

Easy marks. Although it is based in the context of a company, the requirement in part (a) is really generic. You should score highly providing your answer covers all four perspectives of the balanced scorecard.

Marking scheme

				Marks
4	(a)	Perspectives		
		Explanation for each perspective	1.5	
				6
	(b)	Goals and measures		
		Each goal/measure/explanation	2	
		Presentation and structure	1	
				9
	Total Marks			15

(a) The balanced scorecard focuses on **four different perspectives**, as follows.

Customer perspective

The customer perspective considers how new and existing customers view the organisation. This perspective should identify targets that matter to customers such as cost, quality, delivery, inspection and so on.

The customer perspective is linked to revenue/profit objectives in the financial perspective. If customer objectives are achieved, it is likely that revenue/profit objectives will also be achieved.

Internal perspective

The internal perspective makes an organisation consider what processes it must excel at in order to achieve financial and customer objectives.

The perspective aims to improve internal processes and decision making.

Innovation and learning perspective

The innovation and learning perspective requires the organisation to consider how it can continue to improve and create value.

Organisations must seek to acquire new skills and develop new products in order to maintain a competitive position in their respective market(s) and provide a basis from which the other perspectives of the balanced scorecard can be accomplished.

Financial perspective

The financial perspective considers whether the organisation meets the expectations of its shareholders and how it creates value for them.

This perspective focuses on traditional measures such as growth, profitability and cost reduction.

(b) **Goals and measures**

Customer perspective

Goal Ensure that flights land on time

Measure Improve on the 'on time arrival' ranking of seventh best in the country's aviation authority ratings.

If Jamair can improve its 'on time arrival' record and rise up the rankings, customers will perceive it to be a reliable airline and choose Jamair over its competitors.

Internal perspective

Goal Improve the turnaround time on the ground

Measure Reduction in 'on the ground' time from 50 minutes

The company can increase the number of flights and/or improve their on time record by reducing their 'on the ground time'. It should be done in a way that does not compromise customer safety.

Innovation and learning perspective

Goal Reduce employee absentee rate

Measure Reduction in the number of days absent per employee from current level of 4.5 days per year.

The higher absentee rate has led to the cancellation of flights. Therefore an improvement to this figure should lead to increased reliability.

Financial perspective

Goal *Increase seat revenue per plane*

Measure *Revenue per available passenger mile*

Jamair is competing with other low cost airlines mainly on price. Therefore the aim should be to increase the revenue by getting more people on the planes, than by increasing the price, which may have a negative effect on profits.

5 The Safe Soap Co

Text reference. Mix and yield variance analysis is covered in Chapter 11.

Top tips. Clearly label and include all of your workings in part (a). Remember, the mix variance compares actual quantities (standard mix v actual mix) whereas the yield variance compares the standard quantity with the actual quantity (standard mix). It is important to understand the relationship between the mix and yield variance in order to complete part (b). In addition, it is important to recognise that the information in respect of quality cannot be conveyed completely by the mix and yield variances.

Easy marks. There are easy marks available in part (a), providing you know the variance proformas.

Marking scheme

				Marks
(a)	Variance calculations			
	Mix variance		4	
	Quantity variance		4	
				8
(b)	(i)	Variances		
		Marks per variance explained	2	
				4
	(ii)	Discussion		
		Per valid point	1	
				3
Total marks				15

(a) **Mix variance**

The mix variances in quantities are converted into a money value at the standard price of the materials.

	Actual usage kg	*Actual total usage in standard mix (0.25:0.6:0.5)* kg	*Mix variance* kg	*Standard price* $ per kg	*Mix variance* $
Lye	34,080	33,613.33	466.67 (A)	10	4,667 (A)
Coconut oil	83,232	80,672.00	2,560.00 (A)	4	10,240 (A)
Shea butter	64,200	67,226.67	3,026.67 (F)	3	9,080 (F)
	181,512	181,512.00	0		5,827 (A)

Yield variance

	Standard quantity Standard mix kg	*Actual total usage in standard mix (0.25:0.6:0.5)* Kg	*Mix variance* kg	*Standard price* $ per kg	*Mix variance* $
Lye	34,000	33,613.33	386.67 (F)	10	3,867 (F)
Coconut oil	81,600	80,672.00	928.00 (F)	4	3,712 (F)
Shea butter	68,000	67,226.67	773.33 (F)	3	2,320 (F)
	183,600	181,512.00			9,899 (F)

(b) (i)

A mix variance occurs when the actual mix of materials used in production differs from the standard mix. In October, Safe Soap Co used a more expensive mix of products than the standard mix, thus resulting in an adverse mix variance.

A yield variance occurs when the actual production output differs from the standard output which would have been expected from the actual input. In October, Safe Soap Co's actual output was higher than expected.

As a consequence of using a more expensive mix of materials, it is possible that the output/yield will be more than the standard output. In other words, an adverse mix variance may result in a favourable yield variance, as has happened with Safe Soap Co.

(ii)

Generally speaking, quality issues cannot really be dealt with by this variance analysis. In the short term, it is difficult to deduce that the adverse sales volume variance is as a direct result of mix and yield variances. Any sales volume variance that does arise as a result of poor quality products is likely to arise in a different period from the one in which the mix and yield variances arose, and the correlation will then be more difficult to prove.

The sales manager asserts that a change to the ingredients mix in September may have affected sales demand in October, however, there may be other factors at play, such as increased competition or failure of marketing strategy. However, the customer complaints support the sales manager's assertions and therefore they should be strongly considered.

ACCA examiner's answers: June and December 2014

Note. The ACCA examiner's answers are correct at the time of going to press but may be subject to some amendments before the final versions are published.

1 (a) Full budgeted production cost per unit using absorption costing

Product	X	Y	Z	Total
Budgeted annual production (units)	20,000	16,000	22,000	
Labour hours per unit	2·5	3	2	
Total labour hours	50,000	48,000	44,000	142,000

Overhead absorption rate = $1,377,400/142,000 = $9·70 per hour.

Product	X	Y	Z
	$ per unit	$ per unit	$ per unit
Direct materials	25	28	22
Direct labour	30	36	24
Overhead ($9·70 x 2·5/3/2)	24·25	29·10	19·40
Full cost per unit	79·25	93·10	65·40

(b) Full budgeted production cost per unit using activity based costing

Product	X	Y	Z	Total
Budgeted annual production (units)	20,000	16,000	22,000	
Batch size	500	800	400	
Number of batches (i.e. set ups)	**40**	**20**	**55**	**115**
Number of purchase orders per batch	4	5	4	
Total number of orders	**160**	**100**	**220**	**480**
Machine hours per unit	1·5	1·25	1·4	
Total machine hours	**30,000**	**20,000**	**30,800**	**80,800**

Cost driver rates:

Cost per machine set up $280,000/115 = $2,434·78
Cost per order $316,000/480 = $658·33
Cost per machine hour ($420,000 + $361,400)/80,800 = $9·67

Allocation of overheads to each product:

Product	X	Y	Z	Total
	$	$	$	
Machine set up costs	97,391	48,696	133,913	280,000
Material ordering costs	105,333	65,833	144,834	316,000
Machine running and facility costs	290,100	193,400	297,836	781,336*
Total	492,824	307,929	576,583	1,377,336
Number of units produced	20,000	16,000	22,000	
Overhead cost per unit	$24·64	$19·25	$26·21	

Total cost per unit:	$ per unit	$ per unit	$ per unit
Direct materials	25	28	22
Direct labour	30	36	24
Overhead	24·64	19·25	26·21
ABC cost per unit	79·64	83·25	72·21

*A difference of $64 arises here as compared to the cost pool total of $781,400 because of rounding differences. This has been ignored.

(c) When activity based costing is used, the cost for product X is very similar to that cost calculated using full absorption costing. This means that the price for product X is likely to remain unchanged because cost plus pricing is being used. Demand for product X is relatively elastic but since no change in price is expected, sales volumes are likely to remain the same if ABC is introduced.

However, the cost for product Y is almost $10 per unit less using ABC. This means that the price of product Y will go down if cost plus pricing is used. Given that demand for product Y is also elastic, like demand for product X, a reduced selling price is likely to give rise to increased sales volumes.

The cost of product Z is nearly $7 per unit more using ABC and the price of product Z will therefore go up if ABC is used. Given that demand for product Z is relatively inelastic, this means that sales volumes would be expected to be largely unchanged despite an increase in price.

2 (a) Optimum production plan

Define the variables

Let x = number of units of Xeno to be produced.
Let y = number of units of Yong to be produced.
Let C = contribution.

State the objective function

C = 30x+ 40y

State the constraints

Build time: 24x + 20y ≤ 1,800,000
Program time: 16x + 14y ≤ 1,680,000
Test time: 10x + 4y ≤ 720,000

Non-negativity constraints:

x, y ≥ 0

Sales constraints

x ≤ 85,000
y ≤ 66,000

Draw the graph

Build time:

If x = 0, y = 1,800,000/20 = 90,000
If y = 0, x = 1,800,000/24 = 75,000

Program time:

If x = 0, y = 1,680,000/14 = 120,000
If y = 0, x = 1,680,000/16 = 105,000

Test time:

If x = 0, y = 720,000/4 = 180,000
If y = 0, x = 720,000/10 = 72,000

Solve using the iso-contribution line

If y = 40,000, C = 40,000 x $40 = $1,600,000
If C = $1,600,000 and y = 0, x = $1,600,000/$30 = 53,333·33

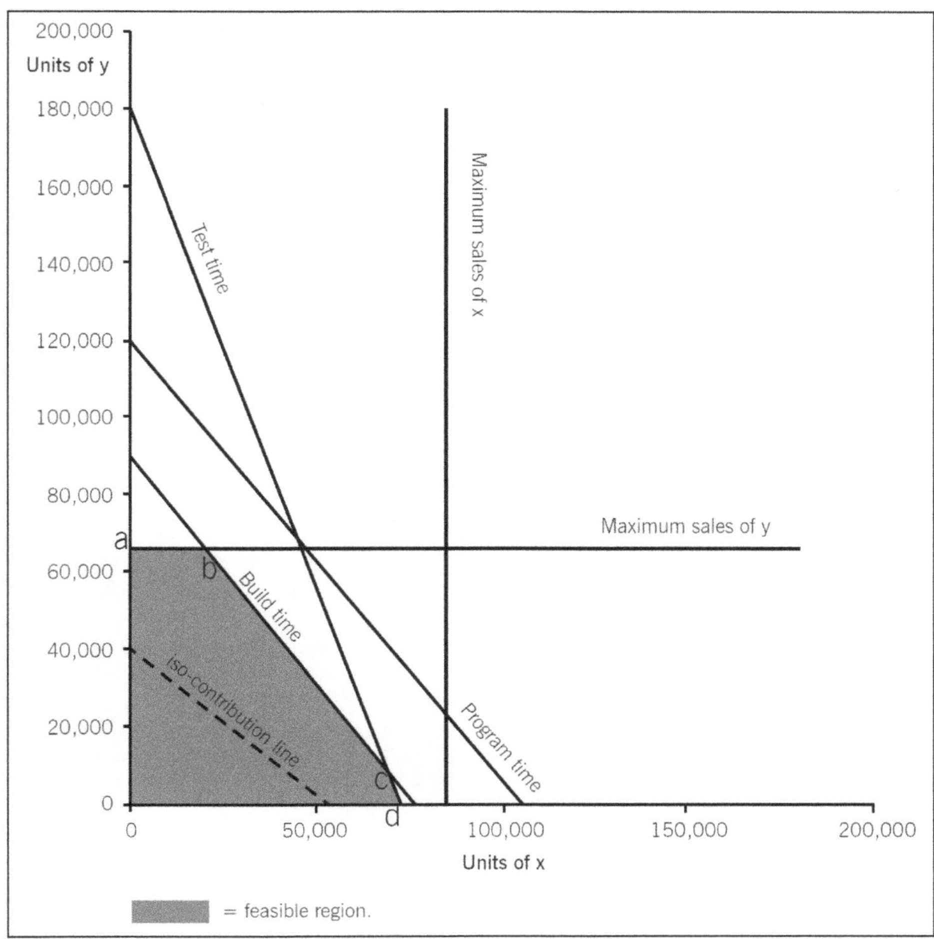

Moving the iso-contribution line out to the furthest point on the feasible region, the optimum production point is b. This is the intersection of the build time constraint and the sales constraint for y. Solving the simultaneous equations for these two constraints:

y = 66,000
24x + 20y = 1,800,000
24x + (20 x 66,000) = 1,800,000
24x + 1,320,000 = 1,800,000
24x = 480,000
x = 20,000

C = (20,000 x $30) + (66,000 x $40)
= $600,000 + $2,640,000 = $3,240,000

Fixed costs = 3 x $650,000 = $1,950,000.
Therefore profit = $1,290,000.

(b) Slack resources

Test time used = (20,000 x 10)/60 + (66,000 x 4)/60 = 7,733 hours.
Therefore slack hours = 12,000 – 7,733= 4,267 hours.

Program time used = (20,000 x 16)/60 + (66,000 x 14)/60 = 20,733 hours.
Therefore slack hours = 28,000 – 20,733 = 7,267 hours.

The slack values for test time and program time mean that there are 4,267 and 7,267 hours of each respective department's time unutilised under the optimum production plan. If possible, this time could be used by the organisation elsewhere or subcontracted out to another company.

3 (a) Ratios

(i) ROCE = operating profit/capital employed x 100%

		$'000	ROCE
W Co	Design division	6,000/23,540	25·49%
	Gearbox division	3,875/32,320	11·99%
C Co		7,010/82,975	8·45%

(ii) Asset turnover = sales/capital employed x 100%

		$'000	Asset turnover
W Co	Design division	14,300/23,540	0·61
	Gearbox division	25,535/32,320	0·79
C Co		15,560/82,975	0·19

(iii) Operating profit margin = operating profit/sales x 100%

		$'000	Operating profit
W Co	Design division	6,000/14,300	41·96%
	Gearbox division	3,875/25,535	15·18%
C Co		7,010/15,560	45·05%

Both companies and both divisions within W Co are clearly profitable. In terms of what the different ratios tell us, ROCE tells us the return which a company is making from its capital. The Design division of W Co is making the highest return at over 25%, more than twice that of the Gearbox division and nearly three times that of C Co. This is because the nature of a design business is such that profits are largely derived from the people making the designs rather than from the assets. Certain assets will obviously be necessary in order to produce the designs but it is the employees who are mostly responsible for generating profit.

The Gearbox division and C Co's ROCE are fairly similar compared to the Design division, although when comparing the two in isolation, the Gearbox division's ROCE is actually over three percentage points higher than C Co's (11·99% compared to 8·45%). This is because C Co has a substantially larger asset base than the Gearbox division.

From the asset turnover ratio, it can be seen that the Gearbox division's assets generate a very high proportion of sales per $ of assets (79%) compared to C Co (19%). This is partly because the Gearbox division buys its components in from C Co and therefore does not need to have the large asset base which C Co has in order to make the components. When the unit profitability of those sales is considered by looking at the operating profit margin, C Co's unit profitability is much higher than the Gearbox division (45% operating profit margin as compared to 15%). The Design division, like the Gearbox division, is also using its assets well to generate sales (asset turnover of 61%) but then, like C Co, its unit profitability is high too (42% operating profit margin.) This is why, when the two ratios (operating profit margin and asset turnover) are combined to make ROCE, the Design division comes out top overall – because it has both high unit profitability and generates sales at a high level compared to its asset base.

It should be noted that any comparisons between such different types of business are of limited use. It would be more useful to have prior year figures for comparison and/or industry averages for similar businesses. This would make performance review much more meaningful.

(b) Transfer prices

From C Co's perspective

C Co transfers components to the Gearbox division at the same price as it sells components to the external market. However, if C Co were not making internal sales then, given that it already satisfies 60% of external demand, it would not be able to sell all of its current production to the external market. External sales are $8,010,000, therefore unsatisfied external demand is ([$8,010,000/0·6] – $8,010,000) = $5,340,000.

From C Co's perspective, of the current internal sales of $7,550,000, $5,340,000 could be sold externally if they were not sold to the Gearbox division. Therefore, in order for C Co not to be any worse off from selling internally, these sales should be made at the current price of $5,340,000, less any reduction in costs which C Co saves from not having to sell outside the group (perhaps lower administrative and distribution costs).

As regards the remaining internal sales of $2,210,000 ($7,550,000 – $5,340,000), C Co effectively has spare capacity to meet these sales. Therefore, the minimum transfer price should be the marginal cost of producing these goods. Given that variable costs represent 40% of revenue, this means that the marginal cost for these sales is $884,000. This is therefore the minimum price which C Co should charge for these sales.

In total, therefore, C Co will want to charge at least $6,224,000 for its sales to the Gearbox division.

From the Gearbox division's perspective

The Gearbox division will not want to pay more for the components than it could purchase them for externally. Given that it can purchase them all for 95% of the current price, this means a maximum purchase price of $7,172,500.

Overall

Taking into account all of the above, the transfer price for the sales should be somewhere between $6,224,000 and $7,172,500.

4 (a) Profit outcomes

Unit contribution	Sales price per unit	
	$30	$35
Up to 100,000 units	$18	$23
Above 100,000 units	$19	$24

Sales price $30

Sales volume	Unit contribution	Total contribution	Fixed costs	Advertising costs	Profit
	$	$'000	$'000	$'000	$'000
120,000	19	2,280	450	900	930
110,000	19	2,090	450	900	740
140,000	19	2,660	450	900	1,310

Sales price $35

Sales volume	Unit contribution	Total contribution	Fixed costs	Advertising costs	Profit
	$	$'000	$'000	$'000	$'000
108,000	24	2,592	450	970	1,172
100,000	23	2,300	450	970	880
94,000	23	2,162	450	970	742

(b) Expected values

Sales price $30

Sales volume	Profit	Probability	EV of profit
	$'000		$'000
120,000	930	0·4	372
110,000	740	0·5	370
140,000	1,310	0·1	131
			873

Sales price $35

Sales volume	Profit	Probability	EV of profit
	$'000		$'000
108,000	1,172	0·3	351·6
100,000	880	0·3	264
94,000	742	0·4	296·8
			912·4

If the criterion of expected value is used to make a decision as to which price to charge, then the price charged should be $35 per unit since the expected value of this option is the greatest.

(c) Maximin decision rule

Under this rule, the decision-maker selects the alternative which offers the most attractive worst outcome, i.e. the alternative which maximises the minimum profit. In the case of Gam Co, this would be the price of $35 as the lowest profit here is $742,000 as compared to a lowest profit of $740,000 at a price of $30.

(d) Reasons for uncertainty arising in the budgeting process

Uncertainty arises largely because of changes in the external environment over which a company will sometimes have little control. Reasons include:

- Customers may decide to buy more or less goods or services than originally forecast. For example, if a major customer goes into liquidation, this has a huge effect on a company and could also cause them to go into liquidation.
- Competitors may strengthen or emerge and take some business away from a company. On the other hand, a competitor's position may weaken leading to increased business for a particular company.
- Technological advances may take place which lead a company's products or services to become out-dated and therefore less desirable.
- The workforce may not perform as well as expected, perhaps because of time off due to illness or maybe simply because of lack of motivation.
- Materials may increase in price because of global changes in commodity prices.
- Inflation can cause the price of all inputs to increase or decrease.

- If a company imports or exports goods or services, changes in exchange rates can cause prices to change.
- Machines may fail to meet production schedules because of breakdown.
- Social/political unrest could affect productivity, e.g. the workforce goes on strike.

Note: *This list is not exhaustive, nor would candidates be expected to make all the points raised in order to score full marks.*

5 (a) Variances

(i) The sales mix contribution variance

Calculated as (actual sales quantity – actual sales quantity in budgeted proportions) x standard contribution per unit.

Standard contributions per valet:
Full = \$50 x 44·6% = \$22·30 per valet
Mini = \$30 x 55% = \$16·50 per valet
Actual sales quantity in budgeted proportions (ASQBP):
Full: 7,980 x (3,600/5,600) = 5,130
Mini: 7,980 x (2,000/5,600) = 2,850

Valet type	AQAM	AQBM	Difference	Standard contribution	Variance
				\$	\$
Full	4,000	5,130	(1,130)	22·30	25,199 A
Mini	3,980	2,850	1,130	16·50	18,645 F
					6,554 A

(ii) The sales quantity contribution variance

Calculated as (actual sales quantity in budgeted proportions – budgeted sales quantity) x standard contribution per unit.

Valet type	AQBM	BQBM	Difference	Standard contribution	Variance
				\$	\$
Full	5,130	3,600	1,530	22·30	34,119 F
Mini	2,850	2,000	850	16·50	14,025 F
					48,144 F

(b) Description

The sales mix contribution variance
This variance measures the effect on profit of changing the mix of actual sales from the standard mix.

The sales quantity contribution variance
This variance measures the effect on profit of selling a different total quantity from the budgeted total quantity.

(c) Sales performance of the business

The sales performance of the business has been very good over the last year, as shown by the favourable sales quantity variance of \$48,144. Overall, total sales revenue is 33% higher than budgeted ((\$319,400 – \$240,000)/\$240,000). This is because of a higher total number of valets being performed. When you look at where the difference in sales quantity actually is, you can see from the data provided in the question that it is the number of mini valets which is substantially higher. This number is 99% ((3,980 – 2,000)/2,000) higher than budgeted, whereas the number of full valets is only 11% ((4,000 – 3,600)/3,600) higher. Even 11% is still positive, however.

The fact that the number of mini valets is so much higher combined with the fact that they generate a lower contribution per unit than the full valet led to an adverse sales mix variance of \$6,554 in the year. This cannot be looked at in isolation as a sign of poor performance; it is simply reflective of the changes which have occurred in Strappia. We are told that disposable incomes in Strappia have decreased by 30% over the last year. This means that people have less money to spend on non-essential expenditure such as car valeting. Consequently, they are opting for the cheaper mini valet rather than the more expensive full valet. At the same time, we are also told that people are keeping their cars for an average of five years now as opposed to three years. This may be leading them to take more care of them and get them valeted regularly because they know that the car has to be kept for a longer period. Thus, the total quantity of valets is higher than budgeted, particularly the mini valets.

Also, there is now one less competitor for Valet Co than there was a year ago, so Valet Co may have gained some of the old competitor's business. Together, all of these factors would explain the higher number of total valets being performed and in particular, of the less expensive type of valet.

Note: *Other valid points will be given full credit.*

Fundamentals Level – Skills Module, Paper F5
Performance Management

June 2014 Marking Scheme

			Marks
1	(a)	**Full absorption cost**	
		Overhead absorption rate	1·5
		Cost for X incl labour and materials	0·5
		Cost for Y incl labour and materials	0·5
		Cost for Z incl labour and materials	0·5
			3
	(b)	**Activity based cost**	
		Correct cost driver rates	4·5
		Overhead unit cost for X	1
		Overhead unit cost for Y	1
		Overhead unit cost for Z	1
		Adding labour and materials costs	2
		Total cost for X	0·5
		Total cost for Y	0·5
		Total cost for Z	0·5
			11
	(c)	**Discussion**	
		Effect on price	3
		Effect on sales volume	3
			6
		Total marks	**20**
2	(a)	**Optimum production plan**	
		Stating the objective function	0·5
		Defining constraint for built time	0·5
		Defining constraint for program time	0·5
		Defining constraint for test time	0·5
		Non-negativity constraints	0·5
		Sales constraint x	0·5
		Sales constraint y	0·5
		Iso-contribution line worked out	1
		The graph:	
		Labels	0·5
		Build time line	0·5
		Program time line	0·5
		Test time line	0·5
		Demand for x line	0·5
		Demand for y line	0·5
		Iso-contribution line	0·5
		Feasible region identified and labelled/shaded	1
		Optimum point identified	1
		Equations solved at optimum point	3
		Total contribution	0·5
		Total profit	0·5
			14
	(b)	**Slack values**	
		Test time calculation	1·5
		Program time calculation	1·5
		Defining and identifying slack resources	1·5
		Discussing implication of slack resources	1·5
			6
		Total marks	**20**

			Marks
3	(a)	Ratios	
		Calculating ROCE	1·5
		Calculating asset turnover	1·5
		Calculating operating profit margin	1·5
		Per valid comment	1
			10
	(b)	Transfer pricing	
		Each valid comment/calculation	1 or 2
			10
		Total marks	**20**
4	(a)	Profit outcomes	
		Unit contribution up to 100,000 units	1
		Unit contribution above 100,000 units	1
		Each line of table for price of $30 (3 in total)	1
		Each line of table for price of $35 (3 in total)	1
			8
	(b)	Expected values	
		Expected value for $30	1
		Expected value for $35	1
		Recommendation	1
			3
	(c)	Maximin	
		Explanation	2
		Decision	1
			3
	(d)	Uncertainty	
		Each point made	1
			6
		Total marks	**20**
5	(a)	Calculations	
		Sales mix contribution variance	4
		Sales quantity contribution variance	4
			8
	(b)	Description	
		One mark per description	2
	(c)	Discussion on sales performance	
		Calculations – each one, max 2	0·5
		Maximum for each point made	2
			10
		Total marks	**20**

Section A

1 A

Division A: Profit = $14·4m x 30% = $4·32m
Imputed interest charge = $32·6m x 10% = $3·26m
Residual income = $1·06m

Division B: Profit = 8·8m x 24% = $2·112m
Imputed interest charge = $22·2m x 10% = $2·22m
Residual income = $(0·108)m

2 D

All costs are included when using life cycle costing.

3 A

This is the definition of a basic standard.

4 B

The first statement is describing management control, not strategic planning.

5 C

Number of units required to make target profit = fixed costs + target profit/contribution per unit of P1.
Fixed costs = ($1·2 x 10,000) + ($1 x 12,500) – $2,500 = $22,000.
Contribution per unit of P = $3·20 + $1·20 = $4·40.

($22,000 + $60,000)/$4·40 = 18,636 units.

6 A

Product	A	B	C	D
Selling price per unit	$160	$214	$100	$140
Raw material cost	$24	$56	$22	$40
Direct labour cost at $11 per hour	$66	$88	$33	$22
Variable overhead cost	$24	$18	$24	$18
Contribution per unit	$46	$52	$21	$60
Direct labour hours per unit	6	8	3	2
Contribution per labour hour	$7·67	$6·50	$7	$30
Rank	2	4	3	1
Normal monthly hours (total units x hours per unit)	1,800	1,000	720	800

If the strike goes ahead, only 2,160 labour hours will be available.
Therefore make all of D, then 1,360 hours' worth of A (2,160 – 800 hrs).

7 B

460 – 400 = 60 clients
$40,000 – $36,880 = $3,120
VC per unit = $3,120/60 = $52
Therefore FC = $40,000 – (460 x $52) = $16,080

8 B

Increase in variable costs from buying in (2,200 units x $40 ($140 – $100)) = $88,000
Less the specific fixed costs saved if A is shut down = ($10,000)
Decrease in profit = $78,000

9 A

Only the first statement is correct. Traditional absorption costing tends to over-allocate costs to high volume products, not under-allocate them.

10 B

By definition, a shadow price is the amount by which contribution will increase if an extra kg of material becomes available. 20 x \$2·80 = \$56.

11 C

Neither statement is correct. Responsibility is not assigned solely to senior managers as, for example, in a TQM environment quality is everybody's responsibility. In addition, standard costing can be difficult to apply in dynamic situations.

12 A

The second statement is talking about flow cost accounting, not input/output analysis.

13 D

Target 1 is a financial target and so assesses economy factors. Target 2 is measuring the rate of work handled by staff which is an efficiency measure. Target 3 is assessing output, so is a measure of effectiveness.

14 B

In comparison to participative budgeting, an advantage of non-participative budgeting is that it should be less time consuming, as less collaboration will be required in order to produce the budgets.

15 C

The target costing process always begins with the target selling price being set. The required profit is then determined and deducted from the target selling price to estimate the target cost. The target cost is then compared to the estimated current cost and the cost gap is then calculated.

16 A

This is a description of an incremental budget.

17 A

New profit figures before salary paid:
Good manager: \$180,000 x 1·3 = \$234,000
Average manager: \$180,000 x 1·2 = \$216,000
Poor: \$180,000 x 1·1 = \$198,000

EV of profits = (0·35 x \$234,000) + (0·45 x \$216,000) + (0·2 x \$198,000) = \$81,900 + \$97,200 + \$39,600 = \$218,700
Deduct salary cost and EV with manager = \$178,700
Therefore do not employ manager as profits will fall by \$1,300.

18 B

Set-up costs per production run = \$140,000/28 = \$5,000
Cost per inspection = \$80,000/8 = \$10,000
Other overhead costs per labour hour = \$96,000/48,000 = \$2

Overheads costs of product D:

	\$
Set-up costs (15 x \$5,000)	75,000
Inspection costs (3 x \$10,000)	30,000
Other overheads (40,000 x \$2)	80,000
	185,000

Overhead cost per unit = 185,000/4,000 = \$46·25

19 A

This is an example of feedforward control as the manager is using a forecast to assist in making a future decision.

20 A

If demand is inelastic or the product life cycle is short, a price skimming approach would be more appropriate.

Section B

1 Chair Co

(a) Learning curve formula = $y = ax^b$

Cumulative average time per unit for 8 units:
$Y = 12 \times 8^{-.415}$
= 5·0628948 hours.
Therefore cumulative total time for 8 units = 40·503158 hours.

Cumulative average time per unit for 7 units:
$Y = 12 \times 7^{-.415}$
= 5·3513771 hours.
Therefore cumulative total time for 7 units = 37·45964 hours.

Therefore incremental time for 8th unit = 40·503158 hours – 37·45964 hours = 3·043518 hours.

Total labour cost for 8th unit =3·043518 x $15 = $45·65277
Material and overheads cost per unit = $230
Therefore total cost per unit = $275·65277
Therefore price per unit = $413·47915

(b) (i) Actual learning rate

Cumulative number of seats produced	Cumulative total hours	Cumulative average hours per unit
1	12·5	12·5
2	?	12·5 x r
4	?	12·5 x r^2
8	34·3	12·5 x r^3

Using algebra: $34{\cdot}3 = 8 \times (12{\cdot}5 \times r^3)$
$4{\cdot}2875 = (12{\cdot}5 \times r^3)$
$0{\cdot}343 = r^3$
$r = 0{\cdot}70$

The learning effect was 70% as compared to the forecast rate of 75%, meaning that the labour force learnt more quickly than anticipated.

(ii) Adjusted price

The adjusted price charged will be lower than the original price calculated in part (a). This is because the incremental cost of the 8th unit will be lower given the 70% learning rate, even though the first unit took 12·5 hours. We know this because we are told that the cumulative time for 8 units was actually 34·3 hours. This is lower than the estimated cumulative time in part (a) for 8 units of 40·503158 hours and therefore, logically, the actual incremental time for the 8th unit must be lower than the estimated 3·043518 hours calculated in part (a). Consequently, total cost will be lower and price will be lower, given that this is based on cost.

2 Glam Co

(a) Bottleneck activity

The bottleneck may have been worked out as follows:

Total salon hours = 8 x 6 x 50 = 2,400 each year. The capacity for each senior stylist must be 2,400 hours, which equates to 2,400 cuts each year (2,400/1). Since there are three senior stylists, the total capacity is 7,200 hours or 7,200 cuts each year. Using this method, the capacity for each activity is as follows:

	Cut	Treatment
Assistants	48,000	16,000
Senior stylists	7,200	4,800
Junior stylists	9,600	9,600

The bottleneck activity is clearly the work performed by the senior stylists.

The senior stylists' time is called a bottleneck activity because it is the activity which prevents the salon's throughput from being higher than it is. The total number of cuts or treatments which can be completed by the salon's senior stylists is less than the number which can be completed by other staff members, considering the number of each type of staff available and the time required by each type of staff for each client.

(b) TPAR

	Cut	Treatment
	$	$
Selling price	60	110
Materials	0·60	8 (7·40+0·6)
Throughput	59·40	102
Throughput per bottleneck hour	59·40	68
Total salon costs per BN hour (w1)	42·56	42·56
TPAR	1·4	1·6

Working 1: Total salon costs

(3 x $40,000) + (2 x $28,000) + (2 x $12,000) + $106,400 = $306,400

Therefore cost for each bottleneck hour = $306,400/7,200 = $42·56

Note: *Answers based on total salary costs were $80,000 were also equally acceptable since the wording of question was open to interpretation.*

3 Hi Life Co

		Note	$
Direct materials:			
Fabric	200 m² at $17·50 per m²	1	3,500
Wood	20 m at $8·20 per m	2	164
	30 m at $8·50 per m	2	255
Direct labour:			
Skilled	50 hours at $24 per hour	3	1,200
Semi-skilled	300 hours at $14 per hour	4	4,200
Factory overheads	20 hours at $15 per hour	5	300
Administration overheads		6	–
Total cost			9,619

1 Since the material is in regular use by HL Co, it is replacement cost which is the relevant cost for the contract.

2 30 m will have to be ordered from the alternative supplier for immediate delivery but the remaining 20 m can be used from inventory and replaced by an order from the usual supplier at a cost of $8·20 per m.

3 There is no cost for the first 150 hours of labour because there is spare capacity. The remaining 50 hours will be paid at time and a half, which is $16 x 1·5, i.e. $24 per hour.

4 HL Co will choose to use the agency workers, who will cost $14 per hour, since this is cheaper than paying existing semi-skilled workers at $18 per hour ($12 x 1·5) to work overtime.

5 None of the general factory costs are incremental, so they have all been excluded. However, the supervisor's overtime pay is incremental, so has been included. The supervisor's normal salary, on the other hand, has been excluded because it is not incremental.

6 These are general overheads and are not incremental, so no value should be included for them.

4 Jamair

(a) The four perspectives

Financial perspective – this perspective is concerned with how a company looks to its shareholders. How can it create value for them? Kaplan and Norton identified three core financial themes which will drive the business strategy: revenue growth and mix, cost reduction and asset utilisation.

Customer perspective – this considers how the organisation appears to customers. The organisation should ask itself: 'to achieve our vision, how should we appear to our customers?' The customer perspective should identify the customer and market segments in which the business will compete. There is a strong link between the customer perspective and the revenue objectives in the financial perspective. If customer objectives are achieved, revenue objectives should be too.

Internal perspective – this requires the organisation to ask itself: 'what must we excel at to achieve our financial and customer objectives?' It must identify the internal business processes which are critical to the implementation of the organisation's strategy. These will include the innovation process, the operations process and the post-sales process.

Learning and growth perspective – this requires the organisation to ask itself whether it can continue to improve and create value. The organisation must continue to invest in its infrastructure – i.e. people, systems and organisational procedures – in order to improve the capabilities which will help the other three perspectives to be achieved.

(b) Goals and measures

Financial perspective

Goal	Performance measure
To use fewer planes to transport customers	Lease costs of plane per customer

Explanation – operating efficiency will be driven by getting more customers on fewer planes. This goal and measure cover the cost side of this.

Goal	Performance measure
To increase seat revenue per plane	Revenue per available passenger mile

Explanation – this covers the first part of achieving operating efficiency – by having fewer empty seats on planes.

Customer perspective

Goal	Performance measure
To ensure that flights are on time	'On time arrival' ranking from the aviation authority

Explanation – Jamair is currently number 7 in the rankings. If it becomes known as a particularly reliable airline, customers are more likely to use it, which will ultimately increase revenue.

Goal	Performance measure
To reduce the number of flights cancelled	The number of flights cancelled

Explanation – again, if flights are seen to be cancelled frequently by Jamair, customers will not want to use it. It needs to be perceived as reliable by its customers.

Internal perspective

Goal	Performance measure
To improve turnaround time on the ground	'On the ground' time

Explanation – less time spent on the ground means fewer planes are needed, which will reduce plane leasing costs. However, it is important not to compromise the quality of cleaning or make errors in refuelling as a consequence of reducing on the ground time.

Goal	Performance measure
To improve the cleanliness of Jamair's planes	The percentage of customers happy with the standard of the planes, as reported in the customer satisfaction surveys.

Explanation – at present, only 85% of customers are happy with the standard of cleanliness on Jamair's planes. This could be causing loss of revenue.

Goal	Performance measure
To develop the online booking system	Percentage downtime.

Explanation – since the company relies entirely on the booking system for customer booking of flights and check-in, it is critical that it can deal with the growing number of customers.

Learning perspective

Goal	Performance measure
To reduce the employee absentee rate	The number of days absent per employee

Explanation – it is critical to Jamair that its workforce is reliable as, at worse, absent staff lead to cancelled flights.

Goal	Performance measure
To increase ground crew training on cleaning and refuelling procedures	Number of days' training per ground crew member

Explanation – if ground crew are better trained, they can reduce the number of minutes that the plane stays on the ground, which will result in fewer planes being required and therefore lower costs. Also, if their cleaning is better, customer satisfaction and retention will increase.

Note: *Only one goal and measure were required for each perspective. In order to gain full marks, answers had to be specific to Jamair as stated in the requirements.*

5 Safe Soap Co

(a) Variance calculations

Mix variance

Total kg of materials per standard batch = 0·25 + 0·6 + 0·5 = 1·35 kg
Therefore standard quantity to produce 136,000 batches = 136,000 x 1·35 kg = 183,600 kg
Actual total kg of materials used to produce 136,000 batches = 34,080 + 83,232 + 64,200 = 181,512 kg

Material		Actual quantity Standard mix	Actual quantity Actual mix	Variance	Standard cost per kg	Variance
		kgs	kgs	kgs	$	$
Lye	181,512 x 0·25/1·35 =	33,613·33	34,080	(466·67)	10	(4,666·70)
Coconut oil	181,512 x 0·6/1·35 =	80,672	83,232	(2,560)	4	(10,240)
Shea butter	181,512 x 0·5/1·35 =	67,226·67	64,200	3,026·67	3	9,080·01
		181,512	181,512			(5,826·69)A

Yield variance

Material		Standard quantity Standard mix	Actual quantity Standard mix	Variance	Standard cost per kg	Variance
			kgs	kgs	$	$
Lye	0·25 x 136,000 =	34,000	33,613·33	386·67	10	3,866·70
Coconut oil	0·6 x 136,000 =	81,600	80,672	928	4	3,712
Shea butter	0·5 x 136,000 =	68,000	67,226·67	773·33	3	2,319·99
		183,600	181,512			9,898·69F

(b)

(i) A materials mix variance will occur when the actual mix of materials used in production is different from the standard mix. So, it is inputs which are being considered. Since the total mix variance is adverse for the Safe Soap Co, this means that the actual mix used in September and October was more expensive than the standard mix.

A material yield variance arises because the output which was achieved is different from the output which would have been expected from the inputs. So, whereas the mix variance focuses on inputs, the yield variance focuses on outputs. In both September and October, the yield variance was favourable, meaning that the inputs produced a higher level of output than one would have expected.

(ii) Whilst the mix and yield variances provide Safe Soap Co with a certain level of information, they do not necessarily explain any quality issues which arise because of the change in mix. The consequences of the change may well have an impact on sales volumes. In Safe Soap Co's case, the sales volume variance is adverse, meaning that sales volumes have fallen in October. It is not known whether they also fell in September but it would be usual for the effects on sales of the change in mix to be slightly delayed, in this case by one month, given that it is only once the customers start receiving the slightly altered soap that they may start expressing their dissatisfaction with the product.

There may also be other reasons for the adverse sales volume variance but given the customer complaints which have been received, the sales manager's views should be taken on board.

Fundamentals Level – Skills Module, Paper F5
Performance Management

December 2014 Marking Scheme

			Marks
Section A			
2 marks per question			40
Section B			
1	(a)	Price	
		Cumulative average time per unit for 8 units	1
		Total time for 8 units	0·5
		Cumulative average time per unit for 7 units	1
		Total time for 7 units	0·5
		Incremental time for 8th unit	0·5
		Cost for 8th unit	0·5
		Total cost	0·5
		Price	0·5
			5
	(b) (i)	Learning rate	
		Calculating learning rate	2·5
		Saying whether better or worse	0·5
			3
	(ii)	Effect on price	2
		Total marks	**10**
2	(a)	Calculation and justification of bottleneck	3
		Explanation of bottleneck	1
			4
	(b)	TPAR	
		Throughput	1
		Throughput per bottleneck hour	1
		Total salon costs	1
		Cost per hour	1
		TPAR	2
			6
		Total marks	**10**
3		Fabric calculation	0·5
		Fabric reason	0·5
		Wood calculation	1
		Wood reason	1
		Skilled labour calculation	1
		Skilled labour reason	1
		Semi-skilled labour calculation	0·5
		Semi-skilled labour reason	1
		Factory overheads calculation	0·5
		Factory overheads reason	1·5
		Administration overheads reason	1
		Total relevant cost (lowest cost estimate)	0·5
		Total marks	**10**

			Marks
4	(a)	Perspectives	
		Explanation for each perspective	1·5
			6
	(b)	Goals and measures	
		Each goal/measure/explanation	2
		Presentation and structure	1
			9
		Total marks	**15**
5	(a)	Variance calculations	
		Mix variance	4
		Quantity variance	4
			8
	(b) (i)	Variances	
		Marks per variance explained	2
			4
	(ii)	Discussion	
		Per valid point	1
			3
		Total marks	**15**

Review Form – Paper F5 Performance Management (04/15)

Name: ______________________ **Address:** ______________________

____

____

How have you used this Kit?
(Tick one box only)

☐ Home study (book only)
☐ On a course: college ______________
☐ With 'correspondence' package
☐ Other ______________

Why did you decide to purchase this Kit?
(Tick one box only)

☐ Have used the complementary Study text
☐ Have used other BPP products in the past
☐ Recommendation by friend/colleague
☐ Recommendation by a lecturer at college
☐ Saw advertising
☐ Other ______________

During the past six months do you recall seeing/receiving any of the following?
(Tick as many boxes as are relevant)

☐ Our advertisement in *Student Accountant*
☐ Our advertisement in *Pass*
☐ Our advertisement in *PQ*
☐ Our brochure with a letter through the post
☐ Our website www.bpp.com

Which (if any) aspects of our advertising do you find useful?
(Tick as many boxes as are relevant)

☐ Prices and publication dates of new editions
☐ Information on product content
☐ Facility to order books off-the-page
☐ None of the above

Which BPP products have you used?

Text	☐	*Passcards*	☐	*Home Study Package*	☐
Kit	☑	*i-Pass*	☐		

Your ratings, comments and suggestions would be appreciated on the following areas.

	Very useful	*Useful*	*Not useful*
Passing F5	☐	☐	☐
Questions	☐	☐	☐
Top Tips etc in answers	☐	☐	☐
Content and structure of answers	☐	☐	☐
Mock exam answers	☐	☐	☐

Overall opinion of this Kit *Excellent* ☐ *Good* ☐ *Adequate* ☐ *Poor* ☐

Do you intend to continue using BPP products? *Yes* ☐ *No* ☐

The BPP author of this edition can be emailed at: accaqueries@bpp.com

Please return this form to: Head of ACCA & FIA Programmes, BPP Learning Media Ltd, FREEPOST, London, W12 8AA

Review Form (continued)

TELL US WHAT YOU THINK

Please note any further comments and suggestions/errors below.